MULTIANNUAL MACROECONOMIC PROGRAMMING TECHNIQUES FOR DEVELOPING ECONOMIES

MULTIANNUAL MACROECONOMIC PROGRAMMING TECHNIQUES FOR DEVELOPING ECONOMIES

Paul Beckerman

Independent Consultant, USA

 **World Scientific**

NEW JERSEY · LONDON · SINGAPORE · BEIJING · SHANGHAI · HONG KONG · TAIPEI · CHENNAI

Published by

World Scientific Publishing Co. Pte. Ltd.

5 Toh Tuck Link, Singapore 596224

USA office: 27 Warren Street, Suite 401-402, Hackensack, NJ 07601

UK office: 57 Shelton Street, Covent Garden, London WC2H 9HE

British Library Cataloguing-in-Publication Data
A catalogue record for this book is available from the British Library.

ISBN-13 978-981-4289-02-3
ISBN-10 981-4289-02-7

Printed by FuIsland Offset Printing (S) Pte Ltd. Singapore

This book is dedicated to the memory of my late father, Mr. Samuel Beckerman. A certified public accountant, he found the issues this book discusses, interesting from technical and ethical perspectives. This book reflects many conversations we had over the years.

Preface

Many finance ministries and central banks, as well as many public and private financial institutions, maintain and apply computer-based multiannual macroeconomic programming exercises. The World Bank's "Revised Minimum Standard Model" ("RMSM," or "RMSM-X" in its Excel version) and the International Monetary Fund's "monetary-programming" exercise are among the better-known examples. Some governments have adapted versions of these exercises for their own use, and some have developed, or have had consultants develop, their own exercises. Analysts have several typical uncertainties when they begin working with such exercises. "Having switched on the computer and opened the Excel file, where do we start?" "How do we proceed — indeed, what are we trying to accomplish through the projection work?" "How do we know we are 'done'?" — or, "How can we tell whether we have formulated a 'good' projection?" And then, of course, many analysts want principles and ideas to enable them to construct their own projection exercises. This book's core purpose is to provide some of the basics to help analysts with these matters.

University economics programs don't always cover practical macroeconomic programming techniques adequately. People with economics degrees who go to work with governments and financial institutions sometimes realize this when first assigned — say — to estimate the future external financing requirements implied by given policy programs. Macroeconomic projection analysis is a practical necessity for policy-makers in financially constrained developing economies, as well as for financial and development institutions who lend to them and monitor their performance. To learn macroeconomic programming techniques, those able do so should make every effort to attend the International Monetary Fund's and World Bank's specialized courses. Not everyone can, unfortunately. This book describes an approach that is in some ways similar and in some ways different, which some readers may find useful for practical needs, and which may in any case provide a helpful alternative perspective.

This book is based on several seminars I have presented since 2000. It began as notes for a three-day seminar on medium-term macroeconomic projection methods presented in Guatemala, July 30– August 2, 2000. The participants were officials and analysts from various public-sector entities, brought together by the SIAF-SAG program, a World Bank-funded project to modernize Guatemala's public-sector management. An initial draft of the book served as the basis of a three-week course I presented in Kigali, Rwanda, June 3–21, 2002. The participants were analysts from Rwanda's Ministry of Finance and Economic Planning, the Rwanda Revenue Authority, and the National (central) Bank of Rwanda. The African Development Bank provided financing.

Over the latter half of 2002 and then during various visits to Santo Domingo in 2003, 2004 and 2005, I had yet another opportunity to apply, test, and revise the approaches this book describes, while working as consultant for the Dominican Republic's "Integrated State Financial Management Program," funded by the Inter-American Development Bank. Over 2004 I helped develop a projection exercise for Perú's Ministry of Economy and Finance, under a project financed by the United States Agency for International Development. In late 2004 I helped develop a projection exercise for Ecuador's Ministry of Finance, under a project financed by the United Nations Development Program. In February 2005 I led a five-day seminar in macroeconomic projection for Nigerian public officials in Kaduna, Nigeria, and in May 2006 I led a two-week seminar in macroeconomic projection for public-sector officials in Luanda, Angola. Both seminars were funded by the U.S. Agency for International Development. In August 2007 I presented a one-week seminar for analysts in the economic analysis unit of the Dominican Republic's Technical Secretariat of the Presidency. Most recently, in May 2008 I presented a three-week course on macroeconomic projection techniques for public-sector analysts in

Georgetown, Guyana, again with funding from the U.S. Agency for International Development.

Because this book is based on experience in different institutions and country settings, I owe thanks to many more people than I could name here. I would like particularly, however, to record my gratitude to Punam Chuhan, Magín Díaz, Frank González, Mark Gallagher, Jariya Hoffman, Raju Kalidindi, Ricardo Lago, Katherine W. Marshall, Gardiana Melo, Mariana Naranjo, Oscar Masabo, Prosper Musafiri, Lars Pedersen, Bisa Octavién Samali, Andrés Solimano and William Tyler for relevant advice, challenging questions, and valued dialogue. I would like also to record my gratitude to the Guatemala, Rwanda, Dominican Republic, Nigeria, Angola, and Guyana course organizers and participants, as well as to many different people in the corresponding finance ministries and central banks. Their interest and enthusiasm persuaded me to complete the spreadsheet exercise and write the book. Of course I alone am responsible for all errors of fact and judgment. Views this book expresses do not necessarily reflect those of any institutions with which I am now or have been associated. I must also record thanks to Azucena and Edward Beckerman for many different kinds of support, especially for cheering up and broader perspectives when these were much needed.

Paul Beckerman

Contents

List of Tables

List of Figures

Abbreviations and Acronyms

Acronym	Meaning	See
ADB	Asian Development Bank	Section 5.3
BAD	African Development Bank	Section 5.3
BIS	Bank for International Settlements	Section 5.4
CIDA	Canadian International Development Agency	Section 5.3
CPI	consumer price index	Section 3.3
CIF-FOB	cost, insurance, freight - free on board	Section 6.4
DSA	debt sustainability analysis	Section 5.3
EBRD	European Bank for Reconstruction and Development	Section 5.3
EDPRS	economic development and poverty-reduction strategy	Section 1.3
GDP	gross domestic product	Section 3.2
GNP	gross national product	Section 3.2
HIPC	Highly-Indebted Poorest Countries Initiative	Section 5.3
IADB	Inter-American Development Bank	Section 5.3
ICOR	incremental capital-output ratio	Section 6.2
ICPOR	incremental capital-*potential* output ratio	Section 6.2
IMF	International Monetary Fund	Section 5.3
LIBOR	London Inter-bank Offer Rate	Section 5.2
MDRI	Multilateral Debt Reduction Initiative	Section 5.3
MTEF	medium-term expenditure framework	Section 1.4
NDP	net domestic product	Section 3.1
NPV	net present value	Section 5.3
OPEC	Organization of Petroleum Exporting Countries	Section 5.3
RMSM	Revised Minimum Standard Model	Section 1.4
SDR	Special Drawing Rights	Section 5.2
USAID	United States Agency for International Development	Section 5.2
WEO	World Economic Outlook	Section 10.2
WPI	wholesale price index	Section 3.3

1 Introduction

If the only tool you have is a hammer, you tend to see every problem as a nail.

— Abraham Maslow (1908–70, American psychologist)

1.1 Macroeconomic programming exercises

This book describes a methodology to formulate multiannual macroeconomic programming exercises for developing economies. The approach is broadly in line with standard methodologies that have evolved since the 1940s, largely through practice by the World Bank and the International Monetary Fund. As discussed below, however, it includes some innovations, at broad and detailed levels.

Macroeconomic-programming exercises can serve many different purposes (see Section 1.3 below). For this book, however, the fundamental objective is to help an economy's policy-makers determine whether their overall multiannual macroeconomic program is *financially feasible*. At any moment, a government's multiannual macroeconomic program may be defined as comprising its multiannual programs for (i) the evolution of the main macroeconomic variables, including real-GDP growth, inflation, and the exchange rate; (ii) government non-financial expenditure flows; (iii) tax and other policies that determine government revenue and affect economic incentives; and (iv) the evolution of the public sector's external and internal financing flows, all set out in a context formed from assumptions about the future "state of the world." In a developing economy, these programs would presumably be set out with a view to bringing about development and poverty-reduction objectives. In these terms, the fundamental objective of the projection exercise this book describes would be to determine, on the basis of quantitative criteria, whether the multiannual macroeconomic program is likely to prove *financially feasible*. If so, then, at least on this criterion, the government could implement the program. If not, the program would have to be revised before it could be implemented.

1

To be sure, at any given moment not all governments have all the components of a multiannual macroeconomic program in explicit form. Even when they do, the different components may be inconsistent, or incomplete. For some economies, the World Bank, the International Monetary Fund, and other international entities will maintain their own versions of particular economies' multiannual macroeconomic programs. This book argues that by having such programs and ensuring their financial feasibility, governments can improve the quality of their policy formulation and persuade their various "stakeholders" that their development and poverty-reduction programs merit confidence. While multiannual macroeconomic projection exercises are costly to develop and maintain, the benefits are likely to be substantial.

In the exercise this book describes, quantitative "programming" assumptions — encompassing macroeconomic-performance, government-policy, and real government-expenditure objectives — are applied to base-year data to project out a multiannual macroeconomic program. This program is then used to formulate a full set of macroeconomic projections, structured in national, external, fiscal, and monetary accounts. These projections incorporate financial-feasibility indicators, which analysts and policy-makers can then evaluate.

More precisely, for each projection year, the macroeconomic "program" comprises

a. projection assumptions for relevant *exogenous external variables*, including international variables such as world interest rates, growth rates of world commerce volumes, and growth rates of world prices;

b. projection assumptions for relevant *exogenous internal variables*, such as population growth;

c. programming assumptions for *basic macroeconomic variables*, including growth rates of the real gross domestic product, the price level, and the exchange rate;

d. programmed policy settings for the determinants of *government revenue*, *external-accounts flows*, and *monetary policy*;

e. programming assumptions for **government non-financial expenditure** in real (i.e., purchasing-power) terms, based on national development and poverty-reduction objectives; and

f. a **financing program for the public sector**, comprising anticipated flows of external and internal debt and assets to and from the public sector.

For any projection year, a multiannual policy program may be characterized as "financially feasible" if

a. implied **real non-government (private) per-capita consumption levels** would remain minimally acceptable on political, social, and ethical criteria;

b. implied **external financing requirements** would be within what the rest of the world would be willing and able to provide;

c. implied **public-sector financing requirements** would be within what external and internal financial markets would be willing and able to provide; and

d. the implied **monetary-policy program** would be feasible, in the sense that the monetary authority could bring about the required money supply without excessively large policy interventions.

If the program and projection results are presented in appropriately structured tables and charts, they should reveal transparently how the programming variables "lead to" the feasibility indicators.

The projection exercise this book describes is not, and should not be confused with, the basic IMF monetary-programming exercise. True, any reader who has studied or worked on IMF programming exercises will recognize some of the techniques, or at least their style. But the fundamental purpose is different. The programming procedure described here aims to ensure that a government's multiannual macroeconomic and development programs are likely to prove consistently feasible in financial terms, over several future years. The basic IMF programming exercise, in contrast, is shorter-term, and aims basically to reverse a

foreign-exchange reserve loss. An IMF program centers on nearer-term
monetary programming, ensuring that the monetary system's net foreign
assets increase relatively more while net domestic assets increase
relatively less. The exercise described here focuses relatively more
on the national, external, and fiscal-accounts projections, precisely
because they embody the national-development program, and the core
objective is to determine how much financing this program would
require.

This book illustrates the projection methodology it describes
with a spreadsheet exercise constructed from "data" and assumptions for
a hypothetical developing economy called "Pacífica." This exercise is
intended mainly to show how this book's concepts can be applied
practically. The spreadsheet exercise can be applied to actual economies,
however, with adaptations as appropriate for specific country
circumstances and structures. As such, it has several features that make
it competitive with other macroeconomic projection spreadsheet exercises:

> the spreadsheet calculates consistent, linked projections for the
> balance of payments, external debt, public-sector internal debt,
> national accounts, the non-financial public-sector accounts,
> and the monetary accounts, using the kind of base-year
> macroeconomic data available from such standard sources
> as the International Monetary Fund's *International Financial
> Statistics* (IFS) and the World Bank's *Global Development
> Finance* (GDF) tables along with assumptions regarding future
> policy and behavioral variables;

> the exercise distinguishes, and consistently projects, *year-end*
> and *year-average* values of such macroeconomic variables as the
> exchange rate, the price level, and the money stock. These
> variables figure in the full range of any economy's
> macroeconomic projections;[1]

---

[1]   Incorporation of the exchange rate in the exercise makes it possible to project the
exchange rate required, for example, to hold a coming year's balance-of-payments
current-account deficit to some specified level, or, indeed, to hold a public deficit to some
specified amount.

the spreadsheet solution uses analytical, not iterative, solution procedures "to close" the various accounts systems. Consequences of changes in assumptions can therefore be determined directly. More important, the use of analytical rather than iterative solution procedures makes it possible to close more than one accounts system. That is, the calculation procedure can close the fiscal and monetary accounts as well as the balance-of-payments accounts;

fiscal projections are carried out for disaggregated public-sector entities, including a central government, sub-national governments, public enterprises, and a public pensions system. (For specific country adaptations the fiscal structure could be disaggregated even further.) Among other things, this enables the exercise to analyze and project public external debt by borrowing entity;

the monetary projections take account, *inter alia*, of the central bank's profit-and-loss accounts, and also of the monetary consequences of movements in the public-sector deposit accounts;

the exercise is structured to be useful for debt-sustainability analysis and to gauge the consequences of debt-reduction exercises;

the updating procedure is complicated, unfortunately, but relatively straightforward compared with others;[2]

---

[2] Computer projection models are typically set up with historical and projection periods. Suppose a spreadsheet's historical period is 1995–2005 and the projection period 2006–2010. After 2006 concludes, its outcomes must be included in the historical period and 2007 then made the new initial projection year. This updating procedure can be difficult and complicated in some projection exercises.

the exercise has been developed to be as transparent and user-friendly as possible, explicitly showing its "bottom-line" feasibility measures.

In this introductory chapter, Section 1.2 summarizes how the macroeconomic projection exercise works. Section 1.3 discusses practical applications of multiannual macroeconomic policy planning. Section 1.4 discusses some general characteristics and principles of macroeconomic *"consistency"* analysis. Section 1.5 discusses the exercise's programming assumptions in general terms. Finally, Section 1.6 introduces the hypothetical economy of "Pacífica," projections for which are used to illustrate the book's points. Finally, Section 1.7 provides an overview of the book's structure.

1.2   The projection exercise, in summary

As noted, the basic purpose of the projection procedure this book describes is to help policy planners determine whether, taken together, their overall multiannual macroeconomic and government-expenditure program is likely to prove "financially feasible." Such a program may be said to be financially feasible if the financing resources the program requires — taxation proceeds, external and internal financing and non-government saving — are within what could reasonably be expected to be available. In particular, one would want to be sure that the projected financing and saving requirements would not follow an explosive trajectory (as percentages of GDP).[3]

Suppose a nation's policy planners have set out assumptions for relevant exogenous world economic conditions, such as interest rates and export-market conditions, and for relevant "exogenous" internal conditions, such as population growth. (Exogenous conditions are those determined outside the macroeconomic system of the projection exercise.) Suppose they have set out a program for the evolution of the

---

[3]   In this book, the expression "saving" refers to saving flows, while the word "savings" is used to refer to accumulated savings stocks.

key macroeconomic variables, including year-by-year objectives for real-GDP growth, inflation, exchange-rate evolution. Suppose that they have projected policy settings for determinants of government revenue, external trade, and the monetary system.

In this context, suppose the authorities propose a quantitatively specified multiannual government expenditure program, encompassing what they believe must be spent on education, health, and social welfare; public infrastructure formation and maintenance; and other essential government services. These real spending flows would be based on the specific development and poverty-reduction objectives. Finally, suppose the authorities propose a quantitatively specified multiannual external-debt program, covering borrowing and amortization flows by and to public-sector borrowers and external financing sources.

The projection exercise consists of applying these programming assumptions to base-year data to calculate projected (i) national, (ii) fiscal, (iii) external, and (iv) monetary accounts, making use of various assumed "behavioral parameters." In the process, the exercise determines the residual financing flows required "to close" the accounts structures in each set of accounts. Each year's overall financing flows give rise to debt-servicing requirements in subsequent years, which in turn affect the overall financing flows necessary to close those years' accounts.

Judgments can then be made about whether the required financing flows, and hence the macroeconomic program, would be feasible. General rules for making such judgments are difficult to set out, but analysts who know a given economy well should be able to form views based on their knowledge of the economy's circumstances and the willingness and ability of foreign and internal entities to provide financing. In some degree, the feasibility criteria are matters of common sense. Slow (not to mention negative) growth in per-capita real non-government consumption growth is likely to be acceptable at most for a year or two, in the context of a temporary crisis, not for the longer term. Foreign creditors may be reluctant, in some circumstances, to provide positive transfers (i.e., disbursements exceeding total debt service), or even positive flows (i.e., disbursement exceeding repayment). In any case, they would probably be uncomfortable seeing their own credit exposure, or all credit outstanding to a country, grow faster than the country's GDP. It may not be feasible, let alone desirable, for a government to demand a large, or fast-growing, share of internal credit resources to finance its deficit. Similarly, it may be neither feasible nor desirable for a central bank to carry out large, continuing volumes of open-market operations to absorb money.

By running and re-running a projection exercise with modified assumptions, analysts should be able to devise a multiannual macroeconomic and fiscal program that is consistent in all respects — i.e., consistent not only with the government's development objectives, but also with the financing flows likely to be available from all sources. They should then be able then to use the results not only to guide policy settings and expenditure programs, but also to communicate their assumptions and intentions to other "stakeholders." By showing the program's consistency and feasibility, they can help persuade all concerned that the program has a high likelihood of working as hoped — and thereby help maximize the likelihood that all concerned will play their roles as assumed.

1.3   Uses of multiannual macroeconomic programming exercises

Projection exercises of the kind this book describes can be useful in various ways to the different observers of a nation's macroeconomy. Current and potential external creditors, for example, could use such projection exercises to estimate future borrowing needs, or to gauge the risk in their exposure. International companies contemplating or engaged in investment activities can use the exercise to determine whether the fiscal and external accounts are likely to be fully financed — and, therefore, to what extent they face such risks as tax increases, adverse exchange-rate adjustment, inadequate internal growth, or macroeconomic instability.

The basic application this book envisages, however, is governments' own macroeconomic and fiscal policy programming. Many developing economies' governments have been persuaded that is useful to maintain rolling multiannual macroeconomic and fiscal "frameworks" — standing, continually updated projection exercises — and to use these to help formulate financially feasible policy and expenditure programs that address development objectives. A growing number of governments have made efforts to develop and implement multiannual expenditure frameworks, often with assistance from the World Bank, the International Monetary Fund, and other international agencies. This book is intended to contribute to and advance on such work.

A government that maintains a multiannual macroeconomic "framework" — that is, a standing procedure for formulating and evaluating macroeconomic programs — should be able to work more effectively with the World Bank, the International Monetary Fund, and other international agencies. The World Bank has developed a practice of organizing its operations with countries on the basis of its "Country Assistance Strategies," medium-term business plans that Bank staff work out with governments every few years. (Many other international agencies have strategies themselves, or make use of the Bank's Country Assistance Strategies to set the bases for their own programs with governments.) To the extent a government can articulate its own multiannual macroeconomic program, it can participate more effectively in the formulation of the Bank's strategy. Similarly, it stands to reason that, if a government must develop a program with the IMF, it can work more effectively and efficiently with IMF staff if it has a macroeconomic program of its own. There is every reason to suppose that World Bank and IMF programs will work better to the extent governments have genuinely participated in their formulation.

For similar reasons, multiannual macroeconomic programs are, or should be, essential components of "economic-development and poverty-reduction" strategies (EDPRS). Many governments have disseminated such strategies as formal documents in recent years, setting out multiannual policy and government-expenditure programs requiring substantial foreign-financing flows. Such strategies should be considered incomplete unless they include projection exercises showing not only that their policy and expenditure programs are likely to bring about their intended economic-development and poverty-reduction objectives, but also that the programmed economic-growth patterns and government expenditure are macroeconomically feasible — that is, that the external and internal and financing flows they require are feasible. The techniques this book describes can be applied to carry out the required analysis.

To be sure, many governments formulate multiannual projections for revenue, expenditure, and external and internal financing. Similarly, central banks routinely formulate projections for their external accounts and for their monetary programs. One point of a macroeconomic projection exercise is to ensure that all these programs are mutually consistent, and then together financially feasible. As an overall macroeconomic program is developed, an integrated projection exercise helps ensure that *all* aspects of the macroeconomic projection remain financially feasible. Once a macroeconomic program has been developed, the output of the projection exercise can be used to demonstrate its general consistency and feasibility.

For a government engaged in dialogue with external financing entities, the value of having a multiannual macroeconomic "framework" is obvious, and difficult to overstate. Perhaps less obviously, multiannual macroeconomic programming exercises can, indeed should, play vital and routine roles in nations' annual budget-preparation exercises. The basic way that a multiannual projection exercise can "add value" to an annual budget process may be understood as follows. Preparation of a given's year's budget typically takes place over the course of the year immediately preceding the budget year. In a conventional budget exercise, government analysts and policy-makers set out with assumptions for such basic macroeconomic programming variables as real-GDP growth, inflation, and the exchange rate, as well as for such exogenous variables as the growth rates of world trade, the world dollar price level, key commodity prices, and relevant world interest rates. They then use these to project the "envelope" of available resources, comprising the flows of tax and non-tax revenue and (net) external and internal financing. Next, they calculate the flow of expenditure to which they are legally or contractually committed. This includes remuneration for staff already on the payroll, government services, transfer payments to other governmental entities, transfer payments outside the government, and interest due. The difference between the resource envelope and the total committed expenditure is the scope for "discretionary" expenditure, that is, expenditure that the government is *not now* committed to make, but could choose to make.

The key point is that a large proportion of the discretionary expenditure that the government chooses to make will give rise to non-discretionary expenditure in subsequent years.[4] Teachers hired, roads constructed, loans taken on this coming year will commit the government to additional expenditure for staff remuneration, road maintenance, and debt service in subsequent years. The government's and legislature's evaluation of this year's budget is therefore incomplete unless it addresses subsequent years' budgets and their financial feasibility. Indeed, even if an austerity-minded government decides to undertake *no* discretionary expenditure this year, it should still want to consider how the non-discretionary expenditure deriving from previous years' discretionary choices will play out in future years. For this reason, the documentation accompanying the current annual budget on its approval process through the legislature should include a multiannual projection indicating its future financial feasibility, as a matter of "best practice."

Two broad issues for which a multiannual projection can be especially useful may be summarized in the terms "sustainability" and "vulnerability." Economists have defined "sustainability" differently in the economics literature, but for present purposes a macroeconomic program may be deemed "sustainable" if its projected financing requirements — broadly defined to include internal saving and perhaps private bank credit — can be reliably projected to remain within what is likely to be available — and, in particular, not grow explosively (as percentages of GDP).

For developing economies with substantial public-debt stocks, the sustainability issue has both fiscal and external aspects. For the

---

[4]   "Discretionary" is, perhaps, a relative term. One criterion for whether a given expenditure is "non-discretionary" could be that, if it were not carried out, the amount not paid would have to be added to the government's stock of arrears. Even so, a government might decline, say, to carry out vital road maintenance. It may be that no arrears would arise as a consequence, but until the expenditure is made the road might be exceedingly dangerous, and, at least in principle, could expose the government to legal liability in the event of an accident.

fiscal aspect the essential question is, "Over coming years, can the government simultaneously maintain adequate expenditure on essential "developmental" programs and maintain reasonably business-friendly tax policies, *while* maintaining its debt-servicing commitments?" For the external aspect the essential question is, "Over coming years, can the economy as a whole maintain an adequate external-saving flow for its development needs, *while* maintaining its debt-servicing commitments?" A well-formulated macroeconomic-consistency projection exercise should help policy-makers simultaneously address *both* the fiscal and external questions, as complete debt-sustainability analyses always should. Should policy-makers find that their fiscal and/or external accounts are unsustainable in these senses, they may consider not only policy adjustments, but perhaps also a request for debt relief, in which case the exercise can help determine how much and what kind would suffice to ensure sustainability.

A well-formulated projection exercise can help policy-makers address their macroeconomy's "vulnerability" by making it possible to test contingency plans for alternative "states of the world." Particularly in economies subject to export-price volatility and other sources of uncertainty, policy-makers are likely to want to determine how different export- and import-price arrays would affect their fiscal and external financing requirements. They may find it useful to sketch policy responses in advance. A projection exercise with different "scenarios" should enable policy-makers to plan responses to such contingencies as oil prices turning out significantly higher (or, for oil-exporting economies, lower), or external interest rates turning out higher, than the "base" scenario assumes.[5]

When formulating projection exercises for sustainability and vulnerability issues, it is important that analysts be clear about the specific questions such exercises are meant to address. This helps

---

[5]   In recent years, policy-makers have become increasingly aware of the dangers of "contingent" liabilities — i.e., expenditure programs a government may have to undertake in the event certain imaginable contingencies materialize (see Polackova 1999). A projection exercise can be used to plan a financing strategy in the event a government must carry out a large expenditure program to cope with a conflict or a major disaster.

determine the specific way each particular exercise is set up — in particular, the structure of the sensitivity analysis (see Section 10.5). Broadly speaking, the analyst will aim to determine, under the different versions of the "assumption array," whether and how the external and fiscal accounts could be feasibly and sustainably financed and whether and how private real per-capita consumption could grow adequately. Policy-makers and analysts are likely to focus on different sets of projection scenarios in different contexts. For example, policy-makers preparing a budget for the coming year may want to ask whether, if they undertake certain expenditure programs that would continue over several years, the resulting public deficits would exceed what foreign and internal sources could feasibly finance, especially after taking account of the interest on the accumulating public debt. Or, policy-makers may be concerned about the economy's vulnerability to shocks. Suppose, for example, that after one year oil prices were to surge (in the case of an oil importer) or to plunge (in the case of an oil exporter). How would public-sector and external financing requirements be affected? How large a real-effective exchange-rate depreciation might prove necessary to bring about the necessary changes in public and external financing requirements? Alternatively, how large a debt-stock reduction might be needed to accomplish the same?

1.4 Macroeconomic "consistency" analysis

The projection exercise this book describes is a "consistency" analysis, in several different senses. The most important is that, unlike projection exercises that simulate economic processes and, as appropriate, adjustment to equilibrium, the analysis described here aims only to determine the financing flows *consistent with* programmed macroeconomic and public-expenditure objectives, to determine whether these would be *consistent with* what is likely to be available.

"Consistency" is a recurring theme in this book, but the word comes up in several different ways. First, it has a practical mechanical significance. When constructing a macroeconomic projection, if particular variables figure in different sets of accounts for the same year, care must be taken to ensure that their values are consistent. Thus, for example, dollar flows of external-debt flows (disbursements and repayment) to and from the government must be consistent in the fiscal and the external accounts; net international-reserve flows must be consistent in the monetary and external accounts; exports and imports of goods and non-factor services must be consistent in the national and the external accounts[6]; and so on. (Section 2.7 discusses this point in more detail.)

Moreover, since accounting "identities" — equivalence relationships that must always be true — govern the different sets of accounts, projected values must be consistent with these identities. Thus, for example, the central bank's stock and flow balance-sheet identities must hold at all moments and over all time intervals. Similarly, each year's non-government consumption flow must be consistent through the national-accounts "expenditure" identity (see Chapter 6) with net exports of goods and non-factor services, gross investment, and government consumption. In addition, year-average and year-end exchange rates, or year-average and year-end price-index values, must be mutually consistent, and in general should not "oscillate" (see Section 3.7 below).

"Consistency" goes beyond simple adding-up considerations, however. One of the book's themes is that policy-makers should endeavor to formulate macroeconomic programs with financially feasible outcomes in all aspects of the macroeconomy. That is, projections must be consistent with resources likely to be available. Will private consumption grow adequately (and so allow a sufficient flow of private saving to take place)? Will adequate financing flows be available for the external accounts and the fiscal accounts? Will government expenditure be consistent with the economy's development objectives? Is the current macroeconomic program likely to do well enough for a time but then

---

[6]   Note, however, that (for example) the dollar value of exports of goods and non-factor services for a given year in the balance of payments may not be precisely match the national-currency value in the national accounts, converted at the year-average exchange rate. If the exchange rate varies over the year, and exports happen not to be spaced evenly over the year, then the actual average exchange rate for exports over the year may differ from the recorded average of the daily averages.

lead to financing problems several years later? A program that is inadequate in these regards is likely, sooner or later, to prove unworkable.

A repeated lesson from experience since the international "debt crisis" of the 1980s has been that an economy's fiscal, monetary, and exchange-rate policies must balance a broad range of objectives. A minimal list would include (a) economic growth, (b) improvement of private-consumption standards, (c) physical- and human- capital formation and maintenance, (d) control of public debt, (e) price and exchange-rate stability, and (f) internal financial stability. Excessive emphasis on one objective tends to distort overall macroeconomic evolution. Thus, for example, nations whose policy-makers over-emphasized external-debt management (e.g., Romania in the 1980s) limited their growth rates, impaired their populations' living standards, and ran down their physical and human capital stocks. Nations whose policy-makers relied on aggressive exchange-rate adjustment to meet balance-of-payments objectives (e.g., Brazil in the 1970s and early 1980s) often incurred the penalty of high inflation. Nations whose policy-makers relied on "hard" exchange-rate policies to meet stabilization objectives (e.g., Argentina in the 1990s) often suffered diminished growth performance and excessive external-debt accumulation. Economies that relied too heavily on tight monetary policy to limit inflation starved productive sectors of credit, and so reduced real growth and living standards.[7]

Experience of this kind suggests that policy-makers could use programming exercises, first, to ensure that they are not over-emphasizing one set of macroeconomic objectives at the expense of others, and, second, to ensure that they are not storing up unmanageable

---

[7] Some analysts believe that monetary authorities should dedicate themselves fundamentally to the objective of price-level stability. Most monetary authorities, however, even those whose charters direct them to prioritize price-level stability, in fact pursue a triad of objectives: (i) adequate availability of bank credit at tolerable interest rates; (ii) adequate foreign-exchange reserves; and (iii) price-level and exchange-rate stability. They typically aim for a practical balance of emphasis among these variables, aiming for the lowest possible inflation rate *subject to* minimum levels of credit adequacy and foreign-exchange reserves.

trouble for the future.[8] Put differently, macroeconomic programs must satisfy conditions of consistency with available resources in *all* aspects of the macroeconomy — as revealed by the national-, external-, fiscal-, and monetary-accounts identities.

"Consistency" has yet another, perhaps more subtle, significance in the approach this book describes. Financial-programming exercises of the kind this book describes differ in an important sense from other kinds of economic "model." Broadly speaking, economic models *simulate* the economic processes they describe, mathematically representing economic systems' movement toward equilibrium through price movements and stock and flow adjustments. For example, a general-equilibrium macroeconomic model might represent an economy's adjustment to a terms-of-trade "shock" by showing the period-by-period adjustments of prices and quantities in domestic financial markets, export and import markets, foreign-exchange markets, the market for external financing resources, and other markets. A "consistency exercise," in contrast, would calculate the changes in the net external financing inflow that would be *consistent with* the post-shock prices, making it possible to determine whether this inflow would be feasible — i.e., whether the programmed GDP growth and exchange rate would be still be possible, or would have to be adjusted to be consistent with available financing resources.[9]

Academic economists sometimes disparage such consistency exercises as "mere" accounting rather than genuine "modeling" exercises. This book takes the view, however, that there is no reason to consider consistency exercises any less "valid" than general-equilibrium models. Consistency exercises are simply *different* instruments of analysis. They may be more appropriate for certain practical questions that policy-makers often need to address — in particular, the financial-feasibility issues on which this book focuses. Like all instruments of

---

[8]   Analysts sometimes use the expression "time consistency" to refer to this issue. That is, macroeconomic policy needs to be set with a view to ensuring consistency "over time."

[9]   Consistency exercises like the one this book describes are often referred to as "models," but this is loose usage. It is more appropriate to describe them as "projection exercises."

analysis, they should be used when appropriate, and not used when inappropriate, or less appropriate than some alternative instrument. Well-designed consistency exercises are well suited for determining the financial feasibility of multiannual macroeconomic programs, and this book therefore recommends their use for that purpose.

Among the better-known macroeconomic consistency "models," the World Bank's "Revised Minimum Standard Model" (the "RMSM-X") has become widely familiar, not only within the Bank but among government analysts who have applied it, or considered applying it, in their own economies. The International Monetary Fund's standard programming procedure, with the "performance targets" on which it has traditionally conditioned its basic lending programs, is also a consistency exercise (see Annex 9.2). Many governments and financial institutions have come to use similar approaches in their own projection work. Commercial banks and other financial institutions that provide finance with developing economies have also developed and applied financial-programming exercises for their own purposes. Many of these are grounded in an approach articulated in the early 1980s, at the outset of the debt crisis, by William Cline (see Cline 1983). Macroeconomic consistency exercises of the kind discussed here work in broadly similar ways. The specific exercise this book describes is intended to be typical, so that readers who understand how this one works may find it easier to understand how others work.

To help understand the distinction between "equilibrium" and "consistency" models, recall the well-known Leontief fixed-coefficients input-output system (see Leontief 1951).[10] Although the Leontief system is sometimes presented in university economics courses as one kind of "general-equilibrium model," it is surely more appropriate to describe it as a consistency "model." It aims only to determine whether an economy's available productive resources would be *consistent with* final-output objectives, assuming that the estimated or assumed input-output

---

[10] For a given set of net final outputs an economy intends to produce, the Leontief system determines the gross output that must be produced, taking account of the reality that some of the gross output must be used as inputs in the production of the final outputs. In the Leontief system, each unit of any output requires a fixed unit of the various types of input.

coefficients apply. Although widely considered a helpful planning exercise, in its basic version, as has often been pointed out, it incorporates no adjustment mechanism by which the productive structure would move to "equilibrium."

In this book's projection exercise, in each aspect of the macroeconomic structure, year-by-year projections are carried out so as to yield *residuals* — typically, (a) non-government consumption and capital formation for the national accounts, (b) the "gap-filling financing" required "to close" the external accounts, (c) internal public debt accumulation for the fiscal accounts, and (d) the required monetary-policy stance. A key point of the methodological approach is that *these residuals are evaluated for feasibility.* Thus, for example, if the projected external accounts require more external financing than foreigners could be expected to provide, it would be appropriate to revise the programming assumptions — e.g., to reduce the programmed real GDP growth rate, or to program a more depreciated real-effective exchange rate, so as to reduce import demand.

Three additional points should be noted here. First, it cannot be too strongly emphasized that it would be methodologically inappropriate to use consistency analysis, of any kind, for *prediction.* The fact that the exercise indicates, say, that a given public deficit would be consistent with a given set of programmed macroeconomic outcomes by no means implies that the deficit and outcomes will, or are even likely to, occur. What a consistency exercise can provide is confirmation that a particular programmed government expenditure program *would be* financially feasible within the context of a macroeconomic program — specifically, that the resulting public deficit and balance of payments *could* be financed, that the banking system *could* provide sufficient credit to support the assumed GDP growth, and that the required flow of non-government saving *would* be feasible. Broadly speaking, a projection that satisfied consistency criteria *could* occur; a projection that failed to satisfy consistency criteria presumably could not.[11]

---

[11]   The exercise this book describes calculates "projections," not "forecasts." That is, the exercise is intended as a policy-planning instrument, not a device for formulating predictions.

Second, while a macroeconomic consistency exercise can help gauge the financial feasibility of a government's overall multiannual expenditure program, it would not generally be useful for determining the efficiency, much less the effectiveness, of government expenditure. Nor would it be likely to be much help in addressing issues of expenditure equity. Again, the general point is that macroeconomic consistency exercises are useful to address *some*, but not *all*, relevant issues facing policy-makers. When evaluating multiannual government expenditure programs, macroeconomic consistency exercises should be used *in conjunction with* medium-term expenditure framework (MTEF) exercises. If available, the MTEF is the appropriate instrument for expenditure effectiveness, efficiency, and prioritization; the macroeconomic projection exercise is the appropriate instrument for determining the financial feasibility of the combined macroeconomic and expenditure program.

Third, financial feasibility is not the only kind of feasibility that matters for a government-expenditure program. As in any economy, capital expenditure plans, and indeed many kinds of current expenditure, should be reviewed for technical feasibility. In some economies with weak execution systems, it is prudent to review some kinds of expenditure to determine whether they are likely to reach their intended beneficiaries — another dimension of feasibility. Particularly for developing economies, however, there is a wide range of expenditure-feasibility characteristics that are often summarized in the expression "absorption capacity." Expenditure planners, especially those with inadequate knowledge of country circumstances, can easily overlook these. It may be financially feasible for a government to hire more teachers for rural schools, but in a developing economy qualified teachers willing to work in rural areas may be in short supply. The current national investment program may be within the government's financial-resource "envelope," but qualified project administrators, or engineers or workers with relevant skills, may be in short supply. Financial feasibility is pretty much the only kind of feasibility the macroeconomic exercise this book describes can address, however.

1.5   Programming assumptions

When working with macroeconomic consistency exercises, it is essential
to bear in mind that they characteristically use programming assumptions
not only for policy settings and "exogenous" international and internal
economic conditions, but also for the *outcomes* of such key
macroeconomic variables in each projection year as the real gross
domestic product (GDP), the inflation rate, and the exchange rate —
even if the exchange rate is floating. Analysts sometimes find it peculiar,
at least at first, *to assume* values for the GDP, inflation or exchange-rate
outcomes: it would seem more natural to suppose that these should be the
results of a macroeconomic projection exercise. The point is that
consistency exercises characteristically work by setting programming
assumptions for objectives and outcomes, and then determining the
requirements — productive inputs in the case of the Leontief system,
financing flows in the case of the exercise this book describes — that
would be *consistent* with them.

The programming assumptions on which macroeconomic projection
exercises are based may be grouped in four categories:

(1) "**structural parameters**," i.e., parameters that quantitatively
define the relationships among variables, such as (a) elasticities
of export and import volumes with respect to world market
growth, real-GDP growth, real capital-formation growth, and
"real-effective" prices (prices adjusted for projected exchange
rates and prices), (b) parameters defining the relationships
among capital formation, real-GDP growth and labor-force
growth; (c) parameters defining the demand for money and cash-
deposit ratios; and others;

(2) relevant **world economic conditions and internal exogenous
variables**, such as the real growth rates of export and import
prices and markets; world inflation and interest rates; and growth
rates of internal exogenous variables such as oil-production
flows;

(3) **macroeconomic programming objectives**, such as real-GDP
growth, inflation, the exchange rate, internal interest rates, and
so on; and

(4) **macroeconomic policy settings**, including such fiscal parameters as tax rates and other public-revenue determinants, employment and remuneration rates for public workers, and such monetary parameters as reserve ratios and interest rates set by the monetary authority. Policy settings, broadly defined, also include the sizes of the government's non-interest expenditure programs and the government's program for external and internal financing.

While this taxonomy of assumption settings is useful for discussions of projection techniques and of particular projection exercises, it is important to note that the distinctions are not always hard and fast. Particular assumptions may sometimes fall into more than one category. For example, consider the elasticity of (say) the volume of cotton exports with respect to the world cotton-trade volume. Export elasticities are presumably "structural parameters." Since a value exceeding one would imply an increase in market share, (see Section 6.4), such an assumption could stand for (a) declining cotton exports from competing economies — i.e., an exogenous world condition, *or* (b) a government program to stimulate cotton exports — i.e., a policy setting. An exchange-rate assumption is another example: it could be either a policy objective or a policy setting, depending on the projected exchange-rate policy. Under a freely-floating exchange rate, for example, the assumption would be a policy objective; under a conventional fixed exchange rate, in contrast, it would be a policy setting.

As always in economic projection work, the results of exercises of the kind this book describes require careful interpretation. Analysts interpreting given results must examine not only the "bottom-line" financial-feasibility indicators, but also the full range of projection results, to understand which assumptions "drive" the results obtained. Determining the implications for policy feasibility requires a measure of judgment regarding (say) how much external financing would be available or how much private consumption or public-sector wage rates could rise or be "compressed" as the case may be. The spreadsheet exercise itself cannot do this. A *computer*-based exercise should be able to show a more complicated range of connections among economic variables than most human minds ordinarily comprehend. After examining the results, however, the analyst must apply judgment, skill and experience to understand out their significance.

1.6   Pacífica's macroeconomy

To illustrate the techniques it discusses, this book describes a projection exercise for a hypothetical economy. The "Republic of Pacífica" is imagined to be a mid-sized economy in the Western Hemisphere. Its estimated mid-2008 population was 8.2 million and its 2008 GDP was US$26.6 billion, for a per-capita GDP just under US$3,260. Pacífica's merchandise exports comprised crude oil, bananas and manufactured products, together amounting in 2008 to 24.6 per cent of GDP. Crude-oil production, estimated at just under 210,000 barrels a day for 2008, has been an important foreign-exchange earner, although it provides Pacífica little influence in world oil markets.

Like many other developing economies, Pacífica has been struggling for decades with inadequate and variable real growth, persisting poverty, high external debt, and export-commodity dependence. In recent years, however, economic liberalization, structural reform, and disciplined macroeconomic policy, together with favorable world export conditions, have brought about some growth. The onset of world recession in 2008 and 2009 has raised concerns for the future, however.

The projection exercise is assumed to be carried out in June 2009. At this moment, historical data are complete through 2008, although subject to further revision. (The base year for the projections is 2008 and the initial projection year is 2009.) Table 1 gives summary indicators for the economy's performance in the last five historical years, 2004–2008.

The world economic crisis of 1998 had interrupted Pacífica's growth from the early 1990s, and the economy recovered relatively slowly over subsequent years. After 2003, however, ***real-GDP growth*** significantly exceeded annual population growth (estimated at 2 per cent). For 2006–2008, real growth rates were 5.5, 5.7 and 6.0 per cent respectively. Rising oil-export prices figured heavily in bringing about this growth. Pacífica's policy-makers were all too aware in 2009 that sharply declining oil prices and world-trade volumes imply that real growth will be most likely be negative in 2009 and very low in 2010.

Gross fixed capital formation was about 19.7 per cent of GDP in 2008, slightly lower than in 2005, 2006 and 2007. Capital formation has been lackluster, but has exceeded the 16.6 per cent rate recorded in 2001. The ***net exports of goods and non-factor services*** account, which had shown deficits of about 1 per cent of GDP in 2004 and 2005, recorded surpluses of 2.3, 1, and 0.9 per cent in 2006–2008. In 2008, ***real per-capita non-government consumption*** stood at about US$1,934, measured at the 2005 exchange rate and price level. This represented an annual average increase of 1.8 per cent over the 2003 value, a disappointingly low growth rate. Even so, the overall ***poverty incidence*** diminished from 20.5 per cent in 2004 to 17 per cent in 2008 while the extreme-poverty incidence diminished from 9.4 per cent to 7.4 per cent. Policy-makers were well aware in 2009, however, that it would be difficult to make additional progress until the recession passes.

The price level and exchange rate were essentially stable after 2004. Consumer prices had risen at annual rates on the order of 9–11 per cent from 1996 through 2000, and had risen 5.8 per cent in 2003. From 2004 through 2008, however, disciplined monetary policy reduced the inflation rate from 4.1 per cent in 2004 to 2.7 per cent in 2008. Meanwhile, both the nominal- and real-effective exchange rates remained steady. In 2009 policy-makers remained determined to hold inflation consistently at world levels over coming years, but were well aware that the exchange rate was coming under pressure to depreciate, in both nominal and real-effective terms.

With the improved trade performance, Pacífica's long-standing deficit in ***the current account of the balance of payments*** became a surplus. The current-account deficits had been 1.2 and 1.3 per cent of GDP in 2004 and 2005, but these were followed by surpluses exceeding 1 per cent of GDP in the following two years and a surplus of 1.4 per cent in 2008, when average oil-export prices were particularly high. Capital and financial inflows over the period 2004–2008 averaged

2.2 per cent of GDP. Multilateral and bilateral institutions maintained steady support, but direct foreign investment flows averaged about 2 per cent of GDP. Gross foreign-exchange reserves, which stood at 3.8 and 3.7 months' of imports of goods and non-factor services respectively at the ends of 2004 and 2005, rose to 5 months by the end of 2008. In 2009, however, the authorities were prepared for some deterioration in the current account, and expected to allow foreign-exchange reserves to diminish somewhat.

In 2006 and 2007 rising real-GDP growth enabled Pacífica's authorities to hold the *central-government deficit* within 1 per cent of GDP. In 2008 the deficit improved to 0.4 per cent of GDP. Total central-government revenue amounted to 20.7 per cent of GDP. Of this total, 3.9 percentage points derived from oil, and 12 percentage points from sources not directly associated with oil. Total central-government expenditure amounted to 21.4 per cent of GDP. Of this total, 14.1 percentage points corresponded to current non-interest expenditure, 2.7 percentage points to external and internal interest, and 4.7 percentage points to government capital expenditure.

Measured at 2005 prices and at the 2005 year-average exchange rate, per-capita real *non-oil tax and tariff revenue* rose steadily, from about US$519 in 2004 to about US$602 in 2008. The 2008 figure represented an annual average increase of 3.6 per cent over the 2003 figure. Meanwhile, per-capita real overall government expenditure rose from about US$658 in 2004 to about US$791 in 2008, a 4.9 per cent annual average increase from 2003. Per-capita real government external interest due rose from about US$72 in 2004 to about US$78 in 2008. In 2009 the authorities were well aware that slower future growth was likely to reduce tax revenue and widen the central-government deficit. They considered standing proposals to increase the value-added tax rate from 12 to 14 per cent, but were reluctant to raise tax rates at a time when the economy faced recession.

To finance substantial fiscal- and external-accounts deficits in the late 1990s, Pacífica took on a substantial stock of *external debt*. At the end of 2003 Pacífica's overall external-debt stock amounted to 30 per cent of GDP. The public and publicly guaranteed part of this — all of which was owed by the central government — amounted to 26.5 per cent of GDP. Neither figure was especially high by comparison with the most heavily indebted developing economies, but they were high enough to merit careful monitoring by policy-makers.   External interest due amounted to 1.9 per cent of GDP in 2003, of which 1.8 per cent corresponded to the public and publicly guaranteed debt. Over the next five years, Pacífica achieved some reduction in its overall external-debt stock as a percentage of GDP, in part because GDP growth was relatively strong.   At the end of 2008 Pacífica's overall external-debt stock amounted to 25.2 per cent of GDP, of which 22 per cent of GDP was public and publicly guaranteed. External interest due amounted to 1.7 per cent of GDP, of which 1.4 per cent corresponded to the public and publicly guaranteed debt. In mid-2009, however, policy-makers were aware that slowing real-GDP growth would make it difficult to sustain progress on reducing the debt stock and interest bill as percentages of GDP.

One worrisome trend has been that the **central-government internal debt** has been rising as a percentage of GDP. At the end of 2003 the central government's gross internal debt had reached 18.5 per cent of GDP.   The central government had internal financial assets (deposit accounts in the central bank and commercial banks) amounting to 2.4 per cent of GDP, so its net internal debt amounted to 16.1 per cent of GDP.   The internal debt continued to grow after 2003, because central-government policy-makers tried to reduce their reliance on external borrowing to finance the deficit. At the end of 2008 the central government's gross internal debt had reached 23.5 per cent of GDP. The central government's internal financial assets amounted to 3.1 per cent of GDP, so that its net internal debt amounted to 20.4 per cent of GDP. Policy-makers were concerned about this problem in mid-2009, and hoped that they could find ways to limit if not reverse the growth of the government's net internal-debt stock.

Pacífica's price and exchange-rate stability after 2003 resulted largely from effective **monetary policy**. The economy's monetization has steadily deepened: the year-end money stock rose as a percentage of GDP from just under 50 per cent for 2003 to 52.4 per cent for 2008, while the monetary base rose as a percentage of GDP from 15.3 per cent for 2003 to 16.9 per cent for 2008. The central bank's year-end net

international-reserve holdings over the period increased from 5.7 per cent
of GDP for 2003 to 12.1 per cent for 2008. Through skillful monetary
policy, the central bank's net domestic assets fell as a percentage of GDP
from 9.5 per cent for 2003 to 4.8 per cent for 2008.

Questions for which policy-makers and foreign observers would
presumably seek answers from a multiannual projection exercise include
the following:

(1) Take as given the projection exercise's assumed structural
parameters and exogenous variables. The authorities anticipate
that real GDP will decline about 4.5 per cent in 2009, but that the
growth rate will rise gradually to about 5 per cent per year by
2015. Meanwhile, inflation will continue to run roughly at world
rates. They expect the average nominal exchange rate to
depreciate gradually from 9 per U.S. dollar in 2009 to 9.60 in
2011. At the same time, they intend to carry out adjustments to
the government's expenditure flows favoring education, health,
and infrastructure. If the other main macroeconomic policy
settings remain basically unchanged, how would the (a) current-
account deficit, (b) non-financial public-sector deficit,
(c) "unprogrammed" external-debt inflows, and (d) per-capita
real private consumption evolve? Would they evolve
unsustainably, in the sense that the implied external and internal
financing requirements would become unfeasibly large?

(2) Suppose that the answer to this first question is that the
macroeconomic program would prove unsustainable, in the sense
that the external and/or internal debt-GDP ratios would tend to
grow explosively. What policy changes would bring about
sustainability? Suppose that the authorities are willing to
consider less ambitious macroeconomic objectives. What
combination of reductions in programmed real GDP growth and
increases in programmed inflation rates would enable them to
reduce the prospective external and internal financing
requirements? What combination of changes in macroeconomic
objectives and policy variables could they consider, and what

consequences could these be expected to have? In particular, should the authorities consider increasing the value-added tax rate? Would it help to seek debt relief?

(3) Suppose that the answer to the first question is that the macroeconomy would evolve sustainably under its assumptions. Would it evolve sustainably under less favorable assumptions? In particular, how vulnerable is the macroeconomy to conceivable "exogenous shocks"?

(4) Finally, suppose that the results of the analysis suggest that no feasible policy change is likely to lead to sustainable evolution of the macroeconomy. It might then be necessary to consider arrears in debt service or negotiated debt reduction. The analysis could be used to consider the amount of debt reduction necessary to bring about sustainability.

This book's remaining chapters describe how macroeconomic consistency analysis could be used to address these questions.

1.7   The book's structure

This book is organized as follows: Chapter 2 presents a *summary overview of the projection procedure*. (Annex 2.1 lists the steps in the calculation procedure, and Annex 2.2 sets out a *simplified version of the projection procedure* in equations.) Chapters 3, 4, and 5 then describe the main components of the *macroeconomic program* that forms the basis of the projection analysis. Chapter 3 discusses the *"basic" macroeconomic assumptions* underlying each year's projections, including real GDP growth, the year-average and year-end price level, the year-average and year-end exchange rate, and their relationships. Chapter 4 discusses techniques for programming *government expenditure*. Chapter 5 discusses techniques for programming *external and internal-government financing*.

Chapters 6, 7, 8 and 9 then describe how the macroeconomic program can be used to formulate national-, external-, fiscal-, and monetary-accounts projections. Chapter 6 sets out a basic **national-accounts** framework to help determine whether an adequate non-government saving flow is likely to be available, given the assumptions for programmed government consumption and capital-formation expenditure. Chapter 7 presents a consistency framework for the **external accounts**, focusing, in turn, on the non-debt external accounts, the external accounts involving debt, and reconciliation of "above-" and "below-the-line" balance-of-payments projections. This reconciliation procedure aims to determine the external financing required, to see whether the balance of payments could be feasibly financed under the policy assumptions. Chapter 8 discusses the projection exercise's **fiscal-accounts** aspects. The basic idea is to determine the public sector's overall internal borrowing requirement, to see whether it could be feasibly met. Chapter 9 describes a programming methodology for the **monetary accounts**. Building on the previous chapters, it describes the links between the monetary- and the national-accounts, fiscal and external projections. It describes a procedure to determine whether the projected medium-term monetary program would need to be unfeasibly contractionary to hold inflation to the programmed level. In each of these chapters, one section illustrates the projection techniques using the "Pacífica" exercise.

Finally, Chapter 10 discusses some of the **practical issues** that arise in projection work. These include the criteria for setting out parameter assumptions, the use of econometric estimation techniques, and "fudging." The final part of the chapter discusses sensitivity analysis, with examples from the "Pacifica" exercise.

On the topic of "practical issues," one final note concludes this chapter. The methodology and specific techniques this book describes aim, above all, to be practical, to serve the cause of sound and efficient policy-making. Practical projection methodology should always be grounded in solid economic theory. In some instances, however, practicality and simplicity require compromises with full theoretical correctness. In such instances, every effort is made to be transparent.

2　Overview of the projection procedure

Trying to make things easier leads to great difficulties.

– attributed to Lao-Tse

2.1　The projection procedure

As Chapter 1 explained, the multiannual macroeconomic projection methodology this book describes consists of

(1) setting out programming assumptions over several future years regarding (a) exogenous external and (b) internal variables (the "state of the world"); (c) basic macroeconomic variables; (d) policy settings for revenue, external flows, and monetary policy; (e) government non-financial expenditure; and (f) public-sector financing programs; then,

(2) using these assumptions to generate projections of the (i) national, (ii) fiscal, (iii) external, and (iv) monetary accounts, and, finally,

(3) evaluating these projections for financial feasibility.

The four sets of accounts are projected separately but consistently — that is, on the basis of common assumptions, and in such a way that, in any projection year, common accounts are consistent. In each set of accounts, for each year, one account is determined residually from the other accounts, on the basis of the "identity" governing that set of accounts. "Financial feasibility" is then evaluated by determining whether this "residual" account would be too large or small.

In principle, what is "too large or small" is a judgment call. Analysts may sometimes find it difficult to say whether a specific future required financing flow would be unfeasible. Rapidly rising external and internal public debt would usually be a worrisome sign, as would slow real per-capita private consumption growth. Some judgment calls would

be easy enough.   A particular macroeconomic program and a
government-expenditure program for a given year might be "consistent,"
say, with net new external borrowing amounting, say, to 35 per cent of
the economy's GDP, but this would obviously be far larger than any
actual national economy could obtain or want.   External lenders taken
together would not want to increase their exposure so quickly to any
single economy, and a national economy could not absorb so large a flow
of new debt in one year.   The projection exercise itself would show that a
large lending flow in any given year would imply larger debt-servicing
charges in subsequent years.   Policy-makers and external lenders would
generally want to limit the economy's public and private borrowing,
among other reasons because the debt-service commitments would
increase the likelihood of unfeasibly large financing requirements in
those subsequent years.

This chapter outlines a sequence of steps through which each
year's projection is, in principle, formulated.[12]   Section 2.2 briefly
describes how the assumptions constituting the macroeconomic program
would be set out.   The four sections following summarize how the
macroeconomic program would then be used to formulate projections of
the national (Section 2.3), external (Section 2.4), fiscal (Section 2.5), and
monetary (Section 2.6) accounts.   Section 2.7 reviews the consistency
relationships among these sets of accounts.   Section 2.8 gives some
concluding observations. Chapters 3–9 below then describe the procedures
outlined in this chapter in greater detail.

To be sure, the actual calculation procedure for the four sets of
accounts is simultaneous, not sequenced: each set of accounts draws
from and contributes to the other sets of accounts.   Thus, for example,
the fiscal-accounts projections require the projections of (tariff-
generating) imports, which are carried out with the external-accounts; the
monetary-accounts calculation requires the external-accounts projections
involving the central bank's external assets and liabilities; and so on.   To
help understand it, though, it can be helpful to think of the projection

---

[12]   The contents of the steps are unequal. They range in complexity from a simple line
of assumptions to project the annual increases in the economy's inventory stocks to
setting all of the projection exercise's structural parameters.

procedure as if it had a logical sequence. To make it work, the cross-relationships are therefore somewhat simplified.

This chapter has three annexes. Annex 2.1 gives a summary listing of the solution procedure. Annex 2.2 sets out a simplified version of the projection exercise in algebraic equations. Annex 2.3 extends the simplified version of the exercise to incorporate the banking system, in particular, the banking system's credit-provision capacity.

2.2 Programming assumptions

This section summarizes the first seven steps in the "sequence" through which the projection is formulated for each year. The first step sets up the projection exercise, and the next six steps set out the macroeconomic program. Sections 2.3, 2.4, 2.5 and 2.6 following describe the subsequent steps, which explain how the macroeconomic program generates the national-, external-, fiscal-, and monetary-accounts projections.

The *first* step in the projection procedure is to set the assumptions for the exercise's **structural parameters**. These encompass a broad range of parameters that figure in the national, external, fiscal and monetary accounts, including the incremental capital-output ratio, the elasticities of the various import elasticities with respect to real GDP, the "collection efficiencies" of various kinds of tax, and the elasticity of the demand for money with respect to real GDP. These parameters, so to speak, "transform" the programmed key macroeconomic variables into the full set of projections.

Many of these structural parameters have "default," or "neutral" values — that is, values which it is usually best to use unless there are good, specific reasons to use different values. Thus, for example, it is usually best to assume that the projected values of the elasticity of the volume of intermediate imported goods with respect to real GDP will be one — that is, that the real volumes of such imports will grow at the same rate as real GDP. The reason this would be the "default" assumption is that, all other things being equal, assuming a higher (lower) value than one would tend, all other things being equal, to generate a rising (falling) ratio of such imports to GDP. This would tend to generate a growing (diminishing) balance-of-payments financing requirement as a percentage of GDP. *As a general rule, analysts should take care to avoid setting assumptions that tend to produce projections of deterioration (or improvement).* In special circumstances, when (say) an import surge is anticipated with recovery from recession, it may be reasonable to assume a moderately higher elasticity for one or two future years, but then have the elasticity revert to, or toward the default value for subsequent years (see Section 10.3).

In particular, it is best to use such default values rather than econometric estimates (see Section 10.3). For developing economies, econometric estimates calculated from historical data are likely to have wide confidence intervals, and the point estimates may well be inappropriate for projection exercises of the kind this book describes. Empirical structural parameters are likely to be unstable in developing economies, and so the past is often a dubious guide to formulating projection assumptions.

Discussions of the most appropriate assumptions for structural parameters are given with the discussions of the national-, external-, fiscal-, and monetary-accounts projections in Sections 2.3, 2.4, 2.5, and 2.6 below and in more detail in Chapters 6–9.

The *next six* steps in the procedure correspond to articulation of the macroeconomic program. As noted in Section 1.1 above, the macroeconomic program that forms the basis of the projection, and which the projection "tests" for feasibility, may be set out in six groupings: (a) assumptions for exogenous international and (b) internal variables, (c) basic macroeconomic assumptions, (d) policy settings, (e) programmed government expenditure, and (f) the public-sector financing program. Each of the next six steps in the procedure corresponds to one of these six groupings.

Accordingly, the *second* step is the formulation of assumptions for **exogenous external variables**. Among these, several would rank as "key" assumptions — that is, assumptions that affect a large number of projection variables or/and for which relatively small changes might produce significant changes in projection results. Among "external" variables, the growth rate of world trade, the world U.S. dollar price level, and world interest rates — in particular, "LIBOR", the London

Inter-bank Offer Rate[13] — are likely to count as key assumptions. The world oil price is likely to be a key assumption both for oil exporters and importers. The price of a nation's principal export commodity (e.g., copper for Chile, oil for Venezuela, coffee for Viet Nam) would also be a key assumption. The "key" assumptions are presumably those the user would want to vary in sensitivity analysis. The idea would be to construct different conceivable "scenarios," comprising sets of year-by-year assumptions for the key variables, and determine their respective financial feasibility. (Section 10.5 discusses sensitivity analysis.)

The best general recommendation about formulating assumptions for exogenous external variables is to set them *conservatively*. Future world-oil prices, for example, should be assumed to be relatively high for oil-importing and relatively low for oil-exporting economies; world interest rates should be assumed either to rise to or remain at relatively high levels. On the whole, it is advisable to make simple assumptions: thus, for example, growth rates of future world-oil prices should be assumed to remain relatively steady in U.S. dollar or real terms, or to grow in real terms on a simple trend, rather than to undergo complicated patterns of evolution.[14]

The *third* step would be to set out assumptions for ***exogenous internal variables***. The most important of these would be demographic variables. The population growth rate should be a key exogenous assumption, given its importance for projected per-capita values.[15]

---

[13]   The London Inter-bank Offer Rates are the deposit rates offered by banks operating in London, in different currencies and maturities, as recorded through a survey taken at 11:00am every business day. It has come to be used as a reference rate for variable-rate loans (see Section 5.2).

[14]   If available, it may be useful to apply assumptions for world variables generated by international agencies such as the International Monetary Fund and World Bank. For some world prices and market conditions, analysts may want to consult specialized government and business analysts.

[15]   This book generally takes population growth rates to be exogenous. Some governments have programs to limit (or, in a few cases, to increase) population growth. Sensitivity analysis could take such programs into account by considering scenarios with different population growth rates. To be sure, though, while government population programs can affect longer-term population growth rates, it is doubtful that they could make much difference in the medium term (i.e., the coming three to five years).

Growth rates of population cohorts may also be important, however —
for example, the growth rate of the school-age population would
obviously be helpful to program education expenditure (see Annex 4.1).
(If demographic variables are used extensively in the projection exercise,
it may be useful to consult with demographic specialists.)

If the projection exercise incorporates assumptions regarding
growth rates and deflators in productive sectors, however, these values
might also be in the category of exogenous internal conditions. It may
be best, however, to program real sectoral growth rates by relating them
to the overall real-GDP growth rate, and/or to program assumptions for
the growth rates of sectoral deflators by relating them to the growth rate
of the overall GDP deflator. (Section 3.4 describes techniques for doing
so.) Even if a specific economy's exercise does not include a full set of
sectoral output projections, it may include assumptions regarding
important specific sectors. Assumptions regarding the evolution of
hydrocarbons or mining production, for example, may fall into the
category of exogenous internal variables. If the output of specific sectors
is particularly important, it may be useful to formulate the relevant
assumptions on the basis of industry information or on the basis of
analysis by specialists.

In economies where oil exports are significant, it may be
advisable to use "auxiliary" projection exercises to project output,
exports, and government revenue deriving from oil. Oil sectors are
especially complex, because output depends on complicated geological
circumstances and revenues are related to world prices through what are
often highly intricate contracts. Moreover, in many oil-exporting
economies the relevant information is not publicly available. If no
auxiliary oil-sector exercise is used, the growth rate of output can be
assumed, and exports and government revenue then projected by means
of additional assumptions.

The *fourth* step would be to set out programming assumptions
for the **key macroeconomic variables**. Chapter 3 discusses this aspect of
the programming process in detail. These assumptions are likely to be
the most important in the exercise. Analysts and policy-makers will
want to know whether the given combination of real-GDP, price-level,

and real-effective exchange-rate growth rates *per se* will prove feasible, given world circumstances. These variables will also figure in the full range of the macroeconomic program, including government expenditures, other policy settings, and the external and internal financing program.

The principle that assumptions should be set conservatively applies to these assumptions, but, given their importance, they are likely to be the assumptions varied in sensitivity-analysis exercises. One of the uses of the exercise may be to determine just how far policy-makers can go in bringing about favorable macroeconomic performance — whether they can bring about faster growth while reducing inflation and maintaining exchange-rate stability without running into financing limitations. It is important, though, that the basic programming assumptions be set realistically: few countries have managed to sustain real-GDP growth rates above 6 or 7 per cent for more than a few years without running into supply constraints, and, without extraordinary measures, inflation rates may prove difficult to bring down quickly.

Among the basic programming assumptions, the growth rates of real GDP, the price level, and the (real-effective) exchange rate would rate as key variables for just about any economy. (As Chapter 3 explains, because they serve different purposes in the projection procedure, the year-*average* and year-*end* inflation and exchange rates will differ in general, but must be projected consistently.) In addition, the central bank's year-end gross international reserve holdings — customarily set out in terms of months of imports of goods and non-factor services — would be yet another key programming assumption, since this variable figures fundamentally in both the external and monetary accounts.

The key macroeconomic variables would also include the growth rates of each sector's output and deflator, if these are taken into account in the projection exercise. (Section 3.4 discusses this aspect of the programming process in detail.) Incorporation of the sectoral growth rates is optional for the projection exercise as this book describes it. Note that if they are incorporated, if the programmed overall growth rates of real GDP and the GDP deflator vary in sensitivity analysis, then the programmed sectoral growth rates would have to vary as well.

The *fifth* step would be to set assumptions for **policy variables**, such as tax rates, tariff rates, minimum required reserve ratios for banks, and others (other than those involving government expenditure, which is the following step). As noted in Section 1.5, the real-effective exchange-rate assumption may be considered a macroeconomic programming assumption if it is to be market-determined, a policy assumption if the authorities intend to manage it, or both at once, and the same is true of some of the other assumptions. Some of these settings may be key assumptions, depending on their importance in current circumstances. For example, if the possibility of raising the value-added tax rate is under discussion, it may be useful to have it as a key assumption, subject to variation in sensitivity analysis.

The *sixth* step would be to set out assumptions for **government non-interest current and capital expenditure**. Chapter 4 discusses this aspect of the programming process in detail. Assumptions for future government expenditure should be formulated not simply as percentages of GDP, but on the basis of anticipated needs, especially if the authorities intend to carry out expenditure programs directed to development and poverty-reduction objectives. Ideally, expenditure should be programmed on the basis of the personnel and capital-formation requirements in the various aspects of the government's budget as necessary to achieve those objectives. Expenditure projections should take realistic account of demographic projections (after all, if government services are provided to citizens, it stands to reason that expenditure on government services will be related to the number of citizens), and of the (real) remuneration of government staff.

Assumptions regarding non-interest government expenditure flows should be set out in three "economic" categories, (i) consumption expenditure, defined as recurring staff remuneration and expenditure on current goods and services; (ii) gross fixed capital-formation expenditure; and (iii) other non-interest expenditure. Consumption and gross fixed capital-formation expenditure figure in the national-accounts expenditure accounts, while all three categories of expenditure figure in the expenditure side of the fiscal accounts. "Other non-interest expenditure" includes the various categories of income transfer from government to non-government entities, including subsidies. (This is discussed in more detail in Section 4.2.)

The *seventh* and last step in the task of setting out the assumption base would be to set out programming **assumptions for government external and internal debt**. Chapter 5 discusses this aspect of the programming process in detail. Under the specific approach this book recommends, *"identified"* future *external*-debt disbursements and repayments would be programmed creditor by creditor. Indeed, they would be programmed creditor-by-creditor under the various *debtor* categories, such as the central government, sub-national governments, public enterprises, and the central bank.

The assumptions for *identified* external-debt flows affect financing accounts in both the fiscal and the external accounts. As this chapter's Section 2.4 explains, however, total external-debt disbursements *to non-government entities* would be calculated to include possible *unidentified* external-debt disbursements. These would fill any positive external-accounts financing gap, and so ensure that the balance-of-payments identity is satisfied. Similarly, as this chapter's Section 2.5 explains, total *internal-debt* disbursements to the government would be calculated to include possible *unidentified* disbursements from internal creditors. These would fill any positive fiscal-accounts financing gap, and so ensure that the fiscal-accounts identity is satisfied.

Table 2 lists the basic macroeconomic programming assumptions and assumptions regarding key world economic conditions for Pacífica in the projection period. These figures are the "Pacífica" projection exercise's most important programming assumptions. In 2009, annual-average world U.S. dollar prices would remain unchanged. They would grow about 1 per cent in 2010, and thereafter would grow at a 2 per cent annual rate. Meanwhile, (real) world commerce would decline 4.5 per cent in 2010, grow 2.5 per cent in 2010, and grow after that at a 5.5 per cent real annual rate. LIBOR would average 1.7 per cent for 2009, and then rise gradually to 4 per cent by 2015. The *real* world oil price would decline by just over 30 per cent in 2009, but then recover partially by 7.7 per cent in 2010 and continue rising from there at 0.8 per cent per year.

In Pacífica's "base" programming scenario, real GDP would decline 4.5 per cent in 2009. It would then recover gradually over subsequent years, reaching 5 per cent in 2015. Consumer prices would rise 2.2 per cent between December 2008 and December 2009, but would have leveled off before the end of the year. They would not grow at all between December 2009 and December 2010. After that they would grow at a 2 per cent annual rate (the same as world U.S. dollar prices). The annual average real-effective exchange rate is assumed to depreciate 0.8 per cent over 2009, bringing the nominal exchange rate to 9.60 per U.S. dollar at the year's end (compared with 9.00 per U.S. dollar at the previous year's end). The nominal exchange rate would thereafter remain unchanged, which would imply an annual-average real-effective depreciation of 3.2 per cent in 2010 and just under 1 per cent in 2011. After that, since Pacífica's inflation rate would be the same as the world U.S. dollar inflation rate and the nominal exchange rate would remain unchanged, Pacífica's real-effective exchange rate would remain unchanged. Year-end central-bank foreign-exchange reserves would be allowed to decline in terms of months' worth of imports of goods and non-factor services from five at the end of 2005 to four at the end of 2010. The authorities would then target this year-end reserve level for subsequent years. Finally, the population is assumed to continue growing at its long-standing 2 per cent annual rate.

To be sure, these are only the more significant projection assumptions. Many more assumptions are required. These "key" assumptions figure heavily in the national-, fiscal-, external-, and monetary-accounts projections, however. They enter into virtually all the Pacífica projections summarized in the following sections of this chapter, through the assumed relationships explained in detail in the remainder of the book. This chapter's remaining sections summarize how the key assumptions are used to calculate the various accounts projections and their residuals. Chapters 3–9 then describe the full range of assumptions and calculations used to complete the projections for each of the four groupings of accounts.

Once the program assumptions are in place, the projection exercise then proceeds through the national, fiscal, external and monetary accounts, as described in the sections following, to formulate the basic projections and to determine the residuals used to gauge the program's feasibility.

2.3   National-accounts projections

For each projection year, five steps may be identified in the national-accounts projection procedure (described in detail in Chapter 6). The *first* would be to determine each year's **gross capital formation**. This is done by applying an assumed relationship between programmed real GDP growth in subsequent years and the current year's capital formation.[16] The exercise assumes, in effect, that the capital stock is the binding physical constraint on the economy's real-GDP growth (see Section 6.2). While other factors of production, not to mention such things as weather, affect any economy's output flow, the exercise effectively assumes that capital formation is the basic requirement for and constraint on longer-term growth.

The *second* step in the national-accounts projection procedure would be to apply an assumption regarding the economy's **increase in inventory holdings** over the year. For a developing economy, one approach is to assume that the increase in inventory holdings in any given year will be a fixed percentage of the increase in nominal GDP, which would keep inventory stocks constant as a percentage of GDP (see Section 6.3). Basic macroeconomic theory holds that inventory holdings reflect the business cycle, diminishing in expansionary phases and expanding in recessionary phases. While the exercise this book describes is not intended to project business cycles, assumptions for nearer-term years may reflect the current and projected business-cycle phases. If so, the analyst may wish to make the corresponding assumptions for inventory accumulation.

---

[16]   Any given year's capital formation could be projected independently from subsequent real-GDP growth. Nevertheless, it seems sensible to posit *some* relationship between real-GDP growth and capital formation in the projection exercise. One of the presumable implications of higher programmed future real-GDP growth is that it would require more productive capacity, hence higher capital formation. See Chapter 6, Section 6.2.

The *third* step would be to project ***exports and imports of goods and non-factor services***. In this step, the assumptions regarding world international conditions and the main programming variables — in particular, real GDP growth and the (real-effective) exchange rate — are applied using assumed elasticities to determine the flow volumes of exports and imports. (Section 6.4 describes the details of the procedures used to make these calculations.)

The *fourth* step would be to bring the projected totals from the government's non-interest expenditure program — i.e., ***government consumption and capital-formation expenditure*** — into the national-expenditure accounts.

The *fifth and last* step in the national-accounts projection procedure would be to calculate the ***non-government consumption and non-government capital formation*** flows. These flows are calculated residually. Non-government capital formation is determined by subtracting the programmed government capital formation from total capital formation. If this figure is very large as a percentage of GDP, or by comparison with its real value in earlier years, the analyst may conclude that the programmed real growth rate might not be feasible. Non-government consumption is determined by subtracting programmed government consumption, total investment, and net exports of goods and non-factor services from total GDP.

The population-growth and inflation assumptions can then be applied to the non-government consumption flow to project per-capita *real* non-government consumption — average "living standards" — and its growth rate over the preceding year. If this figure is very low or negative, the analyst may conclude that the programming assumptions would not be feasible. The macroeconomic programming assumptions might then have to be adjusted — for example, by programming some combination of (a) lower future real GDP growth (to reduce total capital formation) and (b) a more appreciated real-effective exchange rate (to reduce net exports of goods and non-factor services). These changes would affect the other sets of accounts. For example, the reduction in exports could increase the external-accounts financing gap. For some economies, at some moments, it may be challenging to achieve satisfactory balance among the feasibility standards for all four sets of accounts.

One way to approach the question of whether the projected improvement of living standards is too low would be to calculate how many years it would take for per-capita real non-government consumption to double. A variable that grows at 7.2 per cent growth rate would roughly double in about ten years; a 3.6 per cent growth rate would produce doubling in about twenty years.[17] The analyst or policy-maker would presumably have a sense of how fast the society "expects" living standards to improve. The projection results can be evaluated by comparing them with the society's expectations, as best these can be estimated.

2.4   External-accounts projections

For each year, the balance-of-payments projection procedure may be described as having five steps (described in detail in Chapter 7). The *first* is to bring the U.S. dollar values of the projections of ***exports and imports of goods and non-factor services*** from the national-accounts exercise into the balance-of-payments projections. The *second* step would be to formulate the projections of ***all other "above-the-line" non-debt accounts*** in the balance of payments, including unrequited transfers and non-debt capital-account flows (including the foreign-investment, short-term capital, and net errors-and-omissions flows). (This book takes the "above-the-line" balance-of-payments accounts to be the current, capital, financial, and errors-omissions accounts, and the "below-the-line" accounts to be the international-reserve accounts: in effect, the above-the-line accounts "explain" the below-the-line accounts.) Except for projection lines with special information and circumstances, the general procedure for projecting such accounts is simply to make assumptions regarding their respective future real growth rates. For some countries, depending on the level of detail the analyst finds

---

[17]   Set $(1 + .072)^n = 2$, take logarithms of both sides — that is, set $n \ln(1 + .072) = \ln(2)$ — and solve for "n": $n = \ln(2)/\ln(1 + .072)$, which is approximately equal to 10.

appropriate for their circumstances, different procedures may be appropriate for some of the lines (see Section 6.4).

The *third* step would be to bring the various programmed ***external-debt flows***, by class of creditor, from the external-debt program into the balance-of-payments projection. For each creditor, the main debt *flows* are disbursements, repayment of the debt stock outstanding at the start of the projection period, repayment of disbursements during the projection period, "valuation changes" to the debt stocks, and interest charges. (Chapter 5 discusses techniques for projecting external debt.)

From these projections, a *preliminary* "above-the-line" projection of the current and financial accounts may then be calculated. (Since the standard presentation of the balance of payments shows the current account, financial accounts and errors-and-omissions flow adding up to equal, or "explain," the net international-reserve flow, the current and financial accounts and errors-and-omissions flow taken together are customarily considered to be "above the line" and the net international-reserve flow "below the line.") The *fourth* step would be to calculate the overall "below-the-line" ***increase in net international reserves*** — in particular, to determine the increase in the central bank's foreign-exchange holdings (for example, to a level measured in months' worth of imports of goods and non-factor services).

The *fifth* step in the external-accounts projection procedure would be to ***reconcile the above- and below-the-line accounts***. This is accomplished by calculating (i) the required flow of net unidentified borrowing, if the preliminary below-the-line projection exceeds the preliminary above-the-line projection; or (ii) the required "unprogrammed" reserve accumulation, if the preliminary above-the-line projection exceeds the preliminary below-the-line projection. The unidentified private non-guaranteed external borrowing flow or the unprogrammed reserve increase would be the residual account for the external-accounts projection.

If the unidentified private non-guaranteed borrowing required to reconcile the balance-of-payments projections exceeds what foreign lenders would be willing and able to provide (in addition to what they are projected to provide in the "identified" lending projections), the analyst would conclude that the macroeconomic program is not feasible. The program would then have to be adjusted, through some combination of (i) a reduction in the real GDP growth rate, (ii) a more depreciated real-effective exchange rate, (iii) a reduction in the increase in net international reserves, and (iv) other changes in the projection assumptions. On the other hand, if the unprogrammed reserve increase required to reconcile the balance-of-payments projections is very large, the program assumptions could be adjusted in the opposite sense: for example, the real-effective exchange rate could be more appreciated and real GDP growth could be higher, which would increase the projected import flow. Alternatively, the projections of identified external financing could be reduced.

When making changes to programmed macroeconomic objectives, it is important to remember that the changes may affect the other macroeconomic sub-systems. (This is very much the point of the consistency methodology.) All other things being equal, the reduced import flow would increase the private-consumption flow. In addition, a larger reserve accumulation (or smaller reserve loss) would bring about a larger increase in the money supply, which may require (a larger amount of) offsetting contractionary monetary policy to meet the inflation objective. These particular kinds of change would be examined through the monetary-accounts projection (discussed in Section 2.6 below).

2.5   *Fiscal-accounts projections*

To simplify the present discussion, take the "fiscal" accounts here to be synonymous with the "general-government" accounts. (Chapter 8 discusses the fiscal projection procedure in greater detail, and also discusses methods to project such disaggregated components of the non-financial public-sector accounts as sub-national governments, state-owned enterprises, and national pension systems.) For each year, five steps may be identified in the government-accounts projection procedure. The *first* would be to project **tax and non-tax revenue**, on the basis of the real-GDP, inflation, exchange-rate, exports, and imports projections, together with the various behavioral parameters and policy assumptions (including tax rates) through which these variables determine the revenue flows.

The *second* step would be to bring in the assumptions regarding **non-interest expenditure flows**. As noted above, these are programmed on the basis of the development objectives and government services to be provided, taking account of relevant demographic projections and the assumptions regarding wage rates and government employment growth.

The *third* step would be to bring in the programmed **net external-debt flows to and from the government** — encompassing disbursements, repayment, and interest charges. These would come from the programming assumptions regarding net debt flows and from the calculations of interest due in the external-accounts projections. (Again, Chapter 5 discusses techniques for projecting external debt.)

The *fourth* step is to project the (programmed) **net internal debt flows to and from the government**, encompassing disbursements, repayment, and interest charges. (Again, Chapter 5 describes these procedures.)

With these projections, a *preliminary* "above-the-line" projection of the government surplus (or deficit) may then be calculated. (Since the standard "fiscal" presentation of the government accounts shows revenue subtracted from expenditure to equal, or "explain," the financing of the deficit, the expenditure and revenue accounts taken together are conventionally taken to be "above the line" and the financing flows "below the line.") Accordingly, the *fifth* step in the fiscal-accounts projection procedure is to **reconcile the above- and below-the-line accounts**. This is accomplished by determining (i) the required flow of net "unprogrammed" internal borrowing, if the preliminary above-the-line projection exceeds the preliminary net borrowing projection; or (ii) the required increase in the government's deposit stock, if the preliminary net borrowing projection exceeds the preliminary above-the-line projection. This unprogrammed internal borrowing or deposit accumulation would then be the "residual" for the fiscal-accounts projection, to be examined for feasibility.

If the internal borrowing required to reconcile the fiscal projections exceeds what the economy's financial system is likely to be able and willing to provide, the analyst would conclude that the macroeconomic projection is not feasible, and that it must then be adjusted through changes in the projection assumptions. Alternatively, if the unprogrammed increase in the government deposit balance required to reconcile the fiscal projections is very large, the analyst could conclude that the macroeconomic projection could be adjusted through combinations of reductions in projected revenue flows, and reductions in identified net external borrowing, and increases in government expenditure.

2.6   Monetary-accounts projections

For each projection year, five broad steps may be identified in the monetary-accounts projection procedure (discussed in detail in Chapter 9). *First*, the assumptions regarding real-GDP growth, inflation, and the exchange rate would be applied to generate projections of the **year-average and year-end money stocks** that the public would be willing and able to hold — the so-called "demand for money" — as well as the change over the year in the money stock. From this, along with assumptions regarding (a) the cash-deposit ratio the economy's "agents" together choose in the aggregate and (b) commercial banks' reserve holdings, the corresponding **flow increase in the monetary base** — the central bank's monetary liability stock — may be projected.

The *second* step would be to bring in the programmed flow increase in the central bank's **net international assets** from the external-accounts projection (i.e., the U.S. dollar flow value is multiplied by the period-average exchange rate). If the exchange rate changes over the projection year, some intricacies may arise in the calculation of the flow increase in the central bank's net international assets (discussed in Section 9.2). (If the exchange rate varies over the period, the national-currency and U.S. dollar values of exports and imports may differ somewhat, because the timing of exports and imports could cause the average exchange rate at which they take place to differ from the period-average exchange rate. See Section 2.7 below.)

The *third* step would be to project the flow increases in the central bank's **net internal assets**. The central bank's internal assets encompass the government's and financial system's net liabilities to the central bank. The net increase in government liabilities to the central bank is equal to the flow increase in the central bank's holdings of government liabilities, less the increase in the government's deposit account at the central bank. (Note that over any time period the central bank's net acquisition of government liabilities includes what it purchases from financial markets — the so-called "secondary markets" — as well as what it may purchase from the government.) The net increase in the liabilities of the financial system (including the banking system) to the central bank is equal to the flow increase in the financial system's net borrowing from the central bank, less the increase in its holdings of central-bank non-monetary obligations.[18]

The *fourth* step in the monetary-accounts projection procedure would be to calculate the central bank's implied *"average monetary-policy stance"* for each projection year. To understand how this would be done, assume for simplicity that the central bank's net worth remains unchanged over the year, apart from the effect of exchange-rate depreciation on the central bank's external assets and liabilities. (This assumption is made only to simplify the present discussion. Section 9.3 explains how changes in the central bank's net worth, particularly those resulting from the central bank's own profits or losses, can be taken into account.) With this assumption, the central bank's flow balance-sheet identity implies that (a) the projected flow increase in the monetary base, *less* (b) the projected flow increases in the central bank's *external* net-asset position, *less* (c) the projected flow increases in the central bank's net position *vis-a-vis* the fisc, is equal to the flow increase in the central bank's net-asset position *vis-a-vis* the economy's financial markets.

This flow increase in the central bank's net-asset position *vis-a-vis* the economy's financial markets *is* the central bank's monetary-policy stance. In essence, monetary policy amounts to setting this flow: that is, given the external and internal net-asset flows, monetary policy consists of adjusting the central bank's net-asset position *vis-a-vis* financial markets so that the monetary base, and therefore the broad money supply, comes out as targeted. The smaller (larger) the central bank's net-asset position *vis-a-vis* financial markets, the more contractionary (expansionary) monetary policy would be. In this sense,

---

[18]   Note that commercial-bank deposits and holdings of vault cash are *not* negative components of the central bank's net internal assets, because they are part of the monetary base.

the monetary-policy stance is the residual for the projection of the central bank's flow accounts.

If the required tightening of the central bank's monetary-policy stance is very large, when measured against GDP or compared with the size of the economy's financial markets, the analyst would conclude that the programmed macroeconomic projection is not feasible. In the monetary-projection assumptions, a smaller amount of foreign-exchange accumulation by the central bank, or a smaller amount of net borrowing by the government from the central bank, would reduce the required amount of monetary-policy tightening. Alternatively, acceptance of a higher inflation rate would provide some room for money creation, hence base-money issue, to be larger, which would also reduce the required degree of monetary-policy tightening. (Chapter 9 discusses criteria for evaluating whether the implied average monetary-policy stance should be considered more restrictive than would be feasible.)

In one sense this way of characterizing a central bank's policy stance is a bit misleading. In fact, many central banks carry out open-market operations through purchases and sales of government obligations from their (asset) holdings, rather than through purchases and sales of their own obligations. Fortunately, this makes little difference for purposes of formulating a projection. If the projection shows that the central bank would have to carry out a large volume of contractionary open-market operations, it would make little difference for the monetary feasibility of the program if the required policy were carried out, so to speak, from the central bank's liability or asset side.[19]

The assumption that the flow increase in the central bank's net worth is zero can be, and in general should be, relaxed to take account of such things as the central bank's payment of dividends, receipt of capital contributions, and increases (decreases) to net worth arising from its profits (losses). A central bank has profits or losses on account of its net interest flows, the effects of exchange-rate movements on its own

---

[19] The main difference would be that the interest rate the central bank pays on its obligations might differ from the rate it would receive on its holdings of government obligations. If a large differential is projected, then the projection can be checked to see whether it would make a significant difference to the outcome if the central bank's holdings of government obligations is assumed to be larger or smaller.

accounts, earnings from exchange operations, its own operating expenses, and other things. These can be projected along with the overall monetary program. It is important to do so in any economy in which such profits and losses are significant, for at least two reasons. First, a profit (loss) flow is a source of monetary absorption (expansion), which needs to be taken into account when calculating the open-market operations required to reconcile money demand and supply. Second, the evolution of a central bank's own capital position can be a macroeconomic variable of some significance (see Section 9.3).

The *fifth* step in the monetary projection would be to formulate a projection of the flow balance sheet of the consolidated commercial banks, using an additional set of assumptions. This projection can provide an additional feasibility check: the idea would be to ensure that the average real stock of bank credit could grow in line with real GDP. (Annex 2.3 describes, in summary, how this can be done using the simplified projection exercise described in Annex 2.2. Section 9.4 describes a more detailed commercial-bank projection exercise.)

2.7   Consistency relationships among the national, external, fiscal and monetary accounts projections

The national, external, fiscal, and monetary accounts projections summarized above should be consistent among themselves, in the first place, because they are formulated from common assumptions about the key macroeconomic programming variables and about world conditions. In addition, these accounts systems should be consistent because certain accounts figure in two accounts systems. Accounts falling into this category should be projected just once, in the context of one set of accounts. The results should then be passed into any other sets of accounts in which they figure.

Thus, for example, government consumption and government gross fixed capital formation figure in both the fiscal accounts and the national accounts. Government consumption (conventionally defined as recurring staff remuneration and expenditure current goods and services) and government gross fixed capital formation are programming assumptions, based in part on the key macroeconomic assumptions but fundamentally on the government's development and poverty-reduction plans. The projected future values go into the two sets of accounts, with equivalent national-currency values for each projection year.

Similarly, exports and imports of goods and non-factor services figure in both the external and national accounts. Their future values are projected on the basis of the assumptions regarding key macroeconomic variables and exogenous variables. The balance-of-payments projections incorporate their dollar values while the national accounts incorporate their national-currency values, with the latter calculated from the former using the projected average exchange rate. (To be sure, the exchange rate used to calculate the national-accounts values from the balance-of-payments projections may diverge from the projected average exchange rate, if the exchange rate is projected to vary within each projection year and exports and imports take place non-uniformly over the year. Thus, for example, Argentina's grain exports are concentrated in the early months of the calendar year. The average exchange rate at which they occur may therefore differ from the annual average exchange rate. Given the importance of grain exports, a national-accounts projection for Argentina might need to be adjusted for this reality. The projected exchange rate applicable for such exports would then be the average of the first four or five months of each year, rather than the whole year.)

A particularly important group of projections that figure in both the fiscal and the external accounts is the external-debt flows. Interest payments on external debt owed by government figure in national currency in the fiscal accounts and in U.S. dollars in the external accounts. Similarly, external-debt disbursements to and repayment by government figure in national currency in the fiscal accounts and in U.S. dollars in the external accounts. No less important, projected net flows of international reserve assets and liabilities figure in U.S. dollars in the external accounts and in national currency in the monetary accounts. In all these instances, the pairs of values for each future year must therefore be consistent.

Net deposits by government to its central-bank account are recorded in the fiscal and monetary accounts, and the projected values must accordingly be consistent. Similarly, projected net borrowing by government from the central bank must be consistent on the fiscal and monetary accounts. There is an important subtlety here, though. Net "direct" borrowing by government from the central bank must be consistent on the two sets of accounts. But if the government issues bills and bonds, a central bank may purchase or sell such securities from the "open market." This means that the movement in the central bank's holdings of government obligations in any projection year need not have a matching figure in the fiscal accounts.

Figure 1 below is a diagrammatic representation of the overall macroeconomic structure as described in this chapter. The rectangle in

Figure 1. Diagram: Macroeconomic consistency structure

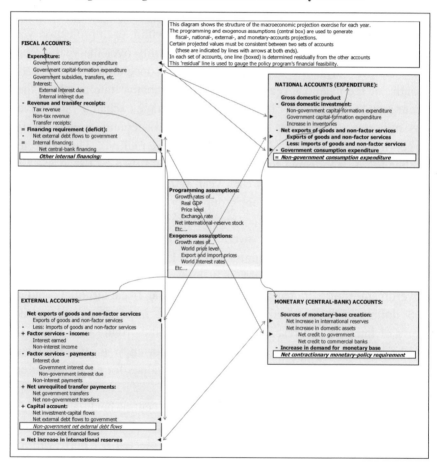

the center of the diagram represents the combined programming assumptions, encompassing a macroeconomic programming assumption set, a government-expenditure program and a government external-debt strategy set, within a context of world economic conditions. These assumptions "feed" the four main sets of accounts, the national, fiscal, external, and monetary accounts. Each set of accounts has a residual account, which is determined from the others through the relevant identity. In addition, the diagram's double-arrowed lines link accounts in different systems that must be projected consistently.

2.8   Concluding observations on the solution procedure

This chapter may be summarized as follows: A macroeconomic program, comprising a set of year-by-year macroeconomic programming assumptions, a government-expenditure program, and a public-sector financing program, within the context of assumed "exogenous" economic conditions, may be evaluated for "feasibility." This is done by applying the macroeconomic program to generate a projection, and then determining whether (i) per-capita real non-government consumption could grow at an adequate rate, (ii) the required external financing would be available for the economy as a whole, (iii) the fiscal deficit could be financed, and (iv) the authorities could implement the required monetary policy. To the extent these "residuals" are unfeasibly large or small as the case may be, the macroeconomic objectives and the programmed government policies would need to be revised before they could be implemented.

The exercise as this book presents it may be considered the "core" of a full macroeconomic consistency projection analysis. To be sure, as described here, it misses some aspects of the macroeconomy's performance. For example, it touches on, but does not fully address, the question of whether the assumed real-GDP growth rate is physically possible, given the economy's physical resource base. It describes one way to address the question of whether the capital stock will be adequate (see Section 6.2), but does not really consider whether resources other than capital capacity (for example, rainfall) might constrain real growth.

Although the capital stock is likely to be the binding constraint to longer-term growth for most developing economies, resource depletion, skills shortages, and other "supply" phenomena may turn out to be binding constraints at any point.

Moreover, as it now stands, apart from the monetary and banking system discussed in Chapter 9, the exercise incorporates no wider financial-system projection. Although interest rates on external and internal debt figure in the fiscal, external, and monetary projections, in the present version of the exercise their values are programmed or assumed, not endogenously determined as they could be if the financial system were more fully represented. The main motive for not discussing financial markets beyond the banking system is to limit the exposition's complexity, since bringing the non-bank financial markets into the exercise would introduce many additional linkages and intricacies. Furthermore, projected financial-sector performance depends heavily on the assumed parameters of the various financial-asset demand functions, which tend to be particularly difficult to estimate. (Once a basic projection analysis has been set up for an economy, it may then be useful and desirable to incorporate the financial system as well. Discussion of how to do so is taken to be beyond the scope of the present book, however.)

Another aspect of an economy this exercise does not discuss is non-financial private-enterprise performance. (The one exception is public-enterprise performance, briefly discussed in Section 8.4.) Again, simplicity is the motive for this omission: representation of the economy's microeconomic productive structure can add considerable complexity. All the same, when evaluating any policy program for financial feasibility, it is important to take account of likely consequences for non-financial private-enterprise performance. Historically, some economies' adjustment exercises led to more real economic disruption than they should have, because took inadequate account of the consequences for enterprises' performance. The present exercise might, for example, show that a policy program involving heavy exchange-rate depreciation could be feasible, but in practice such a program could prove overwhelmingly damaging to enterprises with substantial amounts of external liabilities — and also to the domestic commercial banks exposed to them. Once a basic projection analysis has been set up for an economy it may be useful and desirable then to analyze typical non-financial corporations, to see how they might be affected. Again, however, discussion of how to do so is taken to be beyond the scope of the present book.

(As noted above, Annex 2.1 provides a summary listing of the solution procedure. Annex 2.2 provides a simplified version of the projection exercise this book describes. Annex 2.3 describes an extension of the projection methodology described in Annex 2.2 to cover the full banking system, rather than just the central bank's flow balance sheet.)

3 Basic programming variables

Everything should be as simple as it can be . . . not simpler.
                              – attributed to the poet Louis Zukofsky

3.1 Introduction: Basic programming variables

As it is constructed, the most important programming assumptions in the exercise this book describes are (i) the real GDP growth rates, (ii) the (December-December) price-level growth rates, (iii) the growth rates of the real-effective exchange rate, (iv) the population growth rates, and (v) the increases in the central bank's foreign-exchange reserve holdings. These assumptions figure heavily in all aspects of the projection exercise.

The assumptions for these basic programming variables could be set out in somewhat different ways. For example, instead of programming the real-effective exchange rate and calculating the implied year-average and year-end exchange rates, the analyst could program the year-end nominal exchange rate and determine the implied year-average nominal and real-effective exchange rates. Nevertheless, this writer's experience suggests that for most projection exercises the listing given above will generally be the most helpful way to set out the macroeconomic programming objectives. This chapter discusses these assumptions in more detail, and then describes how they can be used together to calculate mutually consistent projections of such variables as GDP in real, national-currency, and U.S. dollar terms; the year-average and year-end price levels; the real-effective, and year-average and year-end exchange rates.

Analysts carrying out projection exercises of the kind this book describes may be working with a government's current macroeconomic program for the coming year (or two). Governments with annual budget exercises, for example, may publicize the main macroeconomic assumptions used for the budget exercise.[20] Analysts whose governments

---

[20] To be sure, governments and central banks *generally* prefer to avoid publicizing nominal exchange-rate assumptions if they involve any appreciation or depreciation. One obvious exception is pre-announced exchange-rate policies.

have programs with the IMF will typically apply the program assumptions and performance indicators (see Annex 9.6), at least in their "base" projection scenarios.

The exercise described here is intended for what is often characterized as a "medium-term" perspective, three to as much as seven years past the current year. Again, it aims to ensure that the short-term program for the current and coming years — the "inner" projection years, so to speak — lead into a sustainable program for the "outer" projection years. Any multiannual projection can always be lengthened, of course, to take a longer-term perspective covering a decade or more. The "confidence intervals" of variables projected for "outer" years would inevitably be wider than for "inner" years. Projection assumptions for "inner" and "outer" years may be set in different ways. For example, much more will be known about World Bank lending programs for "inner" years — the disbursements are likely to be specifically programmed. For later years (as explained in Section 5.2), it would probably be easiest simply to assume a growth rate for the debt stock.

In this chapter, Section 3.2 discusses the programming assumptions regarding "real economic activity" — i.e., the gross domestic product — and its growth rate. Section 3.3 discusses programming assumptions regarding the price level and exchange rate. (They are discussed together because there are similarities in projection techniques and also because they are related through the real-effective exchange-rate concept.) Section 3.4 discusses projection techniques for the productive structure's sectors and sub-sectors. Section 3.5 briefly discusses programming assumptions having to do with international-reserve holdings, and Section 3.6 regarding population and labor-force growth. Section 3.7 discusses algebraic relationships among the basic assumptions and macroeconomic variables derived directly from them, in particular the relationships between period-average and period-end values. Finally, Section 3.8 describes the assumptions used for the "Pacífica" exercise.

3.2 Gross domestic product and its growth rate

Real-GDP growth rates figure fundamentally in most economies' aspirations and in their policy-makers' objectives. Because so many of the projection exercise's assumptions and results depend on it, each year's assumed real-GDP growth rate may be said to be the projection exercise's "central" assumption. A case could be made that the focus on real growth is misplaced, and that policy-makers should focus more on average living standards, or on the living standards of relatively poorer people. Still, the view that "a rising tide lifts all boats" — i.e., that fast growth is probably the best hope for most poor people — is widespread, and in line with much experience. (To be sure, though, natural-resource based economies — oil-boom economies in particular — have sometimes been characterized by fast growth and worsening distributions of living standards.) With all appropriate caveats and cautions, then, one of the projection exercise's core purposes is to determine how fast the economy could grow, given constraints set by available financing, saving, external credit, internal resource availability, and world economic conditions.[21]

It is useful to review some basic definitions. An economy's **gross domestic product (GDP)** for any period "t" is the total value of *final products* — that is, goods and services not used as inputs for other products — produced during the period within the economy's geographic frontiers (see Annex 3.1). Each final product's total value is estimated by multiplying the estimated total quantity produced by the estimated average unit price. Total GDP is then estimated by summing all the estimated product values. Algebraically, if q_{it} represents the quantity of product "i" produced in period "t," and p_{it} the average price of product "i" during period "t," then GDP in period "t," Y_t, is the sum over "i" of the product values,

$$Y_t = \Sigma(p_{it}\, q_{it}).$$

By definition, Y_t is the *"nominal" GDP* over period "t" — that is, GDP in national currency, calculated using each product's period-average prices. Clearly, nominal GDP can rise or fall between any two periods through changes in quantities produced, changes in average product

---

[21] As noted in Section 1.4 above, though, the methodology this book describes does not take explicit account of "absorption-capacity" constraints on government expenditure.

prices, or both. For many purposes, however, what matters is the economy's "real," rather than its nominal, performance — that is, the evolution over time of the real, physical quantities produced rather than their value. The conventional method "to filter out" price changes is to calculate GDP using *"base-period"* rather than the period-average prices. If the total values of each kind of product are calculated for two different periods using the *same* prices, then the total GDP values would be comparable as *real* magnitudes. For this, a base period is selected, and each period's GDP is calculated using the base period's average prices, rather than the period's actual average prices. Thus, if the base period is $t = 0$, *"real" GDP* for period "t" (more precisely, "period-t GDP at period-0 prices") is given by

$$y_t = \Sigma(p_{i0} \, q_{i0}).$$

The (lower-case) "y" is used here to indicate that this is the GDP in real terms, or "GDP valued at the base-period prices."

The so-called *"implicit GDP deflator"* for period "t," p_t, is defined by

$$p_t = \alpha \, Y_t / y_t,$$

where α is, in principle, *any* constant (see Annex 3.4). Since p_t is an index number, the calculated values of p_t for all periods could be multiplied by any constant coefficient and the result would still be an equivalent GDP-deflator series. The conventional practice is simply to set α to 100, so that for the base period ($t = 0$), p_0 is 100. (Since $y_0 = Y_0$, $p_0 = Y_0/y_0 = 1$, and so having α equal to 100 sets the base-period value p_0 to 100.) The deflator for any period can be used, of course, "to deflate" the period's nominal GDP value to its corresponding real value: divide both sides of the previous formula by p_t and multiply both sides by y_t to obtain

$$y_t = \alpha \, Y_t / p_t.$$

For any year, the overall *real-GDP growth rate* (g_y) is given, as noted, by

$$1 + g_y = y/y_{-1},$$

and the growth rate of the implicit deflator (g_p) is given by

$$1 + g_p = p/p_{-1}.$$

The ***nominal-GDP growth rate*** (g_Y) is given by

$$1 + g_Y = Y/Y_{-1} = (1 + g_y)(1 + g_p).$$

The choice of base period can make a difference (see Annex 3.2): for historical data, calculated real GDP growth rates will differ depending on the base year selected. As a practical matter, however, real-growth patterns over time will tend to be similar regardless of the base year chosen. The precise figures will differ, but rates for higher-growth years will be relatively higher and for lower-growth years relatively lower.

The gross domestic product and other national-accounts aggregates are estimated from survey data. Their true values are never known precisely. This is perhaps especially true for developing economies, where survey methodologies and coverage are more likely to have inadequacies, but it is also very much the case for developed economies. Even in developed economies, historical national-accounts data may be far enough from their "true" values to make some statistical conclusions questionable. It is important to bear in mind that relatively credible real-GDP growth-rate data are subject to distortions, one-time events, and other special circumstances. For example, Ecuador's 1987 real GDP declined 6 per cent in 1987 on account of an earthquake that shut down the Transandean crude-oil pipeline for five months; recovering from that trough, 1988 real GDP was 10.5 per cent higher. Since 2000, several countries have experienced unusually high growth rates in communications sectors simply because of surging purchases of cellular telephones. Events of these kinds are likely to have different consequences for such variables as consumption, imports and money demand and their relationships with measured real GDP compared with presumably more "normal" kinds of real-GDP fluctuation.

Over the past fifty years, nations' annual real GDP growth rates have varied widely. In particularly bad years, some nations have undergone massive real declines. In 1982, for example, Chile's real GDP declined 13.5 per cent, and then another 3.3 per cent in 1983. In

1983, battered by the effects of "El Niño" rains and climate changes on export crops and fishing production, Perú's real GDP plunged ten per cent. On the other side, sustained real growth rates exceeding seven or eight per cent constitute strong performance. Over the five "miracle" years 1969–1973, for example, Brazil's real GDP growth averaged 9.7 per cent. South Korea, one of the world's faster-growing economies, managed real growth averaging 7.9 per cent from 1970 through 1995.

Real GDP growth rates must be evaluated along with population growth (see Section 3.6 below). The difference between real GDP growth and population growth is (approximately equal to) the growth rate of per-capita real GDP.[22] (As noted in Section 2.3, a 7.2 per cent per-capita annual real GDP growth rate doubles per-capita real GDP in about ten years; a 3.6 per cent per-capita annual real GDP growth rate doubles per-capita real GDP in about twenty years.)

Analysts accustomed to working with macroeconomic models that solve for the real GDP growth rate as a *prediction* result sometimes find it disconcerting to work with a projection exercise that *sets out* with "programmed" real-GDP growth rates. To repeat, the basic purpose of the exercise described here is to gauge the financial feasibility of a macroeconomic program and an associated government expenditure program. The exercise is accordingly intended to be carried out with some trial and error. All other things being equal, a long-term annual real GDP growth rate of seven per cent may prove financially unfeasible for a particular economy, but lower growth rates — say, four or five per cent, might be feasible. To be sure, "all other things might not be equal": the seven per cent rate might prove financially feasible[23] with a more depreciated long-term exchange rate, which would help offset the higher imports that the higher growth rates would otherwise induce. Then too, it is always important to bear in mind that "absorption-capacity"

---

[22]   If g_y represents real-GDP growth and g_N population growth, then the corresponding growth rate of per-capita real GDP is given by $[(1 + g_y)/(1 + g_N)] - 1$, which is approximately equal to $g_y - g_N$ for values of the two growth rates below 10 per cent.

[23]   For some economies, however, higher imports may be needed for the higher growth rates. That is, the depreciated real exchange rate might make the higher real GDP growth rate more financially feasible, but the reduced imports might make the growth rate less feasible for physical and technological reasons.

constraints may be "more binding" than financial constraints (as noted in Section 1.4 above). Before assuming that an economy can grow at an annual seven per-cent rate, the analyst would want to be fairly certain that the economy has spare capacity, workers, and natural resources sufficient to permit growth that high in a physical sense.

At any given moment, for many, perhaps most, economies, there is a rough consensus of internal and external opinion regarding the range of the current and coming years' real GDP growth rates.[24] This will inevitably affect analysts' projection assumptions for the coming year or two: projection assumptions that are far from the norm tend to be taken less seriously. Unless the current real-GDP rate is already relatively high, analysts tend to assume that real GDP growth will rise in subsequent years, perhaps gradually, until it reaches a long-term "steady state" some years into the future. A core objective of the projection exercise is to see whether this longer-term growth rate is likely to be feasible in the sense described above — to see whether it would pose a danger of a continuing build-up of public and non-public debt, whether the required fiscal financing flows would be too high, and whether the required rates of capital formation and non-government saving would be realistic. If it is not feasible in this sense, of course, an analyst might conclude either that it have to be lower or that adjustment policies might be necessary.

3.3   The price level and the exchange rate

In exercises of the kind this book describes, changes in assumptions regarding the future inflation trajectory tend to have limited consequences for the projected external, fiscal and national accounts. This is because the projection formulas are generally built on the assumption that economic behavior is affected by *real* rather than *money*

---

[24]   Analysts are often struck by the degree of unanimity regarding a given economy's prospects at any moment, and also by how rapidly and sharply this view can shift. Even veteran analysts were struck by the speed with which economic analysts throughout the world revised their views on economic prospects as recession took hold during 2008.

variables. (Stated differently, the implicit assumption is that economic decision-makers have no "money illusion" — that they always deflate any economic information they have in a more or less appropriate way.)

There are some important exceptions to the general principle that assumed inflation rates make little real difference, however. For example, as noted above, the exercise usually works with projection assumptions for real-effective exchange rates. If the exchange-rate assumption is set in nominal terms, however, differing inflation assumptions will imply different real-effective exchange rates. This can have significant consequences for the projected external, fiscal and national accounts. The one set of accounts for which inflation assumptions should always make a significant difference is the monetary accounts, since the price level affects, and is affected by, people's willingness to hold money (as explained in Section 9.2).

In the macroeconomic program, assumptions regarding future inflation rates are set out in terms of the GDP deflator and the consumer price index (see Annex 3.4). The GDP deflator is often considered the best indicator of an economy's price level. The wholesale and consumer price indices are usually regarded as fairly good, but not fully adequate, indicators of the price level.[25] The fixed weights are one reason such indices are suspect: consumer demand presumably shifts toward commodities whose prices are falling and away from commodities whose prices are rising, but fixed-weight indices ordinarily do not reflect this.

As in the case of the real GDP growth rate, it is important to remember that measured inflation rates are subject to distortions, one-time events, and other special circumstances. For one telling example, in the mid-1970s agricultural-supply constraints sometimes affected Brazil's consumer-price indices. In years when drought sharply reduced production of certain agricultural commodities, their prices would rise sharply. Production, hence sales and consumption, of such commodities would drop precipitously, in one famous instance by more than ninety

---

[25] See, for example, Braverman 1979, Chapter 6 ("Index Numbers").

per cent,[26] but the fixed-weight price indices still carried their sharply increased prices according to base-year consumption levels.

As in the case of the real GDP growth rate, in most economies, at any given moment there is likely to be a consensus of internal and external opinion regarding the likely range of the current year's inflation rate. Unless this rate is already low, or unless there is reason to believe that policy-makers are unable to control it, analysts characteristically assume that inflation will decline in projection years until it reaches a long-term "steady state" some years into the future.

In the present exercise, the December-December growth rates of the consumer price index are set as programming assumptions. These are then used to derive consistent projections of year-average growth rates of consumer prices and of the GDP deflator (Section 3.7 below presents the algebra used in the derivations).

Along with real GDP growth, the growth rate of the (real-effective) exchange rate is a particularly important assumption for each year's projections. (Annex 3.6 describes the real-effective exchange-rate concept.) This stands to reason, in view of the importance of the exchange rate in policy planning and its effects on all the sub-sectors of an open economy's macroeconomic system. The exchange rate, in both its nominal and real-effective versions, figures centrally in the national, external, monetary, and fiscal accounts. In virtually all economies, the exchange rate is a key component of prime cost. The flows of exports and imports of goods and non-factor services, the mix of the external and internal saving flows, the monetary flows, and indeed the fiscal accounts all depend on it.[27]

---

[26]   A vegetable called *chuchú*, a salad ingredient grown mainly on marginal land, was especially problematic for Brazil's price indices. Because it consists largely of water, drought conditions reduced output and so caused large price-index rises. Measured monthly inflation was especially important then because of Brazil's use of financial index-linking. In the 1970s the authorities instituted a practice of reducing inflation adjustment by amounts they deemed to have resulted from this and other kinds of supply disruptions. Many people considered this arbitrary, however, and it damaged the reputation of price indices and indexation.

[27]   One practical use for exercises like the one this book describes is to help estimate the longer-term real-effective exchange rate likely to be appropriate for the macroeconomic and government-expenditure objectives taken together.

To help formulate assumptions for future exchange-rate evolution, the analyst may take account of the recent history of the economy's real-effective exchange rate. The International Monetary Fund has published real-effective exchange-rate series for many nations, in some cases going back several decades. If data are available, estimates can be constructed as well (see Annex 3.7). If the present real-effective exchange rate happens to be distant from historic values, the analyst may conjecture, for example, that the economy will gradually return to those, or else that policy-makers will make an effort to maintain the current values, by managing the currency and the money supply in appropriate ways. On the other hand, the analyst may conjecture that the real-effective exchange rate will adjust, gradually or rapidly, to different values from those currently prevailing, as a consequence of policy, market conditions, or both.

For the national- and external-accounts projections, any given real-effective exchange-rate policy can be expected to have its main effects through exports and imports of goods and non-factor services. In the projection exercise, these will be governed by the assumptions regarding real-effective price elasticities (see Section 6.4), which are structural parameters. The real-effective exchange rate may affect some of the other external-accounts projections, depending on the precise assumptions used to generate them (see Section 7.2). It is important to remember, however, that the real-effective exchange rate is likely to have significant fiscal consequences, depending on the precise structure of revenue and expenditure. This can be one of the more interesting aspects of the kind of exercise described here, because it depends so much on the particular characteristics of the economy in question. In general, for example, a more depreciated exchange rate can be expected to improve tariff revenue, so long as it does not too heavily discourage imports. At the same time, however, it will increase the domestic-currency equivalent of external debt-service expenditure. In addition, the exchange rate is likely to drive other revenue, expenditure, and financing accounts. As a consequence, the overall fiscal consequences of exchange-rate depreciation or appreciation will depend on which effects predominate. They are therefore likely to be highly specific to each economy. Examination of this issue may be an especially important application of the exercise this book describes.

Annex 3.6 describes the real-effective exchange rate concept, and Annex 3.7 explains how a historical real-effective exchange-rate series can be calculated for a given economy. As an example, Annex 3.10 discusses the eventful evolution of Ecuador's real-effective exchange rate from 1970 into 2001, and the broad consequences for the country's exports and imports of goods and non-factor services. All other things being equal, a more appreciated (real-effective) exchange rate discourages exports and encourages imports. A more appreciated (real-effective) exchange rate tends accordingly to imply a larger financing gap for the balance of payments. At the same time, there are consequences for the expenditure side of the national accounts. All other things being equal, a more appreciated (real-effective) exchange rate allows for a higher non-government-consumption level. In addition, exchange-rate appreciation produces deflationary pressure. The monetary policy required to achieve a given monetary-base target with a more appreciated exchange rate and a lower inflation rate should tend to be relatively "looser." This is basically because, all other things being equal, a more appreciated exchange rate would induce a smaller international-reserve inflow, and therefore a smaller amount of money creation.

One other kind of variable that may be classed as a macroeconomic programming variable is internal interest rates. These can play a role in a projection exercise because the government and central bank may pay them or receive them on financing issues. Techniques for programming their values are discussed with the programming of government internal financing (in Section 5.5 below).

3.4   Sectors and sub-sectors of the gross domestic product

It is possible to carry out a projection exercise only with programmed aggregate real- and nominal-GDP assumptions, but for many purposes it can be useful to work with projections of real and nominal output in the various sectors and sub-sectors. Many economies' national accounts classify their products as "primary" (agricultural, extractive), "secondary" (industrial), and "tertiary" (services), and report the total amounts produced in each sector. Others use different sectoral classifications more appropriate for their specific realities. Products within each sector may be grouped in sub-sectors — agriculture, livestock, mining, and others for the primary sector; manufacturing, electricity generation, and others for the secondary sector; commerce, government and others for the tertiary sector. (Mining and oil production are sometimes classed as primary and sometimes as secondary — if as secondary, they are typically characterized as "extractive industry.")

Suppose that an economy's products have been grouped into sectors (or, as the case may be, sub-sectors) "j," so that for year t

$$Y_t = \Sigma(p_{jt}\, q_{jt})$$

and

$$y_t = \Sigma(p_{j0}\, q_{jt}),$$

where p_{jt} represents the price deflator and q_{jt} the real output in sector j. The quantities produced and average prices in the various sectors can be projected using assumptions for their growth rates. By definition,

$$1 + g_{q(j)} = q_{(j)}/q_{(j)-1}$$

and

$$1 + g_{p(j)} = p_{(j)}/p_{(j)-1}.$$

Projections of sectoral output flows at current and base-year prices — that is, in nominal and real terms — can be calculated by applying assumed growth rates for sectoral and sub-sectoral outputs and deflators to base-year data. Overall GDP flows at current and base-year prices can then be projected by summing sectoral output flows at current and base-year prices.

For example, suppose that, during 2009, primary, secondary and tertiary output accounted, respectively, for 35, 25 and 40 per cent of an economy's GDP. Suppose that for 2010 the three sectors' real growth rates are projected to be 4, 6, and 5 per cent respectively. If total 2009 GDP was (say) 100, the three sectors' 2009 outputs would have been 35, 25 and 40 respectively. The implied growth rate of GDP *at 2009 prices* (that is, the real-GDP growth rate) would be (approximately) 4.9 per cent. This is calculated by applying the three *real* growth rates to the respective 2009 sectoral output figures, summing the results, and then calculating the percentage by which this sum exceeds 2009 GDP.

Suppose that average prices in the three sectors are projected to rise 8, 6, and 7 per cent respectively between 2009 and 2010. The projected (decimal) growth rate for any sector *at current prices* — that is, the *nominal* sectoral growth rate — could be calculated by multiplying $(1 + g)$ and $(1 + x)$, where "g" is the sector's (decimal) real-growth rate and "x" the sector's (decimal) price-growth rate, and then subtracting one from the result. For the assumed growth rates given, the implied growth rate of GDP *at current prices* would be (approximately) 12.3 per cent. This is calculated by applying the three nominal growth rates to the respective 2009 sectoral output figures, summing the results, and calculating the percentage by which this sum exceeds 2009 GDP. The growth rate of the implicit GDP deflator would be (approximately) 6.9 per cent, calculated (in decimal terms) by dividing $(1 + 0.123)$ by $(1 + 0.049)$ and subtracting one from the result.

When carrying out overall and sectoral growth projections, it may be more convenient to make assumptions for overall real GDP growth and for the real growth rates in all sectors except one, and *then* determine the growth rate in the remaining sector residually — that is, so as to be consistent with the other assumed real growth rates. One reason this approach may be more convenient is that the analyst wishes to change the programming assumptions, it is easier to just change the assumed year-by-year *overall* real-GDP growth rate rather than change *all* the assumed year-by-year *sectoral* growth rates. To be sure, it is important to check that the calculated future residual-sector growth rates are reasonable — i.e., not unrealistically high or low.

In the preceding example, suppose that the primary and secondary sectors have been projected, as before, to grow 4 and 6 per cent in real terms respectively, but that overall real GDP has been projected to grow 5 per cent. The tertiary sector's implied real growth rate can then be *calculated residually*, as (approximately) 5.3 per cent. The calculation consists of applying the real growth rate of 5 per cent to 2009 GDP to obtain 2010 GDP at 2009 prices, applying the real growth rates of the primary and secondary sectors to their respective 2009 values, and subtracting these last two results from 2010 GDP at 2009 prices.

Suppose that the primary and secondary sectors' deflators have been projected, as before, to grow 8 and 6 per cent respectively, but that overall nominal GDP has been projected to grow 12 per cent. The tertiary sector's implied nominal growth rate would then be (approximately) 11.5 per cent. This can be calculated by applying the nominal GDP growth rate — i.e., 12 per cent — to 2009 GDP to obtain 2010 GDP, then applying the nominal growth rates of the primary and secondary sectors to their respective 2009 values, subtracting these last two results from 2010 GDP, and calculating the percentage by which this value exceeds the 2009 value for the tertiary sector.

If nominal GDP grows 12 per cent and real GDP grows 5 per cent, the GDP deflator would grow (approximately) 6.7 per cent. This value is calculated (in decimal terms) by dividing $(1 + 0.12)$ by $(1 + 0.05)$ and subtracting one from the result. Similarly, if the tertiary sector's nominal output grows 11.5 per cent and its real output grows 5.3 per cent, its deflator would grow (approximately) 6.3 per cent.

In sum, suppose the economy in question consists of "n" sectors. Programming assumptions can be set out for the real growth rates of overall nominal and real GDP and for the growth rates of nominal and real GDP in n-1 of the sectors. For each future period, the value of output in the residual sector *at base-year prices* would be the difference between projected GDP and the sum of output in the n-1 sectors, all at base-year prices, and the value of output in the residual sector *at current prices* would be the difference between projected GDP and the sum of output in the n-1 sectors, all at current-year prices.

Projection assumptions for the various sectors and sub-sectors can be formulated in various ways. For many economies, particular sectors' and sub-sectors' growth rates can be projected, at least for the current and "near-future" years, by using information about sectoral performance. For the agricultural sector, for example, government agencies may release information about current or anticipated crop output. Analysts may be able to formulate estimates for different kinds of production on the basis of interviews with sector specialists, or by applying public or private information of different kinds. For longer-term projections, analysts may be able to project, or program, differing performance among the various sectors. Suppose, for example, that an economy is expected gradually to evolve so that (say) its primary sector will become relatively less important and its secondary and tertiary sectors will become relatively more important. In this case, it would be appropriate to assume that primary real growth rates would be relatively lower and secondary and tertiary real growth rates relatively higher.

One approach to accomplish this would be to set projection assumptions for sectoral growth rates in function of the assumed overall growth rates. Thus, for example, the assumption setting for each sector's real growth rate, "h," can be set in relation to the assumed overall real growth rate "g" using the formula

$$1 + h = (1 + g)^{\eta},$$

where η is a projection assumption. The value of η could be set to values less than one for sectors whose growth is assumed to be relatively slower and higher than one for sectors whose growth is assumed to be relatively higher. For the residual sector, the implicit value of η can be determined from that sector's calculated growth rate, and checked to be sure it is reasonable — i.e., not excessively large or small. If the residual sector's calculated growth rate is h*, the preceding formula implies that the sector's implicit elasticity η* would be given by

$$\eta^* = ln(1 + h^*)/ln(1 + g).$$

Moreover, the value of η for any particular sector may be projected to evolve over future periods. Thus, suppose that the value of η is projected to evolve from a value of η^S in the base period S toward a final value of η^T in period T. Each intermediate value of η^t could then be given by

$$\eta^t = \eta^{t-1} \, [\eta^T/\eta^S]^{[1/(T-S)]}$$

(since there are T – S periods between period S and period T, the value of η would evolve gradually, by an equal percentage change over each time period). The value of η^T could be assumed to be one, which would imply neutral growth — that is, that this sector would grow in real terms at the same rate as the economy generally, and so maintain its relative importance in the economy. (The value of output produced by a sector whose real product and average prices grew at the same rates as the overall economy's real growth and average prices would remain at a constant percentage of nominal GDP.)[28]

---

[28] Setting out from the sectoral growth-rate projections, it is possible to carry out a rough sector-by-sector employment projection by making sector-by-sector projections of labor-productivity growth. If "g" represents a sector's projected real growth rate and "h" its projected labor-productivity growth in any given year, then the growth rate of labor demand could be projected as [(1+g)/(1+h)] – 1. Assuming the base-year employment in the sector is known or can be estimated, the projected future growth rates can be applied to give the evolution of employment in the sector. This can be compared with the projected growth rate of the labor force, to determine whether the unemployment rate is likely to increase or diminish. It is difficult, unfortunately, to make persuasive sector-by-sector labor-productivity growth projections. Such projections would presumably be based on capital formation, not only within the sector in question but in other sectors. Thus, for example, labor productivity in manufacturing would depend in significant measure on power and other infrastructure investment.

3.5   *Central-bank international-reserve holdings*

The assumed year-end stock of foreign-exchange reserve holdings for any projection year qualifies as a "key" assumption, because it plays a significant role in the external- and monetary-accounts projections. All other things being equal, the larger the projected year-end foreign-exchange stock, the larger that year's external financing requirement will be. In addition, all other things being equal, a larger foreign-exchange inflow to the central bank implies a larger amount of money creation: all other things being equal, the larger the foreign-exchange inflow to the central bank, the larger the amount of offsetting contractionary policy the monetary authority must carry out to meet any given money-creation target.

Experience is generally the best guide to the quantity of foreign exchange a central bank should hold. Central banks hold foreign-exchange reserves to ensure orderly conditions for international transactions, basically to ensure that internal business enterprises can make credible foreign-exchange payment commitments. In certain crisis conditions, the authorities may need to allow their holdings to diminish from the usual levels, at least temporarily; later on, as the economy emerges from crisis, the authorities may find they must raise their holdings above the usual levels to help build confidence. Projection exercises can take account of this.

The size of an economy's foreign-exchange reserve holding is typically gauged in terms of "months of imports of goods and non-factor (i.e., final) services."[29] The intuitive idea here is that if an economy's foreign-exchange inflows were for some reason to decline sharply and suddenly, the economy could draw from its reserves to maintain its current flow of goods and non-factor services imports, at least for this number of months. This would presumably allow it time to arrange an exceptional loan or some other means of confronting the crisis. Depending on their precise circumstances, financial markets appear to

---

[29]   Some authorities prefer to use the number of months of imports of goods and *all* services, including interest payments due. They may even prefer the number of months of *all* debt service due.

prefer that central banks hold foreign exchange equivalent to at least three or four months' imports of goods and non-factor services. Some central banks prefer to maintain more. Between 2000 and 2008, central-bank reserve holdings increased significantly throughout the world, partly because central banks viewed them as means of defending their policy independence, partly because the United States runs external- and fiscal-accounts deficits financed with fiscal obligations that other central banks consider secure as reserves.

The key disadvantage of holding large reserve stocks is that the opportunity cost can be high. To qualify as such, reserve holdings must be "liquid," either short-term deposits in overseas banks or readily marketable fiscal obligations of developed economies. Assets of these kinds typically offer low yields. Policy-makers must continually weigh the costs of maintaining a low-earning asset against the advantages in business confidence that reserves provide.

3.6   Population and labor force

The assumed population and labor-force growth rates may also be regarded as "key" assumptions. The population growth rate is one determinant of the growth rates of per-capita real values in the national-income accounts. In addition, population growth should affect the projections of a range of government-expenditure accounts. For a given production flow and production technology, labor-force growth affects the unemployment rate. The labor-force growth rate may also affect various government revenue accounts, in particular those involving public pension contributions.

Across economies, annual population growth rates range between roughly zero, in certain advanced industrial economies where people have small families and immigration rates are low, to 3–4 per cent in the developing nations with the highest population growth rates. Kenya's population grew at an annual average 4.1 per cent rate from 1970 through 1995, one of the world's highest rates. In contrast, Uruguay's population grew at an annual average 0.7 per cent rate, among the lower growth rates among economies classed as developing.

(Italy's annual-average population-growth rate was just 0.3 per cent.) Labor-force growth rates are likely to be on the same order of the population growth rates, but there are instances in which demographic events in earlier years temporarily make labor-force growth rates higher or lower than the concurrent population growth rates. For projection analysis running three to five years into the future, it is usually good enough simply to extrapolate the population and labor-force growth rates of the previous five to ten years. Longer-term projections may require more elaborate demographic analyses and projections. Sensitivity analysis with different population growth rates can, of course, be highly revealing.

3.7   *Algebraic relationships among year-average and year-end GDP, price indices, and exchange rates*

To discuss the projection methodology in coming chapters, it is helpful to describe the algebraic relationships among the (i) year-average and (ii) year-end price-index values, the (iii) year-average and (iv) year-end exchange rates, and (v) real, (vi) nominal and (vii) U.S. dollar GDP. In particular, the year-average and year-end exchange rates and the year-average and year-end price-index values must be projected consistently.

The table below lists symbols used to represent the basic assumption variables. Several conventions are used. A prime following a variable indicates a year-end value. Absence of a prime indicates a year-average or "year-flow" value. An asterisk following a symbol indicates that its units are U.S. dollars. The symbols x_t or x'_t represent "x" during and at the end of period "t," respectively. Except where otherwise indicated, a variable with no subscript is taken to apply to the current period. The symbol Δx stands for "change in x from the preceding period." The symbol g_x is read "growth rate of x." By definition,

$$\Delta x = x - x_{-1},$$

$$g_x = \Delta x/x_{-1} = (x/x_{-1}) - 1, \text{ and}$$

$$x = x_{-1} (1 + g_x).$$

Algebraic symbols representing economic variables and parameters are consistent within, but not always among, the chapters of this book. (There are simply more variables in the exercise than letters available in the alphabet.) Variables presented in the list immediately following, however, *are* used consistently throughout this book:

Y	nominal gross domestic product (GDP);
y	real GDP;
Y*	nominal GDP measured in U.S. dollars;
p	period-average internal price index;
p'	period-end internal price index;
p*	period-average U.S. dollar world price index;
e	period-average exchange rate (domestic currency per U.S. dollar);
e'	period-end exchange rate; and
N	period-average population.

For each projection year, the exercise this book describes takes the following as the "core list" of the "key" macroeconomic variables characterizing a macroeconomic program:

g_y year-over-year growth rate of real GDP;

$g_{p'}$ December-December growth rate of consumer prices;

g_E year-over-year growth rate of the year-average real-effective exchange rate (E), defined so an increase in E represents real-effective *depreciation* of the national currency (see Section 3.3), where

$$1 + g_E = g_{ep*/p} = (1 + g_e)(1 + g_{p*})/(1 + g_p);$$

and

g_N year-over-year population growth rate.

A slightly different listing could be used to characterize and set out a multiannual macroeconomic program. For example, as noted above, for some economies it may be easier to set an assumption for the year-end exchange rate rather than the year-average real-effective exchange rate, and then derive the other required assumptions consistently. For many analysts, the list above has turned out to be the most convenient to set out a macroeconomic program.

Given the assumptions listed above, projected values for each future year's (i) year-average and (ii) year-end price-index values, the (iii) year-average and (iv) year-end exchange rates, and (v) real, (vi) nominal and (vii) U.S. dollar GDP may be computed from the previous year's values and the assumptions for the projected growth rates, as follows. First, by definition, the *year-end* price index is given by

$$p' = p'_{-1} (1 + g_{p'}).$$

Monthly consumer-price indices are generally compiled in the middle of the month in question, so the "year-end" price index is understood here to be the December index. To maintain consistency with the price index, the "year-end" exchange rate is understood here to be the December average.

The *year-average* price index is taken to be a weighted geometric average of the two period-end price-index values,

$$p = p'^{(1-\alpha)}_{-1} \, p'^{\alpha},$$

where α is a weighting coefficient, presumably between zero and one. This weighting coefficient can take account of the possibility that the price index evolves unevenly over the course of the year.[30] If the price index rises evenly over the year, the value of α would be 0.5.[31] If the price index rises more rapidly earlier in the year than in the later part of the year, α would exceed 0.5. The value of α can differ, of course, from year to year.

---

[30]   I am grateful to Luis Serven for suggesting this formulation for weighting the average.
[31]   To be sure, the converse is not necessarily true: a value of α equal to 0.5 could be consistent with uneven price-level evolution over a year.

Since p' = p'_{-1} (1 + $g_{p'}$), this last expression may be rewritten

$$p = p'_{-1}{}^{(1-\alpha)} [p'_{-1} (1 + g_{p'})]^{\alpha}$$
$$= p'_{-1} [(1 + g_{p'})]^{\alpha}.$$

Since $1 + g_p = p/p_{-1}$, dividing both sides of the preceding equation by p_{-1} gives a formula for the growth rate of the year-average price index g_p in terms of the growth rate of the year-end price index $g_{p'}$:

$$1 + g_p = p/p_{-1} = (p'_{-1}/p_{-1}) [1 + g_{p'}]^{\alpha}.$$

Note that the previous year's average and year-end values of the price index are needed to compute the growth rate of the average price index given the growth rate of the year-end price index. This formula can be "reversed" into a formula for the growth rate of the year-end price index $g_{p'}$ in terms of the growth rate of the year-average price index g_p:

$$1 + g_{p'} = [(p_{-1}/p'_{-1}) (1 + g_p)]^{(1/\alpha)}.$$

Next, the growth rate of the *year-average* nominal exchange rate follows from the assumed growth rates of the *year-average* real-effective exchange rate and the *year-average* international price index, together with the growth rate of the *year-average* internal price index just discussed. Since

$$1 + g_E = (1 + g_e) (1 + g_{p*})/(1 + g_p),$$
$$1 + g_e = (1 + g_E) (1 + g_p)/(1 + g_{p*}).$$

If β gives the exchange-rate weighting average such that

$$e = e'_{-1}{}^{(1-\beta)} e'^{\beta},$$

the growth rate of the year-end exchange rate could be calculated from the growth rate of the year-average exchange rate just calculated, using the ("reverse") formula

$$1 + g_{e'} = [(e_{-1}/e'_{-1}) (1 + g_e)]^{(1/\beta)}.$$

Projections involving period-average and period-end variables can sometimes produce "oscillation." Projected year-end exchange rates, for example, may move up and down, or grow at rates that move up and down, rather than follow an upward or downward trend. A simple example clarifies the typical reason. Suppose the exchange rate e' was 2 pesos per dollar at the end of the base year and is projected to take (arithmetic) average values of 3 pesos per dollar for the next four projection years. If the period-end values for the projection years are calculated on the basis of the usual formula for an arithmetic average,

$$e = (e'_{-1} + e')/2,$$

and

$$e' = 2e - e'_{-1}.$$

If e'_{-1} is 2 and "e" is 3, e' will be 4; if e' is 4 and e_{+1} is then 3, e'_{+1} will return to 2. That is, the projected values of e' will simply alternate between 4 and 2.

Oscillating projections of this kind should not be considered sensible. There is simply no reason for an exchange rate to rise and fall over alternate twelve-month periods in this way. A reasonable remedy in this particular example would be to change the programmed average values slightly. Thus, in the numerical example given, if the first projection year's assumed average value were 2.5 rather than 3 pesos per dollar, the subsequent assumed average values would be 3 pesos per dollar and no oscillation would occur: the year-end values would all be 3 pesos per dollar. In general, when setting out assumptions affecting the price level and exchange-rate, it is best to watch for unrealistic oscillation, and to change assumptions to eliminate it.

Thus far this section has spoken of *the* price index. If the price index is understood to be roughly synonymous with the GDP deflator, however, it is important to remember that by definition this variable has only year-average values. Since the consumer-price index is calculated monthly, it would have December and year-average values (the average of the twelve months' values). To project the GDP deflator, it may be reasonable enough to assume that it will evolve in the same way — i.e., at the same growth rates — as the year-average consumer price index. *For the remainder of this section only*, let "c" represent the year-average consumer price index. If the December consumer price index is given by c', then

$$c = c'_{-1} (1 + g_{c'})^{\omega},$$

where — again, *for the remainder of this section only* — ω is the consumer-price averaging coefficient for the year. Divide both sides by c_{-1} to obtain

$$1 + g_c = c/c_{-1} = (c'_{-1}/c_{-1}) (1 + g_{c'})^{\omega},$$

or

$$g_c = (c/c_{-1}) - 1 = [(c'_{-1}/c_{-1}) (1 + g_{c'})^{\omega}] - 1.$$

For each projection year, the growth rate of the GDP deflator could then simply be assumed to equal g_c.

A more sophisticated approach would be to project the GDP deflator as a weighted (geometric) average of the growth rates of (i) consumer, (ii) capital-goods, (iii) export, and (iv) import prices. *For the remainder of this section only*, let "c" represent year-average consumer prices, "k" year-average capital-goods prices, "e" the year-average exchange rate, x* year-average export prices in U.S. dollars, and m* year-average import prices in U.S. dollars. The growth rate of the GDP deflator could be calculated as

$$1 + g_p = [1 + g_c]^{\kappa} [1 + g_k]^{\lambda} [(1 + g_e) (1 + g_{x*})]^{\mu} [(1 + g_e) (1 + g_{m*})]^{\nu}$$

$$= (1 + g_c)^{\kappa} (1 + g_k)^{\lambda} [(1 + g_{x*})^{\mu}/(1 + g_{m*})^{\nu}] (1 + g_e)^{(\mu + \nu)},$$

where, *for this discussion only*, κ, λ, μ and ν are averaging weights (ν would be less than zero). One advantage of this approach is that it permits separate projection assumptions for consumer prices and capital-goods prices. This may be useful — the analyst may wish to consider the consequences if their growth rates diverged. Another advantage is that it enables the projection to take account of the effect on the GDP deflator of movements in exchange rates and world prices.

It is important to bear in mind that when national-currency export and import prices rise, they can be expected directly to affect the prices of the economy's other "tradable" goods. For that matter, they will probably also affect non-tradables sooner or later as well. That is, if projection assumptions include higher national-currency export and import prices (whether on account of world prices or the exchange rate), projection assumptions for consumer and capital-goods prices should *also* reflect these assumptions.

As noted above, the growth rate of the nominal exchange rate is given by

$$1 + g_e = (1 + g_E)(1 + g_{p*})/(1 + g_p),$$

where E represents the real-effective exchange rate and p* the world price index. Substituting this into the preceding expression and solving for the growth rate of the GDP deflator,

$$1 + g_p = \{(1 + g_c)^\kappa (1 + g_k)^\lambda [(1 + g_{x*})^\mu/(1 + g_{m*})^\nu] [(1 + g_E)(1 + g_{p*})]^Q,$$

where $Q = 1/(1 - \mu - \nu)$.

The values of κ, λ, μ, and ν may be projected as the respective proportions by value of total consumption (including change in inventories), investment, exports and imports in total expenditure during the preceding year.

Finally, real GDP is given by

$$y = y_{-1}(1 + g_y);^{32}$$

the domestic-currency value of GDP is given by

$$Y = Y_{-1}(1 + g_Y), \text{ where}$$

$$(1 + g_Y) = (1 + g_y)(1 + g_p);$$

---

[32] See Annex 3.2, however, which shows that the real-GDP growth rate in any given year may depend on the base year chosen.

and the U.S. dollar value of GDP is given by

$$Y^* = Y^*_{-1} (1 + g_Y)/(1 + g_e), \text{ or, equivalently, by}$$

$$Y^* = Y/e.$$

3.8   Basic macroeconomic programming variables for "Pacífica"

Table 2 (first discussed in Chapter 2 above) lists the key macroeconomic programming assumptions for "Pacífica." Nominal and real GDP, the consumer-price index, the exchange rate, and so on are given for the base year, i.e., the final year of "historical" data and the year immediately preceding the first projection year. The base year in this exercise is 2008. As noted, the exercise is being carried out in June 2009, and the year 2009 is the initial projection year, using assumptions corresponding to available estimates for the year.

The 2008 column of Table 7 gives the values of the basic macroeconomic programming variables for the base year. As noted in Section 3.8 above, real GDP growth rates are projected to climb gradually to 5 per cent by 2015, which would produce modest growth in per-capita real GDP since the population would continue to grow at 2 per cent a year. Consumer prices would grow at 2.2 per cent in 2009, zero in 2010, and thereafter at about 2 per cent per year, the same rate as the assumed international dollar inflation rate. After depreciating from 9 to 9.60 over 2009, the exchange rate would hold steady at an average annual value of 9.60 per U.S. dollar. The average real-effective exchange rate would depreciate from 2009 through 2011, then remain unchanged thereafter. Finally, over the years 2009–2015, the central bank's gross international-reserve holdings would hold steady at about 4 months' worth of imports of goods and non-factor services.

Figures in the projection years following 2008 are calculated from the base-year data and the assumptions in Table 2, applying the formulas given in Section 3.7 above. These are the basic programming values used to formulate the projection scenario, as discussed in the chapters following.

Paul Beckerman

Figure 2. Pacífica: Basic macroeconomic projection variables (percentage growth rates), 2008–2015

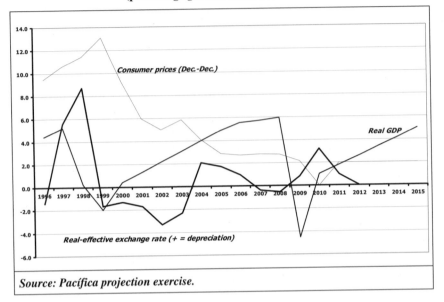

Source: Pacífica projection exercise.

4 Programming variables: Non-interest government expenditure

When outrageous expenditures are divided finely enough, the public will not have enough stake in any one expenditure to squelch it.

– from Murphy's Law[33]

4.1 Introduction: Non-interest government-expenditure projections

It would be perfectly possible, of course, to formulate a multiannual government current-expenditure projection simply by setting assumptions for overall (real) growth rates for each future year, or for the ratios of expenditure to GDP. A projection formulated in this way could actually be useful for many purposes. If the purpose is to determine the feasibility of development objectives, however, it makes sense to program government expenditure so that it addresses these objectives. Thus, for example, if development policy calls for all primary-school-age children to be attending school , say, ten years from now, then projected expenditure on teachers and supervisory staff should be quantitatively consistent with that objective (see Annex 4.1). In effect, the purpose of the overall exercise would be to help determine the financial feasibility of carrying out the expenditure necessary to achieve this and other development objectives.

That is, the fundamental reason for a developing economy's policy-makers to carry out a macroeconomic programming exercise is that they (a) have development objectives, (b) have a macroeconomic and government expenditure program calibrated to attain these objectives, and (c) need to determine whether, or show that, the expenditure program would be financially feasible. The idea would be to

---

[33] Cited as "The Guppy Law," in Bloch, Arthur, "Murphy's Law Complete: All the Reasons why Everything Goes Wrong" (p. 143). (A "corollary": "Enough guppies can eat a treasury.")

estimate the required future external and internal borrowing and then determine whether it would be feasible.

Suppose that government analysts carry out a preliminary projection and find that their development program's overall financing requirements are larger than they could hope to fill. They could revise in several ways. They could scale back the development objectives, devise a smaller government-expenditure program that more efficiently addresses the development objectives, take steps to secure more financing, or do some combination of these. In order to make an increased estimate of future financing credible, policy-makers might appeal to the international donor community to increase aid flows. Policy-makers may be able to strengthen their case by explicitly showing (a) quantitative development objectives, (b) a macroeconomic and expenditure program to attain those objectives, and (c) a quantitative argument that the macroeconomic and expenditure program would be financially feasible with the additional aid requested.

In this way of understanding the programming exercise, the formulation of a government expenditure program that addresses specified development objectives is clearly crucial. That is, in principal, to carry out the feasibility calculation, analysts must first set out (or be given) all relevant development objectives, and then use these to derive the programs of growth and government expenditure that will bring the objectives about. Unfortunately, at this writing, techniques for doing this are not yet well established. For some aspects of the calculation, such as the primary-school payroll projection summarized in Annex 4.1, they are likely to be relatively straightforward. For others, though, connections between specific development outcomes and government expenditure programs are harder to describe quantitatively. This book focuses on *macroeconomic* feasibility, and so a full answer to the question of how to determine what government expenditure would be necessary to address given development objectives is beyond the book's chosen scope. Nevertheless, this chapter offers some partial answers, listing a range of techniques that would at least help an analyst formulate a multiannual government expenditure program.

Government budgets, and specifically budgeted expenditure programs, are often said to be the financial expressions of a government's policies and priorities. This oversimplifies in an important sense. Most government current-expenditure programs are, in practical terms, on-going programs. At any instant, a government has large staffs of teachers, health workers, police, soldiers, tax and customs collectors, registry officials, and so on. At the moment it carries out its programming exercise, the government will have "inherited" them. By design, their activities are likely to be stable and continuing. As "civil servants," they probably have quite substantial degrees of tenure. This means that for most governments, at most times, expenditure "policies" and "priorities" are matters of the "margin" — of relatively larger or smaller increases in expenditure in different areas. In setting its annual budget, a government gives expression and effect to its policies and priorities through *relative increases* in expenditure programs. Thus, for example, a government that prioritizes education over defense will propose proportionally larger *increases* for education than for defense. This reality is reflected in the expenditure-programming techniques described below.

This point is closely related to a distinction often made regarding government expenditure. At any moment, as a government's legislative and executive branches formulate budget appropriations, certain on-going expenditures *must* be included, given laws and explicit and implicit contractual relationships in force. Such expenditures are said to be "non-discretionary": unless the relevant laws and contracts can be abrogated, revised, or re-interpreted, government decision-makers have no discretion to cut them from the budget. A large proportion of just about any government's expenditure program is likely to be non-discretionary in this sense. Remuneration for workers previously hired and tenured, expenditure for a broad range of goods and services (water and electricity services for government buildings, for example), subsidies and transfers "mandated" under previous legislation, and previously contracted payments (including external and internal debt service) are likely all to be legally or practically non-discretionary.

In fact, one way a multiannual programming exercise can turn out unfeasible is for its non-discretionary components to swell beyond available resources. One purpose of the projection exercise is to help policy-makers ensure that nothing like this happens during the projection period.[34]

Section 4.2 focuses on techniques to project non-interest current government expenditure, encompassing consumption and non-consumption "recurrent" expenditure categories. Section 4.3 focuses on capital and other "non-recurrent" expenditure. Section 4.4 returns to the Pacífica projection exercise to describe its government expenditure projections. (Annex 4.1 outlines a simple, illustrative procedure for carrying out medium-term projections of public primary-education programs.)

4.2   *Non-interest current-expenditure projections*

Many government budgets classify government expenditure accounts into "recurrent" and "non-recurrent," or "current" and "capital, categories." As the word implies, recurrent expenditure comprises activities that continue year after year, perhaps in smaller or larger amounts, but in the same basic categories. Recurrent expenditures include the standing government payroll, on-going expenditure on goods and services, interest charges on debt, and regular transfer payments made by the government. Non-recurrent or capital expenditure encompasses what is spent under "projects" and other one-time expenditures. In many economies, different procedures are used to prepare the recurrent and non-recurrent budgets. The International Monetary Fund and other international agencies generally advise governments to integrate preparation procedures, to ensure that they are developed together against the same overall financing constraint.

This section focuses on programming techniques for recurrent non-interest expenditure (Chapter 5 discusses interest expenditure, and

---

[34]   At this writing, for example, many observers in the United States are concerned about the possibility that "entitlements" programs, especially the Federal pensions and old-age health-care programs, could overtake the entire Federal budget. In developing economies, concern is more likely to focus on the government payroll: this year's discretionary expenditure on a new hire leads to subsequent years' non-discretionary expenditure on tenured staff.

Section 4.3 below focuses on non-recurrent expenditure). Current government expenditure, excluding transfers to non-government entities, subsidies and interest, is conventionally classified as *government consumption* expenditure in the national accounts. Or, put differently, government expenditure on recurrent staff remuneration and on purchases of current goods and services is considered synonymous with, and, in principle, equal to, government consumption as given in the national accounts. In fact, in historical data, discrepancies can arise between government-consumption figures in the national and government accounts, for several reasons. One of the most important is that the national accounts use accrual accounting (see Annex 8.1), whereas government accounts may record such expenditure partially or entirely on a cash basis. In addition, in some economies, different criteria may be used in compiling data for the national and government accounts.[35]

For historical periods, the expenditure data ideally would be "budget-execution" data — again, on an *accrual* basis, that is, what the government ought to have paid under its contractual arrangements for goods and services it received. For example, if teachers had not been fully paid in the base year, government budget figures should show what they should have been paid, not what they had been paid, as a base for projections. (Since executed budget data often take some time to finalize, estimates may have to be used for recent years, and revised as and when data are finalized.)

Assume, for now, that the government in question is "unitary," in the sense that there are no separate regional, provincial, sectional, or municipal governments. (Government operations at these levels would presumably be carried out by the single central government.) For present purposes, a functional-*cum*-economic classification would be the most

---

[35] In an economy in which total government consumption in the government accounts differs from the national-accounts figure, it may be convenient to add or subtract the difference to the total goods-and-services expenditures in the government accounts, so as to make total government consumption as shown in the government accounts the same as in the national accounts. This would then become the base for projections of government expenditure on goods and services. If this is done, this "reconciling" account should be clearly shown and labeled, and projected if its magnitude is significant.

useful way to set out and project non-interest government expenditure.[36]
That is, historical and projected expenditure data would first be classified
by *"functional category"* — e.g., as expenditure *for the purposes* of
education, health, internal security, and so on. The categories could be
more or less detailed — for example, instead of "education" being
an expenditure category, "pre-school," "primary" and "secondary
education" could each be expenditure categories. Expenditure under
each functional category would then be *sub-classified* by the
expenditure's *economic character* — that is, as payroll, expenditure on
current and capital goods and services, transfers, and so on.

For many developing economies' governments, unfortunately, a
precise functional classification is difficult to formulate, since the full
range of expenditures would have to be analyzed to determine with
which function they are most appropriately associated. For such
economies, an *institutional* classification — e.g., education ministry,
health ministry, and so on — should be a reasonable approximation to a
functional classification. It is important to remember, though, that in
many governments expenditure carried out by any given ministry may
include expenditures for functions other than those usually associated
with that ministry. Thus, for example, a defense ministry may carry out
education and health services for military personnel and their families.

For programming, recurrent expenditure under each kind of
functional or institutional category could be projected either to grow
(i) at some assumed rate or (ii) at a rate derived from the government's
substantive objectives, such as educating some number of schoolchildren
or providing some number of vaccinations each year. The economic sub-
classification would then take account of the different kinds of economic
expenditure that each functional category encompasses. For most

---

[36] A "functional" classification categorizes expenditure according to purpose — e.g.,
education, defense, etc. An "institutional" classification categorizes expenditure
according to the government agencies that carry it out. An "economic" classification
categorizes expenditure according to what it purchases — e.g., staff remuneration,
current goods and services, transfers, etc. A functional-cum-economic classification
categorizes expenditure by function, but categorizes the expenditure under each function
in economic categories — e.g., staff remuneration in education, current goods and
services in education, etc.

functional or institutional recurrent-expenditure categories, the most important economic "lines" would be staff remuneration and expenditure on goods and services. In some functional or institutional recurrent-expenditure categories, expenditure on goods and services may be related to the number of people on staff, depending on the sector. Thus, for example, expenditure on water and power for government buildings is likely to be related to the number of staff people that work in offices. In education, however, expenditure on goods and services might be more closely related to the number of students than to the number of teachers. In some functional or institutional recurrent-expenditure categories, other economic lines, particularly transfer and capital expenditures, may take on particular importance.

Recurrent expenditure can be programmed to reflect a government's "priorities," its evolving needs, its medium- or longer-term development program, or a combination of these. "Priorities," as noted above, tend to be expressed in government expenditure programs as relatively larger or smaller increases "at the margin" — that is, expenditure lines to be prioritized in the current budget would be programmed to grow faster than others.

The elaboration of a full multiannual government expenditure program from a given set of national development objectives is a relatively complicated analytical exercise. A substantial proportion of the expenditure associated with development objectives would be for capital formation and other non-recurrent expenditure, discussed in Section 4.3 below. Nevertheless, the flow of current expenditure is likely to undergo substantial change over any development process, and programming should reflect this evolution. Expenditure on education will grow as more students receive primary education and attend high school and higher-level institutions. Expenditure on public health services is likely to depend, at least in part, on the population growth rate, but also on the growth rates of demographic groups with specific health-care needs, such as women of child-bearing age and older people. (Inevitably, health expenditure will be affected by the simultaneous evolution of the private health sector.) Expenditure on internal security — police and investigative entities — may be regarded as "developmental," since maintenance of public order, traffic management and emergency services are likely to become more demanding and complex as economies develop. Tax collection is likely to require additional staff as an economy develops and as tax receipts grow in real terms.[37] Government office staffs can be expected to grow in general as government work becomes more complex. Meanwhile, even as development proceeds, the government will also be called upon to maintain the current flows of other, less obviously developmental expenditure. Even certain kinds of current defense expenditure can be considered "developmental" — among other things, expenditure on military infrastructure may have developmental consequences. Expenditure on executive-branch staffs, the legislature, and the judiciary will also grow with development, as their functions become more wide-ranging and complex.

For many if not most types of expenditure, regardless of whether the projection focuses on reflecting priorities, service provision, or meeting development objectives, it will make the most sense to program expenditure flows for staff and for goods and services to grow with population groups that presumably benefit from them. Thus, for example, expenditure on primary education would presumably grow with the number of children of primary-school age — or perhaps faster if the government aims to increase the proportion of children of primary-school age who attend school (see Annex 4.1). Health expenditure associated with hospitals, clinics, and public-health programs generally is likely also to be associated with the growth of population generally and with the growth of specific age cohorts. Specific health issues, such as malaria eradication or management of specific illnesses, may require different, more specific programming procedures. Tax and customs staff sizes are more likely to be associated with the number of contributors and with the overall values of GDP and imports.

In functional or institutional terms, education, health, police, and defense are likely to account for the bulk of any government expenditure program. Given their "labor-intensive" character, these sectors are likely to account for the bulk of the payroll expenditure. Expenditure can be

---

[37] For this reason, full elaboration of a tax-administration expenditure projection requires a revenue projection. See Section 8.2.

grouped by functional (or institutional) category in different ways. A functional grouping this writer has found useful for expenditure is as follows:

    a. armed forces (excluding police);

    b. internal security;

    c. financial-administration (including tax collection, customs, etc.)

    d. "economic" services (excluding public works)[38]

    e. public works;

    f. education;

    g. health and other social sectors; and

    h. administrative, legislative, and judicial services.

By grouping expenditure into these categories, a multiannual expenditure-programming exercise can work with a relatively small number of persuasive assumptions covering these "super"-sectors and their economic sub-classifications.

Under most functional or institutional expenditure categories, *staff remuneration* is likely to be the most important economic expenditure category. The programmed size and (real) remuneration rates of a government's staff are likely to be among the crucial determinants of whether any economy's multiannual fiscal program will prove feasible. Whether for the government as a whole or for a specific functional purpose, staff remuneration can be programmed on the basis of assumptions for the growth rates of the number of people on the

---

[38] The "economic" *functional* category should not be confused with the economic sub-classifications of expenditure. The economic functional category includes expenditure by ministries overseeing particular economic sectors, including agriculture, industry, commerce, tourism, and so on.

payroll, real wage rates, the price level, and "turnover" effects in the sector in question. If U represents the nominal payroll in any specified functional expenditure category "j," "W" the average nominal wage rate, "w" the average real wage rate, "n" the number of workers on the payroll, "p" the year-average price level, and "z" the effects of turnover,[39] the growth rate of U in this expenditure category would be given by

$$1 + g_U = (1 + g_W)(1 + g_n)(1 + g_z),$$

with

$$1 + g_W = (1 + g_w)(1 + g_p).$$

That is, the value of g_U for staff remuneration under a particular functional line may be formulated from assumptions for g_w, g_p, g_n, and g_z for that line. "Turnover" refers to the consequences of new hiring, promotions to higher grade levels, and retirements, and presumably explains whatever growth in U is not explained by the growth rates of (nominal) wages and staff size.

Suppose, for example, that an analyst is programming the growth rate for the coming year's armed-forces payroll. Suppose that policy-makers have decided that the number of people in the armed forces will remain unchanged as a ratio to total population, and that the average nominal pay rate will be 10 per cent higher in the coming year than this year. If the population growth rate is expected to be 2 per cent, then the armed forces staff would grow 2 per cent. Suppose that policy-makers have also decided that the payroll will grow by only 11 per cent. The formula above for g_U implies that the armed forces would have to

---

[39] *Ex post*, if data are available for a given payroll in a given year for the growth rates of the average wage, the number of workers on the payroll, and the price level, then the growth rate of the payroll can be decomposed into the growth rates of employment, real wages and the price level. Any residual would presumably be the result of changes in employees' average wage scales as a consequence of staff turnover. Note that it is unnecessary actually to know the staff size in the base year in order to formulate the projection using growth rates in this way: the staff size can be projected as an index number.

undertake a program of retirement, promotions, and new recruitment whose effect would be to reduce the growth rate of the payroll from what it would be if it resulted only from the growth of staff and of nominal wages:

$$1 + g_z = (1 + g_U)/[(1 + g_W)(1 + g_n)]$$
$$= (1 + 0.11)/[(1 + 0.10)(1 + 0.02)],$$

so that

$$g_z = -0.107$$

— that is, the "turnover" adjustment would have to be programmed to reduce the armed-forces payroll by 1.07 per cent.

Assumed values for the growth rates of nominal (g_W) or real wages (g_w) in functional or institutional sector "j" may be formulated in various ways. For nearer-term projection years, there may be a specific government wage policy or plan. (The nominal or real wage for this calculation would be the *average* over the year, and the growth rate would be the increase in the average in the current year over the average in the preceding year. A ten per cent nominal increase in January, for example, does not necessarily imply that the year-average wage rate would be ten per cent higher than the average for the preceding year, since there may have been one or more wage increases during the preceding year.)[40] For years further in the future, it may be reasonable to assume that real wages would grow, say, at the same rate as overall labor productivity for the economy as a whole, or at the growth rate of the ratio of real GDP to the labor force as a whole. For some years it may be easier to program the growth rate of the nominal wage rate (and calculate the real wage rate using the assumption for the growth rate of the average price level); for some years it may be easier to program the growth rate of the real wage rate (and calculate the nominal wage rate using the assumption for the growth rate of the average price level).

---

[40]   If wage rates rose during the base year, for example, and/or wages rates are expected to rise during the initial projection year, it may be necessary to go to the trouble of constructing an index for the 24 months of the two years and use this to calculate the growth rate of their *nominal* annual average.

The assumption for the growth rate of staff (g_n) in functional or institutional sector "j" could be related in turn to the population growth rate, or to a more relevant demographic growth rate. If the relationship is to be with population growth, then the programming assumption could be the elasticity of the growth rate of staff with respect to the population growth rate, λ, so that

$$1 + g_n = (1 + g_N)^{\lambda}.$$

The assumed average price-level increase (g_p) would of course be the basic assumption for the average increase in the price level. The assumed value of the "turnover" growth rate (g_z) would depend on what is known or projected for changes for in the composition by wage level of staff involved in functional expenditure "j." That is, the analyst would uses the value of g_z to adjust the growth rate of g_w to take account of the effect of new hires, promotions, and retirement on the total wage bill.

Government staff-remuneration expenditure includes social-insurance contributions. Such contributions are typically shared, with the employer — in this case, the government — paying part, and the recipients paying part. The part that is the government's responsibility may be programmed along with the payroll, either as additional pay to workers or as a transfer — either an intragovernmental transfer to the social-security institution (see below) or payment to non-governmental retirement savings institutions.

Current expenditure on **goods and services** in each functional or institutional category can be programmed by projecting its real growth rate and assuming that its cost will grow at the (year-average) inflation rate. Since some goods-and-services expenditure is for contracted personnel services and some is for "materials," it may be desirable to project these economic categories separately, especially if a significant part of the "contracted services" is for workers who are not part of the "tenured" government staff. In this case, it may be appropriate to project the contracted services in the same way as regular staff remuneration. If "X" and "x" represent nominal and real goods-and-services expenditure in functional or institutional sector "j", they can be programmed using

$$1 + g_x = (1 + g_N)^{\mu}$$

and

$$1 + g_X = (1 + g_x)(1 + g_p),$$

where μ is the assumed elasticity of real goods-and-services expenditure with respect to population (N).

Projection of current **transfers and subsidies** requires somewhat different approaches. Expenditures described as transfers fall broadly into two categories. The first comprises transfers to *other government* entities, while the second comprises transfers to *non-government* entities. Certain subtleties arise where transfers to other government entities are concerned. First, in many economies, some of what government budgets list as "transfers" consists of appropriations for government agencies outside the "ministerial" structure. These typically include regulatory commissions, government research and development agencies, motor-vehicle administrations, and public educational institutions. They may even include regional or local administrations where these are part of a unitary central government. Such agencies typically maintain their own financial-management systems, distinct from the central government's treasury. They may even have "own" revenues that are not passed back to the national treasury[41] (and may not even count in total government revenue). Although the "*intra*-government transfers" to them are almost always, in reality, government expenditure on staff or goods and services at one remove, they tend not to be classified as government consumption expenditure. (The national accounts may or may reflect them as such.) In principle, final expenditures of this kind on payroll and on goods and services by such agencies should be recorded as government consumption expenditure. Unfortunately, information on such entities' performance is often incomplete. In some instances, though, it may be possible to calculate or estimate, and then program, a breakdown of such expenditure as going to staff or goods and services.[42]

---

[41] In Latin America entities of this kind are often called "*autarquias.*"

[42] Some countries have agencies of government that are outside the basic ministerial structure and do not even receive transfers from the national budget, relying on own revenues to cover their costs. Their expenditure may or may not be reflected consistently in the government and national accounts.

Inter-government transfers, i.e., transfers to governmental entities other than the central government (or, for that matter, from sub-national governments to the central government, if any) differ from *intra*-government transfers. For one thing, for the transferring government, these are expenditure flows, but neither consumption nor capital-formation expenditures; for the receiving government, they are non-tax revenue flows. When consolidated over all government entities, they would therefore add nothing to overall government consumption and capital-formation flows.

For an economy that has central and separate sub-national governments, it would of course be desirable for the projection exercise to encompass them all. Among other reasons, this would be necessary for consistency between the fiscal and national accounts, since the national-accounts data and projections of government-consumption and — capital formation would cover all government entities.

Current transfers within the government sector, whether intra- or inter-governmental, should be projected according to whatever rules of legislation or customary practice happen to govern them. Thus, for example, where a central government is required by law to provide transfers to municipal governments equal to some percentage of its total revenue, that percentage could be incorporated as an adjustable programming assumption. If there are no specific rules, and the amounts are subject to policy-makers' discretion, the analyst may be able to work with simple assumptions (e.g., that the central government will provide a constant percentage of GDP in such transfers.)[43]

Current transfers and subsidies *to non-governmental entities* can be projected according to the programs' specific characteristics. For example, income-transfer payments to poor people could be projected on the basis of assumptions about the growth rates of the magnitudes of the

---

[43] Revenue sharing with sub-national governments may be represented either (i) by showing the sub-national governments receiving revenue on the basis of the projected taxes or (ii) by showing the central government transferring the required amounts to the sub-national governments in question. These should be equivalent, although it may make a difference for certain calculated values — e.g., for summations of total tax revenue received by sub-national entities.

payments and of the number of recipients.[44] A cash subsidy to all households with students in school, for example, could be projected according to assumptions about the evolution of the number of households with students in school and the subsidy's unit value. Similarly, subsidies to enterprises to enable them to sell a particular good or service at a low price could be projected according to assumptions about production costs and demand volume.[45]

Finally, some governments' current expenditure includes lines that are non-recurrent, and yet not classified as "capital" expenditure. These are sometimes described as "exceptional" current expenditures, since, although non-recurrent, they are not prepared with the capital budget, and are usually not developmental in character. Examples include war-time pay for military personnel (or demobilization after a war), relief and other temporary expenditures in times of natural disaster, and security costs associated with exceptional entertainment or sporting events. Such expenditures must be programmed — or guessed — according to the best information available.

If exceptional expenditures have been carried out in the base year, or are to be introduced in the initial projection year, it may be possible to program their future evolution. Demobilization payments, for example, might tail off and end after a certain time; disaster relief may wind down gradually over a year or two. For the longer term, exceptional expenditures are by their nature difficult to project. Some analysts have come to describe future exceptional expenditures as "contingent liabilities" — i.e., expenditures that the government would be obliged to carry out in the event of certain contingencies whose occurrence is a matter of probability (see Polackova 1999). The simple

---

[44] The projected number of recipients may require an income-distribution projection. Annex 6.6 describes a methodology for projecting the distribution of per-capita real non-government consumption. A similar approach could be used to project per-capita real non-government income, and this could be used to program income-support subsidies.

[45] A subsidy provided in this way should not be confused with a different kind of subsidy, under which a government-owned enterprise is simply *directed* to sell its output at a low price. In such instances, the enterprise earns lower profits than it otherwise would, and so either accumulates less capital or pays less in taxes and dividends than it otherwise would. This is the form in which the subsidy is effectively provided. Government accounts would not directly reflect this form of subsidy.

reality is that conflict, natural or financial disasters, and other "contingencies" can force governments to undertake large expenditures. While the nature and timing of such contingencies may be unpredictable, some are more predictable than others. Nations located in earthquake or hurricane zones, nations with growing financial systems, and nations that have disputes with other nations must plan and prepare for contingencies. Standing armed forces, civil-defense agencies, deposit-insurance schemes, and the like are among the better-known means of planning and preparing for such contingencies. (It may also be necessary to prepare financing plans, possibly involving such things as insurance, credit facilities that can be quickly activated, and disaster-relief arrangements.)

4.3   Capital and other non-recurrent expenditure

As with current expenditure, it is perfectly possible to formulate a multiannual projection of capital, or non-recurrent, expenditure using assumed (real) growth rates for each future year, or assumed ratios of such expenditure to GDP. Such a projection may be useful for many purposes. Again, though, if the purpose is to address the financial feasibility of expenditure on development objectives, it would be better to program government capital expenditure so as to address these objectives. Government capital expenditure is generally defined as comprising not only (i) government gross fixed capital formation, but also (ii) government "investment" expenditure for purposes other than physical capital formation, (iii) payments for land, buildings, equipment, shares in enterprises, and other capital assets, and (iv) capital transfers.[46]

"Gross fixed capital formation" is the creation of *physical* capital, comprising "equipment" and structures. In most economies, a large part of the government's capital formation consists of "infrastructure" — roads, bridges, air and water port facilities, dams, and

---

[46] It is important not to make the error of assuming that all expenditure under a government's "capital," "non-recurrent," or "investment" budget is part of the national-accounts flow of gross fixed capital formation. (Among other consequences, if the overall capital-formation flow is given, over-estimating the government's share would imply under-estimating the non-government share.)

the like. "Other" investment or non-recurrent expenditure consists of "one-time" expenditure for such things as technical advice, consulting advice, training, and other specialized services. Significant proportions of the expenditure under government projects are likely to be for such purposes, rather than for physical capital. Expenditure of this kind is *not* be included in the national accounts' gross fixed capital formation. Some of this expenditure may, or should, count as government-consumption expenditure (another reason why the government- and national accounts' government-consumption figures may diverge), and the remainder would then be non-consumption current expenditure.

Government capital expenditure also includes one-time payments for land, buildings, acquisition of capital positions in enterprises, and other previously existing capital assets. Such expenditure would *not* count as national-accounts expenditure of any kind, since it would not be for goods currently produced.[47] Finally, "capital transfers" are transfers to other public entities and even to the private sector for physical capital formation, other kinds of non-recurrent expenditure, and asset purchases.

Precisely because they are non-recurrent, the various components of a government's non-recurrent expenditure flow can be difficult to project. If non-recurrent expenditure is programmed without reference to a national development program, it could use assumptions such as the following: (i) government gross fixed capital formation will grow at a fixed (or gradually increasing) real rate; (ii) government gross fixed capital formation will be a constant (or slowly increasing) percentage of GDP; (iii) government gross fixed capital formation will always be a given percentage of total gross fixed capital formation (determined at the economy level using techniques discussed in Section 6.2). Similar approaches may also work well enough for non-physical capital expenditure — that is, government capital expenditure that would not be included in gross fixed capital formation under the national accounts.

---

[47] In principle, such payments could be considered "negative" financing items for the government, in the same way that asset sales should be regarded as financing flows. See Chapter 8, Section 5.5 below.

Where a government has an investment program intended to bring about development, however, the projection would need to be more detailed. It may be possible to draw on medium- or longer-term planning exercises, in which the development objectives are used to elaborate multiannual programs of physical and human capital formation to achieve them. Many governments maintain "public investment programs," often as components of official budgets. Such exercises are set out in different ways, but those that are most useful (a) classify projects by sectors — i.e., electrical power, roads, school construction, and so on; (b) indicate the expenditure flows for each project over coming years, (c) indicate how the expenditure flows will be spent — i.e., on structures, equipment, training, studies, project management, and so on; and (d) show how the expenditure flows are likely to be financed — that is, with disbursements of external loans (by lender), external grants, government "counterpart" funds, and so on. The expenditure flows would presumably be related to project objectives. Thus, a power-facility project would bring about an increase in the quantity of available kilowatt-hours.

Projected project expenditures should take realistic account of likely execution rates. Project execution frequently slips behind programmed time "profiles," and it is best to take realistic account of this in programming exercises.

As these observations suggest, non-recurrent expenditure projections can be carried out in less or more complicated ways. At this writing, it seems fair to say that standard methodologies for projecting investment expenditure remain some way from being fully developed. In any case, they are bound to be somewhat country-specific. Unfortunately, full discussion of these techniques is beyond the scope of the present discussion.

Formulation of persuasive projection assumptions for government non-recurrent capital transfers and asset purchases is probably even more difficult than for physical capital formation — again, precisely because of their non-recurrent nature. Inter- and intra-government capital transfers and asset purchases are even less likely than current transfers to be governed by specific continuing rules that can be used to generate assumptions. Precisely because such expenditure is generally "one-off" in character, recent experience is likely to be unhelpful. For nearer-term expenditure programming, the best procedure is to obtain information for the government about specific plans. For the longer term, it may be best to use rough assumptions, such as given percentages of GDP or real per-capita expenditure. (It may be best to set such assumptions somewhat on the high side for a "conservative" projection.)

It may be possible to indicate specifically how certain capital and even current expenditure lines would be financed, and to link particular expenditure lines to specific kinds of financing. Specific expenditure projections may be classified into amounts to be financed from (i) specified (or unspecified) external-debt disbursements, (ii) grants by external donors, (iii) internal debt, (iv) asset sales, and (v) (residually) general budget resources. This would be particularly useful for capital formation and other investment expenditure financed under specific projects, and would also would help with the programming of the government's projected external debt (see Chapter 5 below). It may be useful, moreover, to set out different assumption scenarios: one scenario, for example, could have higher government capital-formation expenditure and correspondingly higher disbursement flows from, say, the World Bank. (It is important to remember in this connection that donors characteristically finance less than the full value of any project, and require governments to provide "counterpart" financing from their own resources. This implies that, since the disbursements will cover only part of a project's expenditure, disbursements of financing for projects can widen a government's financing requirement.)

"Donor financing" to a given economy in any given year can be classified in four broad categories: (1) loans and (2) grants for projects and (3) loans and (4) grants for general (i.e., unspecified) budget support. In the fiscal program, the total value of project expenditures for which project loans and grants would be provided may be shown "above the line" in the fiscal accounts. The corresponding total flow of disbursement would be given below the line and the total flow of grants would be given under grant revenue, usually above the line. For any given year, the total quantity of project loans and grants would be less than total project expenditure. The difference would be the amount financed by the government, the so-called "counterpart" financing. Ideally, the presentation of the fiscal-accounts projection would show these amounts.

4.4   Pacífica's government expenditure

Table 8 lists the assumptions regarding Pacífica's central-government expenditure. These are taken to comprise expenditures in the sectors of (1) armed forces, (2) internal security, (3) financial administration (including tax and customs collection), (4) "economic" sectors (including public works, agriculture, tourism, and industry), (5) education, (6) health and other social services, and (7) administrative, legislative and judicial services. (This classification is illustrative. In applications for actual economies more detailed disaggregation of government expenditure programs would probably be desirable.) Under each of these "functional" categories, the assumptions cover the growth rates of the payroll and expenditure on goods and services, transfers, capital goods, and so on as percentages of GDP. The growth rates of payrolls are each calculated from assumptions covering the growth rates of real wages, employment, and a "promotion" factor. The growth rates of employment are related in turn to the assumed population growth rate through assumed elasticities.[48] The growth rates of the various categories of real goods-and-services expenditure are also related to population growth through assumed elasticities. Transfer expenditures and capital expenditures under each functional category are projected as assumed percentages of GDP.

Table 9 gives the "functional-cum-economic" structure of Pacífica's central-government expenditure, from the base year on through the projection period, with the projections constructed from the projection assumptions given in Table 8. Expenditure structures vary from economy to economy, and while there is probably nothing like a "typical" structure, the structure given here would be far from unusual

---

[48]   Note that the payroll projection in any expenditure category can be carried out in this way even if the number of workers in the base-year is unknown. It is likely to be useful, of course, to know, or at least estimate, and then project the number of workers.

for a developing economy. Central-government non-interest expenditure would rise from 19 per cent of GDP in 2008 to 20 per cent of GDP in 2013 and thereafter. The largest functional component would be education, accounting for about 25 per cent of overall non-interest expenditure. More than half of education expenditure would go for staff remuneration. The remainder would be largely for goods and services — school materials and such services as water, electricity, and the like — and for capital expenditure, basically for construction and repair of educational facilities. Health and other social services expenditure — on government hospitals, clinics, and special programs (presumably to cope with specific problems such as malaria, tuberculosis, and AIDS) — would account for about 16 per cent of overall non-financial expenditure.

Expenditure for the armed forces and for police services together — "security services" — would account for about 17 per cent of non-financial expenditure. Defense expenditure varies widely among countries, of course, since specific security situations differ. (It is important to remember that defense expenditure may include substantial amounts for education, health and other social services, not only for current armed-forces personnel and their dependents but also to veterans and their dependents.) Expenditure on government financial services, which would account for just over a sixth of total non-interest expenditure, includes the substantial staff involved in tax and customs services, as well as the staff that work for the treasury and other aspects of government financial management. (As a broad generalization, the five categories of education, health, armed forces, police, and financial management — including tax and customs collection — are likely to account for the bulk of any central government's staff and, indeed, overall recurrent expenditure.)

Finally, the "economic" expenditure categories, (typically) including expenditure on services for agriculture, tourism, industrial promotion, and the like, as well as the important category of public works and maintenance, would account for about 7 per cent of total non-financial expenditure. The importance of this expenditure will depend, in general, on the size of the government's role in economic sectors generally and in infrastructure in particular. To the extent infrastructure — including electrical power, transport, communications, and water and sanitation — is in the private or public-enterprise sectors, of course, central-government expenditure would be smaller.

The number of people on staff in the functional expenditure categories and real expenditure on goods and services is assumed to vary with population. The programmed elasticities with respect to population of the number of people on staff and of real expenditure differ: they would be higher for education and for health and other social services, and lower for the armed forces and for administrative services, reflecting policy-makers' present priorities. Real wages are assumed to rise with real *per-capita* GDP. Capital and other non-consumption expenditures are projected to remain roughly the same as percentages of GDP.

Under the projection assumptions, total non-interest central-government current expenditure would rise as a percentage of GDP from 14.4 per cent in 2008 to 15.4 per cent in 2015. Capital expenditure would remain at 4.8 per cent of GDP throughout the projection period.

Different programming assumptions would produce different expenditure projections, of course. It is important to note, however, that the elasticities of staff size and real goods-and-services expenditure would have to differ very much from one to produce very significant shifts in the expenditure composition. This reflects the point made in Section 4.1 above, that, unless a very radical restructuring of government expenditure were to occur, shifts in expenditure priorities tend to take place at the margin.

5 Programming variables: External debt and internal government debt

If you owe your bank a hundred pounds, you have a problem. But if you owe a million, it has.

– attributed to John Maynard Keynes

If you owe your bank a billion pounds everybody has a problem.

– The Economist[49]

5.1 Programming external and internal debt

In the projection exercise this book describes, the disbursement and repayment flows of the various kinds of *identified* external and internal government debt are programming assumptions. As noted in Chapters 1 and 2, the basic methodological approach is to formulate a macroeconomic program comprising assumptions for basic macroeconomic variables, government expenditure, and government external and internal debt, and then determine whether this would be feasible. The feasibility indicators include the *unidentified* external debt required "to close" the year-by-year balance-of-payments projections, as well as the *unidentified* internal debt required "to close" the year-by-year fiscal accounts — that is, *to reconcile* the above- and below-the-line balance-of-payments and fiscal projections. Chapter 7 below describes the calculation of *unidentified* external debt in each year's external-accounts projection, and Chapter 8 below describes the calculation of *unidentified* internal debt in the fiscal-accounts projection. This chapter focuses on the *programming* of *"identified"* government external and internal debt.

As noted in Section 4.3 above, some programmed government expenditure for investment projects may have associated external-debt disbursements — the expenditure and the disbursements are coordinated,

---

[49]   See the *Economist*, February 13, 1982, page 11.

so that either both or neither occur. In general, however, the approach described here consists of programming, first, the future evolution of the various kinds of external debt, including those going to the government, the non-government public sector, and the private sector; and then the future evolution of the various kinds of internal government debt. The overall financing program would form part of the overall macroeconomic program to be examined for feasibility, along with the macroeconomic programming assumptions discussed in Chapter 3 above and the government-expenditure program discussed in Chapter 4 above.

Historical external-debt data for a given economy are usually best obtained from the country's official sources. Even so, in the same way that the International Monetary Fund's *International Financial Statistics* are a useful source of data on macroeconomic variables for most developing economies, the World Bank's annual publication *Global Development Finance* is a useful source of external-debt data. To be sure, figures drawn from *Global Development Finance* may need to be adjusted on the basis of country-source data. (Annex 5.1 describes the structure of developing economies' external debt, as set out in the data tables of *Global Development Finance*.)

Figure 3 shows the generic structure of a nation's external debt in a diagrammatic format, following the *Global Development Finance* structure.

Figure 3. Diagram: External debt classified by creditor

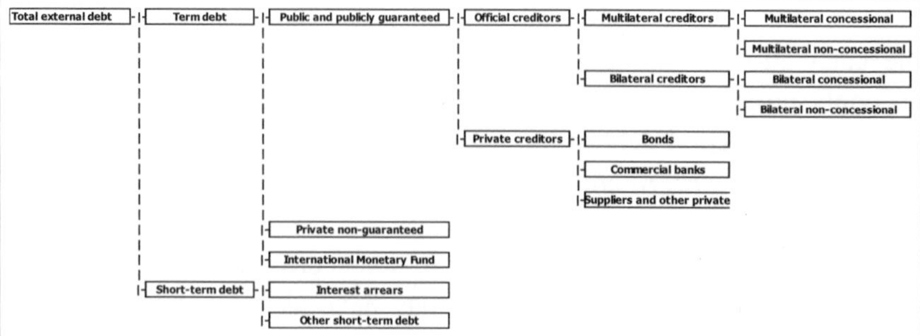

Source: Annex 5.1

In this chapter, Section 5.2 describes techniques for "programming" the evolution of an economy's future external debt. Section 5.3 presents a thumbnail sketch of the recent world history of external debt, and in this way introduces some of the concepts associated with debt rescheduling and reduction. Section 5.4 discusses concepts associated with recent "debt-relief" initiatives, notably the Highly-Indebted Poorest Countries (HIPC) initiative and the MDRI (Multilateral Debt Relief Initiative). Section 5.5 discusses the projection of net internal government-financing flows. Section 5.6 discusses Pacífica's external debt and internal government debt.

5.2   *External-debt programming techniques*

This section describes techniques for programming external "term-debt" operations — that is, operations involving external debt with maturity longer than one year that is repaid in installments (usually called "amortization" or simply "repayment"). Toward the end, however, it also describes some methods for projecting short-term debt, including interest arrears on external term debt.

For any given year, for any given class of debt — that is, debt owed by any identifiable internal entity (or group of entities) to any specific external creditor (or class of creditors) — let $D^{*\prime}$ represent the year-end debt stock outstanding and disbursed, L^* the disbursement flow, A^* the repayment flow, and I^* the interest paid, all in U.S. dollars. Let D^* represent the average debt stock during the year, taken here to be given by

$$D^* = [(D^{*\prime}_{-1} + D^{*\prime})/2]$$

$$= D^{*\prime}_{-1} + \Delta D^{*\prime}/2$$

where

$$\Delta D^{*\prime} = D^{*\prime} - D^{*\prime}_{-1}.$$

The debt-programming exercise works from four basic assumptions for each kind of external debt:

(i) let $g_{D*'}$ represent the assumed growth rate of the year-end debt stock. By definition,

$$g_{D*'} = \Delta D^{*\prime}/D^{*\prime}_{-1} = (D^{*\prime}/D^{*\prime}_{-1}) - 1.$$

Next,

(ii) let "s" represent the assumed interest rate on new loan disbursements. (For simplicity, take this to be a fixed U.S. dollar interest rate. An adjustment to take account of floating-rate debt is described below). In addition,

(iii) let "a" represent the proportion of the base year's (year-end) debt stock to be amortized in any projection year. (For each kind of external debt, the values of "a" must add up over all projection years to a total less than or equal to one.) Finally,

(iv) let "v" represent the percentage increase in the valuation of the previous year-end debt stock over the year. "Valuation changes," which may be positive or negative, arise from (a) changes in "cross-currency" exchange rates between the U.S. dollar and other currencies, where debt stocks are partially or wholly denominated in currencies other than the U.S. dollar; and (b) events like debt forgiveness (for which, of course, the value of "v" would be negative).

The different categories of external debt may be drawn from the list of the different kinds of debt that happen to be significant for the economy in question. An economy's external debt may be classified by creditor (see Annex 5.1), or by creditor and debtor. For example, it is generally useful to sub-classify debt of particular creditors, or classes of creditor (e.g., commercial banks), by such debtor categories as government, non-government non-financial public sector, central bank, and private-sector. Some economies may have only a limited range of external debt, owed by the central government to multilateral and bilateral agencies. Other economies, in contrast, may have a wide and complicated range of creditors and debtors. For now, consider a single class of debt, owed by a specified kind or class of debtor to a specific kind or class of creditor.

Assume first, for simplicity, that no interest arrears have accumulated and that none will over the projection period, and that repayment will take place only on debt already outstanding at the end of the base year (that is, that no repayment obligations will arise in the projection period from disbursements in the projection period). The four assumptions — g_{D*}, "s," "a," and "v" — should then suffice to formulate a complete year-by-year debt projection, consisting of the debt stock, interest, disbursement and repayment. (Projection of interest arrears and projection of repayment of debt disbursed after the base year are discussed below.)

For each category of debt, the projection exercise sets out from the previous year-end debt stock, represented by $D_{-1}^{*\prime}$. By definition, the year-end debt stock ($D^{*\prime}$) is given by

$$D^{*\prime} = D_{-1}^{*\prime} + V^* + L^* - A^*,$$

where $V^* = v\, D_{-1}^{*\prime}$. That is, the debt stock varies over the year by the difference between the net flows of disbursement and repayment and by the net increase in "valuation."

The value of "v," the percentage *valuation increase in the debt stock*, will be larger to the extent the debt in question is denominated in currencies other than the U.S. dollar and these currencies are projected to appreciate *vis-a-vis* the dollar. In addition, anticipated debt forgiveness would give rise to a negative value for "v." (*Ex-post* values of V^* and "v" may be determined implicitly from historical data by subtracting the net flows from the difference between the year-end and previous year-end debt stocks.)

Suppose, for example, that the proportion "h" of a particular year-end debt stock is denominated in British pounds and the remainder is denominated in dollars. Suppose that the U.S. dollar is assumed to depreciate against the pound, such that the exchange rate in dollars per pound will increase by "w." The projected value of "v" would be given by

$$1 + v = (1 + w)^h.$$

An important example here would be loan stocks denominated in SDRs, since IMF loans are denominated in this unit. The value of the SDR is a composite of currencies, with the U.S. dollar accounting for 44 per cent and the euro and the Japanese yen accounting for the remainder. Accordingly, the U.S. dollar value of a debt stock denominated in SDRs increases — that is, the SDR becomes more expensive in dollars — as the dollar depreciates against the other currencies. If over a given period the dollar depreciates by "m" against the other currencies in the SDR, the value of "w" in the preceding formula would be given by

$$1 + w = (1 + 0)^{0.44} (1 + m)^{0.56}$$

$$= (1 + m)^{0.56}.$$

As noted above, ***repayment flows*** (A*) are assumed for simplicity to be made only on debt already outstanding — i.e., on debt outstanding at the end of the current projection's base year. For any projection year, the value of repayment of debt outstanding at the end of the base year 0 would be given by

$$A^* = a \, [Z/Z_0] \, D_0^{*\prime},$$

where "a" represents the percentage of the base-year repayment programmed for that year and Z is a "valuation index,"

$$Z = Z_{-1}(1 + v).$$

That is, if the programmed repayment would be A* if there were no future valuation adjustment, it would be A* Z/Z_0 after taking account of such adjustment.

Disbursement flows (L*) may be programmed in several ways. For some creditors, it is possible to program a given year's flow on the basis of commitment "pipelines." Multilateral entities like the World Bank disburse loans in "tranches," programmed at the moment the loan is approved. Disbursement may be delayed relative to what was programmed upon commitment if projects or policy programs proceed more slowly than anticipated — in particular, if disbursement "conditionalities" have not been met. Nevertheless, information about programmed disbursement profiles can be used to estimate disbursement flows over the first few projection years, especially if time likely to be necessary to satisfy the disbursement conditions can be taken into account. Other lending entities have more or less formalized lending programs, and to the extent these are known or estimated or known they may be used to project disbursement flows. Note that if disbursements L* are estimated in these ways, the *assumption* for $g_{D*'}$ would overridden, and the growth rate of the debt would be calculated instead as

$$1 + g_{D*'} = D^{*'}/D^{*'}_{-1} = (D^{*'}_{-1} + V^* + L^* - A^*)/D^{*'}_{-1},$$

with

$$g_{D*'} = (V^* + L^* - A^*)/D^{*'}_{-1}.$$

Alternatively, disbursements may be projected, as indicated above, on the basis of an assumption for $g_{D*'}$:

$$L^* = A^* - V^* + g_{D*'} D^{*'}_{-1}.$$

That is, using this formula to project the value of L* for any particular class of debt would imply that the debt stock would grow by the (decimal) growth rate $g_{D*'}$.

If $g_{D*'}$ is set equal to the growth rate of the U.S. dollar value of GDP, then the debt stock in question would remain at the same percentage of GDP as at the end of the preceding year. The assumption that $g_{D*'}$ is equal to the growth rate of the U.S. dollar value of GDP would be a more or less "neutral" assumption, since lenders' "exposures" to economies are often described in terms of the ratio of the outstanding debt stock to GDP and this assumption would hold the ratio unchanged. There is an important caveat here, however. For any year in which real-effective exchange-rate depreciation is significant, it is better to have the external debt grow according to the U.S. dollar of GDP valued *at a constant purchasing-power exchange rate*. This is because foreign lenders would presumably not increase (or reduce) their lending just because a large exchange-rate appreciation increased (or depreciation reduced) the U.S. dollar value of GDP. Perhaps more important, if the debt stock is assumed to grow with the unadjusted U.S. dollar GDP, any increase in the assumed real-effective exchange-rate depreciation would reduce the dollar flow of disbursements.   In general, it would seem inappropriate to assume such a link between the dollar value of GDP and the disbursement flow for any particular kind of debt. Having a debt stock grow at the same rate as GDP valued at a constant purchasing-power exchange rate is a straightforward way to remove it.

In general, better information on loan commitments and disbursement plans is likely to be available for projection years nearer to the present. This suggests that, for most kinds of debt, it may be reasonable to program disbursements for nearer years on the basis of specific information about projects and borrowers' and lenders' plans, and then to program disbursements for subsequent years on the basis of assumptions about the growth rates of the debt stock. (Note that these disbursement flows may be associated with specific project expenditure, as discussed in Section 4.3 above.)

Once the valuation-change, repayment, and disbursement flows are projected, the basic stock-flow formula

$$D^{*\prime} = D^{*\prime}_{-1} + V^* + L^* - A^*$$

can be used to calculate the **year-end debt stock**. The year-average debt stock can then be projected as the arithmetic average of the two year-end debt stocks:

$$D^* = [(D^{*\prime}_{-1} + D^{*\prime})/2].$$

The following procedure may be used to project **interest due** on each kind of external debt. First, to simplify, assume that the interest rate is a simple annual percentage rate (in particular, not a spread over a reference rate such as LIBOR). Projection of the interest bill on any kind of external debt for any given year begins with a calculation of the previous year's implicit *ex-post* interest rate, taken to be given by

$$i_{-1} = I^*_{-1}/[(D^{*\prime}_{-2} + D^{*\prime}_{-1})/2]$$

$$= I^*_{-1}/D^*_{-1},$$

where

$$D^*_{-1} = [(D^{*'}_{-2} + D^{*'}_{-1})/2],$$

i.e., the arithmetic average of the debt stock over the previous year.

Assume that disbursement and repayment in each projection year take place June 30, half way through the year. The interest payment in the projection year should then be the weighted average of i_{-1} and "s,"

$$I^* = D^{*'}_{-1} [(1 + (v/2)] - (A^*/2)\} \, i_{-1} + (L^*/2) \, s.$$

This may be used to determine the value of "i" to be used to calculate the projected interest payment for the subsequent year.

This last formula can be adjusted to take account of the reality that interest rates on many external loans — particularly credit from private commercial banks and bond issues — are "LIBOR-based," i.e., computed at a rate equal to the current LIBOR plus a spread. For such loans, the value of "s" would represent spreads over LIBOR rather than conventional interest rates. Let "m" represent the value of LIBOR lagged six months (since interest paid will typically have been set on the basis of the LIBOR prevailing six months earlier). The preceding formula for the interest flow would now become

$$I^* = \{D^{*'}_{-1} (1 + (v/2)] - (A^*/2)\} \, (i_{-1} - m_{-1} + m) + (L^*/2) \, (s + m).$$

If there are no interest arrears, this formula indicates both interest due and interest paid.

Summarizing thus far, setting out from base-year values for a particular class of debt, it is straightforward to calculate projections of year-end and year-average debt stocks ($D^{*'}$ and D^*) and flows of disbursement (L^*), repayment (A^*), interest (I^*) and valuation change (V^*), on the basis of four year-by-year projection assumptions: (i) the growth rate of the debt stock (g_{D^*}), (ii) the interest rate on new disbursements (s), (iii) the proportion of the base-year debt stock repaid (a), and (iv) the valuation change in the debt stock ("v").

Interest arrears may be projected as follows. Let H*' represent the accumulated stock of interest arrears on a given kind of debt at the end of a year and let the projection assumption "j" represent the proportion of the interest currently due that is actually paid. The accumulated stock of interest arrears is a short-term debt stock, which generates interest due itself. The stock can be reduced, of course, through repayment. If the total amount of interest due on the term-debt stock is given by

$$I^* = \{D^{*'}_{-1}\,(1 + (v/2)] - (A^*/2)\}\,i_{-1} + (L^*/2)\,s\,,$$

interest actually paid would be given by

$$J^* = j\,I^*,$$

and the increase in the in the arrears stock would be

$$(1 - j)\,I^*.$$

The year-average interest rate would still be given by

$$i = I^*/D^*.$$

Let the projection assumption "k" represent the percentage of the interest-arrears stock that is paid down in any year. Over the year, then, the change in the interest-arrears stock would be given by

$$\Delta H^{*'} = (1 - j)\,I^* - k\,H^{*'}_{-1}\,,$$

while the year-end accumulated interest-arrears stock would be given by

$$H^{*'} = H^{*'}_{-1} + \Delta H^{*'}$$

$$= (1 - j)\,I^* + (1 - k)\,H^{*'}_{-1}.$$

The formulas for ΔH^* and H^* could be further adjusted, if useful, to take account of assumptions for penalty interest and valuation changes arising from cross exchange rates and forgiveness.

Most economies make use of ***"contractual" short-term debt***, mainly export financing and short-term bank credit lines. Such debt is never counted as "public and publicly-guaranteed debt," which is term debt. ("Non-contractual" short-term debt consists of payments arrears, including accumulated interest arrears, although, by convention, *not* accumulated principal in arrears. Principal arrears are discussed below.) The year-end outstanding stock of contractual short-term debt may be projected by relating it through an assumed elasticity with respect to the sum of merchandise exports and imports. The interest rate on such debt could be projected directly (ordinarily as a spread over LIBOR), and the interest flow would be this interest rate multiplied by the average of the year-end and the previous year-end debt stocks.

Thus far, projected repayment flows have been assumed to arise only from debt outstanding at the end of the base year. To take account of **repayment flows arising from future disbursements**, projection assumptions must be set for the (average) grace and maturity periods for disbursements made in each future year. If loan disbursements totaling L_t^* are made in year t with average maturity periods of M years and grace periods of G years, then repayment payments amounting to $L_t^* (z/z_t)/(M - G)$ would take place in years $t + G + 1$ through $t + M$. In each projection year, repayment payments would be made on debt of various "vintages," that is, debt disbursed in different preceding projection years. These repayment payments would be in addition to repayment payments made on the base-year year-end debt stock.

Taking account of repayment flows arising from future disbursements causes some complexities for spreadsheet projection. It may not always be necessary. First, if the projection period is relatively short, repayment based on future disbursements is likely to be small, since the new loans' grace periods may extend past the projection period. Second, if future disbursements are projected using assumed debt-stock growth rates, the assumed repayment flow will make no difference for the evolution of the debt stock and no more than a second-order difference for interest rates and charges. Accordingly, for some projection exercises, careful projection of repayment flows arising from future disbursements may simply not be worth the effort. (The Pacífica exercise includes it, however.)

The discussion thus far has not covered several external-debt concepts that play a limited role in the projection exercise but sometimes matter in debt negotiations and more detailed debt projections. For example, the discussion has discussed interest arrears, but not ***principal arrears***. To the extent a debtor is projected to fail to pay principal when due, the present exercise simply shows a smaller repayment and the debt stock does not diminish. (In a more detailed projection exercise, though, the amount not repaid could pass to a different debt category, "principal arrears." Principal arrears may carry a penalty interest rate. As noted, unlike interest arrears, principal arrears are conventionally not considered short-term debt, although in fact their accumulated stock is due, in principle, immediately.)

Debt outstanding, whether in arrears or not, may be ***rescheduled***. In the present exercise, for a given debt category, this simply involves revising the projected repayment pattern (see Section 5.3 below). In a more detailed projection exercise, however, the amount rescheduled could pass to a different category of debt, "rescheduled debt," which may carry a different interest rate.

When loans are provided in multiple disbursements, their contracts may commence as "***commitments***," under which lenders and borrowers agree to execute the loan. Disbursement schedules are typically subject to "conditionality" — that is, borrowers may have to satisfy certain conditions or have their projects reach certain stages in order for each disbursement to proceed. Until such loans are disbursed, loan agreements may provide that borrowers pay ***commitment fees*** on undisbursed balances. These are characteristically relatively small, and are not taken into account in the present exercise. Again, though, commitment fees and undisbursed balances could be taken into account in more detailed exercises. Finally, lenders sometimes collect ***commissions*** of various kinds as well as interest. These are also usually small, and so are disregarded in the present exercise, but could be taken into account in more detailed exercises.

In the discussion thus far, disbursements are based entirely on programming assumptions. Such disbursements, which could be projected by borrower and lender, are characterized as "identified" — lenders may or may not have agreed in any sense to carry them out, but the analyst would identify them by name, at least generically (e.g., "multinational" lenders). Section 7.3 below introduces disbursements of "unidentified" debt. These disbursements are the financing required "to fill the gap" between above- and below-the-line balance-of-payments projections. As unidentified debt, the lenders would not be named.

5.3 External debt-rescheduling and -reduction concepts

To understand the key concepts associated with external debt, a summary review of the history of external lending by developing economies over recent decades may be helpful. National governments have borrowed from external sources for centuries. In the decades following World War II, however, lending by official entities to relatively poorer economies grew rapidly. In this context, the term "official entities" refer to those belonging to developed economies' governments, either individually or together.[50] The World Bank and International Monetary Fund were founded in 1944, and commenced operations soon after the war ended. The World Bank's original purpose was to help finance reconstruction of war-devastated economies, but in the late 1940s it began lending heavily to developing economies. The International Monetary Fund's original purpose was to provide financial support to economies undergoing balance-of-payments difficulties, and thereby reduce the likelihood that they would resort to exchange-rate depreciation. Later, regional development banks, including the Inter-American Development Bank (IADB), the Asian Development Bank (ADB), the African Development Bank (*Banque Africaine de Developpement*, or BAD), and the European Bank for Reconstruction and Development (EBRD), were founded and undertook growing volumes of lending operations. Meanwhile, bilateral entities, such as the United States Agency for International Development (USAID), the Canadian International Development Agency (CIDA), and various European entities came into being and undertook significant lending operations with developing economies.

During the 1960s and 1970s, international commercial banks significantly increased their operations with developing economies, including term lending. In the 1970s they self-consciously took on a role

---

[50] Loans by entities owned by a single government are defined as "bilateral," while loans by entities owned by more than one government are defined as "multilateral."

"recycling" — i.e., lending — funds that oil exporters, flush with cash following the price increases toward the end of 1973, placed on deposit with them. They lent almost exclusively, even to developing economies, at variable interest rates, linked either to the U.S. "prime" rate on bank loans or to the London Inter-bank Offer Rate (LIBOR), thus ensuring that their interest earnings would cover their interest charges on deposits. The rapid growth of the Organization of Petroleum Exporting Countries' (OPEC) deposits placed the banks under heavy pressure to lend large amounts in this way. They lent large amounts to the larger, more dynamic developing economies: oil-importing economies needed loans to help finance oil purchases, but oil-exporting economies also borrowed heavily in the hope that they could accelerate their own development.

Perhaps inevitably, even before the 1980s, some developing economies slipped into payments difficulties, both on debt to official and to private creditors. The experience creditors and debtors acquired from the "workouts" affected subsequent lending practices and modalities. In 1956, Argentina slipped into difficulties repaying bilateral creditors and appealed to them to "reschedule" its amortization payments, to enable it to repay over a longer time period. To coordinate their response, creditors met as a group with Argentine government representatives in Paris, in a meeting chaired by a French Finance Ministry official. This turned out to be the first "Paris-Club" rescheduling. Since then, many countries finding themselves in repayment difficulties have met their bilateral creditors as a group in Paris. Since that first one, Paris Club meetings, usually lasting no more than a day, have been convened to negotiate general principles for rescheduling amortization due by particular countries, one country at a time. The principles so agreed have then been applied in separate, subsequent accords worked out between the country and each creditor. From the outset, and for several decades thereafter, the Paris Club agreements covered rescheduling of repayment, but not debt-stock forgiveness. Although the Paris Club dealt only with bilateral debt, the IMF and World Bank came to participate in the meetings as observers. Paris Club creditors often insisted that the countries in question agree to Fund programs, presumably to ensure that the countries had macroeconomic-adjustment programs in place that would enable them to meet their new payments commitments.

During the 1970s, several countries slipped into difficulties meeting amortization due to private creditors, notably Perú and Costa Rica. Since these nations owed money to a large number of creditors, the workout processes became complicated exercises, involving coordinated responses by all affected banks. Such coordination was necessary on account of the "cross-default" clauses in loan contracts, which provided that defaults on loans to one creditor would be deemed defaults on all loans covered by such clauses. (Such clauses are intended to prevent borrowers in payments difficulties from favoring some creditors over others.) As the workouts proceeded, the international banks and the countries in question developed mechanisms of coordinated negotiations and sharing information. The IMF came to play an increasingly important role in these processes: as with the Paris Club, the banks increasingly made it a condition that the countries agree to Fund programs, in the hope that the programs would improve the countries' payment prospects.

Despite the occasional crises involving specific economies, banks continued to lend heavily throughout the 1970s to developing economies. In the early 1980s, however, the international-lending system slid into a generalized, "systemic" crisis. The crisis had two basic causes: the 1979 round of world oil-price increases and the United States Federal Reserve's unprecedented monetary-policy tightening, which combined to produce a world-wide recession that affected most debtor economies. Developing economies' export earnings declined, even as their interest bills swelled on account of their floating-rate debt. Policy-makers took drastic steps to adjust their economies, with sharp exchange-rate devaluations and tightened fiscal and monetary policies. Even so, during 1982 and 1983 Mexico, Argentina, Brazil and many smaller economies slid into deep payments difficulties involving what were then massive debt stocks.

In the years following the onset of what rapidly came to be known as the "debt crisis," international commercial banks, pressured and supported by their national governments and the IMF, undertook coordinated efforts "to lend through" the crisis. They undertook concerted operations, sometimes involving large numbers of banks already heavily exposed to specific economies, in massive syndications.

The idea was to lend sufficient resources to cover interest due, if not more, to enable the economies to sustain growth and make it possible for regulators to rate their loans as "performing." This approach came to be known as the "Baker Plan," after the U.S. Treasury Secretary James Baker articulated the U.S. Government's support for it in 1986. The hope was that over time such debt-burden indicators as the debt-GDP ratio and the debt-service ratio (i.e., the ratio of debt service to net exports of goods and non-factor services) would stabilize, albeit at relatively higher rates, but with growing real GDP. Baker Plan-style deals that countries reached with their commercial-bank creditors typically involved "new money" (i.e., fresh, concerted disbursements by all previously exposed banks), rescheduling of amortization due, and arrangements to maintain export credit and other short-term credit lines, all worked out through intricate negotiations.

Despite the continual lending operations, by 1988 and 1989, developing economies' debt indicators remained unstable and tending upward. Economic growth was still unsteady, at least on part because of the uncertainty produced by the external debt. Many economies, notably Argentina and Brazil, were undergoing severe inflation and continual exchange-rate depreciation.[51] Accordingly, beginning in the early 1990s, the commercial banks decided to change their approach. Instead of lending, the commercial banks decided both to reduce and to securitize the debt, which would enable them "to exit" from their exposure. The essential idea was to conclude deals with developing economies under which outstanding debt was converted into sovereign bonds, either at a discount or with improved terms from debtors' viewpoints. Some of the bonds were collateralized with U.S. Treasury bonds that countries purchased using funds borrowed from the World Bank and other official lenders.

---

[51]   There was much debate about whether and how nations' macroeconomic instability was related to the external debt. In retrospect, the relationships were strong. Thus, for example, Brazil's inflation was plainly related to the authorities' efforts to maintain a severely depreciated exchange rate, the idea of which was to sustain a strong trade surplus and so limit the country's external financing requirement. In general, of course, heavy debt-servicing requirements and severe exchange-rate depreciation contributed heavily to fiscal deficits.

This approach came to be known as the "Brady Plan," after the U.S. Treasury Secretary Nicholas Brady articulated the U.S. Government's support for it. (The banks allowed certain smaller countries — for example, Bolivia — to repurchase their outstanding debt at sharply discounted rates, an approach previously regarded as setting an unacceptable precedent, but which now seemed simply practical.) Over the 1990s, a large number of developing economies that owed significant sums to commercial banks succeeded in converting them to "Brady" bonds. For the banks, the most appealing characteristic of the Brady bonds was that they were bearer instruments, and so no longer associated with the banks. The banks could hold or sell the bonds, and would no longer have to participate in concerted lending operations. Indeed, at around this time international markets for developing economies' bonds became far larger: many financial enterprises were actively trading them, and by the early 1990s, financial analysts throughout the world had developed procedures to monitor and report on the various sovereign bonds' performance.

Meanwhile, beginning in the late 1980s, the Paris Club began carrying out debt-stock reduction operations for relatively poorer economies. As it became clear that the international commercial banks would have to bear losses, developed nations' governments and multilateral entities came under pressure "to share the burden" of the debt crisis. Beginning in the late 1980s and continuing into the mid-1990s, the Paris Club began offering the poorest developing economies debt relief in conjunction with rescheduling operations. After the mid-1990s the Paris Club's debt relief came to be provided along and in coordination with multilateral debt relief, under the Highly-Indebted Poorest Countries (HIPC) initiative led by the IMF and the World Bank (discussed below), and later on, after 2002, by the Multilateral Debt Reduction Initiative (MDRI).

Several countries slid into new rounds of payments difficulty following the Brady conversions. For example, Ecuador, which had been affected by a sharp downturn in oil-export prices and the effects of the 1997–8 El Niño weather cycle, failed to meet its September 1999 interest obligations, and called upon bondholders to negotiate. The following year, finding it impossible to carry on substantial negotiations with the mostly anonymous and unorganized holders of Brady bonds, Ecuador's government simply made its bondholders an "exchange offer," under which it would provide new, higher-seniority bonds in exchange for the old bonds at about sixty cents on the dollar. Bondholders accounting for about 95 per cent of the outstanding bonds accepted the exchange, apparently reasoning that their only other choice would be expensive litigation with doubtful prospects. In 2002, Argentina, whose government had borrowed heavily over the 1990s to help defend its fixed exchange rate and to cover its chronic fiscal deficit, carried out a similar exchange offer to reduce its accumulated debt.

The countries that benefited from debt reductions through the "Brady" approach were almost entirely so-called "middle-income" economies, developing economies with relatively higher per-capita incomes than other developing economies. Relatively poorer economies — in particular, sub-Saharan African economies — had generally received few commercial-bank loans. Their external debt was almost entirely to the IMF, the World Bank, regional development institutions, and bilateral sources. Until the mid-1990s, the multilateral institutions kept to a policy of never forgiving debt. This was partly intended to help keep their financial reputations strong and (hence) keep their borrowing costs low. In addition, they argued, unlike commercial entities, they still stood ready to lend to any country that maintained its payments in good order — implying, in effect, that new lending was almost always available to help cover current debt service. In the mid-1990s, however, the multilateral entities agreed to depart from their no-forgiveness policy to benefit the world's poorest economies. Under the leadership of the World Bank and the IMF, they set elaborate processes into motion intended to enable such economies to qualify for debt reduction. The basic idea was to ensure that resources freed from debt service would be applied to development and poverty reduction. Over the late 1990s and the early 2000s, more than forty countries were considered for participation in the "Highly-Indebted Poorest Economies" (HIPC) Initiative (see Section 5.4 below), and more than half eventually benefited from substantial reductions of debt and debt service owed to multilateral and bilateral entities. After 2000, multilateral and bilateral lenders began carrying out even larger debt-reduction operations, under what is now known as the Multilateral Debt Reduction Initiative (MDRI). Some nations benefited to the extent of having virtually all of their multilateral debt eliminated.

Meanwhile, highly-indebted economies not eligible for the HIPC or the MDRI took a variety of approaches to managing their debt. Following Brady deals with creditors in the mid-1990s, for example, Brazil maintained regular payments on its debt, and contracted new debt in the form of sovereign-bond issues. (The large devaluation carried out in 1999 was intended, in part, to reduce its external-borrowing needs.) Sovereign-bond issues, often carried out with sophisticated "road shows" and informative prospectuses, became a standing feature of the international financial landscape. Argentina and Ecuador, as noted, acted unilaterally, reducing their debt through exchange offers. After oil prices rose in the first decade of the new century, some oil exporters simply paid down large proportions of their outstanding debt. Nigeria, for example, paid virtually all of its outstanding debt in April 2006.

The projection techniques described in Section 5.2 above can be used to represent prospective rescheduling and reduction operations. A rescheduling can be represented simply by changing the relevant values of the parameter "a" and the programmed growth rates of the debt stock. A simple debt reduction can be represented with an appropriate negative value for "v" for the relevant year. (Note that this automatically reduces amortization due over subsequent years.) An exchange of one kind of sovereign bond for another with a discount would be a bit more complicated to represent: for the year in question it would comprise a negative value for "v" affecting the stock of the old debt, amortization of as much of the remainder as bondholders accept, and a "disbursement" in the new kind of bond, with its new terms.

5.4   Debt-reduction concepts associated with the Highly-Indebted Poorest Countries initiative

Projections involving HIPC- and MDRI-type operations require certain additional concepts. The fundamental HIPC idea is that any total public external-debt stock that exceeds a certain multiple of annual exports and non-factor services, or whose servicing flows exceed a certain percentage of annual exports and non-factor services, should be deemed "unsustainable." Any total public-debt stock exceeding the "benchmarks" for these "burden indicators" should be reduced until the indicators are below the benchmarks.

One obvious problem with this way of defining sustainability is that the different debt stocks that make up each nation's total public-debt stock have different interest rates and maturities. This means that the debt stocks cannot simply be summed, because a dollar of one kind of debt is not the same kind of burden as a dollar of another kind. To the extent a particular debt is "concessional" — i.e., provided at below-market interest rates and above-market maturities — it is a smaller burden. A million-dollar debt stock at, say, a one per cent annual interest rate and a forty-year average maturity is a lighter burden than the same amount at LIBOR plus 200 basis points (100 basis points equal one percentage point) and a five-year average maturity.

The accepted way to make two debt stocks with different rates and maturity schedules comparable is to calculate their respective net present values (NPVs) using a common discount rate — that is, for each debt, to project all the future debt-service flows, use the common discounting rate to determine the present values of the debt-service flows, and then sum these. (For any given single debt stock, the so-called "concessionality element" can be calculated by subtracting the NPV from the nominal U.S. dollar stock.) Unfortunately, though, such NPVs cannot be calculated unambiguously, for several reasons. First, for many kinds of debt, future debt-service flows cannot be predicted precisely in dollars: debt and debt service denominated in currencies other than the dollar may appreciate or depreciate in dollar terms, and interest due on variable-rate debt depends on the evolution of the reference rate. Second, the appropriate discounting rate is always debatable: the "market" interest rate at any moment is likely to lie within a range of rates. Different projections of reference interest rates and exchange rates as well as different discounting rates could lead to quite different NPV results.

The practical procedure to make each economy's debt stocks comparable (and "summable") is to formulate common projection assumptions and then use the same discount rate to calculate their respective NPVs. The results from these calculations are then applied in two ways. First, the NPV, rather than the nominal dollar value, of the public external debt is used to calculate the burden indicators, and so to estimate by how much the economy's debt is excessive. Second, if debt reduction is then deemed necessary, the reduction can be allocated fairly among creditors according to the NPV of the debt, rather than according to its nominal dollar value. Each hundred dollars of a more concessional debt stock would be reduced proportionately less than each hundred dollars of a less concessional debt stock.

The fact that different debt stocks, and their NPVs, may have different currency units presents further practical difficulties for this calculation. The most important unit of account for external debt is the U.S. dollar, but significant quantities of external debt are denominated in euros, SDRs, pounds sterling, yen, and other units.[52] At least two approaches could be taken to deal with this problem. One would be to convert all future debt-service flows into U.S. dollars using projected exchange rates and then apply a U.S. benchmark interest rate to calculate the NPV of all of the debt. The HIPC initiative took a second approach, however: it calculated the NPVs of debt *in the different currency units* using discounting rates drawn from each currency's home financial market, converted these NPVs to U.S. dollars using recent average exchange rates, and then projected the future evolution of the total debt.

For each economy considered for the HIPC exercise, the appropriate debt reductions (if any) and their allocation among creditors were determined using these techniques. International Monetary Fund and World Bank staff carried out the calculations and reported them in official documents called "debt sustainability analyses" (DSAs). The DSAs reported comparative external-accounts projections carried out without and with specified amounts of debt reduction. The idea was to determine whether the projected ratios to exports of goods and non-factor services of (i) the NPV of the external debt owed to official creditors and

---

[52] Other currencies that come up include the Swiss franc, various Middle Eastern currencies, and the Scandinavian currencies. Eastern European economies are likely to have a large share of their debt in euros.

(ii) the debt service on this debt would be likely to stay within the "sustainability" benchmarks. The benchmarks that the international agencies chose for the HIPC were 150–200 per cent for the ratio of the NPV of the debt stock to exports of goods and non-factor services and 25–30 per cent for the ratio of the debt service to exports of goods and non-factor services. Countries whose ratios exceeded these benchmarks were deemed to merit reductions to bring the ratios to or just below the benchmarks.

Beginning in 1996, the DSAs were carried out in many candidate countries to calculate debt reductions and their allocation among creditors. Many countries benefited from one or two rounds of HIPC reduction. In the first round, mainly in the late 1990s and the early part of the following decade, participating countries were able to bring their public external debt within the benchmarks. In the second round, the so-called "enhanced HIPC," countries were able to reduce their public external debt even further by formulating and taking steps to implement "poverty-reduction strategies," multiannual policy programs intended to show how poverty would be reduced to the 2015 "Millennium" goals that the United Nations set out in 2000. Several years into the decade, the multilateral institutions undertook a much deeper debt-reduction initiative, the Multilateral Debt Reduction Initiative (MDRI), which involved far larger and deeper debt-reduction exercises. Economies benefiting from these reductions received writedowns amounting to 90 per cent or more of their outstanding multilateral debt.

The HIPC, the enhanced HIPC and the MDRI were successful in the sense that they brought about substantial debt-stock reductions. It may be some years before it will be possible to carry out credible analyses of how much these initiatives served to promote development and reduce poverty. Even then, such analyses will always run up against the "counter-factual" problem: it will be difficult to say how the economies in question would have evolved if they had not benefited from debt reduction.

It is clear enough, though, that the HIPC-MDRI approach has turned out to have many methodological weaknesses. It is indisputably good, of course, for a government to have smaller debt-servicing obligations. All the same, debt-relief operations can lead to difficulties for the external and fiscal accounts. These were not always fully anticipated. To understand the nature of the problem, suppose that the debt stock a government owes to an important creditor is reduced. Suppose then that the creditor decides henceforth to reduce lending to the government in question — for example, by reducing its targeted debt stock as a percentage of the economy's exports. The government may then have to find a different financing source, or else reduce the borrowing requirement by reducing expenditure or increasing revenue. That is, the reduction in the lending flow could very well exceed the reduction in the debt-service flow resulting from the debt relief. As a consequence, the economy may have to grow more slowly because its overall net external financing inflow is more limited, and the government may need to either to reduce its expenditure or to substitute internal financing or higher taxation for the diminished external financing. Already, a number of governments benefiting from debt reduction have had to increase internal borrowing or raise taxes. Although some countries have sought additional grant aid to avoid new external borrowing, some have taken on increased financing from commercial sources, on less attractive terms than they might have obtained from concessional lenders.

One of the reasons DSAs sometimes failed to take proper account of these kinds of fiscal problem is that the HIPC sustainability criteria focused on the external accounts. For many economies, though, the external-debt problem was at least as much fiscal as external in character. A DSA projection may indicate external-accounts sustainability, either without or with debt reduction, but it is perfectly possible that a full fiscal-accounts projection would indicate unsustainability, in the form (say) of a growing financing gap (see Chapter 8 below). Once again — as this book argues — full evaluation of a macroeconomic projection comprising (i) a set of target macroeconomic variables, (ii) a government-expenditure program, and (iii) an external-debt program should encompass feasibility tests involving the full range of macroeconomic accounts, encompassing the external, national, fiscal, and monetary accounts.

In principle, the projection methodology this book describes could be used to carry out a HIPC-type DSA. To be sure, though, because the exercise as set out in this book does not classify the debt by currency, a HIPC-type calculation would be have to be simplified. The NPV of the outstanding debt would be determined by applying a single U.S. dollar discount rate to the total projected debt service *denominated in dollars*, using projected exchange rates between the U.S. dollar and the other currencies, and then project its future evolution.

There are several deeper ways in which the present exercise would differ somewhat from the HIPC approach. The HIPC approach has been to gauge sustainability as a matter of whether the debt stock and debt-service flow exceed benchmark ratios to exports of goods and non-factor services. The present exercise gauges debt sustainability by asking whether the economy's future financing requirements are likely to be feasible, given the projected debt-servicing flows. In effect, the present exercise takes debt sustainability to be *dynamic* in character. In any case, its preferred debt-burden indicators are ratios to GDP, rather than to exports of goods and non-factor services. That is, the economy's *size* is taken to be the appropriate standard against which to measure a debt stock.

Using ratios to exports rather than to GDP leads to several problems. Small, open economies, which tend to have large export flows, will be likely to show that even quite large debt stocks are sustainable, whereas economies with small export flows will tend to show that even quite small debt stocks are unsustainable. Economies with large export flows will therefore tend to receive limited debt reduction, whereas economies with small export flows will receive larger debt reduction. Once debt reduction takes place, however, economies with large export flows will be able to take on relatively large amounts of new debt without significantly increasing their indicators, whereas economies with small export flows will increase their debt indicators quickly with relatively small amounts of new debt. (The practice of measuring debt and debt service against exports is anachronistic, a practice that made more sense when currency convertibility was harder, and when export flows were relatively easier and GDP flows relatively harder to estimate.)

5.5   *Projections of internal government debt and financial assets*

Government deficits can be financed, of course, from internal as well as external sources. By definition, external debt is not only denominated, but must also be paid, in foreign currencies. Internal debt, in contrast, is payable in the economy's own currency.[53] A further defining feature of external debt, as opposed to internal debt, is that its legal bases are either international agreements (in the case of debt owed to "official" entities) or contracts subject to foreign courts (in the case of debt owed to private entities). (Developed economies' public debt is more likely to be "internal" in the legal senses. In the case of the United States, government external debt and internal debt are essentially indistinguishable: U.S. Treasury bills and bonds that foreigners hold are no different from what U.S. residents hold.)

Internal financing sources for a government's deficit encompass (i) net debt issues in the form of securities; (ii) net direct borrowing (including overdraft borrowing) from financial institutions, including the central bank, commercial banks, and other financial institutions; (iii) government sales of physical or financial assets, and (iv) net withdrawals from its deposits in the central bank or commercial banks. ("Net" borrowing refers to gross borrowing less repayment.) "Securitized" government debt can be purchased and sold in so-called "secondary" financial markets, whereas loans directly contracted ordinarily cannot be purchased and sold in secondary financial markets. Securitized and direct borrowing should be recorded and programmed in separate lines.

Debt issues may include term debt (i.e., debt with a maturity exceeding one year) and short-term debt. Internal term-debt disbursements, repayments, and year-end stocks may be programmed using techniques similar to those used for external term debt, described in Section 5.5 above. Interest on internal term debt can also be projected using the techniques described above for external term debt. Internal debt issues may also include short-term bills, i.e., instruments issued at a

---

[53]   Internal debt that must be paid in foreign currency could be reclassified as external debt.

discount that have no interest "coupons." Interest due on short-term internal debt may be calculated by applying the assumed year-average interest rates to the respective year-average debt stocks.

With few exceptions, developing economies' financial markets have limited scope to absorb government securities issues. One implication is that any large issue of government securities therefore runs some risk of driving the prices of government securities down and (essentially the same thing) forcing their interest rates up. Even so, government securities play crucial roles in any economy's financial markets, partly because they are perceived to have a low risk of default. Commercial banks and other financial institutions are likely to be significant purchasers of bonds and bills. In addition, non-bank financial institutions and insurance companies may constitute "captive markets" for government obligations, since they may even be required by law to hold liquid government obligations in their technical reserves. Still, any significant government-securities issue is likely to force interest rates up generally. Internal-debt issues may have the effect of "crowding out" private-sector borrowers from credit markets — that is, attracting buyers who might otherwise have used their funds to provide private credit.[54]

Projections of direct loans by the government from commercial banks work in essentially the same way as projections of bills or bonds. The basic difference is that financial institutions, including the central bank and commercial banks, could purchase or sell bills and bonds in the financial markets. A bond or bill issued by the government could be purchased by anyone, whereas a direct loan by the government would, in general, remain on the books of the institution that provided it.

A government's internal-debt "issues" may also include (positive or negative) increases in arrears on interest due to its lenders. As in the case of external interest arrears, accumulated internal interest arrears are short-term debt stocks, which accumulate when interest due goes unpaid and diminish as accumulated balances are paid down. (Indeed, *any* payments arrears — including overdue pay to government staff and

---

[54]   In some instances, governments in developing economies have carried out obligatory placements of bonds — in some instances to pay down arrears to contractors and suppliers.

overdue payments to suppliers and contractors — amount to non-contractual financing flows, and may be treated as such in the projection exercise.)

"One-time" sales of government physical and financial assets are sometimes recorded below the line as financing transactions and sometimes above the line as "capital" or "other" revenues. Practices vary from economy to economy, and are occasionally inconsistent from year to year in a country's fiscal accounts. In principle, since such sales would be "non-recurrent," there is an argument for showing such transactions below the line, so that they do not misleadingly reduce the recorded deficit for the year in which they occur. Privatization sales should, for example, be recorded below the line on this argument.

Withdrawals from — that is, reductions in — government deposit accounts, whether at the central bank or at other financial institutions, are yet another source of financing for a government deficit, and as such should be recorded below the line with other internal financing flows. (Increases in government deposits, like repayment of government debt, would also go below the line, but with a negative sign, since they are "negative financing.")

Programming assumptions for internal financing flows may be set out in different ways. One straightforward approach is to assume that the year-end values of internal debt stocks — bonds, bills, and direct loans will be given percentages of GDP (or, the same thing, to have the stocks grow at the same rate as nominal GDP). This approach can also be used to program the government's internal deposit stocks. The programming approaches for interest-arrears stocks depend, inevitably, on the specific circumstances of particular economies: increases in arrears stocks would depend, in part, on the flows of unpaid interest that feed them, and then on programming assumptions regarding the speed at which they would be paid down.

In setting these assumptions, it is important to remember that banks and insurance companies may require a supply of government securities for their own asset holdings. A government may therefore consider it appropriate to issue a larger quantity of securities than is actually necessary to finance its deficit. Longer-term debt may be issued in conjunction with specific investment projects. Similarly, a government may wish to maintain given deposit stocks as percentages of GDP for transactions purposes. In some instances, governments may maintain relatively large deposit balances in the central bank as a way to assist with monetary control. Sales or purchases of non-financial assets are difficult to project, of course, since they are non-recurrent. Except for specific sales or purchases in coming years (e.g., privatization of enterprises), such transactions are probably best projected to be zero.

Internal interest rates may be programmed in various ways. In general, it is a good idea to project interest rates on bonds and bills in real terms, and then calculate their nominal equivalent using the programmed December-December inflation rate. If "r" represents a projected real interest rate and "x" the projected December-December growth rate of consumer prices, then the nominal interest rate for that year would be given by

$$i = r(1 + x) + x.$$

(If the inflation rate is relatively high, the value of "x" should not be the inflation rate, but the negative of the "real rate of return on money," defined by

$$\pi = g_{p'}/(1 + g_{p'}),$$

see Annex 9.2.) For government term borrowing that works with disbursement and amortization flows, this would be the interest rate applying to new disbursement, and the average interest rate on the total outstanding balance would be a weighted average of the preceding year's and this interest rate (Section 5.2 above describes how the year-average interest rate is calculated for external term debt, and the procedure would be the same for internal term debt). For short-term borrowing, the interest rate "i" would be the applicable average nominal interest rate.

The *real* interest rate on funds borrowed by the government could be projected as an exogenous assumption. More realistically, it could be linked positively with the real-GDP growth rate, or positively with the stock of government debt outstanding as a percentage of GDP — that is, the faster real GDP grows, or, the higher the debt outstanding in financial markets, the higher the interest rate the government should expect to pay to persuade the financial markets to absorb more. Interest rates paid by the central bank and other financial institutions — for example, on the government's deposit balance — could be set as programming assumptions, either in nominal or real terms, as simple policy settings or as the values markets might set in keeping with real-GDP growth or with other determinants of the state of financial markets.

In the approach this book recommends "to close" the fiscal accounts, the internal financing accounts include the fiscal accounts' "residuals." That is, in addition to the *programmed* increases (or decreases) in the various internal financing accounts, the government debt and asset flow accounts also include the *unprogrammed* flows necessary to bring the projected above- and below-the-line fiscal accounts into equality. The magnitudes of the residual flows could then be used to gauge the fiscal feasibility of the macroeconomic-*cum*-government expenditure program. (Section 8.3 describes the methodology for "closing" the fiscal projection and calculating the residuals for any future year, either by having the government take on sufficient new internal debt to cover any positive financing gap, or by having the government's deposit holdings increase if the financing gap is negative.)

5.6   Pacífica's external and internal debt

Pacífica's public and publicly-guaranteed external debt totaled US$5.8 billion at the end of 2008, about 22 per cent of that year's GDP (see Table 10). Just over 46 per cent of this debt was owed to the World Bank and other multilateral creditors. About 16 per cent of this debt was owed to bilateral creditors, and the remainder was owed to private creditors in the forms of sovereign bonds and debt to commercial banks. The central bank owed a relatively small amount to the International Monetary Fund.

Several simple assumptions are applied to project the external debt over coming years. The most important concern the growth rates of the debt stocks. The multilateral, bilateral and sovereign-bond debt stocks are assumed to grow at the same rate as GDP measured at the purchasing-power parity exchange rate. The commercial-bank debt is assumed to decline with its amortization rate, roughly 10 per cent per year of its end-2005 debt stock, reflecting the authorities' decision to phase out public borrowing from commercial banks and to rely more on sovereign-bond issues to raise external financing from private sources. (Since the debt stock would be diminishing while the amortization rate remains at a constant percentage of the base-year stock, this particular debt stock would diminish at an increasing rate.) Future spreads over LIBOR for new credit are projected to remain the same as they were on credit outstanding in 2008. Exchange rates among the dollar, the euro, the yen and other currencies in which the external debt is denominated are assumed to remain unchanged. The 2008 year-end debt stock is projected to be amortized at various rates, but the assumption that future spreads over LIBOR will remain unchanged implies that the assumed amortization rates would make little difference to the debt-stock projection (or, for that matter, to any other aspects of the projection).

Table 10 shows the external-debt projection results in percentage-of-GDP terms. Under the assumptions given, public and publicly-guaranteed debt would rise as a percentage of GDP from 22 at the end of 2008 to 23.4 per cent at the end of 2010, but then decline to 21.3 per cent at the end of 2015. (The unidentified part of the debt is determined by the balance of payments projection, discussed in Section 7.3 below.)

Pacífica's internal government debt had been rising as a percentage of GDP over the years since 1998, and in mid-2009 policy-makers were hoping to limit its growth, at least as a percentage of GDP. Nevertheless, they understood that it would be difficult to prevent internal-government debt from increasing as recession reduces tax revenue. Gross internal government debt totaled 25.6 per cent of GDP at the end of 2008. It would decline slightly to 25.3 per cent of GDP at the end of 2009, but then increase gradually to about 30 per cent of GDP at the end of 2012, and then remain at about this level through the end of 2015.

6 National-expenditure accounts projections

If anything is used to its full potential, it will break.

– from Murphy's Law[55]

6.1 Introduction: National-expenditure accounts projections

As noted in Section 2.3 above, the exercise this book describes works out the national-accounts projections in five steps. The first is to estimate the year-by-year fixed-capital-formation rate on the basis of the programmed real-GDP growth rates. The second is to project the change in inventory stocks. The third step consists of projecting exports and imports of goods and non-factor services on the basis of the macroeconomic programming assumptions and international conditions. The fourth step consists of bringing in the government consumption and capital-formation projections from the fiscal-accounts projections. Finally, in the fifth step, non-government capital formation and consumption are calculated as the projection residuals, applying the national-accounts expenditure identity (see Annex 6.1).[56]

In this chapter, Section 6.2 describes how gross fixed capital formation is projected from the real-GDP growth projection. Section 6.3 discusses the inventory projections. Section 6.4 discusses techniques for projecting exports and imports of goods and non-factor services. Section 6.5 discusses projections of government consumption and capital formation, while Section 6.6 discusses projections of non-government consumption. Section 6.7 returns to the Pacífica projections. (Annex 6.3 summarizes the capital-formation projection procedure. Annex 6.4

---

[55]   Cited in Bloch, Arthur, "Murphy's Law Complete: All the Reasons why Everything Goes Wrong" (p. 235), as "Poulsen's Prophecy."
[56]   In the Excel workbook for the "Pacífica" exercise, the projection exercise for exports and imports of goods and non-factor services is incorporated in the external- rather than in the national-accounts worksheet. In this way, the external-accounts worksheet incorporates all aspects of the external-accounts projection exercise.

discusses aggregate national income and the "terms-of-trade" effect. Annex 6.5 discusses the main saving concepts, including external and internal saving and foreign and national saving. Finally, Annex 6.6 describes a methodology to project the economy's poverty incidence.)

6.2   Capital formation and real-GDP growth

This section discusses methods for formulating capital-formation projections on the basis of assumed real-GDP growth rates. The relationships between projected real-GDP growth and capital formation are among the more important in macroeconomic projection analysis generally, since projected ratios of investment and capital formation to GDP directly and indirectly affect many accounts throughout the macroeconomic structure.

As noted in Chapter 2, the present exercise incorporates rather less than a full "aggregate-supply" projection methodology. In effect, it assumes that the economy's aggregate capital stock is *the* physical constraint to attaining the projected real-GDP growth rates. The exercise focuses on determining whether adequate financing will be available for the capital formation required by the programmed real-GDP growth rates. Other factors of production, such as labor and natural resources, are required, of course, but the exercise assumes that the capital stock is the "constraining" determinant of real-GDP growth. For developing economies generally, this would seem reasonable enough (since less-developed economies are perhaps best defined as those in which physical capital is relatively scarce). Obviously, other factors of production can constrain real growth in reality. Fast-growing economies can run into shortages of skilled or even unskilled labor, or of management capacity, or of particular material resources. To the extent natural-resource constraints are a problem, it may be possible to make them up through imports; the present exercise can then help determine whether the availability of financing for such imports will constrain growth.

This said, the empirical quantitative relationships between capital formation and real-GDP growth are not always so close and positive as common sense would suggest. There are many countries for which relatively high capital-formation rates were associated over long periods with low growth rates (for example, the case of Zambia cited by Devarajan, Easterly and Pack 1999). For a medium-term projection exercise, however, the presumption that real-GDP growth is positively related with gross fixed capital formation, at least on average over the longer term, is difficult to avoid. Thus, if an analyst increases the real-GDP growth rates programmed for future years, it would seem only reasonable also to increase the programmed capital-formation rate in prior years, to ensure that the projection captures the full cost of attaining the growth.

The conventional way to do this is to apply an assumed "incremental capital-output ratio" (ICOR). The ICOR is defined as the ratio of the real flow of capital formation during one year to the (presumably resulting) real increment to GDP in the following year. For the present discussion, let "i" represent real gross fixed investment, "y" real GDP, "g" the real GDP growth rate ($\Delta y_{+1}/y$), and "v" the ICOR. Algebraically, the ICOR is defined as

$$v = i/\Delta y_{+1}.$$

Since

$$i = v/\Delta y_{+1},$$

$$i/y = v\,\Delta y_{+1}/y,$$

or

$$i/y = v\,g_{-1}.$$

Using this formula, for each projection year the exercise would project real capital formation as a percentage of GDP, on the basis of the real GDP growth rate projected for the subsequent year. Again, recalling a point made in Chapter 1, it may seem peculiar to assume a future real-GDP growth rate and then calculate the capital-formation rate *required* in the preceding year. This is characteristic, however, of "consistency" approaches — the objective here is to determine the capital-formation rate *consistent with* a subsequent real-GDP growth rate.

A variant of this approach is to assume that the incremental output in any given year is related to capital formation carried out during several previous years, not just the immediately prior year. The effects on each year's output growth of earlier years' capital-formation flows would have a weighting structure. Put differently, the capital formation in any given year would be related to "incremental" output in subsequent years through

$$v \left[(a_{+1} \, \Delta y_{+1}) + (a_{+2} \, \Delta y_{+2}) + (a_{+3} \, \Delta y_{+3}) \right],$$

where Δy_{+t} is the incremental output "t" years past the year being projected, "v" is the capital-output ratio, a_{+1} and a_{+2} are fractions, and $a_{+3} = 1 - a_{+1} - a_{+2}$. The appropriate values for a_{+1}, a_{+2} and a_{+3} may be econometrically estimated on the basis of earlier experience, or simply guessed. For example, weights of one half, one third and one sixth could be used for a_{+1}, a_{+2} and a_{+3} respectively. This particular weighting structure would give relatively more importance to incremental output in the year immediately following a given capital-formation flow.[57] (The Pacífica exercise uses this weighting.)

Another adaptation of this general approach is to work with the "net" ICOR, to allow the projection to take explicit account of capital depreciation. Thus, capital-formation rates may be projected for each year using (i) assumed *net-basis* incremental capital-output ratios (ICORs) for each year together with (ii) assumed capital depreciation rates, as percentages of the preceding year-end capital stock. Let "δ" represent the depreciation rate over the current year of the previous year's year-end real capital stock (i.e., the proportion of the capital stock that depreciates over the year), and let "v" now represent the *net-basis* ICOR. The "net-basis" ICOR would be defined by

$$v = (i - d)/\Delta y_{+1}$$

---

[57]   It might seem logical to use different ICOR's for capital affecting each future period — that is, to have different ICORs for capital formation in the current projection period affecting output one, two and three years hence. The same effect can be obtained, however, by making adjustments to the variables a_{+t}.

where "d" represents the estimated depreciation flow, equal to $\delta\,k_{-1}$.[58] That is, the increment to GDP in the subsequent year should depend not on the net, not the gross, addition to the capital stock (i.e., the magnitude in the numerator). The investment rate (i/y) required in a given year to attain a real GDP growth of g_{-1} in the subsequent year would then be given by

$$i/y = v\,(g_{-1} + \delta).$$

Depreciation itself may be projected from guesses about the capital stock's longevity. If, for example, the existing capital stock is believed to depreciate on average in ten years, the value of "δ" would be 10 per cent. The capital stock comprises many different kinds of asset, to be sure. Residential housing, for example, might be assumed to last thirty to forty years on average, whereas motor vehicles might average no more than five or ten. Factories and productive machinery might last ten and twenty years on average. By estimating the rough composition of the capital stock and the longevity of its components, a more or less credible estimate could be made for "δ."

In addition to capital depreciation, several other aspects of the projected determinants of aggregate supply may be taken into account. For example, capacity utilization may be taken explicitly into account, as follows. Let "z" represent *potential* real GDP, i.e., the real GDP that would be produced if all existing capital were fully and efficiently used. Let "y" represent real GDP, "k" the real period-end capital stock, "i" real capital formation over the period, and δ represent the capital-depreciation rate. Let "c" be defined then by

$$y = c\,z,$$

with

$$\Delta z_{+1} = i/v - \delta\,k_{-1}/w,$$

---

[58]   More precisely: let $\Delta y_{+1} = i/v - \delta\,k_{-1}/v'$ where "k'" represents the real year-end capital stock, "v" the ICOR and v' the capital-output ratio for the capital existing at the end of the preceding period. Divide this expression through by y to obtain $\Delta y_{+1}/y = (i/y)/v - \delta\,(k_{-1}/y)/v'$, or $g_{+1} = (i/y)/v - \delta$, since, by definition, $k_{-1}/y = v'$.

where "v" is now the incremental capital *potential*-output ratio ("ICPOR," to coin an acronym) and "w" is now the capital-*potential* output ratio. A formula for the growth rate of output in terms of "c," "δ" and the ICPOR may be derived as follows. First,

$$\Delta z_{+1}/z = (i/z)/v - \delta (k_{-1}/z)/w.$$

Since by definition $w = k_{-1}/z$,

$$\Delta z_{+1}/z = (i/z)/v - \delta$$

$$= [i/(y/c)]/v - \delta.$$

It follows that

$$i/y = v [(\Delta z_{+1}/z) + \delta]/c. \qquad (*)$$

Since $y = c z$,

$$\Delta z_{+1}/z = [(1 + g_{+1}/z)/(c_{+1}/c)] - 1,$$

where $g_{+1} = \Delta y_{+1}/y$.

This can be used to solve for i/y in terms of g_{+1}, c_{+1}, and "c" in the expression (*) above:

$$i/y = v \{[(1 + g_{+1})/(c_{+1}/c)] - 1 + \delta\}/c. \qquad (**)$$

The quantitative relationship between real growth and capital formation is a conceptually worrisome aspect of macroeconomic projection exercises. Although the ICOR concept has been used in growth analysis and in practical projection analysis since it was first invented in the late 1940s, it has been criticized on both theoretical and practical grounds (see Devarajan, Easterly, and Pack 1999). Macroeconomic projections can be highly sensitive to the assumptions about the relationship between real growth and capital formation. A projection with one set of annual values of the ICOR may be quite feasible in terms of the required financing; a projection otherwise the same but with a modestly higher ICOR (hence, requiring more capital formation for given real growth rates) may be unfeasible. Econometric analysis may be used to determine the relationship on the basis of past experience, but empirical relationships between capital formation and real growth are notoriously unstable, and it is never possible to be sure that future relationships will be anything like those of the past. Still, the logic of the projection exercise requires that some relationship must hold between capital formation and real growth. Given the uncertainty associated with the quantitative characteristics of the relationship and the sensitivity of the analysis to them, it is advisable to check the robustness of the projection results by varying the ICOR and related variables (see the discussion in Section 10.5 on sensitivity analysis).

Analysts who carry out macroeconomic capital-formation projections should be aware of a more fundamental criticism. In the 1950s, Joan Robinson and several other British economists pointed out that, in economic-growth models and analytical work generally, it is inherently incorrect to state values of capital-formation flows and capital stocks in monetary units, even at base-year prices. This is because the prices are presumably determined within the model — or, put differently, the *quantity* of the capital stock cannot also be a *value*. Otherwise, any analysis involving quantity and value becomes logically circular. This objection gave rise to what came to be called the "Cambridge capital controversy" (because in the mid-1950s it was economists at Cambridge University who maintained the critique while several economists at MIT, in Cambridge, Massachusetts, defended the use of monetary units for capital stocks, more on practical than theoretical grounds.) This writer's personal view is that while the practice is defensible on practical grounds, analysts should keep the Cambridge (England) critique in mind.

At least one additional point needs to be taken into account when projecting capital formation. Until now, this section has discussed real growth and capital formation entirely in real terms. In order to calculate projected capital formation as a percentage of GDP, projected real capital formation must be converted to projected nominal capital formation, at current prices. This, in turn, requires a projected capital-formation price index. The simplest approach is to assume that capital-formation prices will evolve at the same rate as the overall inflation rate. More sophisticated assumptions may be appropriate, however. For example, to the extent capital equipment is largely imported, and to the extent capital equipment figures in total capital formation, the price index will be driven by (i) the import price of capital equipment and (ii) the exchange rate.

Taking proper account of these determinants of capital formation is something of a challenge. Annex 6.3 describes a practical approach to setting up a projection so as to take efficient account of the various points discussed thus far, including the ICOR, multiannual relationships between growth and capital formation, capital depreciation, and the capital-formation price index.

The composition of an economy's capital formation may be worth projecting in some detail, since different kinds of capital formation may have different consequences for projected imports, depreciation, and other macroeconomic flows. The capital stock, and gross fixed capital formation, comprises structures and equipment. The category of "structures" comprises such things as electrical-generation plants, roads, railways, bridges, airports, dams, port facilities, broadcasting towers, and the like, as well as factories, office buildings, and private residences. The category of "equipment" is a similarly broad range of things, including turbines, manufacturing machinery, computers (apart from what are considered to be durable consumer goods), railroad rolling stock, ships, aircraft, and vehicles. Structures create demand for construction materials, some of which may need to be imported. They may also generate employment demand. Equipment, on the other hand, may need to be imported. (While the Pacífica exercise does not represent distinctions among types of capital goods in detail, it may be important to take them into account for particular economies.)

6.3   Inventory holdings

In addition to physical capital formation, investment expenditure includes the increase in firms' inventory holdings over the year. In most economies, additions to inventories are likely never to amount to more than fractions of percentage points of GDP, either positive or negative. Increases are limited by the economy's physical storage capacity (which would increase with gross fixed capital formation), while decreases are limited by the small sizes of inventory stocks relative to GDP.

In general, for most economies, data for year-end inventory stocks are simply unavailable, so that it is not feasible to project them on the basis of, say, an assumed elasticity with respect to GDP. (The order of magnitude of the base-year inventory stock may be guessed by summing the net real increases in inventories recorded over preceding years, but the result is likely to be doubtful at best.) The change in inventories is therefore best — or, perhaps, least badly — projected by assuming that they will be an assumed percentage of the *change in* GDP. The idea is that, in the aggregate, productive and commercial businesses would want to hold inventory stocks roughly at some given percentage of GDP, which would be a projection assumption — very much a guess, to be sure. Inventory holdings generate warehousing and "carrying" expenses, and the analyst may want to assume that the economy will manage its inventories ever more efficiently over time. In this case, the assumed percentage would gradually diminish.

When the projection is for a current or coming year, information about current circumstances may imply a relatively smaller or larger projection, based on what is known of current business conditions. According to basic macroeconomic theory, the business cycle powerfully influences inventory accumulation. Unsold goods presumably accumulate in cyclical downturns, but run down when demand picks up (for example, see Branson 1972). Other kinds of influence can make inventories accumulate or diminish. For example, suppose that a small, open economy's importers are quite certain the exchange rate will depreciate in the coming year. They might respond by increasing imports and adding to inventory, since the national-currency cost of the merchandise would be lower now than after the depreciation. Knowing this, an analyst might project an inventory build-up for the coming year and then perhaps a roughly equivalent inventory draw-down in the subsequent year — after the depreciation has taken place.

6.4   *Exports and imports of goods and non-factor services*

Exports and imports are likely to figure centrally in both the national- and external-accounts projections for most economies. In general, it is

most convenient to project merchandise exports by commodity group
(coffee, tea, manufactures, and the like), and to project imports according
to their economic classification (consumption, non-fuel intermediate,
fuel, and capital goods.).

Projections of export and import values may be calculated from
projections of export and import prices and volumes. Prices may be
projected on the basis of assumed (i) *real* growth rates for the various
export and import prices and (ii) the world price-level growth rate.
Volumes may be projected on the basis of (i) real growth rates of world
trade in the various kinds of export and import, (ii) real-effective prices
of the various kinds of export and import, and (iii) real GDP, using
assumed values for the relevant elasticities. The year-average real-
effective price of a given export or import is defined as (i) the average
U.S. dollar price prevailing over the year (ii) multiplied by the year-
average exchange rate and (iii) divided by the year-average internal price
level, (iv) adjusted for taxes and, (v) in the case of imports, adjusted by
freight and insurance costs.

Once again, some simple algebra is helpful here. Export and
import prices may be projected as follows. Let p* represent the world
price level and p_i^* the U.S. dollar world price of commodity "i." The
projected U.S. dollar unit price of commodity "i" may be calculated as

$$p_i^* = p_{i(-1)}^* \, (1 + g_{p*}) \, (1 + g_{[p*(i)/p*]}),$$

where g_{p*} is the growth rate of the world price level and $g_{[p*(i)/p*]}$ the
growth rate of commodity i's real world price. That is, the unit price in
dollars may be projected as the combined growth rates of the world price
level and the product's relative price. It would be possible, of course,
directly to assume a growth rate for the nominal U.S. dollar price p_i^*.
The main advantage of working with assumptions for the *real* rather than
the *nominal* world prices of the various export and import lines is that
doing so permits the analyst easily to change the assumption regarding
the future evolution of the world price level without having explicitly to
change every assumption regarding the prices of the individual export
commodity lines.

Projection of export and import volumes is more intricate. First, for exports, let "e" represent the year-average exchange rate, "p" the year-average internal price level, q_i^* the volume of *world* trade in commodity "i," and t(i) the export-tax rate on the commodity. In any year, the commodity's average real-effective price is taken to be given by

$$R_i = [1 - t(i)] \, e \, p_i^*/p,$$

which is equal to

$$[1 - t(i)] \, (e \, p^*/p) \, (p_i^*/p^*)$$

or

$$[1 - t(i)] \, E \, (p_i^*/p^*),$$

where E represents the real-effective exchange rate and p_i^*/p^* the commodity's "real world price" (the second expression follows from multiplying the first by p^*/p^*). Note that $E = e \, p^*/p$ is the overall real-effective exchange rate (see Section 3.3) and p_i^*/p^* is the real world price of the export. Thus, the commodity's real-effective price is given by the product of the real-effective exchange rate and the commodity's real world price, adjusted for any export levies.

Let b(i) represent the elasticity of the export volume with respect to the world trade volume in good i and c(i) the elasticity of the export volume with respect to the real-effective price.[59] The growth rate of the export volume "q_i" is taken here to be given by[60]

$$1 + g_{q(i)} = [1 + g_{q^*(i)}]^{b(i)} \, [1 + g_{R(i)}]^{c(i)},$$

---

[59] For any particular year, the world trade volume in the commodity in question must be projected. One approach would be to project the growth rate of the *overall* world trade volume, i.e., in all goods and non-factor services, and then project the world trade volume in the specific commodity in relation to the overall world trade volume — e.g., by projecting the elasticity of the world trade volume in the specific commodity with respect to the overall world trade volume.

[60] The elasticity of a variable "y" with respect to an associated variable "x" is usually defined as the ratio of the growth rate of "y" to the growth rate of "x." Here, however, the precise definition is the value of "a" such that $(1 + g_y) = (1 + g_x)^a$. For small values of "a" the two definitions are nearly equal. See Annex 3.9.

where

$$1 + g_{R(i)} = \{[1 - t(i)]/[1 - t(i)_{-1}]\}\{1 + g_E\}\{1 + g_{[p^*(i)/p^*]}\}.$$

For an export commodity the values of b(i) and c(i) should both be positive, since a growing world market in any given commodity would imply increased demand for this nation's exports and a higher real-effective price would encourage exports. A value of b(i) exceeding one would imply that the country would gain market share in this particular commodity as world trade volume in it grew, while a value of b(i) less than one implies that the country would lose market share in this particular commodity as world trade volume in it grew. The volume in the base year and projection years could be expressed in physical units (e.g., kilograms per year) or as a volume index (e.g., "1995 = 100").[61]

Non-factor service exports could be projected in a similar way, using a volume index rather than a physical unit of account. In particular, tourism exports may be projected by projecting the growth rates in the annual number of tourist arrivals, the average number of days each tourist stays, and the average daily amount each tourist spends.

Export volumes for certain commodities could be projected to depend negatively on real GDP growth, although to keep it simple the formula given above for $g_{q(i)}$ does not include this. Higher internal demand would induce a garment producer to sell internally rather than export, for example. This could be represented in the export-volume formula by incorporating a multiplicative factor

$$[1 + g_y]^{d(i)},$$

where d(i) is presumably less than zero. (One commodity for which this may be useful in many economies is oil: a country that produces oil can be expected to sell more internally and less externally if its real-GDP growth rate increases.)

---

[61]   In some economies, specific kinds of export may be subject to quantitative limits. For a particular export line, this can be taken into account by projecting the limit and then setting any given year's export quantum to the minimum of (i) the quantity indicated by the formulas discussed above and (ii) the projected limit.

A different formulation may be preferable to project export volumes for commodities for which there is significant internal demand. Suppose the country's annual average internal production "q" is exogenously determined. Let the export volume be given by "x", and let internal consumption be given by "c". Let "f" represent the elasticity of internal consumption with respect to real GDP "y". The export volume in any given year could then be projected as

$$x = q - c$$

$$= [q_{-1} (1 + g_q)] - [c_{-1}(1 + g_y)^f].$$

Internal demand could be made to depend in addition on the real internal price. (Ordinarily, the internal price would be the national-currency equivalent of the world price, adjusted for tariffs or export levies according to circumstances. In special circumstances, though, including temporary local shortages and lagging price adjustments, the internal price could diverge from its "parity" value.) For any given year, the export volume resulting from this calculation could be less than zero, meaning that the country would be importing rather than exporting the commodity in question.

For an import commodity, the growth rate of the import volume "q_i" is taken to be given by

$$1 + g_{q(i)} = [1 + g_y]^{b(i)} [1 + g_{R(i)}]^{c(i)},$$

where b(i) represents the elasticity of the import volume with respect to real GDP; c(i) represents (as with exports) the elasticity of the import volume q_i^* with respect to the real-effective price; and

$$1 + g_{R(i)} = \{[1 + t(i)]/[1 + t(i)_{-1}]\}\{[1 + h(i)]/[1 + h(i)_{-1}]\}\{1 + g_E\}\{1 + g_{[p*(i)/p*]}\},$$

with t(i) now representing the import tariff rate and h(i) shipping and insurance charges as a proportion of the import value (the so-called "C.I.F.-F.O.B. factor"). (Note that the tariff rate appears in the import-volume formula preceded by a plus sign, not a minus sign as with the export-tax rate in the export-volume formula.) For an import commodity the value of b(i) should be positive while the value of c(i) should be negative, since a higher (real-effective) price presumably discourages imports.[62]

Capital-goods import volumes would depend on real capital formation rather than real GDP, that is,

$$1 + g_{q(k)} = [1 + g_k]^{b(k)} [1 + g_{R(k)}]^{c(k)},$$

where g_k represents the real growth rate of capital formation (calculated from the national-accounts projection).

It is best to project merchandise imports at their F.O.B. ("free-on-board") values, as opposed to their C.I.F ("cost, insurance, freight") values. Shipping and freight services are non-factor service imports, and should be projected as percentages of the value of merchandise imports, where the percentages are the assumed "C.I.F.-F.O.B. factor." Other non-factor service imports may be projected in the same way as merchandise imports, the main difference being that such non-material imports would be subject neither to tariffs nor freight and shipping charges.

Once exports and imports of goods and non-factor services have been projected in dollar terms, they can usually be converted to national-currency values using the projected year-average exchange rate. It is important to remember that historical data in national currency may differ from the U.S. dollar values converted at the year-average exchange rate. This is because exports and imports may take place unevenly over the year, so that the average exchange rate at which they are transacted may differ from the year-average exchange rate. If projected exports and imports have strong seasonality, and the exchange rate is projected to vary in future years, it may be appropriate to take this into account in the projection. For example, the bulk of Argentina's grain exports take place within the first four months of each calendar year. If Argentina's exchange rate is projected to vary within each year, it may be more

---

[62]   If a given kind of import is subject to quantitative limit, the projection for any given year could be set in the same way as a projection of an export subject to quantitative limit. The procedure would be to project the limit and then set any given year's import quantum to the minimum of (i) the quantity indicated by the formulas discussed above and (ii) the projected limit.

appropriate to convert these exports into Argentine *pesos* using a projected average exchange rate for the first four months rather than the whole year.

Although the practice is increasingly rare, some economies still have multiple exchange rates — that is, different exchange rates for different classes of transaction. In such cases, different exchange rates might apply to different export and import lines. This can be taken into account straightforwardly in the expression for the real-effective price. If, for example, consumer-goods imports must be carried out at special market rate which is at a premium over (i.e., more depreciated than) the basic export rate, the expression for the real-effective price applicable to consumer imports would incorporate a factor $(1 + z)$, where "z" represents the market premium. This premium would then be another projection assumption. If different exchange rates apply to different export and import lines, it may be more appropriate to use these to convert each export and import line into national currency. In general, however, it is usually reasonable to project the national-accounts values of exports and imports by multiplying their projected dollar flows by the projected average annual exchange rate.

Once each year's unit price and volume have been projected for any given export or import, the dollar value of the export or import flow would then be the product of the dollar price per unit volume and the volume exported. Once these values of all exports and imports have been computed, it is straightforward to calculate the sums of total exports and imports of goods, total non-factor service exports and imports, and total exports and imports of goods and non-factor service exports and imports.

The consumption-, intermediate- and capital-goods import volumes presumably depend, respectively, on the real flows of non-government consumption, real GDP, and overall real capital formation. Since non-government consumption is taken to be the residual for the national-accounts expenditure projections, however, the spreadsheet projection cannot have the consumption-imports volume depend on real non-government consumption, since doing so would lead to circularity. There are at least two ways around this problem. One is simply to have the consumption-imports volume depend on real GDP. (This is the approach taken in the Pacífica exercise.) The other is a bit more complex. Start from the national-accounts expenditure identity,

$$C \equiv Y - [I + G + X - Q].$$

Total imports are given by

$$Q = Q^c + Q^i + Q^k,$$

where Q^c represents consumption-goods imports, Q^i intermediate-goods imports, and Q^k capital-goods imports. Substituting and rearranging,

$$C - Q^c \equiv Y - [I + G + X - Q^i + Q^k].$$

The idea would be to have non-government consumption less consumption-goods imports, rather than non-government consumption, be the residual for the national-accounts expenditure identity. Once this value is determined, it would then be possible to calculate values for C and Q^c that would be consistent with the *volume* of consumption imports, with consumption imports depending through an assumed elasticity on real consumption. This would be done through several simultaneous equations. Let p_c represent the consumer-price index, "c" real non-government consumption, p_{qc} the price index of consumption imports (the exchange rate multiplied by the corresponding international U.S. dollar prices), and q^c the volume of consumption imports. Given the values of p_c and p_{qc} and the values of Y, I, G, X, Q^i, and Q^k, the values of C, "c," Q^c, and q^c would follow from solving the following equations simultaneously:

$$C - Q^c \equiv Y - [I + G + X - Q^i + Q^k];$$

$$q^c = f(c, p_{qc}),$$

i.e., q^c is a function of "c" and p_{qc};

$$p_c c - p_{qc} q^c = C - Q^c;$$

$$c = C/p_c;$$

and

$$q^c = Q^c/p_{qc}.$$

6.5 Government capital formation and consumption

In principle, although government capital formation and consumption figure in the national-expenditure accounts, their projected values would be determined in the government-expenditure projections described in Chapter 4 above. Total government expenditure comprises current and capital expenditure. Current expenditure comprises expenditure for staff and "current" goods and services, as well as interest, explicit subsidies, and transfers. Capital expenditure comprises expenditure for capital formation and purchases of land, buildings, and other kinds of asset. In principle, the national-accounts figure for government consumption would be current government expenditure excluding interest, subsidies and transfers. Similarly, in principle, the national-accounts figure for government capital formation would be the same as the capital-formation figure in the government accounts.

In reality, however, as noted in Chapter 4, government consumption and capital formation as recorded in the national accounts may differ somewhat from the figures in the government accounts. The general reason is that the national accounts and government-budget accounts often use different criteria to categorize specific expenditure accounts. An additional reason is that expenditures recorded in the government accounts as having taken place during a particular year may have been recorded for the government accounts as having taken place in the previous or the following year. Yet another reason is that the national accounts are formulated on an accrual basis, whereas government budget figures are likely to given on a cash basis. That is, consumption and investment expenditure is recorded in the national accounts when the "final" purchaser receives the good or service, whereas government consumption and investment expenditure may be recorded in the government accounts only when the government disburses payment. In general, however, the government-consumption and government capital-formation figures from the two sources should be of the same order of magnitude. They should be projected consistently, which may mean either the same or with a projected "discrepancy" component in the national-accounts government-consumption account.

Separation of the national-accounts expenditure flows on consumption and capital formation into government and non-government sectors is standard in most national-accounts methodologies, but has long been recognized as somewhat arbitrary, particularly for economies in which public enterprises are large and significant. The activities of these entities are "non-government," but they are plainly part of the public, not the private, sector. For example, when analyzing aggregate saving flows, there is an obvious case for separating the saving flows of public enterprises from non-government saving more broadly, and including them in what would then become public-sector saving flows. (Annex 6.5 discusses the basic aggregate-saving concepts and their relationships.)

In any case, the classification of some kinds of government expenditure as consumption or investment is in some measure arbitrary. For example, expenditure on education, which accounts for a large proportion of most nations' government expenditure, is conventionally counted almost entirely as government "consumption." Only what the government spends on construction of education facilities and installation of capital equipment should count in the national accounts as government capital formation. Nevertheless, education expenditure is clearly expenditure on human capital, and as such may reasonably be considered a kind of "capital formation." When examining government statistics, it is important to bear in mind that a large share of what is shown as consumption is, in reality, human-capital formation. (All the same, this book follows convention and considers it part of government consumption.)

The components of the government's future expenditure program are considered programming assumptions for the exercise this book describes. They may be based on some of the other programming assumptions: thus, for example, real expenditure on health would be based, *inter alia*, on the population growth rate, while the projected growth rate of prices is likely to figure in the projected determination of government wage rates. Broadly speaking, however, government-expenditure projections should be based on what the government aims to achieve — that is, the number of people required to educate school-age children, roads that need to be built or maintained, communications facilities to be constructed and staff, national defense requirements, and so on (as discussed in Chapter 4 above).

6.6   *Non-government capital formation and consumption*

For any projection year, if the values of GDP (Y), exports (X) and imports (Q) of goods and non-factor services, capital formation (I), the change over the year in inventory stocks (ΔV), and government consumption (G) have been projected, non-government capital formation as a percentage of GDP would be given by

$$(I/Y) - (J/Y),$$

non-government consumption would be given by

$$(I/Y) - (J/Y),$$

and non-government consumption would be given by.[63]

$$C/Y = [Y - (G + I + \Delta V + X - Q)]/Y$$

or

$$C/Y = 1 - [(G/Y) + (I/Y) + (\Delta V/Y) + (X/Y) - (Q/Y)].$$

---

[63]   Some analysts may prefer in this context to project non-government consumption on the basis of an assumed marginal propensity to consume, projected GDP (or national income), and a representative interest rate (say, the average deposit rate). If this procedure is followed, however, the national-accounts projection would be over-determined. Another approach may be recommended here. After determining non-government consumption as a residual, the assumed consumption function may then be solved for the deposit rate. This deposit rate could then be applied in the fiscal and monetary aspects of the exercise.

Non-government consumption and capital formation calculated in these ways may then be evaluated for feasibility.[64] A very large value for non-government capital formation, particularly by comparison with preceding years, would suggest that the subsequent years' projected real-GDP growth might not be feasible.   Non-government consumption may be evaluated in real per-capita terms, applying assumptions for inflation and population growth.   The analyst may conclude that a negative or very low level of real per-capita consumption growth is too low, in the sense that consumers in the aggregate would be unable or politically unwilling to accept so large a reduction in living standards.   These would be grounds to question the feasibility of the projection's macroeconomic programming objectives.

To evaluate the feasibility of a particular year's projection results, it may be useful to make use of the implied macroeconomic saving flows — i.e., the national, foreign, internal and external saving flows. These are discussed in Annex 6.5.

Given the poverty incidence for an initial year, the projected evolution of real non-government consumption can be applied to project the future evolution of the economy's poverty incidence.   Annex 6.6 describes a technique to carry out this calculation.

6.7   National-accounts projections for "Pacífica"

Table 11 gives the main national-accounts projection assumptions (including those given in Table 2). Table 12 gives the projection assumptions for exports and imports of goods and non-factor services.

---

[64]   Some analysts may prefer in this context to project non-government consumption on the basis of an assumed marginal propensity to consume, projected GDP (or national income), and a representative interest rate (say, the average deposit rate).   If this procedure is followed, however, the national-accounts projection would be over-determined.   Another approach may be recommended here.   After determining non-government consumption as a residual, the assumed consumption function may then be solved for the deposit rate.   This deposit rate could then be applied in the fiscal and monetary aspects of the exercise.

Table 13 then gives the basic national-accounts structure and projections for Pacífica based on the assumptions of Table 11 and Table 12.

As noted in Section 2.2 above, after declining 4.5 per cent in 2009, Pacífica's annual real GDP growth rate is programmed to rise gradually from 1 per cent in 2010 to 5 per cent in 2015. The annual growth rate of consumer prices would fall to 2.2 and 0 per cent in 2009 and 2010 before leveling off at 2 per cent through 2015. The real-effective exchange rate would depreciate modestly through 2011 and then remain unchanged through 2015.

The economy's capital stock is assumed to depreciate at a 3.5 per cent annual rate — that is, the economy's capital (including equipment and structures) is assumed to last just over 28 years on average. The ICOR net of depreciation is projected to decline gradually from 7.3 in 2009 to 1.5 in 2015. With the gradual increase in real GDP growth, this would imply an increased capital-formation requirement: gross fixed capital formation would be 19.7 per cent of GDP in 2009 but then reach 21 per cent in 2015. Capital formation in any given year is assumed, a bit arbitrarily, to affect GDP over the subsequent three years, in the proportions one half, one third, and one sixth.[65] After declining 5 per cent in 2009, capacity utilization is projected to rise gradually and modestly, from 74.8 per cent in 2009 to 80 per cent in 2015.

Projections of general-government consumption and capital formation are drawn from the fiscal-accounts projection (see Section 4.2). In addition, to calculate projected saving flows, projections of the balance of payments' current account other than exports and imports of goods and non-factor services are drawn from the external-accounts projection. Projections of exports and imports of goods and non-factor services are based on the assumptions given in Table 12. The first group of assumptions covers the oil sector. The assumptions that cover this sector are pretty much self-explanatory. The real growth rate

---

[65] As noted in Footnote 57, it would be possible to assume that ICORs for capital formation carried out in year t differ for each subsequent year t+1, t+2, and t+3, but it is easier simply to change the proportions in which the capital formation in year t affects output in subsequent years.

of derivatives import prices is projected to be the same as that of crude export prices. The production volume is projected to grow at 5 per cent per year. Oil-derivatives exports are assumed to remain at 2 per cent of total oil-export export volume (measured in equivalent barrels). Demand for imported oil products and internal demand for oil products is projected to grow at the same rate as real GDP. The tax rates on oil exports and internal sales, and the tax rate and collection efficiency[66] on internal sales are projected to evolve as indicated in Table 12.

For export items other than oil, five assumptions are used to project the export volume: the projected growth rates of (1) the international trade volume in and (2) the real price of the good in question; (3) the export-tax rate; and the elasticities of export volume with respect to (4) the international trade volume in and (5) the real-effective price of the good in question. (Internal demand is assumed to be negligible in determining export volumes other than oil.) For import items other than oil, four assumptions are used to project the import volume: the projected growth rate of the real price of the good in question; the tariff rate; and the elasticities of import volume with respect to real GDP (or, in the case of capital-goods imports, with respect to real capital formation) and the real-effective price of the good in question. The elasticities of export volumes with respect to the international volumes of trade are taken to be one. The elasticities of import volumes with respect to real GDP (or, in the case of capital-goods imports, with respect to real capital formation) are also taken to be one. Banana exports are projected to be relatively insensitive, and manufacturing exports somewhat more sensitive, to real-effective prices. Consumption imports are projected to be relatively more sensitive, and intermediate and capital imports relatively less sensitive, to real-effective prices.

Table 13 gives the national-accounts projection results. Capacity utilization is projected to decline 5 per cent in 2009, and gross fixed capital formation is projected to decline as a percentage of GDP to

---

[66]   The collection efficiency of a tax whose yield flow is T, base is Y and rate is "t" is defined as T/tY. See Section 8.2 below.

17.5 per cent (from 19.7 per cent in 2008). Capacity utilization is projected then to recover gradually to 80 per cent in 2015, while gross fixed capital formation is projected to rise gradually to 21 per cent in the same year. Government capital formation would rise slightly from 5.7 per cent of GDP in 2008 to 5.8 per cent of GDP in 2015, while non-government capital formation would rise from 14 to 15.2 per cent of GDP. Net exports of good and non-factor services — the "resource gap" — would diminish from a 0.9 per cent of GDP surplus in 2008 to a 3.8 per cent of GDP deficit in 2015. Real per-capita non-government private consumption would diminish after 2009, and fall to a value 4.3 per cent below its 2008 value by 2011. Thereafter, however, faster real-GDP growth would bring about a recovery in living standards, so that by 2015 real per-capita non-government private consumption would be 2.7 per cent above its 2008 value.

Figure 4. Pacífica: Per-capita GDP and non-government consumption (2005 U.S. dollars), 2008–2015

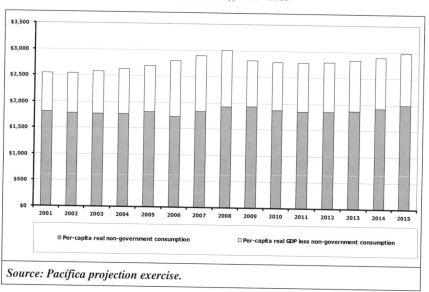

Source: Pacífica projection exercise.

Figure 5. Pacífica: Gross saving and investment (per cent of GDP), 2008–2015

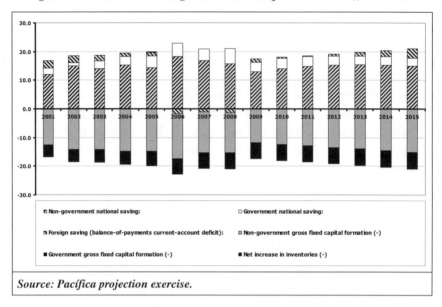

Source: Pacífica projection exercise.

Figure 6. Pacífica: Poverty incidence, 2008–2015[67]

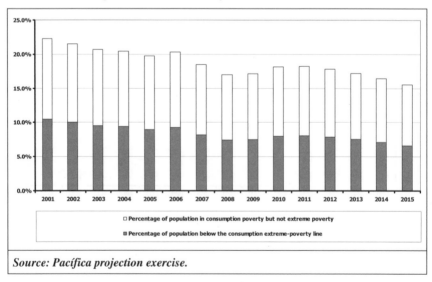

Source: Pacífica projection exercise.

---

[67] Poverty-incidence figures are projected using the methodology outlined in Annex 6.6.

Because of the slow improvement in overall living standards, the poverty incidence would improve only slightly over the projection period. Overall poverty incidence would decline from 17 per cent in 2008 to 15.5 per cent in 2015. Extreme poverty incidence would decline from 7.4 per cent to 6.6 per cent.

The national-accounts projection would appear to be feasible enough, although for any actual economy, the analyst would need to take careful account of political and social conditions in forming such a judgment. The analyst might want to confirm that managers of non-government business enterprises would be sufficiently optimistic to increase capital formation at the rate projected. The analyst would also want to be sure that the slow increase in per-capita non-government consumption would be politically manageable and socially acceptable.

Figure 7. Pacífica: Merchandise trade (per cent of GDP), 2008–2015

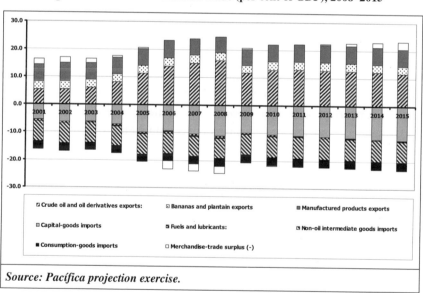

Source: *Pacífica projection exercise.*

7 External-accounts projections

"We will find neither national purpose nor personal satisfaction in a mere continuation of economic progress, in an endless amassing of worldly goods... The Gross National Product measures neither our wit nor our courage, neither our wisdom nor our learning, neither our compassion nor our devotion to our country. It measures everything, in short, except that which makes life worthwhile, and it can tell us everything about America — except whether we are proud to be Americans."

– Robert F. Kennedy, speech at the University of Kansas,
March 18, 1968

7.1 Introduction: External-accounts projections

As noted in Section 2.4, the exercise this book describes works out the national-accounts projections in five steps. The first is to bring in the projections of exports and imports of goods and non-factor services discussed in Section 6.4 above. The second is to formulate projections for the remaining non-debt components of the current-account, capital and financial, and errors-and-omissions components of the balance of payments (that is, the remaining "above-the-line" accounts). The third step is to formulate projections for the debt-flow and interest-flow components of the current-account, capital and financial, and errors-and-omissions components of the balance of payments. The fourth step is to formulate projections for the international-reserve ("below-the-line") flows of the balance of payments. The fifth step is to reconcile the above- and below-the-line accounts, by determining the additional external borrowing or international-reserve accumulation necessary to close the "financing-gap" between them.

Section 7.2 describes projection techniques for the balance-of-payments accounts, focusing on aspects other than the debt flows and the export and import flows covered in Chapter 5 and Section 6.4 above. Section 7.3 describes the basic technique for reconciling the "above-the-line" and "below-the-line" accounts. Section 7.4 returns to the illustrative "Pacífica" exercise to discuss the external-accounts projections.

7.2   Balance-of-payments projections

This section discusses techniques for projecting the various balance-of-payments flows.   The "above-the-line" balance-of-payments accounts can be grouped (see Annex 7.2) into (i) exports and imports of goods and non-factor services; (ii) the non-interest components of the factor-services accounts; (iii) unrequited transfers under the *current account*; (iv) unrequited transfers under the *capital account*; (v) net investment flows; (vi) other non-debt financial flows; (vii) errors and omissions; and (viii) debt flows, including interest, disbursements and repayments. The "below-the-line" balance-of-payments accounts comprise (ix) net international-reserve flows.[68]

Before proceeding, it is important to bear in mind that projections of the different balance-of-payments accounts are interrelated.   It is therefore not quite possible to have the discussion proceed serially through the accounts as listed.   The discussion of the projection procedures for each of these accounts is likely to include some discussion of other accounts.

(i) Exports and imports of goods and non-factor services: Projections of these accounts would be drawn directly from the projections of exports and imports of goods and non-factor services under the national accounts (Section 6.4 above describes the projection procedures).   Note, however, that in particular economies specific export and import projections may be closely associated with other balance-of-payments projections. Examples include capital-goods imports associated with inflows of direct foreign investment or disbursement of debt financing under projects.

---

[68]   As noted in Section 2.4 above, this book takes the "above-the-line" balance-of-payments accounts to be the current, capital, financial, and errors-omissions accounts, and the "below-the-line" accounts to be the international-reserve accounts. The above-the-line accounts are taken "to explain" the below-the-line accounts.

Projections of exports and imports of goods and non-factor services would be centrally important projections for most developing economies — characteristically, the principal source of variation in external financing requirements. Debt flows, comprising interest, disbursements and repayments, are also likely to be among the more important above-the-line balance-of-payments accounts for most economies. Discussion of these flows is postponed, however, to follow the discussion of all the other above-the-line balance-of-payments accounts.

(ii) Non-interest elements of the factor-services accounts, (iii) unrequited transfers in the current and (iv) capital accounts; (v) net investment flows; (vi) other non-debt financial flows; and (vii) errors and omissions: Unlike the projections of net exports of goods and non-factor services, which also figure in the national accounts, and the public-sector debt projections, which also figure in the fiscal accounts, the various "non-trade, non-debt balance-of-payments" accounts figure *only* in the external-accounts projections. The general approach to projecting these accounts, and their sub-accounts, is to formulate and apply assumptions regarding their real (deflated) growth rates. Thus, for example, net non-official unrequited transfer inflows (Z) could be projected as

$$Z = Z_{-1} (1 + g_{p*}) (1 + g_z)$$

$$= Z_{-1} (1 + g_Z),$$

where g_z represents the assumed *real* growth rate of such flows and g_{p*} the assumed growth rate of the world price level. Other balance-of-payments lines, such as official unrequited transfer inflows, direct foreign investment, other non-debt financial flows, and errors and omissions, could also be projected in this general way. The value of g_Z, i.e., the nominal value of Z, could be projected directly as such, of course, but it would then remain unchanged when the projection of g_{p*} is changed.

To be sure, this is just the general approach. For non-official unrequited transfer inflows in particular, and for many of the other non-trade, non-debt balance-of-payments accounts, analysts may prefer to apply more detailed assumptions to formulate the assumptions for the real growth rates in question.

Under the current account, the non-trade, non-interest accounts comprise (i) non-interest factor receipts and payments and (ii) net unrequited transfers. Non-interest factor receipts and payments include cross-border payments of wages, rents, and profits. For most countries, these accounts would be relatively small in magnitude. Receipts are probably best projected by having their real values grow at rates based on real world GDP, while payments are probably best projected by having their real values grow at rates based on real GDP. Under the net-unrequited-transfers heading, remittances from citizens living and working abroad figure significantly in some developing economies' balance of payments. For such economies, the real growth rate of unofficial transfer inflows could be projected on the basis of the assumed growth rates of (a) the number of citizens living abroad and (b) average real annual remittances by each citizen living abroad, which could be based in turn on the projected real-growth performance of the countries in which citizens overseas are working.

For most developing economies, *official* unrequited transfer *outflows* would be insignificant in magnitude. *Official* unrequited transfer *inflows*, on the other hand, are significant for many economies, since these encompass the grants from official entities to non-government and government entities. Grants for non-government and government entities should be projected separately, because while both figure in the balance of payments, only grants to government entities figure in the fiscal accounts. In any case, it is important that grants to official entities be consistent in the external and fiscal accounts. Their values should therefore be projected *either* in the fiscal or the external accounts, and the results should then be transferred to the other set of accounts. (Grants to government entities figure in the fiscal accounts either as (i) above-the-line receipts with "revenue" or (ii) below-the-line financing sources, depending on the specific economy's accounting conventions.)

In order to discuss the projection of official transfers further, however, a digression is necessary to explain certain intricacies in the balance-of-payments accounting. Since the turn of the century, the IMF has urged countries to use a balance-of-payments structure that differs somewhat from what had previously been conventional.   (The new structure is described in the IMF's 2001 *Balance of Payments Manual*). Previously, the above-the-line balance of payments included, in addition to the current and errors-and-omissions accounts, a single set of what were called "capital," "financial," or "capital-and-financial" accounts. In the revised structure, these accounts are divided rigorously into "capital" and "financial" accounts. The "capital" accounts are defined in a new way.

The change in the accounts structure and definitions was intended to address at least two important problems. The first was that, previously, *all* grants were supposed to be recorded with the current-account unrequited-transfers accounts. Developing economies receive significant flows of grants for project finance, however. Many analysts felt that was not quite right to record these as *current* unrequited-transfer inflows. Accordingly, in the new accounts structure, project grants are supposed to be recorded as inflows under the (new) capital accounts. In effect, with this change they count as financing *sources*, rather than as reductions in financing uses as they had previously.

That is, with these changes, official transfers are recorded and projected in two different balance-of-payments accounts. Current grants — in particular, "budget grants," that is, outright cash transfers to governments to reduce their borrowing requirements — are recorded and projected under unrequited transfers, in the current account. For future years closer to the present, current grants can be programmed on the basis of existing and planned donor programs. Analysts can formulate projections by consulting with donors, or with government specialists who work with donors. For years further into the future, current grants can be programmed by directly setting assumptions for their likely real growth rates. Capital grants, on the other hand — in particular, "project grants," that is, project-financing flows — are recorded and projected in the (new) capital account. For future years closer to the present, project grants can be programmed on the basis of projects. For years further into the future, project grants can be programmed, again, by directly setting assumptions for their likely real growth rates.

The second problem the new capital account was intended to address was that, previously, the balance-of-payments indicated debt forgiveness inadequately and inconsistently. This is discussed below, following the discussion of the debt projections in the balance-of-payments accounts.

The remaining above-the-line non-trade, non-interest accounts — the non-debt financial accounts and the errors-and-omissions account — are, in general, difficult to project, because for many developing economies, they have been, and are likely to remain, unstable. For the nearer term, assumptions regarding the real growth rate of direct foreign investment and other investment transactions should be based, ideally, on what is known or can be guessed about the plans of foreign enterprises operating or planning to operate within the economy. For example, exploration and development plans of oil companies in oil-producing economies are likely to be quantitatively significant. For oil and other extractive sectors, it is important to remember that direct foreign investment inflows often take the form of capital-goods imports. (To this extent, for some economies it may be appropriate to link at least part of direct foreign-investment flows with projected capital-goods imports.)

Net portfolio investment inflows are more likely to be related to equity markets' projected performance. Here, the analyst might find it preferable to apply assumptions regarding stock-exchange performance and assumptions regarding the relationship between that performance and net portfolio-investment inflows. It hardly needs saying, however, that external inflows to and outflows from any economy's equity markets' are likely to be volatile. For a conservative projection, it is advisable, if not essential, not to project a large net portfolio investment inflow, particularly over several years. A large net portfolio investment inflow projection would significantly, and probably over-optimistically, reduce the projected unidentified borrowing requirement. A projected net portfolio investment inflow exceeding 0.5 per cent of GDP would probably be excessive.

For many economies, returns on foreign investment are a significant component of the factor-services payment accounts. As a matter of correct accrual methodology, the current account is supposed to record *all* profits on foreign investment as outflows, whether repatriated or not, and the foreign-investment accounts are then supposed to incorporate, either explicitly or implicitly, all reinvested (i.e., non-repatriated) profits. For most economies, even after the fact, profits earned on foreign investment — let alone the accumulated stock of foreign investment on which the profits are based — can only be estimated imprecisely.[69]

One relatively simple way to project the returns on direct foreign investment account is to link its real value to real GDP through an assumed elasticity. Thus, the flow of returns "V" in dollars would be projected as

$$V = V_{-1} \, (1 + g_{p*}) \, (1 + g_y)^c,$$

where "c" would be the elasticity of real returns on foreign investment with respect to real GDP. More sophisticated approaches are possible, of course: for example, the various categories of foreign-investment flow could be accumulated year by year into stocks, and rates of return assumed for each year's average stock. For most economies, however, data limitations and the inherent difficulty of projecting equity markets' performance are likely to make this approach difficult to apply. (In any case, even for economies significant with significant accumulated direct foreign investment and equity markets, the magnitude of this account is likely to be relatively small compared with other external accounts.)

The "other-financial-flows" account comprises non-investment, non-debt financial flows, including financial movements into and out of bank deposits and other short-term financial applications. For most economies, estimation of this account is particularly difficult. Historical values are often less than credible, and it is simply very difficult to project how these accounts will move. At times of macroeconomic stress, fears of sharp devaluation or political disruption tend to drive this

---

[69] One exception is Brazil. Under legislation dating back to the early 1960s Brazil has maintained a registry of direct-foreign-investment inflows, and the data, while far from perfect, offer scope for analysis not possible in most other economies.

account toward net outflow, as people and firms try to move resources outside the economy and its endangered currency unit. Generally speaking, extrapolative projection analysis described here would not assume crises of this kind (although sensitivity analysis may be used to take account of the consequences of heavy capital flight in particular future years, as discussed in Chapter 10). For "base-scenario" projections, simple assumptions would be most appropriate here. If there is an outflow in a base year, for example, the analyst could assume that it would grow at some real growth rate (perhaps zero), or that it would decay "radioactively" (e.g., by half in real terms each year). Again, as for portfolio-investment flows, it is advisable, if not essential, not to project a large inflow, particularly over several years. Again, a inflow projection would significantly, and probably over-optimistically, reduce the projected unidentified borrowing requirement. Again, a projected net portfolio investment inflow exceeding 0.5 per cent of GDP would probably be excessive.

Finally, for all projection years, unless the analyst has specific information or previous years' data show a clear trend, it is usually most advisable to project the errors-and-omissions account as zero. For some economies, however, if the errors-and-omissions account tends generally to be significant and to be characterized by a trend, it may be more realistic to take this into account — say, to project the flow account as a percentage of GDP.[70] Analysts sometimes think of the errors-and-omissions account as consisting of, or at least, reflecting "capital flight" — i.e., transfers of financial resources outside the economy in question for reasons other than what can be specifically identified in the current, capital and financial accounts. Indeed, for many economies the

---

[70] This writer once had an instructive experience on this subject when working in an international organization. One January, he circulated a "projection" of a nation's balance-of-payments accounts for the year just ended, with the errors-and-omissions account "projected" to be zero. Soon afterward, the nation's central bank published initial estimates, including errors and omissions amounting to about 6 per cent of GDP. Several people telephoned to ask why the errors-and-omissions projection had been so far off. To be sure, experience suggested that the magnitude of the errors-and-omissions account would tend to decline sharply as the central bank's estimates underwent revision. The eventual definitive estimate was about 2 per cent of GDP.

errors-and-omissions account does tend to turn more strongly negative in historical years when there have been economic crises. For projections, however, it is generally best to project capital flight as taking place through the relevant accounts under the financial account, the accounts where it would be recorded if fully observed, and project the errors-and-omissions line to be zero.

(viii) Debt flows, including interest, disbursement and repayment: To conclude the discussion of the above-the-line balance-of-payments accounts, the discussion turns now the debt flows. Since the turn of the century, as part of the changes described above, the IMF has urged countries to estimate the "other financial accounts" — including the debt accounts, and any other financial flows not included in the other accounts — in categories, reflecting inflows to and outflows from (a) the monetary authorities, (b) the general government, (c) the banking system, and (d) other sectors. Projections of these accounts would be drawn directly from the projections by debtor of external-debt disbursements and repayment (Chapter 5 above describes the projection procedures). Projected interest due and interest paid would be shown in the current account. (Unpaid interest would be captured as an increase in the stock of accumulated interest arrears.) Disbursement and repayment flows are shown in the debt flows of the financial accounts.

There are several additional issues involved in the projection of external-debt flows in the balance of payments. Some of these have to do with the new capital account. The second problem the new capital account was intended to address was that, previously, the balance-of-payments indicated debt forgiveness inadequately and inconsistently. This was problematic, in view of all the many debt-forgiveness operations that had been carried out since the late 1980s.

In a sense, before the changes in the balance-of-payments concepts, debt forgiveness was not supposed to figure at all in the balance of payments. This was basically because, as simple reductions in debt *stocks*, debt forgiveness involved no actual payments flows. It never seemed quite right, however, for the balance-of-payments to take no account of debt forgiveness: debt forgiveness could be significant in magnitude when it took place, and many analysts wanted the balance-of-payments flows to indicate them. Accordingly, the new capital account records debt forgiveness as an inflow. Since no payment flow takes place, however, other accounts in the balance of payments must record *outflows* summing to the amount of the debt forgiveness. Thus, for example, a debt-stock reduction of US$10 million could be recorded as a US$10 million inflow in the capital account and a US$10 million "repayment" under the financial accounts. Subsequent, and projected, interest and repayment flows would then be adjusted down accordingly, reflecting the reduced debt-service burden and the favorable effects on the current and financial accounts.

In fact, matters are a bit more complicated than this. The debt-stock reduction is *not* recorded in the recording and projection procedure the IMF recommends. Rather, the outflows recorded in the current account for interest and in the financial accounts for repayment continue to include *what would have been paid* on the forgiven debt. The capital account then records (or projects) the forgiven interest and repayment quantities, as offsetting inflows. Thus, in effect, the IMF's recommended procedure is to have the balance of payments show debt relief as applying *year by year* to the forgiven *debt service* rather than to the debt stock on the single occasion when it is reduced. This procedure shows the unrequited transfers effectively provided by donors who reduce debt.

This has some peculiar implications for the debt-flow projections. If the economy in question has had one or more debt-reduction operations in the past, and the balance-of-payments data follows the procedure the IMF now recommends, then the historical financial-account flows would incorporate debt-service flows for debt that had already been written down. These would be offset by precisely equal capital-account inflows reflecting the debt reduction. For projection years, debt service on written-down debt could then continue, along with the corresponding capital-account offset.

The basic objective of the projection exercise is to determine the future external-accounts financing gaps. For this, it would make no difference what values were projected for debt service on written-down debt, since the capital-account flows would precisely offset them, whatever they are. To be sure, though, a moment's thought raises questions about the procedure of recording debt-service flows for debt that has been written down. If interest and repayment flows for written-down debt continue to be recorded, after all, then recorded interest and repayment outflows — and the corresponding current- and financial-account deficits — would be larger than they actually were, or would be in projection years. This may be unhelpful for the purposes of the projection exercise. A case could be made, then, for *removing* (or zeroing) the interest and repayment flows for written-down debt from the financial accounts, along with the corresponding capital-account inflows, in the projection exercise. On the other hand, if interest and repayment flows for written-down debt are kept in, the capital-account inflows would show the effective transfer the economy receives, year by year, through the debt-reduction operation. It is always a simple matter to report "adjusted" values for the interest-due, repayment, current, and financial accounts remove the interest and repayment flows for written-down debt.

To summarize, the above-the-line balance-of-payments accounts are projected by bringing in the net-exports and debt-flow projections from the national-accounts and external-debt projections worksheets respectively, and then formulating and applying projection assumptions for the real growth rates of the remaining "non-trade, non-interest" accounts. In particular, following the IMF's recommended procedures, grants for government projects and the effective transfers arising from debt-forgiveness operations are recorded and projected under what are now called as the "capital" accounts.

(ix) International-reserve flows: For most economies at most times, the most important below-the-line account is the net foreign-exchange international-reserve inflow. It is more or less standard projection practice to program a central bank's year-end foreign-exchange stock, as a policy variable, to end the year at a stock value measured as some number of months of the year's imports of goods and non-factor services (see Section 3.5). The international-reserve *flow* may therefore be projected as the differences between the corresponding year-end stocks. When doing so, however, cross-currency valuation changes should be taken into account. That is, the net dollar inflows would partially reflect changes in the stocks measured in dollars that arise from changes in the

exchange rate between the dollar and the currencies in which the reserve stocks are actually held. The remainder of the flow would be the foreign-exchange inflow measured at the period-average exchange rate.

The intuition behind projecting foreign-exchange reserves in terms of imports and goods and non-factor services in this way (as discussed in Section 3.5 above), is that the economy presumably could maintain an import flow for that number of months, in the hypothetical event that the economy's exports were to stop entirely. In this way, the reserves would amount to a security cushion. Analysts and policy-makers have sometimes relied on a rule of thumb that for most economies three months' "reserve cover" was the minimum necessary, that six months' was prudent, and that higher amounts might be considered excessive, except in exceptional circumstances. That is, it was widely believed that a central bank with less than three months' risked speculative pressure on its currency, while a central bank with more than six months' was using resources wastefully, since rates of return on the overseas deposits and financial instruments in which reserves are usually held are typically relatively low. This approach is only one among many possible, however. The number of months of "cover" that a central bank ought to maintain is very much a matter of economy-specific circumstances. For example, central banks whose economies have heavy external-debt servicing burdens may take the view that they would do better to hold some number of months' worth of debt-servicing payments.

Reviewing the projection procedure described in Section 3.5 above, suppose the central bank in question sets its reserve holding on the basis of net imports of goods and non-factor services. Let A* represent the central bank's year-end foreign-exchange holdings in U.S. dollars, let "m" represent the number of months of imports of goods and non-factor services at which this stock would be programmed to end the year; and let Q* represent the U.S. dollar flow over the year of imports of goods and non-factor services. Let "v" represent the change in the value of the previous year-end reserve stock arising from valuation changes — that is, changes in the dollar value of non-dollar foreign-exchange holdings. The projected year-end value of A would then be given by

$$A^* = [(m/12)\, Q^*]$$

and the corresponding reserve flow would be given by

$$A^* - [A_{-1}^*\,(1 + v)] = [(m/12)\, Q^*] - [A_{-1}^*\,(1 + v)].$$

Other below-the-line, or reserve, accounts could be projected in straightforward ways. Changes in the central bank's year-end holdings of SDRs (Special Drawing Rights, the reserve "money" issued by the IMF), in its reserve position in the IMF, and in its gold holdings could be projected using assumed growth rates in terms of SDRs or, in the case of the gold holdings, in ounces of gold. The year-end values could then be determined in dollars by applying assumed changes in the U.S. dollar value of the SDR, or, in the case of the gold holdings, the gold valuation used by the country. The change in the year-end stocks gives the flow increase over the year.

   The central bank's interest earnings on international reserves figure in the current account, as a component of factor-service income. This account may be projected by applying an assumed interest rate to the average reserve holding of the year, which could be projected as the average of the year-end and the previous year-end stocks. The interest rate may be calculated as a projected spread over the projected value of LIBOR. As noted above, rates of return on central banks' foreign-exchange placements are typically relatively low.[71] A central bank is likely to hold part of its reserve resources in highly liquid, lower-yielding forms, such as checking accounts, available immediately, and the rest in less liquid, higher-yielding forms, such as U.S. Treasury instruments, certificates of deposit, and the like. Inevitably, the maturity and currency mixes for gross international reserves are crucial management issues for any central bank.

---

[71]   To be sure, many central banks engage in fairly active management of reserve placements, and where appropriate, the balance-of-payments projections may take this into account.

Loans received by a central bank from the International Monetary Fund count as "reserve liabilities." A central bank's "net international-reserve" stock at any moment is the difference between its reserve assets and liabilities. (The basic point of the concept is to net out reserve holdings that have been borrowed from the International Monetary Fund, so that the reserves reported are those the central bank has managed to secure through the country's economic activity.) The central bank's borrowing from and repayments to the International Monetary Fund are debt flows, and should be projected accordingly, along with other debt flows (See Section 5.2 above, and, also, see the discussion of central-bank operations with the International Monetary Fund in Annex 9.6.)

To calculate the overall below-the-line balance-of-payments flows to be explained by the above-the-line flows, the pure valuation changes must be subtracted from the overall changes in the central bank's net-asset stocks. That is, suppose the central bank's SDR holdings increased over a given year by US$1 million, but that US$100,000 of this increase resulted from an increase in the U.S. dollar value of the SDR. The overall below-the-line balance-of-payments flows should record only the US$900,000 in inflows. For a projection exercise, the following procedure may be used to decompose a change in an asset stock into a flow change and a valuation change. Let $e*$ represent the year-average and $e*'$ the year-end exchange rate of U.S. dollars per SDR.[72] Let $R*'$ represent the year-end stock of SDRs and let $\Delta R*'$ represent the flow increase over the year in the central bank's SDR stock. The overall change in the central bank's SDR stock would be given by

$$e*' R*' - e*'_{-1} R*'_{-1},$$

---

[72] The projection assumptions for the year-average and year-end SDR-U.S. dollar exchange rates must be mutually consistent. For example, if one would like to assume that the rate will remain unchanged over the projection years (a "default" assumption), the year-average rate for all projection years should be set equal to the preceding year-end rate, and the year-end rates should then be set equal to the current year-average rate.

and the valuation change could then be approximated by

$$[e^{*'} R^{*'} - e_{-1}^{*'} R_{-1}^{*'}] - e^{*} \Delta R^{*}.$$

7.3   Reconciling above- and below-the-line balance-of-payments projections

If the above- and below-the-line accounts are projected as described in Section 7.2 above, the two sets of projection need not be equal. The above- and below-the-line accounts must be reconciled, however, in order for the projection to be meaningful. In the reconciliation approach suggested here, the first step is to determine whether the below-the-line projection exceeds or falls short of the above-the-line projection. If the below-the-line projection exceeds the above-the-line projection, reconciliation would be carried out by increasing the above-the-line projection — specifically, by increasing disbursement under an "unidentified" debt line. If the above-the-line projection exceeds the below-the-line projection, reconciliation would be carried out by increasing the below-the-line projection — specifically, by increasing the projected inflow of unprogrammed foreign-exchange reserves.

Simply assigning the amount of the "gap" to a debt disbursement — or, if the gap is negative, to an increase in foreign-exchange reserves — would not quite close the gap, however. This is because any increase in debt disbursements in any given year would increase interest due above the line, while any increase in foreign-exchange reserves below the line would increase interest earnings above the line. Either way, the calculated amount needed to close the gap must take account of the additional interest paid or earned. The additional interest may be assumed to be a half year's worth, since any "gap-filling" debt disbursement could be taken to occur halfway through the year, and any "gap-filling" increase in foreign-exchange reserves could be assumed to take place evenly over the year.

For a given projection year, let **A** represent the total unadjusted above-the-line projection and let **B** represent the total unadjusted below-the-line projection. Suppose first that **B-A** is greater than zero, so an unidentified loan disbursement would be needed to reconcile the two projections. Let "r" represents the interest rate on new loan disbursements. It can be shown that an unidentified disbursement equal to $(B-A)/[1 - (r/2)]$ would reconcile the above- and below-the-line projections. The reasoning is as follows. The above-the-line projection would increase by $(B-A)/[1 - (r/2)]$ as a consequence of the unidentified disbursement but decrease by $(r/2)(B-A)/[1 - (r/2)]$ on account of the increase in interest due. The adjusted above-the-line projection would therefore become

$$A + (B\text{-}A)/[1 - (r/2)] - (r/2)(B\text{-}A)/[1 - (r/2)]$$

$$= A + [1 - (r/2)](A\text{-}B)/[1 - (r/2)]$$

$$= A + B - A$$

$$= B,$$

thus closing the gap.

Suppose next that **A-B** is greater than zero, so that an unprogrammed foreign-exchange inflow would be needed to reconcile the two projections. Let "r" now represent the interest rate on foreign-exchange reserves. It can be shown that an unprogrammed foreign-exchange inflow of $(A\text{-}B)/[1 - (r/2)]$ would reconcile the above- and below-the-line projections. The below-the-line projection would increase by $(A\text{-}B)/[1 - (r/2)]$, while the above-the-line projection would increase by a half year's interest on this amount, $(r/2)(A\text{-}B)/[1 - (r/2)]$. The above- and below-the-line values would now become

$$A + (r/2)(A\text{-}B)/[1 - (r/2)] \quad and \quad B + (A\text{-}B)/[1 - (r/2)].$$

Multiplying both expressions through by $[1 - (r/2)]$ turns the first expression into

$$A[1 - (r/2)] + (r/2)(A\text{-}B) = A - [(r/2)B]$$

and the second expression into

$$B[1 - (r/2)] - (A - B) = -B(r/2) + A = A - [(r/2)B],$$

which are precisely equal.

In this approach, it is useful to speak of each year's "unadjusted" and the "adjusted" "financing gaps." The *unadjusted* gap is the amount which, if it could simply be added (say) to exports of goods and non-factor services and so to the sum of the above-the-line accounts, would close the gap. That is, for any given year's projection, if this unadjusted gap could be added in some way above the line, no additional debt disbursement would be required and the projected reserve accumulation would be precisely right. The *adjusted* gap is the amount that would have to be added specifically to debt disbursements or to gross international reserves to reconcile the above- and below-the-line accounts. These two financing gaps will differ, in general, because if the *adjusted* gap is filled through increases in an interest-bearing account, additional intra-year interest would arise from the unprogrammed net addition to external debt or foreign-exchange reserves.

In the exercise this book discusses, if there is a positive unadjusted financing gap, the private sector, not the government is assumed to receive the "unidentified" loan that fills it. That is, when the unadjusted above-the-line projection exceeds the unadjusted below-the-line projection, the residual flow account is "unidentified non-guaranteed private borrowing." It is important to remember that this should not be interpreted as a "forecast" or prediction that such borrowing would take place. Rather, it should be understood as the amount of private borrowing that would have to take place given all the other projected balance-of-payments accounts. If in any future year the private borrowing is "very large," this would indicate that the projection assumptions are probably not feasible. The reason it is preferable not to assign the unidentified borrowing to the government is that doing so would affect the fiscal accounts. It is simply easier to program the government's external borrowing and *then* examine the external- and fiscal-accounts projections for feasibility. (Chapter 8 discusses the fiscal-accounts projection.)

At least one complication may be worth introducing into the procedure for closing the external financing gap. The idea may be understood as follows. Suppose that *ex ante* financing requirements are projected to be negative for all projection years through year t-1, but a positive *ex ante* financing requirement is projected for year t. Year t-1 would conclude with a positive balance of unprogrammed gross international reserves. Rather than allow the entire year t gap to be covered with unidentified borrowing, the authorities could first allow accumulated unprogrammed reserves to diminish. If the year t-1 unprogrammed reserves stock sufficed to cover the year t financing requirement, no unidentified borrowing would be needed in year t. If the year t-1 unprogrammed reserves stock were insufficient to cover the year t financing requirement, unidentified borrowing would be needed in year t, but only to cover the difference between the year t gap and the year t-1 unprogrammed reserves stock.

That is, if the *ex ante* financing gap in year t *exceeds* the previous year-end reserves stock (and interest earned on it during year t), unprogrammed reserves could fall to zero in year t, and unidentified borrowing would cover the remaining financing gap. If the financing gap in year t *is less than* the previous year-end unprogrammed reserves stock (and interest earned on it), unprogrammed reserves would decline only by the amount of the financing gap, and no unidentified borrowing would be needed. (If the financing gap in year t were still negative, unprogrammed reserves could rise by the absolute value of the financing gap.)

Naturally enough, if it makes sense to set up the projection exercise so any *positive ex ante* financing gap in year t would be covered first by drawing down accumulated unprogrammed reserves, it might also make sense to have any *negative ex ante* financing flow applied first to pay down any accumulated unidentified debt stock in year t-1. Whatever remained from the negative financing gap could then be added to unprogrammed gross international reserves. Note that if the projection exercise has *both* these procedures are in place — that is, if any positive financing gap is financed first by drawing down accumulated unprogrammed gross international reserves and any negative financing gap is applied first to pay down accumulated unidentified debt — it should be impossible for *both* the accumulated unprogrammed gross international reserve stock *and* the unidentified external-debt stock to end the same projection year greater than zero. In any projection year, at least one of these two stocks would have to be zero.

This can be exploited in the procedure for closing each year's financing gap. If the *unprogrammed reserves stock* in year t-1 exceeds zero (and the unidentified debt stock is therefore zero), the closure procedure for year t would be based on the unprogrammed reserves stock: any positive *ex ante* financing requirement would be met first by drawing from the unprogrammed deposit stock (and interest earned on the unprogrammed reserves stock during year t). Unidentified borrowing would take place only to the extent the financing gap exceeds the previous year-end reserves stock (and interest earned on it during year t). On the other hand, if the *unidentified debt stock* in year t-1 exceeds zero (and the unprogrammed reserves stock is therefore zero), the closure procedure would be based on the unidentified debt stock: the negative value of any *ex ante* financing gap would be applied first to pay down the unidentified debt stock, and any remainder would be added to the unprogrammed reserves stock.

7.4   *External-accounts projections for "Pacífica"*

Table 14 gives the assumptions on which the external-accounts projections are based, apart from the basic macroeconomic assumptions in Table 2 and the assumptions regarding the external-debt flows, discussed below. The programmed value of year-end foreign-exchange holdings expressed in months of imports of goods and non-factor services is one of the more important assumptions for the external accounts. The remaining assumptions in this table cover the other components of the central bank's gross external assets and balance-of-payments lines not covered by assumptions elsewhere. It is often helpful to assume that non-debt financial-account flows other than foreign investment and debt and net errors and omissions will go to zero in the first projection year and remain zero in all subsequent years, and then to carry out sensitivity analysis to observe the consequences of different negative and positive flow quantities.

Table 15, Table 16 and Table 17 show the balance-of-payments current-account, financial-accounts, and reserve-account projections generated from these assumptions. Declining export prices would move the current account into deficit in 2009. The deficit would narrow somewhat in 2010, as export prices began to recover and recession reduced imports, but it would widen over the years 2011–2015, as rising real-growth rates increased import volumes. The 2015 deficit would reach 3.3 per cent of GDP. The goods and non-factor services balance would go from a 0.9 per cent of GDP surplus in 2008 to a 3.8 per cent of GDP deficit in 2015. The deficit on the factor-services account would narrow slightly from 2 per cent of GDP in 2008 to 1.7 per cent over the same period, mainly because interest due on external debt would diminish as a percentage of GDP. On the financial accounts, investment transactions flows would remain roughly unchanged as a percentage of GDP, at about 2.4–2.6 per cent. Net term borrowing would increase as a percentage of GDP. In 2014 and 2015 it would include unidentified private non-guaranteed borrowing. The central bank would accumulate foreign-exchange reserves in amounts ranging between 0.5 and 2 per cent of GDP each year to keep pace with rising imports of goods and non-factor services. This, in addition to the current-account deficit, largely explains the continuing need for external financing over the projection period.

Figure 8. Pacífica: Current account of the balance of payments (per cent of GDP), 2008–2015

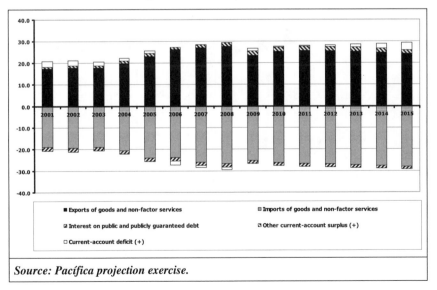

Source: Pacífica projection exercise.

Figure 9. Pacífica: Balance of payments (per cent of GDP), 2008–2015

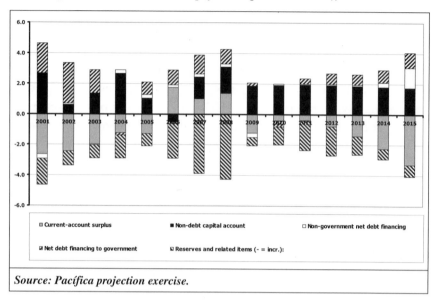

Source: Pacífica projection exercise.

Figure 10. Pacífica: External-debt stocks (per cent of GDP), 2008–2015

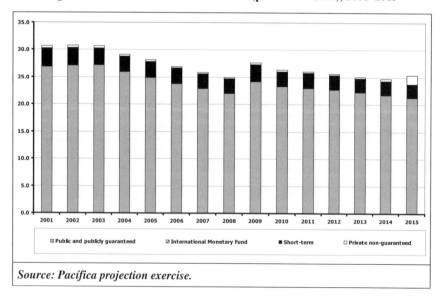

Source: Pacífica projection exercise.

Table 18 shows that the overall year-end external-debt stock would rise slightly from 25.2 per cent of GDP in 2008 to 25.5 per cent in 2015. Public and publicly-guaranteed debt would decline from 22 to 21.3 per cent of GDP over this period. Unidentified disbursements from private sources would need to rise over the period, and the unidentified component of total external debt would reach 1.4 per cent of GDP in 2015.

Table 19 gives the sources-and-uses presentation of the projected balance-of-payments flows. The "uses" portion of the table indicates the relative importance of the current-account deficit, debt repayment, and gross foreign-exchange reserve accumulation in determining Pacífica's overall borrowing requirement. Over the projection period, the financing uses shown amount to about 4.9 per cent of GDP. Term-debt disbursements would finance about 3.1 percentage points, with other capital inflows — including investment transactions — covering the rest.[73] To say whether this would be feasible, the analyst would have to know more about Pacífica's specific circumstances and in particular its relationship with its external creditors. It *seems* feasible, however, on the view that if Pacífica's real GDP and world prices were to grow at real rates assumed, the debt-GDP ratio would be tending to stabilize.

---

[73] This presentation shows the *gross* financing uses and sources — that is, debt repayment is shown as a use of finance. It could be shown, of course, as a negative financing source. If this were done, the uses and sources would be *net*.

8   Fiscal-accounts projections

The less the people know about how sausages and laws [and budgets]
are made, the better they sleep at night.

– attributed to Otto von Bismarck

8.1   Introduction: Financing the fiscal-expenditure flow

This chapter discusses the methodology used for the fiscal projections.
The fiscal aspect of the projection exercise is structured basically to
address the following question. Suppose a government aims to carry out
a given multiannual development-expenditure program, including
selected programs in the social sectors and in infrastructure investment
and maintenance. Suppose that the government intends to maintain a
given tax policy, as well as various non-interest, non-developmental
expenditures. Suppose in addition that the government has a specified
external-debt program, possibly with adjustments it intends to negotiate
with external creditors.   Finally, suppose that the government has
programming assumptions for real GDP growth, inflation, exchange rate,
population growth, and other macroeconomic variables, and also for such
exogenous variables as the growth rates of export and import prices, the
world price level, the real world-commerce volume, and LIBOR (as
discussed in Chapter 3).

Under these assumptions, how would the government's external
and internal debt burden, and in particular its interest bill, evolve? Given
the programmed future net external-borrowing flow, how large would the
implied flow of net *internal* government debt be?   Could the internal
financial markets absorb the projected net government-borrowing flow at
the assumed interest rates?   Would the public sector's overall debt
position be "sustainable" in these circumstances?   That is, over the
projection period, would the government's debt-service burden have to
remain at or rise to high percentages of GDP, or even grow explosively?

In a conventional fiscal-accounts presentation for a given time
interval, the "above-the-line" accounts show revenue inflows and
expenditure outflows. If negative, the difference between total outflows

and inflows — the "deficit" — must be *financed*; if positive, the difference — the "surplus" — must be *applied*. A deficit can be financed from external and internal sources. External sources include net borrowing, net sales of external assets, and net withdrawals from external deposit accounts. Internal sources include net borrowing, net sales of internal assets, and net withdrawals from internal deposit accounts — these last including the government's accounts at the central bank and other commercial banks. A surplus can be applied in external and internal placements. External placements include net repayment of loans, net purchases of external assets, and net external deposits. Internal placements include net repayment of loans, net purchases of internal assets, and net internal deposits. Net borrowing may be further divided into "contractual" and "non-contractual" (i.e., arrears) flows.

The fiscal financing accounts — the "below-the-line" fiscal accounts — are best presented in transparently structured accounts. There are different ways to organize them, but it is usually advisable to divide financing flows into the two broad categories of external and internal financing. Each of these broad categories could then have the sub-categories of net borrowing, net asset sales, and net deposit withdrawals, with net borrowing further divided into contractual" and non-contractual flows.[74]

Suppose a government has set out an expenditure program, as discussed in Chapter 4 above. To finance it, it must use a combination of taxation and financing (including external grants). Some of the financing would be covered by identified net external and internal borrowing. Chapter 5 above describes techniques to program such net borrowing. To complete the discussion of fiscal-accounts projection, then, this chapter discusses taxation and *unidentified* net internal borrowing.

---

[74] Anyone who has worked with many different countries' fiscal presentations has seen many different ways of presenting fiscal financing flows. In many cases they are organized haphazardly, showing lines that happen to be quantitatively (or politically) the most important lines and lumping all other financing flows into catch-all categories. Clear and comprehensive presentations are obviously helpful for analysis of any kind, and essential for projection work.

The fiscal-projection methodology presented here is quite similar to the procedure used for the external accounts. For each year, the exercise sets out by applying the macroeconomic assumptions to project government revenue. The government's non-interest expenditure and external-financing programs are as given (see Chapters 4 and 5). The government's "identified" internal financing flows are projected using assumptions, in ways discussed in Section 5.5 above. The external and internal interest bills are calculated on the basis of interest-rate assumptions applied to the average debt stocks over each year, calculated as the arithmetic average of the initial and year-end debt stocks.

Taken together, the overall government deficit these projections imply for the year could turn out either greater or less than the financing "identified" as forthcoming from external and internal sources. If the deficit exceeds the identified financing, additional, "unidentified" internal borrowing would be needed to cover the gap. If the deficit is less than the projected deficit financing, an addition to government deposits — "unprogrammed" deposit accumulation — would take place to close the (negative) gap. To take account of the "valuation change" in the debt stock resulting from such events as debt forgiveness and changes in the exchange rates of loan currencies *vis-a-vis* the U.S. dollar, the procedure adjusts the previous year-end debt stocks by the assumed percentage changes before adding in the net borrowing over the year to obtain the year-end stock.

The "residual" unidentified borrowing or unprogrammed deposit accumulation may then be evaluated to determine the projection's feasibility. If the additional internal borrowing required is "large," the analyst might conclude that the fiscal projection would not be feasible, and must be revised. If the unprogrammed deposit accumulation is "large," the analyst could conclude either that the government could borrow less than had been identified, or that fiscal policy could be more expansionary than assumed thus far.

As with the external accounts, it is helpful to refer to two "financing gaps" for each year, the "unadjusted" and the "adjusted." The *unadjusted* gap is the amount which, when added to any of the revenue accounts or subtracted from any of the (non-interest) expenditure accounts, would make the projected deficit equal to the sum of *identified* net borrowing from external and internal sources (including asset reductions). That is, for any given year's projection, if this unadjusted gap were subtracted from the programmed developmental expenditure, or added to revenue, the government's "debt-management" objective would be met. The *adjusted* gap is the amount that would have to be added to internal financing to make the projected deficit equal the sum of identified net borrowing from external and internal sources. These will differ, in general, because the *adjusted* gap takes account of the additional intra-year interest arising from the unprogrammed net addition to the debt stock.

Section 8.2 of this chapter describes some relatively simple "macro-level" revenue-projection techniques. Section 8.3 describes the fiscal-accounts reconciliation procedure in algebraic terms. Section 8.4 describes how the projections can be carried out and consolidated for different public-sector entities. Finally, Section 8.5 discusses the fiscal aspects of the "Pacífica" exercise.

To simplify the discussion, assume until Section 8.4 below that the government is "unitary," with no "sub-national" government entities, no public enterprises, and no public pensions system. One problem that arises when analyzing fiscal performance and formulating projections is that for many economies the public-sector goes beyond the central government, and macroeconomic projections may be incomplete without the performance of various sub-national governments and state enterprises. Over the past few decades, with encouragement from the International Monetary Fund, many nations' economic authorities have developed comprehensive non-financial public-sector accounts for macroeconomic programming and monitoring. Some nations have even programmed and monitored the profits and losses of their central banks and other financial institutions.

In economies where the central government is relatively large, it may be useful enough to focus on the central government's deficit alone. It is important to remember, however, that the government accounts of the national accounts incorporate expenditure by all government entities. Consistency with the national accounts accordingly requires that the public accounts incorporate all government expenditure.

8.2 Government-revenue projections

Government-revenue structures differ from economy to economy, and the appropriate projection techniques therefore vary somewhat. This section describes several more or less generic techniques that can be used to project different kinds of revenue flow.

A tax authority would require a highly detailed monthly projection exercise, but the government-revenue aspect of a multiannual macroeconomic projection exercise can be much less elaborate. Thus, for example, a revenue authority may need to project the largest companies' performance, possibly company by company. In contrast, the government-revenue part of a macroeconomic projection exercise is likely to be most useful with a more aggregated, less detailed structure than a revenue authority would use. (In this aspect of a macroeconomic projection exercise as in others, increasing detail implies the need to formulate additional assumptions, and the more assumptions that must be set, the harder the exercise will be to apply practically under deadline pressures.)

The following is one useful classification scheme for the various sources of government revenue:

"Non-hydrocarbons" revenue:
    Tax revenue:
        Tax revenue from internal sources:
            Direct taxes:
                Income taxes:
                    Personal income tax
                    Companies tax
                Property taxes
            Indirect taxes:
                Taxes on specific goods and services:
                    Excises
                    Other specific taxes
                Value-added tax on internal sources

Tax revenue from external sources:
  Export levies
  Import tariffs
  Value-added tax on imports
Non-tax revenue:
  Non-financial receipts:
    Transfers from other government entities
    Earnings from publicly-owned companies
    Other non-financial receipts
  Financial receipts:
    Interest earnings from deposits and other assets
    Other financial receipts
"Hydrocarbons" revenue:
  Contractual royalties
  Taxes on production and exports

This classification is intended to be generically applicable to all government levels, from the national to the "sub-national" (regional, provincial, municipal). In principle, any kind of government could receive revenue under any of these categories. In practice, of course — for example — sub-national governments are more likely to collect property taxes and national governments are more likely to collect import levies. In some economies, different governments share revenue flows, according to legislation and policy rules.

Also, in this classification the expression "hydrocarbons revenue" is intended as a somewhat broader idea. Many governments earn significant revenues from natural resources and other specific natural "endowments" their economies enjoy. The earnings come through special kinds of tax, profits, royalties, and other special flows. In general, projections of revenue in such categories require specific techniques that are often difficult to characterize in generic terms. For most governments, of course, taxation is the basic, conventional non-oil revenue source. Even economies that have significant oil-export revenues are likely to derive significant revenue flows from more "conventional" kinds of tax. This apart, though, some nations have unusual revenue sources. The governments of Panamá and Egypt, for example, receive substantial revenue from canal tolls.

Under the tax-revenue category, one basic distinction classifies receipts into those from internal sources and those from external sources. Internal revenue flows may be classified in turn into "direct" and "indirect" levies. Direct levies are those based on persons' and companies' income and property, while indirect levies are those based on transactions.

Revenue from direct taxes — income and property taxes — may be projected on the basis of the projected values of the underlying variables that presumably drive them. The nominal income-tax flow, for example, may be projected by applying an assumed elasticity to projected nominal personal income, or, alternatively, nominal GDP. This could be done in different ways for the different kinds of income and property tax, depending on the characteristics of each type of tax. For a simple income-tax system, however, the elasticity approach is bound to be the most straightforward. If T represents nominal revenue and Y represents nominal GDP, then

$$1 + g_T = (1 + g_Y)^a,$$

where "a" is the elasticity of nominal revenue with respect to nominal GDP. If the income-tax system has no intra-annual withholding system, the nominal GDP on the right-hand-side of the formula above would be lagged one year, since the tax collected would be based on the previous year's results, so that

$$1 + g_T = [1 + g_{Y(-1)}]^a.$$

In an economy whose income-tax system is developing and improving, the value of "a" would exceed one, although it would presumably decline toward one as rates of development and improvement level off.[75]

---

[75]   For example, the elasticity could be projected to decline from its initial-projection-year value by some percentage each year until it reaches one.

Another reason the value of "a" could exceed one is that the economy may be undergoing "formalization," with a rising proportion of income flowing through taxable rather than informal channels. For any economy for which informality is significant, it may be useful to rewrite the preceding formula:

$$1 + g_T = [(1 + g_f)\,(1 + g_Y)]^a,$$

where "f" is simply the percentage of overall GDP in formal sectors. The value of g_f — that is, the pace of formalization — would then be a projection assumption.

If the income-tax system is progressive but tax brackets are not index-linked, the income-tax yield would increase as the price level rose, because nominal incomes would rise into higher brackets. That is, the elasticity of the income-tax yield with respect to the price level would be greater than one. This may be represented by rewriting the basic formula above to

$$1 + g_T = [(1 + g_y)\,(1 + g_p)^w]^a,$$

where "w" would be greater than one. (Indexation of income-tax brackets should largely eliminate this "bracket drift.")

A different approach is likely to work better for projecting ***value-added and general sales taxes***. Value-added-tax receipts, for example, may be projected for each year by applying the basic tax rate and a "collection-efficiency" factor to projected nominal GDP. If T (now) represents the value-added tax revenue flow, "t" the tax rate, and Y nominal GDP, then "q" would be defined by

$$q = T/(t\,Y),$$

so that

$$T = q\,t\,Y.$$

If "q" were equal to one, the value-added tax would effectively be paid on the total GDP flow. In general, the collection efficiency of a value-added tax will be considerably less than one.[76] The proceeds of any tax with a specified rate and a more or less definable "tax base" can be projected using this "collection-efficiency" approach. Higher values of the collection-efficiency factor would presumably come about through more rigorous tax administration and reduction of the kinds of transaction exempted from the tax. A projection exercise could assume a rising — or, if the circumstances warrant, a diminishing — value for the collection-efficiency factor. Since a rising tax rate may encourage evasion and avoidance, the yield from raising a value-added tax rate could be offset in part by a drop in collection efficiency. A "conservative" projection exercise should take account of this reality.

Value-added taxes generally apply to imports as well as internal transactions. For many economies, imports are disproportionately significant as sources of value-added revenue, basically because they are collected at the same times and places as customs duties. That is, all other things being equal, value-added tax has a higher collection efficiency when collected on imports than on other goods and services. It is useful to project proceeds from "internal" transactions and from imports separately, with collection-efficiency factors applying to GDP and to import flows respectively. The projected year-average exchange rate will figure in the determination of the value-added revenue from imports.

For **excise taxes**, different approaches may be appropriate. Again, a tax authority would want to maintain projections of the value flows of transactions in specific commodities subject to excises, then project the revenue flows using productivities appropriate to each type of excise. Thus, for example, if it collects an excise on beer, the authority could project (i) the value of beer consumption (based on projections of beer prices and quantities consumed), (ii) the beer-excise rate, and (iii) the collection efficiency (typically fairly high, since excises are almost always collected at factories). Indeed, a revenue authority is

---

[76] In developing economies, a domestic value-added tax collection efficiency exceeding 35 per cent would be fairly high, although some small Caribbean economies have even higher rates. For some economies, productivities in the range 20–30 per cent must be considered satisfactory.

likely to find it useful to carry out such projections in detail — for example, at regional levels. This kind of detail should be unnecessary, however, for the government-revenue aspect of a macroeconomic projection exercise. Instead, for excise receipts on consumption goods, a formulation such as

$$1 + g_T = (1 + g_C)^b,$$

where "b" is the elasticity of nominal revenue with respect to nominal non-government consumption, should work well enough. Again, a value of "b" higher than one could be used to represent the idea that the tax authority is increasing its collection effectiveness. (Since excise taxes are usually levied at points of production, there should be no need to reflect issues of formality and informality.)

In high-inflation economies, real tax yields may be significantly reduced by the purchasing-power depreciation of the monetary unit over the "collection lag," i.e., the period between a "taxable event" and the moment the tax is paid (known as the Olivera-Tanzi effect in honor of two noted analysts who drew attention to it — see Olivera 1967 and Tanzi 1977). Suppose that a given tax is subject to a collection lag of "m" months, and suppose that its yield as a percentage of GDP would be R^+/Y if the price level were perfectly stable. With annual inflation running at g_p over the period, the actual revenue flow as a percentage of GDP would be given by

$$R/Y = (R^+/Y)/[(1 + g_p)^{(m/12)}].$$

Having the revenue flows adjusted for inflation in this way enables the revenue projection to reflect the favorable consequences of reduced inflation.

The sources of **non-tax revenue** vary from country to country and by level of government. They may include various types of user fee — charges for such services as civil registry, legal documents, passports, drivers' licenses, and the like. Revenues of this kind may be projected to grow in real terms at the rate of population growth. They may include transferred profits from publicly-owned enterprises. These may be projected to grow at the same rate as nominal GDP, but, if the amounts in question are significant, it may be useful to project the enterprises' performance in detail (see Section 8.4 below). In addition, they may include financial earnings. If the government in question has interest-bearing deposit accounts, or possesses interest-bearing financial securities, their yields should also be included in the government's non-tax revenue flows (see Section 8.4 below).

Revenue from taxes on external transactions may be projected in ways similar to those for internal revenue. Thus, tariff receipts may be projected by applying the tariff rates to the different kinds of merchandise import set out in the import accounts (see Section 6.4). (Non-oil export-tax proceeds, if any, may be projected in similar ways.) The collection-efficiency technique may be applied for tariff and export-tax proceeds. Thus, suppose that a particular class of import carries a tariff rate of "t" and the U.S. dollar flow of such imports over a year is given by Q^*. If tariff were paid on *all* imports in this class, the proceeds would total tQ^* for the year. In reality, the proceeds would be somewhat lower, tqQ^*, where "q" is between zero and one, on account of administrative imperfections and exemptions. Projection assumptions for the collection-efficiency factor "q" could be set for all imports in the aggregate or separately for each kind of import.

For oil-exporting economies, it is obviously essential to project *oil-export revenue*. Realistic projection of oil revenues is intricate, not just because of the difficulties of projecting oil prices and volumes exported, but because the contracts that determine tax and royalty receipts, and especially the sharing of earnings, tend to be complicated. Matters are further complicated if earnings are shared between foreign and internal producing companies. In addition, revenue-flow projections must take account of exogenously projected production from existing, new, and even unproven oil reserves.

If the government applies a fixed percentage tax or royalty rate to oil exports, the national-currency equivalent of this revenue flow may be projected by multiplying the tax rate and the exchange rate by the oil-export proceeds. This is unlikely to be the case, however. If there is no single fixed percentage rate, it may be easiest to work using an assumed elasticity: the dollar revenue flow would grow by

$$g_{R*} = (1 + g_{V*})^h - 1,$$

where R* is the U.S. dollar revenue flow and V* the dollar value of oil exports, and "h" is the elasticity of revenue in U.S. dollars with respect to the dollar value of oil exports.

Finally, at least two additional categories of inflow to governments may be projected. Neither, strictly speaking, are "revenues" in the usual sense. One is *external grants*. Some fiscal accounts' systems show external grants above the line in the fiscal accounts, either as "revenue" or as inflows separate from revenue. External grants may also be shown below the line, however, as a financing flow, albeit a financing flow that produces no change in government assets or liabilities and generates no interest liability. External grants can be projected by setting out assumed growth rates in their dollar value, or by assuming that they will flow at some constant, rising, or diminishing percentage of GDP. For an economy for which the external-grants flow is significant, it may be best to formulate the projection at least for "nearer-term" projection years on the basis of detailed information from the governments and other international entities that provide them.

It is important, of course, to ensure that the external-grants projections in the fiscal accounts are consistent with those in the external accounts. Not all "official transfers" into the economy go to government: some may go to non-government entities (in recent years, for example, the United States Agency for International Development has been providing relatively large aid flows to non-government entities). Moreover, those going to government may flow to sub-national governments.

Another kind of inflow to governments is *capital revenues*. These include proceeds of sales of government-owned capital assets, including infrastructure facilities, land, equity in state-owned companies, and so on. Again, some accounting systems show these as revenues, or as a separate type of inflow along with revenue, above the line in the fiscal accounts. They may also be shown below the line, however, as financing flows — in this instance, financing flows that produce no change in the government's *financial* assets and liabilities. One argument for placing such capital revenues below the line is their "non-recurrent" character. For any year in which such flows occurred, if recorded above the line, they might give a misleadingly optimistic indication of the government surplus — so the argument goes. (For this reason, if such flows are included above the line, it is best to calculate the surplus with and without them.) Because of their non-recurrent nature, capital revenues can be difficult to project. If a government has plans for asset sales — say, a scheduled privatization program — this can be used to formulate a projection, although proceeds can be difficult to guess even in the near term.[77]

8.3   *Reconciling above- and below-the-line fiscal projections*

Having projected the "above-" and "below-the-line" government accounts for any future year, where the above-the-line accounts are total expenditure less total revenue and the below-the-line accounts are net financing, the fiscal-accounts reconciliation procedure consists of calculating the "unidentified" borrowing or "unprogrammed" accumulation of deposit balances necessary to close the "gap" between them. As in the external-accounts projection (see Section 7.3 above), interest due on the unidentified borrowing, or earned on the unprogrammed deposit accumulation, must be taken into account. (The fiscal and external accounts differ slightly in this regard, because the "above-" and "below-the-line" accounts structures differ: the financing flows are above the line in the balance of payments but below the line in the fiscal accounts.)

---

[77]   Governments may prefer not to publish projections of proceeds from asset sales they are about to carry out, to avoid revealing their expectations to potential purchasers.

To describe the procedure algebraically, define the following variables:

T   tax revenue from internal sources;

T*   tax revenue from external sources (mainly import levies; in U.S. dollars);

N   non-tax revenue from internal sources;

N*   non-tax revenue from external sources (in U.S. dollars);

D'   year-end internal government-debt stock;

D*'   year-end external government-debt stock (in U.S. dollars);

A'   year-end government holdings of assets other than deposits at the central bank;

Q'   year-end deposit balance at the central bank;

R, R* interest due on internal and external debt;

r, r* year-average interest rates on internal and external debt;

F   interest received on internal assets;

f   year-average interest rates on internal assets;

J   government developmental expenditure;

H   government non-developmental expenditure;

v, v* percentage valuation change in the internal and external debt stocks over the year; and

e   average exchange rate (national currency per U.S. dollar).

(The prime sign indicates year-end values; the asterisk indicates values in U.S. dollars). Each year's unadjusted financing gap is given by the difference between the above- and below-the-line accounts,

A - **B** respectively, where

$$A = \{[J + H + R] + [R^*/e]\} - \{[N + T + F] + [(F^* + T^*)/e]\},$$

(i.e., the "above-the-line" accounts, expenditure less revenue); and

$$B = [\Delta D' + (\Delta D^{*\prime}/e)] - [\Delta A' + \Delta Q'],$$

(i.e., the "below-the-line," net-financing accounts, the net increase in borrowing less the net increase in asset holdings), where

$$\Delta Q' = Q' - Q'_{-1}, \ \Delta A' = A' - A^{*'}_{-1}, \ \Delta D' = D' - D'_{-1},$$

and

$$\Delta D^{*'} = D^{*'} - D^{*'}_{-1}.$$

Suppose first that **A-B** is greater than zero, so unidentified borrowing would be needed to reconcile the above- and below-the-line projections. Let "r" represent the interest rate on new loan disbursements. It can be shown that unidentified borrowing of equal to $(\mathbf{A\text{-}B})/[1 - (r/2)]$ would reconcile the above- and below-the-line projections. Since the below-the-line projection would increase by $(\mathbf{A\text{-}B})/[1 - (r/2)]$ as a consequence of the disbursement but the above- the-line projection would decrease by $(r/2) (\mathbf{A\text{-}B})/[1 - (r/2)]$ on account of the increase in interest due, the above-the-line projection would diminish to

$$A - (r/2) \, (A\text{-}B)/[1 - (r/2)]$$

while the below-the-line projection would increase to

$$B + (A\text{-}B)/[1 - (r/2)],$$

which would be precisely equal.

Suppose next that **B-A** is greater than zero, so that an unprogrammed increase in government deposits would be needed to reduce total net financing so as to reconcile the two projections. Let "r" now represent the interest rate the government earns on deposits. It can be shown that an unprogrammed addition of $(\mathbf{B\text{-}A})/[1 - (r/2)]$ to deposits would reconcile the above- and below-the-line projections. Since the addition to deposits would reduce below-the-line projection by $(\mathbf{B\text{-}A})/[1 - (r/2)]$ while the increase in interest due would increase the above- the-line projection by $(r/2) (\mathbf{B\text{-}A})/[1 - (r/2)]$, the above-the-line projection would rise to

$$A + (r/2) \, (B\text{-}A)/[1 - (r/2)]$$

while the below-the-line projection would diminish to

$$B - (B\text{-}A)/[1 - (r/2)],$$

which would be precisely equal.[78]

As with the external-accounts projections, it may be desirable to set up a more complex procedure for closing the fiscal financing gap (see Section 7.3). For any projection year, the idea would be to meet any positive *ex ante* financing requirement first by drawing from the accumulated unprogrammed deposit stock (augmented by interest earnings on the deposit stock during half the year), and then having unidentified borrowing only to the extent the financing gap exceeds the previous year-end unprogrammed deposit stock (and interest earned on it). More specifically, if the financing "gap" in year t *exceeds* the previous year-end deposit stock (and interest earned on it), unprogrammed deposits would fall to zero in year t and unidentified borrowing would cover the remainder of the gap; if the financing gap in year t *is less than* the previous year-end unprogrammed deposit stock (and interest earned on it), unprogrammed deposits would decline only by the amount of the financing gap and no unidentified borrowing would be needed. (If the financing gap in year t is negative, unprogrammed deposits could rise by the negative amount of the financing gap.)

Again, as with the external accounts, if it makes sense to set the projection exercise so any *positive* financing gap in year t is covered first by drawing down accumulated unprogrammed deposits, it might also make sense to have any *negative* financing gap applied first to pay down accumulated unidentified debt in year t-1, with whatever remained then being added to the unprogrammed deposit stock. Again, as with the external accounts, if the projection exercise has *both* these procedures are in place — that is, if any positive financing gap is financed first by

---

[78] This can be seen by multiplying both expressions by $[1 - (r/2)]$. The above-the-line expression becomes

$$A [1 - (r/2)] + (r/2) (B\text{-}A) = A + (r/2) B$$

while the below-the-line expression becomes

$$B [1 - (r/2)] - (B\text{-}A) = A + (r/2) B.$$

drawing down accumulated unprogrammed deposits and any negative financing gap is applied first to pay down accumulated unidentified debt — it would be impossible for *both* the accumulated unprogrammed deposit stock *and* the unidentified debt stock to end the same projection year greater than zero. In any projection year, at least one of these two stocks would have to be zero.

As with the external accounts, this can be exploited to program the procedure for closing each year's financing gap. If the *unprogrammed deposit stock* in year t-1 exceeds zero (and the unidentified debt stock is therefore zero), the closure procedure for year t would be based on the unprogrammed deposit stock: any positive *ex ante* financing requirement would be met by drawing from the unprogrammed deposit stock (and interest earned on it during year t), and then having unidentified borrowing only to the extent the financing gap exceeds the previous year-end deposit stock (and interest earned on it during year t). On the other hand, if the *unidentified debt stock* in year t-1 exceeds zero (and the unprogrammed deposit stock is therefore zero), the closure procedure would be based on the unidentified debt stock: the negative value of any *ex ante* financing gap would be applied to pay down the unidentified debt stock, and any remainder would be added to the unprogrammed deposit stock.

8.4   *Taking account of disaggregated public-sector entities*

This chapter has assumed thus far that the government is "unitary," i.e., that the public sector consists of a single government. Most countries, however, have "sub-national" governments — regional, provincial, or municipal governments — with financial structures separate from, if not fully independent of, the central government. In addition, many countries have publicly-owned financial and non-financial enterprises. Publicly-owned financial enterprises include central banks, specialized development-finance institutions, and publicly-owned commercial banks. Non-financial public-sector enterprises range from oil producers and distributors to electricity generators and telephone services. Although many have been "privatized" in recent decades, a relatively large number of enterprises remain partially or wholly in public ownership. Finally, many governments have what may be generically described as "separate government entities." They are not enterprises, but they are nevertheless financially separate from the governments to which they belong. These typically include regulatory agencies, universities, cultural institutions, and special administrative agencies. One especially important type of agency in this category is public-pension institutions. (Annex 8.4 describes a more or less general public-sector structure, and Figure 11 shows a generic public-sector structure in diagrammatic form.)

Figure 11. Diagram: A generic public-sector structure

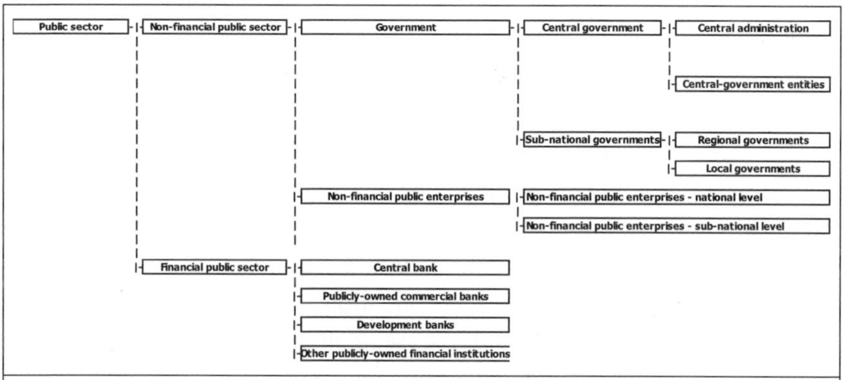

Source: Annex 8.4

(1) *The central-administration accounts* in a non-unitary government system would be structured and projected essentially as described in Section 8.2. The main difference the existence of other government entities would make is that the central administration's revenue accounts could include transfers from, and the expenditure accounts would include transfers to, those other entities. These transfers would be structured and based on assumptions appropriate to each economy's particular circumstances and rules. For example, existing policies and laws might require a central government to transfer a particular percentage of its tax revenue to sub-national governments (assumptions regarding future values of the percentage could be varied in sensitivity analyses). A central government might subsidize the national pensions system (see

below). Particular taxes may be shared between the central and sub-
national governments: for example, total receipts from a value-added tax
could be shared in a ratio of (say) 80–20 between the central and (say)
provincial and municipal governments.

A non-unitary government system would have financial accounts
for each government unit, each with their own revenues, expenditures
and financing flows. "Separate" entities belonging to a central
administration, for example, while part of the central government in an
organizational sense, would have their own financial administration.
Their staff remuneration, for example, would be separate from that of the
central administration. While the central administration might provide
transfers to such entities, they might also have their own revenue
sources. For example, public universities may collect and retain student
fees, which they would retain and use rather than transfer to the central
administration.

Accounts corresponding to a central administration and its
separate entities could, in principle, be consolidated. That is, the central-
administration accounts could be consolidated with the accounts of the
separate central-government entities into a single set of overall central-
government accounts. In the consolidation process, transfers between
the central administration and the separate government agencies, or
among the agencies, would "net" out. The consolidated accounts would
show the government's total revenue and expenditure, rather than just the
part corresponding to the central administration, and would also include
any net financing flows to the separate entities. In many economies,
however, such accounting consolidation may be difficult, possibly
because accounting systems may be incompatible. Many governments
therefore simply budget and project the central-administration accounts,
without attempting to consolidate the independent entities' accounts, and
report and project central-administration transfers to the separate entities.
These transfers may provide a fair order-of-magnitude estimate of the
activities of the entities, but some information is undoubtedly lost: the
separate entities' staff remuneration, goods-and-services expenditure,
revenue, and financing flows would simply not appear in the historical or
projected government accounts.

(2) *Sub-national government accounts* could also be structured and projected, in much the same way as the central government's accounts. (Unlike the central government's separate agencies, sub-national governments are likely to be completely separate governments. In countries where the central government directly governs regions and municipalities, the government entities at the regional and provincial level should not be described as "sub-national governments," although they may function as (financially) "separate entities," receive central-administration "transfers," and have some "own" revenues.) Sub-national governments' expenditures are likely to be for staff and goods and services, and possibly for transfers to separate entities of their own. Some sub-national governments may even own enterprises and receive their dividends. Sub-national governments may raise their own revenue, and may receive central-government transfers. Their financing options may be more limited than those of the central government, but they may include a fairly wide range of possibilities, sometimes including external borrowing.

When projecting sub-national governments' accounts, care must be taken to ensure consistency with other government accounts. Thus, projected transfers to sub-national governments in the central-administration expenditure accounts should be consistent with the corresponding projected receipts in the consolidated sub-national government accounts.[79] For different economies, it may be useful to represent sub-national government accounts in the aggregate or with some disaggregation. For example, quantitatively significant provinces or municipalities could be separately projected.

(3) *Public-enterprise accounts* present a somewhat different set of issues from those of government accounts, both in general and in particular economies' specific circumstances. The first point to note is that the

---

[79] In some economies, transfers from the central government destined for sub-national governments are made to a special fund, and this fund then makes transfers to the sub-national governments. In this case, in any given year, transfers made by the central government might not add up precisely to those received by the sub-national governments.

financial significance of the "bottom-line" flow accounts for non-financial public enterprises differs somewhat from that of governments. A government deficit is the net amount the government must borrow or draw down from its net financial-asset holdings — i.e., the net increase in the government's *net liability position* — over a given time interval. An enterprise's "loss," however, is the amount by which its activities reduce its *net worth* over a given time interval. It would be possible to define an enterprise deficit so as to be conceptually consistent with that of the government — the enterprise's net borrowing less the reduction in its asset position. But while it is often presumed that a higher government deficit indicates "worsening" fiscal performance, there is less likely to be such a presumption about an enterprise's net borrowing. A publicly-owned company is likely, like any enterprise, to borrow to finance capital formation.

One way in which public enterprises differ from private enterprises generally is that profitability may not matter so much for public enterprises. For one obvious example, since a central bank tends to reduce its profitability when it tightens monetary policy (see Section 9.3 below), it would not be sensible to use profitability indicators to evaluate a central bank's performance, much less its staff performance. Other public enterprises may have "missions" that imply limitations to their profitability, such as adequate provision of electrical power throughout an economy, or communications services. It is important to remember, though, that decapitalization will make it difficult for any enterprise, even a public enterprise, to carry on. Accordingly, even when a public enterprise has a basic mission besides profitability, it must nevertheless monitor its profitability and net worth, and take steps to ensure their adequacy.

Many governments calculate a summary indicator of overall public-sector financial performance by adding the non-financial public enterprises' consolidated operating losses (i.e., losses excluding "non-operating" earnings from financial assets, government subsidies, and the like) to the conventional government deficit. Some governments even include the central bank's profit or loss flow. The International Monetary Fund has used such indicators for its programs with some economies. It is worth remembering, though, that such measures, whatever else they show, would not be equal to the reduction in the non-financial public sector's net liability position.

In general, non-financial public-enterprise accounts may be analyzed and projected using methods used for business entities. Analyses and projections of public-enterprise performance (like any corporate performance) may be complicated where public enterprises use unconventional accounting procedures. Some public enterprises operate on a fully commercial basis, more or less as they would if they were in the private sector; others operate as though they were ministries involving business activities. The discussion following summarizes a projection procedure that can be used with a bare minimum of information regarding public-enterprise accounts. Ideally, the analysis would be carried out for each public enterprise, or for groups of public enterprises in the same line of business. It could also be carried out for an economy's public enterprises on a consolidated basis, although this would be more difficult and perhaps less credible.

To formulate non-financial public-enterprise performance projections, it helps to divide the flow accounts into operating and non-operating categories. The precise determinants of the projected accounts will depend on specific characteristics of the enterprises and the economy. Generalizing, however, under the operating accounts, (i) sales volumes may be related to real GDP through assumed elasticities; (ii) unit prices may be governed by policy formulas, related to world prices or and to the internal price level through assumed elasticities; (iii) employment levels may be determined in relation to sales volume, or taken to grow through assumed public-sector employment policies; (iv) input costs may be determined in relation to sales volume; and so on. Non-operating accounts may include transfers and subsidies of various kinds, as well as interest earnings and interest charges on assets and liabilities. They may also include the capital budget — i.e., expenditure on new plant and equipment, non-recurring maintenance and repair charges, and so on.

"Below the line" in the flow accounts, public enterprises' financing requirements would be met through net external and internal borrowing, payments arrears, reductions in financial-asset holdings (such as deposit accounts), and reductions in inventory and fixed-asset holdings. That is, the enterprises' flow balance sheets effectively describe the financing of their operating and non-operating deficits. This may be understood by noting that — abstracting from recapitalization and or dividend receipts — the deficit would equal the reduction in the enterprises' consolidated net worth. The reduction in the enterprises' consolidated net worth would in turn equal the increase in the enterprises' total liabilities less the increase in their total assets.

A methodology similar to that used to determine the government deficit may be applied to determine the public enterprises' net deficit, either separately or in the aggregate. Simplifying, *here only*, let M' represent the enterprises' overall year-end cash position, A' their year-end stock of inventories and fixed assets, L' their year-end outstanding liability stock, and V' their year-end consolidated net worth. Let S represent the above-the-line surplus for the year. Then

$$S = \Delta V' = \Delta M' + \Delta A' - \Delta L'.$$

Let Z represent the part of the surplus excluding interest earned on cash or paid on liabilities, m the interest rate on cash, and i the interest rate on liabilities. Then

$$Z + m\,M - i\,L = \Delta M' + \Delta A' - \Delta L',$$

where M and L are, respectively, the average stocks of cash and liabilities outstanding over the period.

Since $M = M'_{-1} + (\Delta M'/2)$ *and* $L = L'_{-1} + (\Delta L'/2),$

$$Z + m\,M'_{-1} - i\,L'_{-1} = \{\Delta M' [1 - (m/2)]\} + \Delta A' - \{\Delta L' [1 - (i/2)]\}.$$

The values of $\Delta M'$ and $\Delta L'$ could each be taken to have an assumed, or *programmed*, component and a *residual* (or *unprogrammed*) component. The residual component would be non-zero for one or the other, according to whether the equation must be closed by increasing the enterprises' cash position (i.e., the financing gap is negative) or by increasing their outstanding debt (i.e., the financing gap is positive).

Assume for the moment that the programmed components are both zero. The equation above may be solved for $\Delta M'$ or for $\Delta L'$:

$$\Delta M' = [1 - (m/2)] \{Z + m M'_{-1} - i L'_{-1} - \Delta A'\},$$

if

$$Z + m M'_{-1} - i L'_{-1} - \Delta A' > 0, \text{ or}$$

$$\Delta L' = -[1 - (i/2)] \{Z + m M'_{-1} - i L'_{-1} - \Delta A'\}$$

if

$$Z + m M'_{-1} - i L'_{-1} - \Delta A' < 0.$$

A public-enterprise projection must also take account of capital contributions and dividend payments, as well as any taxes that may fall on profit flows. In all, the profit flow adjusted for taxes, dividend payments and capital contributions gives the flow change in the enterprise's capital position. One of the purposes of the projection would be to ensure that the enterprise's capital position will grow as necessary — say, toward or to a specified capital-GDP ratio.

(4) *Public pensions systems'* (i.e., social-security systems') financial performance may also be projected. The structures of pension-system accounts differ significantly from those of government accounts. Analysis and projection of public-pension systems is one of the more intricate aspects of public finances, involving the complexities of demographics and, in most systems, country-specific policies and rules. Because some pension systems constitute significant proportions of overall public expenditure (notably in eastern Europe), because many countries have had to undertake complex pension reforms, and because their finances can be vulnerable to exogenous developments, it is important for many economies to include them in projection analyses of overall public-sector finances. Since the focus of interest for macroeconomic projection is narrowly on their finances, however, it is usually reasonable enough to make use of relatively simple projection techniques.

A pension system's basic operations consist, under the inflow accounts, of contributions and, under the outflow accounts, of benefit payments. Basic determinants of a pension system's operations accordingly include the growth rates of (i) the number of contributors, (ii) each contributor's average annual contribution, (iii) the number of beneficiaries, and (iv) the average annual benefit. Annual projections can be constructed straightforwardly from these four categories of assumption. To the extent the assumptions can be made more detailed — i.e., to the extent the four sets of growth rates can be set out for different groups and cohorts of contributors, and to the extent growth rates of contributors and beneficiaries can be determined through demographic analysis — they can be made more meaningful and credible. Projections of contributors and contributions should distinguish the public and private sectors, since the public-sector expenditure projections would include social-security contributions.

In addition to these basic operational flows, a projection of a public-pensions system's revenue side could also include (a) transfers (apart from contributions) received from governments and (b) interest and other earnings on the system's holdings of financial assets. Expenditures would include administrative costs (which may be linked to the number of contributors and beneficiaries) and interest due on amounts borrowed by the system itself. Projection of the financing lines is similar to the projection of any other public-sector entity: projected flows of assets and liabilities give rise to changes in the corresponding stocks, and hence to interest flows.

As in the case of any other public-sector entity, the fundamental question is whether the financing flows implied by the projections are feasible. For many pension systems, the pension deficit would presumably be financed by a government subsidy. In this case, it is the projected government deficit, including the government subsidy to the pension system, that would be examined for feasibility: the higher the required subsidy, the more likely the government deficit would be too high, and so unfeasible.

Finally, **(5)** *publicly-owned financial institutions* play important roles in most economies. Thus far, this chapter's discussion has focused on the non-financial public sector. Most governments possess central banks, and many governments own commercial banks, development banks, housing banks, and other financial institutions. Section 9.3 below describes the projection of all aspects of a central bank's financial performance, including its profits and losses. Section 9.4 then discusses the projection of commercial banks' operations. The aim is to project the operations of the economy's entire commercial-banking system, but the approach can be applied to project any specific commercial bank's profitability, capital adequacy, and liquidity, including those of any publicly-owned commercial banks. (The Pacífica exercise incorporates no public-sector financial institution apart from that of the central bank.)

8.5   *Fiscal-accounts projections for "Pacífica"*

Table 20 lists the assumptions, in addition to the basic macroeconomic assumptions given in Table 2, on which the public-sector revenue projections are based. The revenue assumptions comprise tax rates, tax productivities,[80] elasticities of tax yields with respect to their bases, revenue flows as percentages of GDP, and so on. They also include the percentages in which the proceeds of particular taxes are allocated to different public-sector entities. (To save space, assumptions for expenditure and financing of other governments, public enterprises, and the public-pension system are omitted here.)

One key revenue assumption concerns the value-added tax rate. Having perceived the likelihood that fiscal deficits would increase over coming years, policy-makers had been considering two-percentage-point increase in the value-added tax rate, from 12 per cent to 14 per cent. Imminent recession persuaded them to postpone making the proposal, because they believed the legislative if not the executive power would be unwilling to go along. They are still considering the consequences of securing the increase beginning in 2011, however, once recovery seems more likely. The base scenario assumes, however, that the value-added tax rate would remain unchanged over the projection period.

---

[80]   The collection efficiency of a tax whose yield flow is T, base is Y and rate is "t" is defined as T/tY. See Section 8.2.

The assumptions governing non-interest central-government expenditure and the resulting projections are given in Section 4.4. (Table 24 gives the summary non-interest expenditure accounts, from Table 8.) Table 21 gives the assumptions governing the financing of the central government. The first set of assumptions is drawn from the external-accounts assumptions (see Section 7.4 above). The (nominal) growth rates of the central bank's internal contractual debt and deposit stocks are given next. The (nominal) growth rates of the flow transfer of earnings from the central bank to the central government and of the central government's capital contributions to the central bank are drawn from the monetary-accounts assumptions (see Section 9.6 below). Assumptions regarding interest rates on the central government's internal contractual debt and deposits are set out in real terms, and reflated using the growth rate of consumer prices. Finally, the assumption regarding the valuation increase in external debt stocks is drawn from the external-accounts assumptions (see Section 7.4 above). The corresponding assumption for the stock of internal debt outstanding is the final line of this set of assumptions.

Table 22 shows Pacífica's projected overall government accounts and Table 23, Table 24 and Table 25 show the central-government accounts. Under the programmed macroeconomic objectives, Pacífica's general-government balance, which recorded a 2.2 per cent surplus in 2008, would remain close to balance throughout the projection period. The central government's finances, however, would show a deficit of about 2 per cent of GDP over the projection period. Revenue would be just under 21 and expenditure just under 23 per cent of GDP. The sub-national governments together would run a surplus of about 2 per cent of GDP over the projection period.

The central government's external-debt stock would decline slightly as a percentage of GDP, from 22 per cent in 2008 to 21.3 per cent in 2015. The internal-debt stock would rise as a percentage of GDP, from 23.5 per cent in 2008 to 27.9 per cent in 2015. The interest bill on the internal debt would rise from 1.2 per cent of GDP in 2008 to 1.4 per cent in 2015. Policy-makers feel this would be a relatively good outcome, given the conservative assumption that real GDP would diminish in 2009 and that recovery would thereafter take some time.

Figure 12. Pacífica: Central-government finances (per cent of GDP), 2008–2015

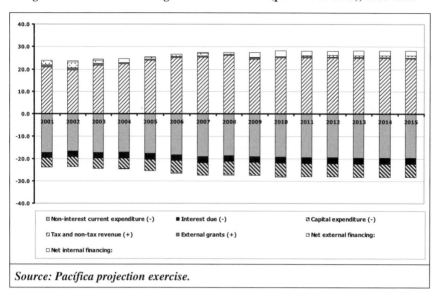

Source: Pacífica projection exercise.

Figure 13. Pacífica: Year-end government debt stocks (per cent of GDP), 2008–2015

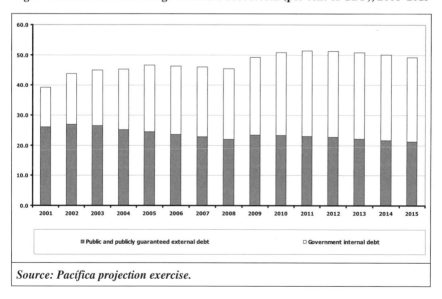

Source: Pacífica projection exercise.

Table 26 shows the central government's accounts in a "sources-and-uses" format, in per-capita U.S. dollars at 2005 prices and exchange rate. Because it is in per-capita real terms, this presentation shows clearly how the central government effectively transforms revenue and financing into expenditure. Per-capita non-interest expenditure would be 4.7 per cent higher in 2015 than in 2008, which should enable the government to sustain credible development and poverty-reduction efforts.

Figure 14. Pacífica: Macroeconomic-balance indicators (per cent of GDP), 2008–2015

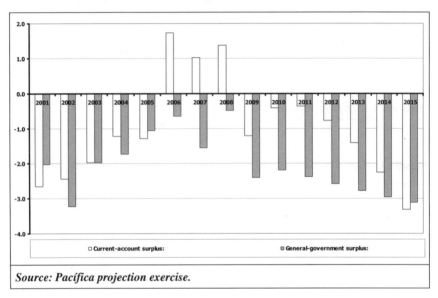

Source: *Pacífica projection exercise.*

9   Monetary-accounts projections

If something cannot go on forever, it will stop.
– attributed to the economist Herbert Stein[81]

9.1   *Introduction: Monetary-accounts projections*

A basic monetary projection may be formulated from base-year
monetary data by applying the macroeconomic assumptions, elements
from the fiscal-, national-, and external-accounts projections, and a set of
additional assumptions regarding monetary behavior. For each future
year, the idea would be to gauge whether the monetary-policy stance
necessary to bring about the macroeconomic assumptions would be
feasible.

This chapter describes a procedure for doing so. In broad terms,
the approach is similar to that applied for the other macroeconomic sub-
sectors. Focusing on the central bank's flow balance sheet, the objective
is to determine whether the authorities would have to issue an unfeasibly
large quantity of open-market instruments in order to ensure that the
money supply remained consistent with the overall programming
assumptions.

By its nature, monetary policy tends to be relatively short-term
in its objectives and focus. This is one reason why longer-term
macroeconomic programming analyses sometimes leave it aside,
focusing on the national, external and fiscal accounts. It is important,
nevertheless, to take account of monetary balance in the kinds of exercise
this book describes. A given macroeconomic policy program may seem
perfectly feasible from the perspective of the criteria discussed in earlier
chapters: the internal and external financing required for the fiscal and
external accounts may be available, and projected private consumption
may be adequate. The monetary projection analysis described in this
chapter asks, in effect, whether the monetary authority would, on
average, have to carry out excessively large doses of contractionary

---

[81]   See the *Economist*, August 2, 2003, p. 66.

policy to make the overall program work. If so, the inflation target might be too ambitious, and might need to be revised upward, to permit more money creation and hence smaller doses of monetary contraction. Alternatively, the foreign-exchange reserve accumulation implied by the external accounts might be too large, implying that the projected external accounts might need to be adjusted. Another possibility is that the central bank's projected net internal credit creation might be too high, and so require too much accommodating money creation.

Section 9.2 presents some of the basics of what has come to be known as "monetary programming." Section 9.3 describes how a monetary programming exercise can take account of a central bank's profit-and-loss account and other sources of capitalization (or decapitalization). (Annex 9.7 discusses conditions under which a central bank could sustain its capital-asset ratio.) Section 9.4 describes a methodology for projecting the performance, profitability, and liquidity of a commercial-banking system. Section 9.5 discusses the consolidated banking-system, or "monetary-survey," accounts. Finally, Section 9.6 discusses the Pacífica exercise's monetary-accounts projections. (Annex 9.6 describes how the programming targets of programs supported by International Monetary Fund operations are calculated.)

9.2   Monetary policy consistent with a given macroeconomic program

In principle, the point of a monetary-programming exercise is to estimate the policy action a monetary authority must carry out over a coming time period to drive the money supply to a value consistent with what the economy is projected to be willing to hold. The core of a monetary-programming exercise is a two-part consistency calculation. The first part determines the increase in the monetary base consistent with the amount of money the economy would be willing to hold — the "demand for money" — given policy-makers' targeted price-level, exchange-rate and real-GDP growth rates. (The "monetary base" is defined as the total stock of monetary liabilities issued by the central bank, including currency issues and commercial banks' deposits at the central bank.)

The second part applies the central bank's flow balance-sheet identity to determine the quantity and sign of open-market operations the central bank must carry out in order to set that increase in the monetary base, given all the other determinants of the increase in the monetary base — including those deriving from the balance of payments and the net borrowing requirements of the government and the banking system.

To simplify the initial discussion, this section assumes that the central bank's own profit or loss flow is insignificant, that it makes no dividend payments or other distributions from its accumulated profit, and receives no new capitalization flows. (Section 9.3 below shows how approach discussed here could be generalized to take account of flows affecting the central bank's capital position.)

Define the following variables:

M   the economy's *period-average* demand for broadly-defined money (that is, the average money stock that the economy is willing and able to hold over the period);

M'   the *period-end* money-demand stock (note the prime, which indicates period-end as opposed to period-average values);

B'   the period-end monetary base;

C'   the period-end stock of currency in circulation;

R'   the period-end stock of bank reserves (including currency holdings);

Q'   the period-end stock of the government deposit account at the central bank;

U'   the period-end stock of central-bank non-monetary liabilities (including open-market intervention instruments issued by the central bank);

V'   the period-end central-bank net worth;

A'   the period-end stock of central-bank gross international reserves measured in domestic currency;

L'   the period-end stock of central-bank gross international liabilities measured in domestic currency;

H'   the period-end stock of central-bank credit outstanding to commercial banks; and

F'   the period-end stock of central-bank credit outstanding to the government.

Except for the broad money supply, these are all components of the central bank's balance sheet:

CENTRAL-BANK BALANCE SHEET

Assets		Liabilities	
Gross external assets	**(A')**	**External liabilities**	**(L')**
Internal assets:		**Internal liabilities:**	
Government obligations	(F')	Monetary base:	(B')
Commercial-bank obligations	(H')	Currency in circulation	(C')
		Bank reserves	(R')
		Government deposit account	(Q')
		Non-monetary internal liabilities	(U')
		Net worth	**(V')**

(To be sure, actual central banks have accounts besides these, including, for example, fixed assets and "special" deposits. Those listed here, however, are a central bank's basic, "defining" accounts.)

The targeted value of the monetary base derives from a projection of the economy's average money holding over the period — the "demand for money." (Annex 9.1 reviews the determinants of an economy's demand for money.) The economy's average money holding over the period, M, presumably depends on the projected real gross domestic product (GDP) and the period-average price level through a "money-demand" relationship such as

$$M = M_{-1} (1 + g_p) (1 + g_y)^\alpha,$$

where g_p, represents the growth rate of the period-over-period price level, g_y the growth rate of the period-over-period price level, and α the elasticity of the demand for money with respect to real GDP, is presumably greater than zero. The values of g_p, and g_y would be programming assumptions for the exercise (see Section 3.7 above).

The relationship of the demand for money with real GDP and the average price level need not be as elementary as the one given here, of course. In addition, interest rates on other financial assets can also be incorporated into the formula — presumably, the higher the interest rates available on other available assets, the less inclined economic agents would be to hold money. The real rate of return on money itself, defined as the percentage increase in money's purchasing power from one end of the relevant time period to the other (see Annex 9.2), can also affect the willingness to hold money. Expected inflation makes the expected real rate of return on holding money negative, of course. All other things being equal, expected inflation — i.e., the expectation of a negative real rate of return on money — reduces money demand. If the real rate of return on money is defined by $-\pi = g_{p'}/(1+g_{p'})$, the demand-for-money formula given above may be rewritten

$$M = M_{-1} (1 + g_p) (1 + g_y)^{\alpha} (1 + \pi)^{\beta},$$

where, as before, g_p, represents the growth rate of the period-over-period price level; α, the elasticity of the demand for money with respect to real GDP, is presumably greater than zero; and β, the elasticity of the demand for money with respect to the negative of the real rate of return on money, is presumably less than zero.

The values of M', the period-end money supply, and ΔM', the increase over the period in M', may then be derived from the values for M'_{-1} and M, using, for example,

$$M = M'_{-1}{}^{(1-\omega)} M'^{\omega}$$

and

$$M' = M'_{-1} (1 + g_{M'})$$

to solve for g_M, where ω is a projected "weighting value" between zero and one. The "programmed" value of ΔM' would then be $M'_{-1} g_{M'}$. This would be the increase in the broad money supply consistent with the projection assumptions for real GDP, the average price level, and whatever other variables are assumed to affect money demand.

If m' represents the *marginal* "money multiplier" (i.e., the ratio of the *change in* the period-end money stock to the *change in* the period-end monetary base),

$$\Delta B' = \Delta M'/m'$$

would give the flow increase in the monetary base over the period. Given the projection assumption for m', the monetary-programming objective would be to drive $\Delta B'$ to this value. (The money multiplier is the presumably stable relationship between the overall money supply and the monetary base that comes about through economic agents' preferences about the proportion of their overall money demand to hold in the form of currency together with banks' decisions to hold bank reserves against deposits. Annex 9.3 discusses the determinants of the money multiplier.)

Once the value of $\Delta B'$ has been determined, the second part of the calculation determines the value of value of $\Delta U'$ from the central bank's flow balance-sheet identity,

$$\Delta U' = [(\Delta F' - \Delta Q') + \Delta H' + (\Delta A' - \Delta L') - \Delta V'] - \Delta B'.$$

The values of $\Delta F'$, $\Delta Q'$, and $\Delta H'$ may be treated as projection assumptions, or their values may be derived from other projection assumptions. For example, the projected net increase in the central bank's lending to commercial banks, $\Delta H'$, can be set equal to

$$\Delta H' = h\,Y,$$

where Y represents GDP. In this case the value of "h" would be the projection assumption. Alternatively, $\Delta H'$ could be given by

$$H' = H'_{-1}\,(1 + g_H),$$

in which case the future values of g_H would be the projection assumptions. Projected values of the net increase in the government's deposit account at the central bank, $\Delta Q'$, could be drawn from fiscal-accounts projections, or, again, simply assumed. Projected values of

ΔF', the net increase in the central bank's holdings of government obligations, need not be consistent in the same way with the fiscal-accounts projections, because the central bank can buy and sell government obligations for and from its holdings in open-market operations. These too could be projection assumptions.

The projected flow increases in the central bank's gross international-reserve and international-liability stocks, ΔA' and ΔL', could be separately assumed or could come from balance-of-payments projections. There are at least two different ways to measure their value in the national currency unit, which give different results if the nominal exchange rate moves over the period in question. Let ΔA*' represent the increase in gross international reserves measured in U.S. dollars and ΔL*' represent the increase in international liabilities measured in U.S. dollars (the asterisk indicates that the variable in question is in dollars). The flow increases measured *in national currency* would be given by

$$e\,(A^{*\prime} - A^{*\prime}_{-1})$$

and

$$e\,(L^{*\prime} - L^{*\prime}_{-1}),$$

where "e" is the period-average exchange rate (national currency per U.S. dollar). The changes in the national-currency stock values, however, would be given by

$$e'\,A^{*\prime} - e'_{-1}\,A^{*\prime}_{-1}$$

and

$$e'\,L^{*\prime} - e'_{-1}\,L^{*\prime}_{-1},$$

where e' is the period-end exchange rate. Although the second pair of expressions indicates the changes in the national-currency balance-sheet values of external assets and liabilities, for this section ΔA' and ΔL' will be taken to be given by the first pair of expressions. This is because, in this initial presentation of the monetary-programming procedure, the central bank's profit (or loss) flow is assumed to be insignificant. (As explained below, however, the difference between the two pairs of expressions above is roughly equal to the profit (or loss) flow arising from exchange-rate depreciation.)

With capitalization flows assumed to be insignificant, $\Delta V'$ is taken to be zero. The value of $\Delta U'$ required to close the central bank's flow balance-sheet accounts — that is, to drive $\Delta B'$ to the value consistent with the economy's demand for money — would then follow residually from the flow balance-sheet identity above. In effect, $\Delta U'$ indicates the monetary-policy "tightness" required to achieve $\Delta B'$, given the net increase in the central bank's net international reserves, net government financing, and net lending to the banking system, as indicated by the other variables on right-hand side of the flow balance-sheet identity. A large positive flow value for $\Delta U'$ — relative, say, to GDP, or to the money supply — would indicate that the monetary authority would have to carry out a quantitatively large amount of contractionary policy to adjust the money stock to the macroeconomy's willingness to hold it. The analyst, or policy-makers, could then make a judgment about whether this value of $\Delta U'$ would be excessive — i.e., a larger placement of central-bank open-market obligations than the financial markets would be able and willing to absorb.[82] A large negative flow value, in contrast, would imply that the monetary authority would be in a position to release base money into the economy — or,

---

[82] Alternatively, the value of $\Delta U'$ could be assumed — e.g., using $\Delta U' = u\,Y$, where the value of "u" is assumed. In this case, the value of $\Delta H'$ could be the residual, and the analyst can judge whether its value would be too small (in particular, excessively negative) — i.e., a smaller flow of net central-bank lending to the banking system than the system would be likely to require. To be sure, many central banks would not (and in some instances legally may not) issue their own liabilities to carry out monetary policy. In effect, if a central bank may not issue sterilization instruments, then any value of $\Delta U'$ greater than zero would indicate that the policy program would not be feasible. Or, instead of having $\Delta F'$ as a projection assumption, it could serve as the residual account, indicating the net flow of open-market purchases of government obligations that the central bank would have to carry out in order to drive $\Delta B'$ to its targeted value. Or, again, $\Delta H'$ could be the residual programming account.

alternatively, release less money into the economy and aim for a lower inflation rate.

A moment's thought should make it clear that the assumption that $\Delta V'$ is zero is at best approximate and at worst illogical. The central bank's assets and liabilities are, in general, interest-bearing, and, as noted, any exchange-rate movement will give rise to profits or losses. In addition, central banks have operating costs, as well as various kinds of earnings besides interest and exchange-rate movement. This means that over any time interval $\Delta V'$ will almost assuredly have a non-zero value. This value can be projected, as discussed in Section 9.3 below.

9.3   Central-bank capitalization and decapitalization flows

The discussion in Section 9.2 above assumed, for simplicity, that the central bank's net worth would remain unchanged, i.e., that $\Delta V'$ is zero. This assumption can and, for many central banks should, be relaxed, not only to take account of accumulation (or reduction) of central-bank capital through the central bank's own profits (or losses), as well as recapitalization and dividend-distribution operations. This section describes a way in which a monetary-programming exercise can do so.[83]

The basic approach may be grasped through a simplified presentation. Consider a simplified period-end central-bank balance sheet consisting of (i) the monetary base (B'), (ii) remunerated monetary-policy instruments (U'), (iii) all other aggregated *net* external and internal assets (represented *for this section only* by Z'), and (iv) net worth (V'). Let r_Z represent, *for this section only*, the average interest rate over the period accrued on the aggregated net assets and let r_U represent the average interest rate over the period due on outstanding

---

[83]   An argument is sometimes made that central banks really need no capital, since, unlike commercial banks, their ability to issue legal tender ensures that they can meet any financial obligation. It is true that a central bank can meet any domestic obligation by creating money, and may be able to use money it creates to purchase enough foreign exchange to meet any external obligation. But a central bank needs to maintain capital adequacy not to avoid "failure" in the conventional sense, but rather to ensure that it has the financial means to manage the monetary unit's value.

monetary-policy instruments. The flow balance sheet over the period is given then by

$$\Delta B' + \Delta U' + \Delta V' = \Delta Z'.$$

For simplicity, assume that the net interest receipts on its net asset holdings and the expenses for the interest on its monetary-policy instruments constitute the central bank's only net income. Suppose the monetary base is targeted to grow by $\Delta B'$ over the period. The profit or loss the central bank perceives over the period implies a (non-zero) value for $\Delta V'$. Let Π represent this profit flow. With no other source of new capital and no dividend payments over the period, $\Delta V'$ would equal Π, and Π would consist of the interest earnings on the period-average stocks of the central bank's net asset holdings and the outstanding stock of monetary-policy instruments. If the *period-average* stocks of the central bank's net asset holdings and the outstanding stock of monetary-policy instruments are given by $(Z'_{-1} + Z')/2$ and $(U'_{-1} + U')/2$ respectively,

$$\Delta V' = \Pi$$

$$= r_Z (Z'_{-1} + Z')/2 - r_U (U'_{-1} + U')/2$$

$$= r_Z [Z'_{-1} + (\Delta Z'/2)] - r_U [U'_{-1} + (\Delta U'/2)].$$

Substitute this expression into the flow balance-sheet identity,

$$\Delta U' = \Delta Z' - (\Delta B' + \Delta V'),$$

to obtain

$$\Delta U' = \Delta Z' - \Delta B' - \{r_Z [Z'_{-1} + (\Delta Z'/2)] - r_U [U'_{-1} + (\Delta U'/2)]\}$$

$$= \Delta Z' - \Delta B' + \{r_U [U'_{-1} + (\Delta U'/2)] - r_Z [Z'_{-1} + (\Delta Z'/2)]\},$$

and then solve for $\Delta U,'$ the monetary-policy action required to bring about the value targeted for $\Delta B'$, given $\Delta Z'$:

$$\Delta U' = \{[1 - (r_Z/2)] \Delta Z' - r_Z Z'_{-1} + r_U U'_{-1} - \Delta B'\}/[1 - (r_U/2)].$$

Since $\Delta V' = \Delta Z' - \Delta B' - \Delta U'$, multiplying both sides by $[1 - (r_U/2)]$ gives

$$\Delta V' \, [1 - (r_U/2)] = \Delta Z' \, [1 - (r_U/2)]$$

$$- \Delta B' [1 - (r_U/2)] - \Delta U' \, [1 - (r_U/2)]$$

$$= \Delta Z' \, [1 - (r_U/2)] - \Delta B' [1 - (r_U/2)$$

$$- \{[1 - (r_Z/2)] \, \Delta Z' - r_Z \, Z'_{-1} + r_U \, U'_{-1} - \Delta B'\}$$

$$= \Delta Z' \, [(r_Z - r_U)/2)] + \Delta B' \, (r_U/2) + r_Z \, Z'_{-1} - r_U \, U'_{-1},$$

so that

$$\Delta V' = \{\Delta Z' \, [(r_Z - r_U)/2)] + \Delta B' \, (r_U/2) + r_Z \, Z'_{-1} - r_U \, U'_{-1}\}/[1 - (r_U/2).$$

These expressions give the increases in $\Delta U'$ and $\Delta V'$ that would be consistent with holding $\Delta B'$ to a targeted value, given Z'_{-1}, U'_{-1}, $\Delta Z'$, r_Z, and r_U. To help see their significance, suppose first that the net assets Z'_{-1}, have been greater than zero and will earn interest for the central bank, while U'_{-1} has been zero (so that the central bank owes no interest on monetary-policy instruments). Suppose that a programming target of zero is set for both $\Delta B'$ and $\Delta U'$. If the monetary base does not increase over the programming period and no monetary-policy instruments are issued, then the increase in the central bank's net-asset position through its interest earnings on net assets would have to come entirely through the capitalization of the earnings into the asset stocks. Moreover, this capitalized interest would itself generate further interest earnings over the period, so that the full amount of the interest earned would be the interest earned on the previous period-end stock multiplied by $1/[1 - (r_Z/2)]$, which exceeds one if r_Z is between zero and one (as it presumably is). The formulas for $\Delta U'$ and $\Delta V'$ above would together imply that

$$\Delta V' = \Delta Z' = Z'_{-1} \, r_Z/[1 - (r_Z/2)],$$

which would be consistent with $\Delta B'$ and $\Delta U'$ being zero.

On the other hand, suppose now that U'_{-1} has been greater than zero, r_Z and $\Delta Z'$ are both zero, and the monetary authority aims to hold $\Delta B'$ to zero over the programming period. In this case, $\Delta U'$ would have to be greater than zero, in order for the central bank to avoid having to issue money to pay the interest due not only on U'_{-1} but also on $\Delta U'$. The balance-sheet offset to $\Delta U'$ would be a reduction in the central bank's net worth:

$$\Delta U' = -\Delta V' = U'_{-1}\, r_U / [1 - (r_U/2)].$$

All other things being equal, any central-bank profit flow is — like any increase in central-bank non-monetary liabilities or any reduction in central-bank assets — a source of money absorption; any central-bank loss is a source of money creation. Note that this is true even when the increase or decrease in the central bank's net-asset position is simply a valuation change — say, an exchange-rate depreciation that increases the value of the central bank's dollar-denominated assets. In this instance, no base money is created because, in effect, the central bank's net worth increases or decreases by precisely the amount of the valuation change.

Projection of the central bank's profits can be combined with the monetary projection described in Section 9.2 above for a more general framework. That section showed that *with the central bank's net worth held constant* the "monetary policy" consistent with (a) the programmed monetary expansion, (b) the increase in the central bank's net international assets, and (c) the central bank's net lending to the public sector, expressed as the difference between the increase in central-bank credit to commercial banks and the increase in non-monetary central-bank obligations, would be given by

$$\Delta U' = [(\Delta A' - \Delta L') + (\Delta F' - \Delta Q') + \Delta H'] - \Delta B'.$$

As in the preceding section, assume that $\Delta V'$ consists entirely of the profit (loss) flow — that is, that neither recapitalization nor drawings from capital (in particular, dividend payments) take place. In addition, assume that the profit flow consists entirely of interest payments and receipts (additional components of profit or loss can also be taken into account, as discussed below). To take account of the profit-and-loss account in the monetary program, subtract $\Delta V' = \Pi$ from the right-hand side — that is, all other things being equal, a larger central-bank profit would absorb *more* base money and make it possible to have *less* contractionary monetary policy. Assume for simplicity that the central bank pays no interest on the monetary base. The monetary policy required to bring about $\Delta B'$ would be given by

$$\Delta U' = [(\Delta A' - \Delta L') - (\Delta F' - \Delta Q') + \Delta H'] - \Delta B' - \Delta V',$$

where

$$\Delta V' = e\,[(r_{A*}\,A*) - (r_{L*}L*)] + [(r_F\,F) - (r_Q\,Q)] + [(r_H\,H) - (r_U\,U)],$$

and where $F = F'_{-1} + (\Delta F'/2)$, $Q = Q'_{-1} + (\Delta Q'/2)$, and so on.

The expression for $\Delta V'$ may be substituted into the previous expression to obtain a more general expression for the monetary policy stance, $\Delta U'$, consistent with the right-hand-side variables:

$$\Delta U' = -\Delta B' + e\,\Delta A*'\,[1 - (r_{A*}/2)] - e\,r_{A*}A^{*'}_{-1}$$

$$- e\,\Delta L*'\,[1 - (r_{L*}/2)] + e\,r_{L*}L^{*'}_{-1}$$

$$+ \Delta F'\,[1 - (r_F/2)] - r_F\,F'_{-1}$$

$$+ \Delta H'\,[1 - (r_H/2)] - r_H\,H'_{-1}$$

$$- \Delta Q'\,[1 - (r_Q/2)] + r_Q\,Q'_{-1}$$

$$+ \Delta U'\,(r_U/2) + r_U\,U'_{-1}.$$

This equation can be solved for $\Delta U'$, the total issue of non-monetary liabilities (central-bank sterilization instruments) that would be required to bring the demand for the monetary base in line with all net sources of monetary issue:

$$\Delta U' = \{ -\Delta B' + e\,\Delta A^{*'}\,[1 - (r_{A*}/2)] - e\,r_{A*}A^{*'}_{-1}$$

$$- e\,\Delta L^{*'}\,[1 - (r_{L*}/2)] + e\,r_{L*}L^{*'}_{-1}$$

$$+ \Delta F'\,[1 - (r_F/2)] - r_F\,F'_{-1}$$

$$+ \Delta H'\,[1 - (r_H/2)] - r_H\,H'_{-1}$$

$$- \Delta Q'\,[1 - (r_Q/2)] + r_Q\,Q'_{-1}$$

$$- r_U\,U'_{-1} \} / [1 - (r_U/2)].$$

Again, interest payments on central-bank liabilities are a source of monetary expansion. The larger they are, the *larger* the contractionary policy would have to be to bring about the targeted monetary-base growth. Interest receipts on central-bank assets are a source of monetary absorption. The larger they are, the *smaller* the contractionary policy would have to be to bring about the targeted monetary-base growth. Note, by the way, that if $\Delta F' = F\,g_F$ and $g_F = r_F$ then $\Delta F' = F\,r_F$, which means that the interest perceived on the central-bank asset F would effectively (or actually) be capitalized into the asset stock. The increase in the asset stock and the interest flow would be precisely equal, implying that there would be neither money creation nor absorption. The same is true for any of the other assets and liabilities.

Central banks can earn profits and take losses in ways besides interest flows, and these can be taken into account in projection analysis. For example, central banks have operating expenses of their own. These can sometimes be significant as a percentage of GDP, especially in relatively small economies. Although the practice is less common than it once was, central banks occasionally have responsibilities for certain types of fiscal expenditure, and, to the extent they are not reimbursed by the government, these too can give rise to losses. Central banks often profit or lose from the difference between the foreign-exchange selling and purchasing prices. Ordinarily, this difference is small, but central banks can make relatively large profits or losses in multiple exchange-rate regimes, where the prices at which they sell and buy foreign exchange differ significantly.

One important kind of profit or loss arises from exchange-rate appreciation or depreciation. As noted above, the changes in the national-currency equivalent of the central bank's external-asset and external-liability positions are given by

$$e' A^{*'} - e'_{-1} A^{*'}_{-1}$$

and

$$e' L^{*'} - e'_{-1} L^{*'}_{-1},$$

where e' is the period-end exchange rate. The only parts of these changes that would affect actual money creation or absorption would be

$$e\,[A^{*'} - A^{*'}_{-1}]$$

and

$$e\,[L^{*'} - L^{*'}_{-1}],$$

where "e" is the period-average exchange rate (or the exchange rate at which the asset and liability exchange transactions actually took place). Where the values of "e," e', and e'$_{-1}$ differ, the effects on the monetary program and on the central bank's finances would be as follows: for the foreign-exchange assets, the increase in their national-currency value would be

$$e' A^{*'} - e'_{-1} A^{*'}_{-1},$$

the sterilization requirement would be higher by the flow

$$e\,[A^{*'} - A^{*'}_{-1}],$$

and the difference

$$e' A^{*'} - e'_{-1} A^{*'}_{-1} - e\,[A^{*'} - A^{*'}_{-1}]$$

would be incorporated in the profit flow. For the foreign-exchange liabilities, the increase in their national-currency value would be

$$e' L^{*'} - e'_{-1} L^{*'}_{-1},$$

the sterilization requirement would be lower by the flow

$$e\,[L^* - L_{-1}^{*\prime}],$$

and the negative difference

$$-\{e'\,L^* - e_{-1}'\,L_{-1}^{*\prime} - e\,[L^* - L_{-1}^{*\prime}]\}$$

would be incorporated in the profit flow.

Central-bank accounts often record profits or losses arising from exchange-rate depreciation or appreciation separately from other profits, accumulating them in designated reserves. While such profits (losses) are "non-operating," and entail no money absorption (creation), they do enhance (diminish) the central bank's capital position in a perfectly real way. That is, they increase (diminish) the net asset backing of the monetary base, enhancing (reducing) the central bank's capacity to carry on monetary policy and so sustain the value of the currency unit.

Let X represent the central bank's flow of operating expenses and let W represent the flow of earnings from the buy-sell differentials in foreign-exchange operations. The overall profit flow taking account of interest paid and received, operating expenses, foreign-exchange operations, and exchange-rate profits would be given by

$$\Pi = e\,[(r_{A*}A^*) - (r_{L*}L^*)] + [(r_F\,F) - (r_Q\,Q)] + [(r_H\,H) - (r_U\,U)]$$

$$- X + W + e'\,A^{*\prime} - e_{-1}'\,A_{-1}^{*\prime} - e\,[A^{*\prime} - A_{-1}^{*\prime}]$$

$$-\{e'\,L^{*\prime} - e_{-1}'\,L_{-1}^{*\prime} - e\,[L^{*\prime} - L_{-1}^{*\prime}]\}.$$

In addition to the profit flow, recapitalization and dividend payments would also affect the central bank's net worth. If S represents the recapitalization flow and T its dividend payments, then of course

$$\Delta V' = \Pi + S - T.$$

Any assumption regarding projected recapitalization must be accompanied by an assumption about the form in which it will be provided. For example, if the government provides the new capital, then it may do so as a transfer of government obligations ($\Delta F'$) or as a transfer from its deposit account ($-\Delta Q'$). A dividend payment by the central bank to the government may be provided as a transfer to the government's deposit account ($\Delta Q'$). If no explicit assumption about the "counterpart transaction" is made, it would implicitly be a change in the monetary base: a recapitalization flow would come through a central-bank cash receipt ($-\Delta B'$), while a dividend payment would come through a central-bank cash payment ($\Delta B'$).

Summarizing, the value of $\Delta U'$ determined by the procedures described here indicates the sign and magnitude of the monetary policy the central bank would need to run in order for the monetary base to grow as programmed. A large value for $\Delta U'$ relative to GDP implies that the monetary authority would have to carry out a quantitatively large amount of contractionary monetary policy to adjust the money stock to the economy's willingness to hold it. A negative flow value would imply that the monetary authority would have to carry out expansionary monetary policy to adjust the money stock to the willingness to hold it — or else could aim for a smaller amount of monetary issue and a lower inflation rate. Taking account of the central bank's profit and loss flows contributes to the comprehensiveness and credibility of the monetary-programming exercise. (Annex 9.7 uses this section's algebra to develop conditions under which a central bank's capital position would be sustainable, given its projected future profit flows.)

9.4   *Projecting commercial-bank performance*

This section describes a spreadsheet projection exercise for a single commercial bank, or for a consolidated commercial-banking sector. The projection procedure simultaneously and consistently determines each future period's (i) flow balance sheet, (ii) net profit flow, and (iii) period-end balance sheet.

By incorporating a projection of commercial-banking performance, the macroeconomic projection analysis takes account of what would otherwise be "loose ends" in the overall macroeconomic-projection exercise. First, in most developing economies, commercial banks are likely to be key holders of government obligations. On the one hand, a consistency check would ensure that they are not projected to hold more government obligations than the government has issued. On the other hand, if their holdings of government obligations are projected to be less than the total stock outstanding, the analyst would want to be fairly sure the difference would be within the holding capacity of wealth-holders outside the commercial-banking system — that is, non-bank financial institutions and other wealth-holders. Second, the projection would enable the analyst to ensure that projected growth rates of (real) GDP and (real) bank credit could be in line with one another, so the credit supply would be growing sufficiently rapidly to support the programmed GDP growth rate. Finally, the projection could address the question of whether commercial banks would be able to maintain their capital adequacy.

The exercise sets out from (i) a base-year balance sheet for the commercial banks and (ii) assumptions regarding growth rates of various balance-sheet items, interest rates on and valuation changes in assets and liabilities, operating costs, taxes, and dividend distribution. It projects the increases in commercial banks' assets, liabilities, and overall net worth, as well as the profit flow. In each period, it solves simultaneously for (i) after-tax and after-dividend profit, (ii) the increase in net worth through profit accumulation, and (iii) the increase in the liquid-asset position consistent with the other balance-sheet items.

It should be helpful to summarize the basic projection procedure, then describe it in more detail. To simplify the initial discussion, assume that the commercial bank's — or consolidated commercial-banking system's — capital position increases only through undistributed profit accumulation. That is, no capital contributions take place during the period in question, no dividend payments are made, and no "valuation" changes affect any of the balance-sheet variables.

Define the following variables:

Z, Z' period-average and period-end net assets (i.e., assets less liabilities) *except* holdings of liquid securities;

i_Z overall rate of return on net assets (i.e., assets less liabilities) except holdings of liquid securities;

S, S' period-average and period-end holdings of government, central-bank, and other non-government liquid — i.e., easily marketable — securities;

i_S rate of return on liquid securities;

Ψ profit flow before tax and dividend distribution;

W period-average net worth;

K net operating costs;

τ tax rate applying to profit; and

δ dividend-distribution rate.

The basic flow balance-sheet identity sets the increase in net worth, ΔW, defined by

$$\Delta W' = W' - W'_{-1},$$

equal simultaneously to (i) the profit flow net of tax and dividend distribution and (ii) the balance-sheet flow increase in net worth:

$$\{[i_Z (Z'_{-1} + Z')/2] + [i_S (S'_{-1} + S')/2] - K\} (1-\tau)(1-\delta)$$

$$= \Psi (1-\tau)(1-\delta)$$

$$= \Delta W'$$

$$\equiv \Delta S' + \Delta Z',$$

where

$$(Z'_{-1} + Z')/2 \text{ and } (S'_{-1} + S')/2$$

are the average balances Z and S over the period. Since

$$(Z'_{-1} + Z')/2 = Z'_{-1} + (\Delta Z'/2)$$

and

$$(S'_{-1} + S')/2 = S'_{-1} + (\Delta S'/2),$$

the preceding equation can be rewritten as

$$\{i_Z [Z'_{-1} + (\Delta Z'/2)] + i_S [S'_{-1} + (\Delta S'/2)] - K\} \xi \equiv \Delta Z' + \Delta S',$$

where $\xi = (1-\tau)(1-\delta)$. This last equation may be rewritten in turn as

$$\xi \{i_Z Z'_{-1} + i_S S'_{-1} - K\} + \xi i_Z (\Delta Z'/2) - \Delta Z'$$

$$= \Delta S' + \xi i_S (\Delta S'/2)$$

or

$$\xi [i_Z Z'_{-1} + i_S S'_{-1} - K] - [1 - (\xi i_Z/2)] \Delta Z' = \Delta S'[1 - (\xi i_S/2)],$$

and solved for

$$\Delta S' = \{\xi [i_Z Z'_{-1} + i_S S'_{-1} - K] - [1 - (\xi i_Z/2)] \Delta Z'\}/[1 - (\xi i_S/2)].$$

That is, if the values of i_S, i_Z, τ and δ are given, and the value of $\Delta Z'$ — the net increase in all the net assets, including deposits, loans, and reserves *except* liquid securities — is programmed, then this last formula gives the net increase in the bank's holdings of liquid securities that would be required to bring that about. The reason for using liquid assets here as the residual, or adjustment, variable is that the values of many of the other possible commercial-bank balance-sheet variables — including deposits, bank reserves, and borrowing from the central bank — will already have been determined (see Section 9.2 above). Moreover, the growth rate of the loan portfolio would be programmed. Of the possibilities remaining, liquid assets seem a more likely adjustment variable than fixed assets.

A practical projection exercise can be constructed using this approach. Define the following (period-end) balance-sheet variables (*for this section only*, except for R', defined in Section 9.2 above):

R'   commercial-bank reserves;
S'   commercial-bank holdings of liquid assets, including government, central-bank, and other non-government obligations (including liquid assets denominated in foreign currencies);

N' loans (including loans to public-sector entities, and including loans denominated in foreign currencies); and

J' other assets, including fixed assets.

Next, define the following balance-sheet liability and net-worth variables (again, *for this section only*, except for D', and H', defined in Section 9.2 above):

D' deposits including government deposits (*including* deposits denominated in foreign currencies);

G' government deposits (included in deposits);

E' borrowing from sources other than the central bank (*including* borrowing denominated in foreign currencies);

H' borrowing from the central bank; and

W' accumulated net worth.

The variables R' and H' are discussed in Section 9.2 above, while the value of D' is the difference between the total money supply (M') and currency in circulation (C'), both discussed in Section 9.2 above. The values of N', E', G', and E' are determined from projection assumptions about their growth rates or relationships with other projection variables. The values of $\Delta S'$ and $\Delta W'$ are determined simultaneously, as explained below. The balance-sheet structure is as follows:

COMMERCIAL-BANK BALANCE SHEET

Assets		Liabilities	
Bank reserves	(R')	Deposits including government deposits	(D')
		of which, government deposits	(G')
Liquid-assets holdings including government, central-bank, and other non-government obligations	(S')	Borrowing, except from the central bank	(E')
Loans	(N')	Borrowing from the central bank	(H')
Other net assets	(J')	Net worth	(W)

Finally, define the following variables relating to capitalization flows:

K   net non-interest cost flow;
v   the non-accrual rate;
τ   tax rate on commercial-bank profit; and
δ   proportion of the profit distributed in dividends.

(For the moment no new capitalization flows are assumed to occur.) The non-accrual rate is simply the proportion of loans on which the bank records no interest income because they are deemed to be in danger of failing to recover their full value. (The value of the principal would not be written down, but any payments received on such loans would be set against principal, never as interest income.) Define $g_{N'}$, $g_{J'}$, $g_{G'}$, and $g_{E'}$ as the growth rates of the variables indicated, and v_R, v_S, v_N, v_E, v_D, v_G, v_E, and v_H as the valuation increases, over each period of the respective asset and liability stocks. Finally, define i_R, i_S, i_N, i_E, i_D, i_G, i_E, and i_H as the period-average interest rates on these balance-sheet variables. The value of each balance-sheet flow variable is calculated from the corresponding assumption for its growth rate, so that $\Delta R' = g_{R'} R'_{-1}$, etc.

Once again, the basic flow balance-sheet identity sets (i) the profit flow net of tax and dividend distribution equal to (ii) the balance-sheet flow increase in net worth (ΔW):

$$\{ i_R [R'_{-1} + (\Delta R'/2)] + i_S [S'_{-1} + (\Delta S'/2)]$$

$$+ [(1 - v) i_N [N'_{-1} + (\Delta N'/2)] + i_J [J'_{-1} + (\Delta J'/2)]$$

$$- i_D [D'_{-1} + (\Delta D'/2)] - i_E [E'_{-1} + (\Delta E'/2)]$$

$$- i_H [H'_{-1} + (\Delta H'/2)] - K$$

$$+ [v_R R'_{-1} + v_S S'_{-1} + v_N N'_{-1} + v_J J'_{-1} - v_D D'_{-1} - v_E E'_{-1} - v_H H_{-1}] \} \xi$$

$$\equiv [\Delta R' + \Delta S' + \Delta N' + \Delta J'] - [\Delta D' + \Delta E' + \Delta H'],$$

where $\xi = (1 - \tau)(1 - \delta)$. This may be solved for $\Delta S'$:

$$\Delta S' = \{\xi[i_R R'_{-1} + i_S S'_{-1} + (1 - v)i_N N'_{-1} + i_J J'_{-1} - i_D D'_{-1} - i_E E'_{-1} - i_H H'_{-1} - K]$$

$$+ \xi[v_R R'_{-1} + v_S S'_{-1} + v_N N'_{-1} + v_J J'_{-1} - v_D D'_{-1} - v_E E'_{-1} - v_H H'_{-1}]$$

$$- [1 - (\xi\, i_R/2)]\,\Delta R'$$

$$- [1 - (\xi\, \gamma\, i_N/2)]\,\Delta N'$$

$$- [1 - (\xi\, i_J/2)]\,\Delta J'$$

$$+ [1 - (\xi\, i_D/2)]\,\Delta D'$$

$$+ [1 - (\xi\, i_E/2)]\,\Delta E'$$

$$+ [1 - (\xi\, i_H/2)]\,\Delta H'\}/\{1 - [\xi\, i_S/2)]\}.$$

The value of $\Delta W'$ would be given then by

$$\Delta W' = [\Delta R' + \Delta S' + \Delta N' + \Delta J'] - [\Delta D' + \Delta E' + \Delta H'].$$

For simplicity, deposits are taken to be a single variable in these formulas. A projection exercise could work with different types of deposit, encompassing demand, saving, and term deposits (these could be represented by D1, D2, and so on). Deposits could be in different units of account. One key distinction between deposits (D') and borrowing (E') is that deposits have reserve requirements.

These formulas incorporate a large number of underlying assumptions, including the growth-rate assumptions that determine the flow increases, the valuation changes, and the various interest rates. To be sure, no assumptions would be made here for the growth rates of bank reserves (R'), deposits (D'), and borrowing from the central bank (H'), since, as noted, their values would already have been determined. In addition, the growth rate of the government deposit stock (G') would be determined with the government-financing projections. The growth rate of the loan portfolio (N') would be a fundamental assumption, however, since the outstanding loan stock would presumably be a relatively large component of any commercial bank's asset stock, and the growth of the commercial banks' loan portfolio is likely to figure heavily in policy-makers' concerns. The assumed growth rate of the loan portfolio could be related to the nominal-GDP growth rate, or to the growth rates of the particular sectors that rely on commercial-bank credit. Similarly, the assumed growths rate of J' and E' could also be related to the nominal-GDP growth rate. In some economies, commercial banks borrow from external sources to finance external trade, and so this borrowing could also be related to the short-term borrowing flows projected with the external debt. Projecting different categories of deposit, borrowing, and loans, the exercise would open the possibility of setting their growth-rate assumptions in different ways. As explained below, however, the growth-rate assumptions of asset and liability stocks must be related to assumptions about their interest rates and valuation changes.

The formulas above have $\Delta S'$ determined residually. In a practical projection exercise, the analyst may prefer to have different categories of liquid asset, with growth rates (and interest rates and valuation adjustments) assumed for all but one of the categories. That residual category of liquid asset would then serve the gap-filling function the formulas here ascribe to total liquid assets.

Assumptions for the interest rates can be set in different ways. Interest rates on bank reserves and on borrowing from the central bank would be policy variables of the monetary authority. Since commercial banks would be holding central-bank open-market obligations and government obligations as part of their liquid-asset portfolio, interest rate on liquid assets should be in line with the assumptions for these. Assumptions for commercial banks' deposit and borrowing rates may be set in real terms, so that the corresponding nominal rates would rise or fall if the inflation assumption is increased or reduced. Assumptions about spreads" between loan and deposit rates could be based on preceding years' experience. Finally, the assumed rates of return on commercial banks' "other assets" would depend on those assets' specific characteristics. If assumed to be mainly structures and equipment, they might be assumed (conservatively) to have no yield.

Assumptions for the valuation changes can be used to reflect different ways in which assets may evolve. For example, assumed valuation changes can be used to reflect the growth in asset or liability values arising from their being denominated in foreign currencies. Suppose, for example, that at the end of the preceding period the proportion q(-1) of the deposit stock D'_{-1} was dollar-denominated. Suppose, for simplicity, that these deposits do not change over the current period in dollar terms. If the exchange rate of national currency for U.S. dollars is assumed to increase by $g_{e'}$ over the period, then the valuation change in the total deposit stock would be

$$v_D = [(1 + g_{e'})^{q(-1)}] - 1.$$

Note that the value of "q" would change over the current period, simply through the change in the conversion rate between national currency and the U.S. dollar. Assume now that the dollar part of the deposit stock grows through a net deposit inflow. If the overall deposit stock grows by g_D and the part of the deposit stock denominated in dollars, qD', grows by $g_{qD'}$ (*including* growth arising from exchange-rate depreciation), then the new value of q would be given by

$$q = q_{-1} (1 + g_{qD})/(1 + g_D).$$

This approach can be used to project valuation change arising from exchange-rate movement, in the national-currency values of liquid assets, loans, other assets, deposits, and borrowings denominated wholly or in part in foreign exchange. Assumed valuation changes could also be used to reflect projected loan loss. Thus, for example, if x per cent of the loan portfolio is expected to be written down, then this would be the value of v_N.

It cannot be emphasized too strongly that the assumed growth rate of any asset or liability stock must take account of the assumed interest rate and the assumed valuation change — that is, the assumption for g_D (for example) must take account of the assumptions for v_D and i_D. Thus, if the national-currency value of a given dollar-deposit stock is expected to increase in a given year because of exchange-rate depreciation, this would affect the assumptions for both g_D as well as v_D. The interest-rate assumption affects the growth-rate assumption if the interest is expected to be capitalized into the asset stock, as would generally be the case. Note that if a banking system had no net deposits into or withdrawals from its deposit accounts, and the deposits were entirely in national currency, then their growth would result entirely from the interest-rate assumption. In this case, the interest due would be given by

$$i_D D'_{-1} + (i_D \Delta D'/2)$$

$$i_D D'_{-1} [1 + (g_D/2)],$$

and, since

$$g_D = (D'_{-1} + I)/D'_{-1},$$

$$g_D = i_D [1 + (g_D/2)],$$

and the value of g_D consistent with the interest rate i_D *in this particular instance* would be

$$g_D = i_D/[1 - (i_D/2)].$$

If there were valuation change in addition to interest, but still no net deposits or withdrawals, the value of g_D consistent with the interest rate i_D and the valuation change v_D *in this particular instance* would be

$$g_D = (i_D + v_D)/\{1 - [(i_D + v_D)/2]\}.$$

If it is also assumed that the deposit stocks in question would grow through net deposits (or diminish through net withdrawals), then the assumed value of g_D would be larger (or smaller) than this last expression. In the case of loans, interest is assumed to be capitalized into the loan balance (except for loans that have been placed in "non-accrual" status).

The non-interest cost flow K could be assumed to grow from year to year by an assumed growth rate g_K. This assumption could be made more detailed, of course. For example, it may be useful to separate such cost categories as staff remuneration, computing costs, and so on, and consider their growth rates separately. Assumptions can be made about the banking system's staff size and pay, perhaps in relation to the to the total loan portfolio and/or deposit base. It may be useful to take account of the number of branches the banking system has, and the average costs of running branches. Analysts may prefer to project a relatively simple set of costs and assumptions, or a more complicated set, depending on the particular projection exercise's objectives.

Each year's projection exercise produces a flow (and therefore a stock) balance sheet for the end of the year as well as a profit flow. As in other projections of accounts systems, the residual account — the flow increase in liquid-asset holdings — can be used to help gauge whether the projection would be feasible. If the liquid-asset stock would have to diminish sharply (or even turn negative), the analyst might conclude that the assumed increase in the loan portfolio would simply be too large, given the available resources and deposit and borrowings. If the liquid-asset stock would have to increase, the analyst might conclude that the loan portfolio could increase more, or that the borrowing flow on the liability side could be reduced.

At the same time, each year's projection exercise calculates a new year-end net-worth position. This can be· compared with the projected required net worth, which would be calculated by (a) multiplying each kind of bank asset by prescribed risk coefficients between zero and one, (b) summing the results, and then (c) multiplying the sum by the prescribed minimum capital-adequacy percentage. Since the late 1980s, most countries' prudential regulators, following (or exceeding) the so-called "Basel guidelines" set down by the Bank for International Settlements, have required commercial banks to maintain net-worth positions equal to or greater than "risk-adjusted" sums of their asset stocks. Under this approach, the weighting coefficients are higher, even one, for assets subject to risk (such as most loans) and smaller, even zero, for assets subject to less risk (such as cash and government obligations). If the net worth is projected to be less than the minimum required net worth, the analyst might conclude that the loan portfolio would have to grow more slowly. If the net worth is projected to be significantly larger than the minimum required net worth, the analyst might conclude that the loan portfolio could increase more.

When working with consolidated banking systems rather than individual institutions, it is important to remember that projections for particular banks or groups of banks may differ considerably from the projection of the consolidated system. At any moment, even if the system's consolidated net worth exceeds the minimum required, one or more commercial banks may be inadequately capitalized.

9.5   Consolidated monetary accounts

The "banking-system," or "monetary-survey," accounts are the consolidation of the central-bank and commercial banks' accounts. The consolidation eliminates the bank-reserve accounts (R') and commercial-bank holdings of central-bank non-monetary obligations, which are commercial-bank assets and central-bank liabilities; and central-bank loans to the commercial banks (H'), which are commercial-bank liabilities and central-bank assets. In the consolidated system, roughly speaking, the banking system's net external assets, net credit to the government, and loans to the private sector, less non-monetary borrowing by the central and commercial banks and the central and commercial banks' aggregate net worth, form the asset base that effectively "backs" the broad money supply:

CONSOLIDATED BANKING-SYSTEM BALANCE SHEET

Assets		Liabilities	
Central- and commercial-bank external assets		Central- and commercial-bank external liabilities	
Central-bank holdings of government obligations	(F')	Broad money supply:	(M')
Commercial-bank liquid-assets	(S')	Currency in circulation	(C')
		Commercial-bank deposits including government deposits	(D')
Commercial-bank loans	(N')	Government deposits at the central bank	(Q')
Other net commercial-bank assets	(J')	Central-bank non-monetary obligations	(U')
		Internal borrowing by commercial banks	(E')
		Borrowing from the central bank	(H')
		Net worth	(V'+W')

Summarizing, the monetary-programming approach recommended thus far would use the projected real-GDP and price-level growth rates to determine the increase in each future year's money demand, and then calculate the monetary policy required to bring about the equivalent increase in the money supply, given the projected money-supply growth that would arise from external and fiscal accounts. For economies with limited financial markets, this approach would probably be the most appropriate. For economies whose financial markets are more developed, however, it may be advisable for the projection to take account of interest rates set in those markets.

In this case, the basic macroeconomic variables would include a projected value for the "basic" interest rate — presumably, the government bond rate — in financial markets. This rate "i" would be included in the money-demand formula:

$$M = M_{-1} (1 + g_p) (1 + g_y)^\alpha (1 + \pi)^\beta (1 + i)^\gamma,$$

where α and β would be greater than zero but γ would be less than zero. (The value of "i" could be set in *nominal* rather than real terms, on the view that the nominal rate is the *spread* between the yield on government bonds and money, and that this is what would matter for people's willingness to hold money.)

9.6 Monetary-accounts projections for "Pacífica"

Table 27 presents the assumptions, in addition to the basic macroeconomic programming assumptions given in Table 2, on which the monetary-accounts projections for Pacífica are based. Table 28 presents the projected monetary accounts. Table 29 presents the central bank's projected capital-account flows, and Table 30 presents the central bank's projected assets and liabilities. Again, the results are given mainly as percentages of GDP, to make them easier to interpret.

The monetary assumptions are straightforward and conventional. Except for the recession years of 2009 and 2010, the elasticity of the demand for broad money with respect to real GDP is taken to be one, which is a "default" assumption (see Chapter 10). For the recession years, the money-demand elasticity is "fudged" (see Section 10.3 below) to maintain a steady increase in the money-GDP ratio. The marginal broad-money multiplier of 2.6 is within the 2–4 range observed in many developing economies. The international-reserve figures are drawn from the external-accounts projections. The monetary authorities are assumed to set relatively low nominal interest rates on the central bank's assets.

Both the broad money supply and the commercial-bank deposit stock are projected to remain steady as percentages of GDP (at about 54 and 37 per cent respectively), essentially because of the assumption that the elasticity of the demand for money with respect to real GDP will remain at one. Given the assumed marginal money multipliers, the flow increase in the monetary base is projected to increase as a percentage of GDP over the projection period, from 0.5 per cent in 2009 to 1.5 per cent in 2015. The central bank's overall asset position is projected to rise as a percentage of GDP as international reserves and internal assets accumulate, from 16.4 per cent of GDP in 2008 to 19.2 per cent of GDP in 2015. The central bank would run a small flow of losses beginning in 2010, about 0.3 per cent of GDP each year. It would arise largely from the central bank's own operating expenses, since the interest differential would remain steady at about -0.1 per cent of GDP through the projection period.

Figure 15. Pacífica: Central-bank balance (per cent of GDP), 2008–2015

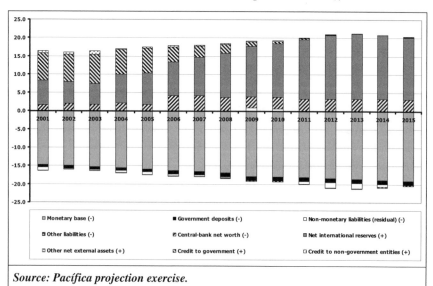

Source: Pacífica projection exercise.

The growth of the central bank's asset and liabilities positions would be such that the open-market operations necessary to secure balance would be limited, averaging about 0.3 per cent of GDP over the projection period. From the monetary-accounts perspective, the overall program would appear to be feasible.

10 Practical programming and projection issues

The future cannot be predicted from the past.

– attributed to Marcel Proust

10.1 Introduction: Practical programming and projection issues

A broad range of practical issues arises in setting up, carrying out, and making use of the kinds of projection exercise this book describes. This chapter discusses some of the more common and important. Section 10.2 discusses some of the practical issues involved in the formulation of a macroeconomic projection exercise. Section 10.3 discusses some issues that arise when formulating assumptions, including "fudging" and approaches to projecting parameter evolution. Section 10.4 describes the way in which the kind of exercise this book describes can play a role in government budget cycles. Section 10.5 begins the discussion of sensitivity analysis, and Section 10.6 describes an illustrative sensitivity analysis for Pacífica. Section 10.7 discusses sensitivity analysis involving debt reduction. Finally, Section 10.8 offers a concluding note on the methodology considered as a whole. Annex 10.1 offers some advice on spreadsheet design, based on this writer's experience. Annex 10.2 describes a simple "open-economy Phillips curve," which could be used to structure the relationship among the (i) real-GDP growth rate, (ii) price level (GDP deflator), and (iii) (real-effective) exchange rate assumed for each year in a projection exercise.

Two related points cannot be emphasized strongly enough. The first is that macroeconomic-projection exercises generally have, and sometimes merit, poor reputations. Policy-makers often simply lose patience with them. Spreadsheets are notorious for acquiring defects, particularly when they are complex and used under time pressure. Analysts sometimes make them too complicated, and then cannot make them perform quickly enough. Economists with a purist bent sometimes object to their perceived theoretical defects. On occasion, to be sure, policy-makers lose patience with them precisely because the projections reveal that their policy programs are not feasible, or even inconsistent.

The second point is that macroeconomic-programming exercises must be practical, or they will simply not work, in the sense that they will not affect policy-making. They must provide insight into questions that policy-makers need, and they must provide material that can be used in ministerial documents. The care and feeding of standing macroeconomic projection exercises is expensive, and they must earn their keep. Above all, they must be practical in "real time": that is, if the authorities require its output quickly (say, for discussions with the IMF or the World Bank), or if a document must be written rapidly, then it must be able to meet the requirements. Macroeconomic-programming exercises must be kept up in disciplined ways, and then be available for use on short notice. The need to have them work in real time means that assumption sets must be relatively small, and limited to what is essential. Analysts must have a thorough understanding of how the assumptions are set and, if necessary, how they can be successfully "fudged." At the same time, they must be capable of interpreting the results meaningfully.

10.2 Setting up a macroeconomic projection exercise: data, assumptions, and presentation of results

A projection exercise — *any* projection exercise — consists of combining base-year data and projection assumptions into projections, and then presenting the results in tables and charts. This section discusses some of the practical issues involved in setting up a macroeconomic-projection exercise, including (i) data requirements, (ii) assumptions, and (iii) presentation of results. Section 10.3 focuses on special practical "strategies" and "tactics" for assumptions.

10.2.1 Historical data

In principle, data are required only for the base year — i.e., the year immediately preceding the initial projection year. In practice, it is helpful to have several years' worth of data, to place projection results in

242   *Paul Beckerman*

perspective, and to permit the calculation of several years' worth of implicit assumption values. Tables and charts showing the projection results will be more persuasive and informative if they include historical experience.

Many of the key historical data series for any economy are available from (i) the International Monetary Fund's *International Financial Statistics (IFS)*, published monthly. These include the monthly exchange-rate, consumer-price, and monetary-aggregates data needed to calculate the series discussed in Chapter 3 above, as well as some of the key annual monetary, balance-of-payments, and national-accounts data.[84] The IFS also provides data on the annual flows of disbursement and repayment ("purchases" and "repurchases"), as well as on LIBOR and on the U.S. dollar-SDR exchange rate. (ii) The World Bank's *Global Development Finance (GDF)* tables, published annually, are a useful source for the external-debt data.[85] (iii) Annual data on the main categories of merchandise exports and imports, public-sector performance, the central bank's profit and loss accounts, the product composition of the GDP must usually come from country sources.

Analysts occasionally find IFS and GDF data series outdated or even inaccurate, and find it necessary to substitute recently revised data for particular accounts. The organization of the data in the IFS and GDF is helpful, however — among other reasons, because it is standardized from country to country. The IMF's and the World Bank's Internet web sites provide some current reports on the economies with which they work, and these may include more current data series. These reports often include data on the main categories of exports and imports of goods and non-factor services, public-sector performance, and the product composition of the GDP. Unfortunately, these data series may also be inaccurate, and sometimes cannot be "matched up" with longer historical data series.

---

[84] For countries with a history of high inflation, IFS data for years preceding the inflation sometimes have the problem that significant figures are truncated, even on the CDs. In such cases, there is no alternative but to turn to the old printed copies of the IFS.

[85] The IMF and World Bank websites provide information about how historical data can be obtained in electronic formats.

For some economies, some historical data series may turn out to be difficult to locate or simply unavailable the first time a projection spreadsheet is developed. Unless the data are unusually deficient, however, it is usually possible to carry on with approximations or guesses for missing base-year data.[86] When the data series are located or compiled, they may then be incorporated.

When constructing a projection spreadsheet, it is advisable to place the historical data series on at least one separate worksheet, in the format in which they are made available. This makes it easier to revise and update them. When doing so, it is advisable to set formulas to ensure that the various data tables sum properly. Thus, for example, for each year the above- and below-the-line balance-of-payments data must be equal. To ensure that this is always so, it is helpful to set the net inflow of international reserves through a formula, as the sum of the reported current, capital, financial, and errors-and-omissions accounts. The calculated figure can be checked against the figure given in the data set. No less important, if the analyst changes, say, a given merchandise-export datum for a given year, the full set of accounts would remain consistent.

The different data worksheets should be kept consistent with one another, if necessary, by substituting one worksheet's data for another's. For example, IFS data for a given economy will show historical values for the "use of Fund credit" in SDRs; the GDF data will show corresponding dollar amounts. Instead of using the GDF data, the dollar values in the worksheet containing the GDF could be calculated instead from the IFS data and the SDR-dollar exchange rate. Similarly, if a country-source worksheet gives balance-of-payments data, values shown in the IFS data worksheet should be made consistent with those shown in the country-source worksheet: either the IFS data lines could be drawn from the country-source worksheet, or the relevant country-source worksheet lines could be drawn from those in the IFS data lines.[87]

---

[86]   Until they become available, missing data that are guessed or approximated can be indicated by, say, using red font for the Excel cells in question.

[87]   For example, suppose that the country-source merchandise-exports total differs from the IFS total. The IFS total could be changed to match the country-source total. Alternatively, the country-source total could be changed to match the IFS total, and one export line in the country-source sheet — "other exports" — could be adjusted to make the total add up.

It is always important to bear in mind that all macroeconomic data are estimates and approximations. National-accounts aggregates are all estimates, constructed on the basis of surveys or rough approximations, applying arbitrary conventions about which activities should be included. Estimates of exports and imports inevitably miss a large amount of border trade, and even the figures on flows through customs sources are subject to substantial error. Estimates of such balance-of-payments accounts as unrequited transfers and private capital flows are best characterized as guesses. While year-to-year figures are generally fair indicators of the direction and order of magnitude of changes (as long as the estimation methods are similar from year to year), it is never possible to be sure they are anywhere near the (never-to-be-known) "true" values. Fiscal, central-bank and commercial-bank data are presumably more reliable, since they derive from structured accounting systems. Even these data are subject to considerable error, however, for reasons ranging from recording errors to conceptual imperfections and inconsistencies. Compilation of aggregate public external and internal debt stocks has proven surprisingly difficult in many economies, and the figures calculated for many developing economies are best regarded as rough approximations. One implication of the approximate character of macroeconomic data is that, while their relationships are presumably governed by rigorous logic, implicit or statistically estimated quantitative relationships among historical data series should never be thought of as exact.

At the same time, it is important to bear in mind that the key results of any multiannual projection exercise may be highly sensitive to base-year values and initial-projection-year assumptions. Put differently, seemingly minor changes in base-year values and the assumptions governing nearer-term projections can significantly affect longer-term projections. (In some instances, this can be the economic-projection version of what meteorologists call the "butterfly effect" — the point that, at least in theory, a single fluttering butterfly can have significant long-term dynamic consequences for large weather patterns, through chains of consequences.) This is especially true if projected real interest rates are high and therefore produce significant compounding effects. One reason this is important to remember is that base-year data are likely to be provisional and incomplete when a multiannual projection is first carried out. Analysts may then sometimes have to decide whether to use poor provisional base-year data or rough estimates, or combinations of the two. They must be prepared for the possibility that revisions to base-year data can significantly change the character of projection results.

This is as good a place as any to mention that historical and base-year data should be recorded as carefully as possible to ensure the quality of calculations and projections. Just about anyone who has experience with projection work can recall occasions when peculiar results turned out to be the consequence of data-entry errors. Obviously, manual data entry increases the likelihood of errors, but errors can also occur in many, often unanticipated ways even when data entry is automatic or electronic. In this exercise, the historical data bases should be entered with calculation checks, to minimize the likelihood of errors. Thus, it is only prudent to ensure that, in the data sets, the national expenditure-accounts, balance-of-payments, fiscal-accounts, and monetary-accounts identities are satisfied, that stock-flow relationships are satisfied, that variables that should never be negative never are, and so on.

10.2.2 Projection assumptions

When carrying out a projection exercise, it is helpful to think of the years involved in four categories: (i) historical years; (ii) recent "estimation" years, (iii) current and near-term future years; and (iv) longer-term future years. For convenience, refer to these as (i) "historical," (ii) "estimation," (iii) "near-term," and (iv) "longer-term" years. Thus, suppose the projection exercise is being carried out in February 2007. The "historical" years would probably be those up to and including 2005. The "estimation" year would be 2006, the "near-term" years would be 2007 and 2008, and the "longer-term" years would then be those beginning with 2009.

Although perhaps subject to revision, data for historical years through 2006 would be essentially complete. Data for the estimation year would be incomplete, and the exercise could treat this year either as historical, with much of the data estimated, or as a projection year, with some of the assumptions "fudged" to produce outcomes in line with what is believed to have actually happened.

As a simple example, suppose that assumptions for central-government expenditure on goods and services are formulated as percentages of GDP. Suppose that for a year just concluded, however, official estimates are available for (i) central-government expenditure on goods and services and (ii) GDP. The "assumed" percentage of GDP for the "projection" of the year just ended could then simply be the ratio of the two official estimates. For another example, suppose that for a year just ended official estimates are available for (i) central-government personal income tax receipts and (ii) GDP, and that the former are projected using an elasticity with respect to the latter. In general, for the longer-term "future" years, projection elasticities ought to be on the order of one. The two official estimates may, however, imply a far different elasticity for the years with estimated figures.

An elasticity of one in this last example could be said to be a "neutral," or "default," assumption, in the sense that it would preserve the ratio of tax collection to GDP. In general, as discussed in Section 2.2 above, for many of the assumptions in all parts of the exercise, there are values that may be characterized as "default," or "neutral" values. Thus, for example, a value of one would be a default assumption for the elasticity of the volume of consumer imports with respect to real GDP. This is because, all other things being equal, this value would preserve the ratio of consumer imports to GDP. A value of one would be a default assumption for the volume of any export commodity to the real growth rate of world trade in the commodity, since, all other things being equal, this value would preserve the country's share of the world market. For many policy settings, the default assumption would be the policy that had prevailed in preceding years. In general, for projection assumptions for which a default value can be defined, this would be the best to use, unless there is a specific reason to use a different value.

In general, as discussed in Chapter 1, the analyst carrying out a projection exercise will be aiming to determine whether, given (i) the economy's assumed *behavioral and production parameters* — i.e., the various elasticities relating macroeconomic variables with one another;

(ii) the medium-term evolution of *world variables* — i.e., export markets, import prices, and interest rates; (iii) policy-makers' *macroeconomic programming objectives*, i.e., for real growth, the exchange rate, the price level; and so on; and (iv) *policy settings*, i.e., those governing expenditure, revenue, and financing; the external and fiscal accounts could be feasibly and sustainably financed and private real per-capita consumption would grow. This way of describing the exercise is useful to help set up a work program an analyst could use to formulate a "base-case" projection. For each of the four kinds of assumption, it is helpful to keep certain principles and "tricks of the trade" in mind.

Structural parameters: The more important structural parameters are (i) export and import elasticities, (ii) the parameters governing monetary behavior, (iii) some of the behavioral relationships that determine public-sector revenue flows, and (iv) the parameters governing the relationships between GDP growth and capital formation. As in the case of the world variables, it is generally advisable to use default assumptions for the projected structural parameters, except where (a) there is a specific reason to do otherwise or (b) no obvious default assumption can be defined.

Thus, for example, consider the export and import elasticities. The default assumption for the elasticity of intermediate-goods imports with respect to real GDP would be one. As noted in Section 6.4, if it were less or greater, all other things being equal, the flow of intermediate goods would fall or rise as a percentage of GDP. The default assumption for the elasticity of banana exports with respect to the real growth rate of world trade in bananas would also be one. Again, as noted in Section 6.4, if it were less or greater, all other things being equal, the economy's share of the world market in bananas would fall or rise. In contrast, there is no obvious default assumption for any projected value of the elasticity of intermediate-goods imports with respect to their real-effective price. It is important to bear in mind that larger absolute values for the real-effective-price elasticities of exports and imports will, all other things being equal, imply larger, perhaps excessively optimistic, consequences for any projected real-effective exchange-rate depreciation. (Section 10.3 below discusses the use of econometric estimates in this context.)

The main monetary behavior parameters are those governing the demand for money, the non-bank public's currency-deposit ratio, and the commercial banks' reserve-deposit ratio. The default elasticity of the real demand for money with respect to real GDP would presumably be one, since, all other things being equal, this elasticity would maintain the demand for money constant as a percentage of GDP. (According to one well-known theoretical analysis, however, if the demand for money is characterized by economies of scale in relation to real transactions, the elasticity should be considerably less than one.[88]) On the other hand, it may be reasonable enough to assume that developing economies will undergo monetary deepening as they grow, and, to this extent, the elasticity of demand for money with respect to real GDP would exceed one. For the elasticities of the demand for money with respect to expected inflation or to (real) interest rates, there is no obvious default value.

The default assumption for the public's currency-deposit ratio would presumably be whatever value it has taken in the recent past — i.e., in the absence of a specific reason, the default assumption would be that this value would remain unchanged. With banking system development, to be sure, the ratio should diminish gradually over the longer term. The bank's reserve-deposit ratio may be viewed as either a policy setting or a behavioral parameter, depending on whether banks are assumed to maintain reserves in excess of their requirement. If not, the ratio would be a policy setting; if so, the ratio would reflect assumed bank behavior. In the latter case, the default assumption would be that the ratio would remain unchanged. Nevertheless, it may be reasonable to assume that banks will come to operate more efficiently, implying that they would maintain their reserve holdings as low as permitted. In one sense, these would be "conservative" assumptions, because they would both imply a larger money multiplier (see Section 9.2), and, all other things being equal, that monetary policy would have to be more contractionary in order to meet any given inflation target.

---

[88] So-called "inventory" approaches suggest that the elasticity of the demand for money with respect to real GDP would be about 0.5. See Baumol 1952.

Although most of the flows that make up the fiscal accounts would be governed by policy settings, assumptions regarding "behavioral" parameters will also matter, particularly for revenue assumptions. For example, the revenue yield from a value-added tax would presumably be governed by the tax rate and the collection efficiency (the ratio of the tax yield to the product of the tax rate and GDP — see Section 8.2). The tax rate would be a policy setting. The collection efficiency would be either a behavioral parameter, characterizing the revenue yield the economy naturally produces from each percentage point of the rate, or a kind of policy setting. Considered as a behavioral parameter, the default setting would be the value of the collection efficiency in the years just before the projection period. Considered as a policy setting, steady increases over the projection period could reflect improving tax administration and, perhaps, removal of exemptions.

As another example, consider the elasticity of internal demand for oil products with respect to real GDP. This parameter would figure in the determination of government tax revenue and public oil-enterprise earnings (and perhaps also in the determination of oil exports or imports). The default projection would presumably be one. It may be more appropriate in some developing economies to use a figure larger than one, however, on the view that real growth would lead to proportionally higher oil-derivatives consumption.

Some of the most problematic structural parameters in a macroeconomic projection exercise are those governing the relationships between capital formation and real-GDP growth. A large proportion of the criticism of macroeconomic consistency modeling focuses on these assumptions — justifiably so, because projections of these parameters are bound to be highly arbitrary and a large number of variables in the structure of the exercise depend directly and indirectly on them. It is difficult to define default values, since past performance is unlikely to be a guide to the future. Indeed, it will always be difficult to claim that the assumption settings for ICORs are anything but arbitrary.

One obvious source of difficulty is the lag structure through which capital formation affects output. Econometric techniques can be used to estimate the lag structure, although the results are likely to be unsatisfactory on statistical criteria. Any economy's investment lag structure is likely to be unstable. Construction of a large dam over several years, for example, could make a significant temporary difference. Smaller-scale changes in the composition of investment can also affect the lag structure significantly. In many exercises, this writer has found the use of an arbitrary lag structure (such as the "one sixth, one third, one half structure mentioned in Section 6.2 above) to be the "least-bad" approach. There simply is no obvious "default" lag structure.

Even if the lag structure is plausible, it is difficult to avoid arbitrariness in projecting other determinants of the relationship between growth and capital formation. The closest thing to a default assumption for the ICOR would presumably be the historical value, determined by calculating the sum of the annual flows of real capital formation over (say) one or two decades of national-accounts data and dividing it by the change in the flow of real GDP between the last year and the year immediately preceding the first year of the same time period. This may then be adjusted for assumed capital depreciation (see Section 6.2 above). There is no obvious default assumption for capital depreciation, unfortunately. Some countries formulate estimates for its historical values, however, and these can be used to guide future assumptions. Otherwise, rough guesses based on the likely life of the existing capital stock must suffice. Similarly, some countries estimate historical capacity utilization, and these may be used to guide future assumptions. Otherwise, again, rough guesses must suffice. Note that if the projection is carried out according to the methodology described in Section 6.2, the relevant assumption would be the assumed *change* in capacity utilization, not the precise starting value.

It may be easiest to set out a plausible projection series for the capital-formation rate, and then try out combinations of assumptions regarding capital depreciation, capacity utilization, and the lag structure "to back out" a fudged assumption for the ICOR. The fairest advice here, however, is that (a) projection results are highly sensitive to the projected relationship between capital formation and real growth, and (b) projections of the relationship between capital formation and real growth are bound to be somewhat arbitrary. In any case, it is likely to be useful to subject projection results to sensitivity analysis involving changes in these variables (see Section 10.5 below).

World and internal exogenous variables: Governments and large institutions may provide their analysts with sets of projection assumptions for world interest and inflation rates, prices and volumes transacted in world commodity markets, and other "state-of-the-world" variables, and recommend or require that these be used to formulate "base-scenario" projections. The IMF disseminates some of its own medium-term assumptions for world economic performance in its *World Economic Outlook* (WEO) publications, and these will generally be uncontroversial. In some instances analysts may be able to use internal projections by the World Bank and other international institutions. Analysts may wish to make their own state-of-the-world assumptions. In doing so, however, they should strive to make the assumptions as uncontroversial as possible. For base-case scenarios, to the extent possible, analysts are best advised to use "neutral" and conservative assumptions, with clear trends. World export prices should either be assumed to remain unchanged in real terms, or to trend up or down according to "consensus" views. World inflation rates should generally be assumed to remain steady at ranges corresponding to recent experience. World commerce should be expected to grow at "moderate" — i.e., not unduly optimistic — real rates. "Conservatism" is obviously a sound principle for assumption formulation: thus, for example, all other things being equal, analysts in an oil-exporting economy would want to set relatively lower assumptions about future oil prices. It is important, of course, to avoid overly optimistic state-of-the-world assumptions about exports that effectively assume away the need for policy choices.

The appropriate assumptions for real growth rates of commerce in world markets are likely to vary considerably from commodity to commodity. Analysts may wish to construct a "tree" of assumptions for export projections, regarding (i) the overall real growth rate of world commerce, (ii) the elasticities of world-trade volume in the different commodities that the particular economy exports to overall world real commerce, and (iii) the elasticities of the economy's export volumes of each kind of commodity with respect to the relevant world trade volumes. In general, again, these should be moderate, steady assumptions, as close to being "neutral" in character as possible.

There are circumstances, of course, in which the presumable default setting for a state-of-the-world assumption would obviously be inappropriate. For example, an oil-exporting economy whose producing fields are undergoing rapid depletion may be unable to keep its exports growing at the same rate as the world oil market. A nation that hosts a large regional sports competition can expect a substantial increase in tourist proceeds that year, and perhaps some decline in the subsequent year.

Certain exogenous internal variables would also figure among the state-of-the-world assumptions. Depending on how the projection analysis is structured, examples could include oil-production flow rates, fishing yields, and so on. One of the most important state-of-the-world assumptions, of course, would be the population growth rate. In most economies, demographers will have a consensus view about the appropriate assumptions for the coming decade, and this would be the appropriate figures for the base scenario.

Macroeconomic programming objectives: The main macroeconomic programming objectives are the real-GDP growth rate, the inflation rate, and the evolution of the real-effective exchange rate, international-reserve holdings in months of imports of goods and non-factor services, and the population growth rate. (Since the financial system is not explicitly modeled in the exercise this book describes, internal interest rates are also taken as programming assumptions.)

In principle, one point of a projection exercise would be to figure out how high real-GDP growth could go before it ran into financing constraints, or before it posed a high risk of forcing heavy exchange-rate depreciation. The programming objectives could be subjected to sensitivity analysis (see Section 10.5 below). If the economy's real GDP has been relatively low, many analysts make it a practice to project gradually reviving growth, until the growth rate reaches what would be a presumably sustainable longer-term rate. Except for "high-case" growth scenarios (which are likely to imply high external-financing requirements), it is usually best to hold projected real-GDP growth to relatively conservative values. Similarly, many analysts make it a practice to program inflation to decline gradually, toward or to world inflation rates. One simple projection technique is to have each year's projected December-December inflation rate be (say) 90 per cent of the preceding year's rate., until it falls to a specified minimum level (such as the assumed world inflation rate). A similar approach can be used for the real-GDP growth rate — i.e., have each year's real growth rate be (say) 1.2 times the preceding year's rate, until it reaches a specified maximum level.

Projection of the real-effective exchange rate may be more complicated. Any economy's real-effective exchange rate is determined through the interaction of policy and market responses both to that policy and other events. All the same, it is important to bear in mind that one of the exercise's purposes is to determine the year-by-year financing flows that would be *consistent with* a particular projected real-effective exchange-rate evolution, however that evolution were to come about. For example, the default setting for the real-effective exchange rate depends very much on the basic exchange-rate policy rule in place. With a flexible exchange rate, for example, the default assumption would be that the real-effective exchange rate would remain unchanged. With a fixed exchange rate, the default assumption would be that the real-effective exchange rate would evolve according to the differential between the internal and world inflation rates. In any case, when projecting significant real-effective depreciation, it is important to use careful judgment regarding the relationship between the nominal exchange-rate depreciation and internal inflation rates. In general, a high nominal depreciation rate and a low internal inflation rate are more likely to require unfeasibly large doses of contractionary monetary policy, bearing out the widespread experience that deep exchange-rate depreciation often generates inflationary pressure.

Policy programming: Any macroeconomic consistency projection exercise incorporates a significant number of assumptions for policy settings. Apart from the exchange-rate assumptions, and certain policy settings for the external and monetary accounts, the most important are associated with fiscal policy and external-debt flows.

In general, unless there are specific reasons to do otherwise, the best settings for the fiscal-policy settings are their default values. For taxation and tariff policies, this would broadly imply that rates and collection efficiency levels would continue roughly as before (or, in the case of the collection efficiencies, with gradual improvement), while that elasticities (such as the income-tax yield with respect to real GDP) would settle at one. For public-sector staff expenditure, the default settings for wage rates would have them grow at the same rate as the price level; the number of workers on staff would grow at the same rate as population (or the number of students in the case of the education sector); and there would be no net "promotion" effect. For non-staff, non-interest expenditure, the default assumption would be either (i) that it would remain unchanged as a percentage of GDP, or (ii) that it would grow in real terms at rates related to population growth.

External-debt assumptions pose a different set of challenges. For each identified class of external debt, the default assumption for the disbursement flow would be whatever amount was necessary to maintain the ratio of the year-end debt stock to GDP (valued at the base-year purchasing-power parity exchange rate), taking account of scheduled repayment and valuation change. If the economy is growing, this would imply a positive "flow" (i.e., disbursement less repayment), although it might not imply a positive "transfer" (flow less interest due). By using this default assumption for all the identified external-debt categories, the analyst can determine whether all the other projection assumptions would then require an increase in unidentified external borrowing that would increase or reduce the overall external debt-GDP ratio.

Where there are significant accumulated arrears or other manifestations of an excessive debt burden, it becomes more difficult to generalize about the appropriate settings for the relevant assumptions. The analyst must then take close account of country-specific circumstances, the disposition of specific external creditors to lend, and the kinds of amelioration and resolution proposals under consideration.

More generally, the formulation of projection assumptions is at least as much of an art as a science. Inevitably, practice, experience, good judgment, trial and error, solid knowledge of country circumstances, and care in drawing conclusions from the analysis can be expected to lead to the "best" — i.e., the most useful, least unreliable — results.

10.2.3 Presenting projection results

As a practical matter, the presentation of projection results is just about as important as the results themselves. One of the purposes of the projection exercise may be to produce output tables and charts that can be used in standard documents, including those used by the IMF and World Bank as well as the government's standard budget documents. In addition, it is important that the projection exercise produce tables that display the essential results and show how they were calculated. In broad terms, the purpose of the exercise this book describes is to inform policy decisions. It follows that the results of the exercise need to be communicated in ways that properly inform policy-makers, that provide them with information and judgments they need for the decisions they must take. Results that are incomprehensibly communicated have about the same consequence and value as no results at all.

Thus, depending on the precise ways in which a given projection exercise is applied, it could be set up to produce, for recent and four to six projection years:

i.   summary tables, showing such key indicators as capital formation, the current account of the balance of payments, and the government deficit as a percentage of GDP, and such feasibility indicators as the unprogrammed external and unprogrammed government internal borrowing requirements,

ii.   more detailed "feasibility" tables, showing not only (say) the unprogrammed government internal borrowing requirement as a percentage of GDP (or in national-currency units), but also, at least in summary, the other main fiscal-accounts lines, such as tax revenue, non-tax revenue, current non-interest expenditure, interest, capital expenditure, and programmed financing, to help the reader see what "drives" the unprogrammed government internal borrowing requirement.

Sources-and-uses presentations can be especially revealing and useful for the external and fiscal accounts (see Annexes 7.3 and 8.3). A sources-and-uses presentation for the external-accounts would show, under "sources," the flows of net borrowing, and, under "uses," the amounts that the net borrowing would be financing — i.e., the current-account deficit, the central bank-s gross reserve accumulation, and net non-debt financial outflows (including "errors and omissions"). The perspective — i.e., the amount of financing and what it is being used to finance" — would be helpful for all stakeholders in the process, including each donor considering providing financing and the economy's authorities.[89] A sources-and-uses presentation for the fiscal-accounts would show, under "sources," the flows of tax and non-tax revenue and the flows of net external and internal borrowing, and, under "uses," the current and capital expenditure that to be financed. Again, this would place the financing arrangements in a singularly helpful perspective.

10.3   Setting projection assumptions

Before proceeding to sensitivity analysis, it is worth mentioning certain generic practical issues that often arise in setting projection assumptions. This section briefly discusses "fudging," econometric parameter estimates, the importance of making feasible projection assumptions, time patterns for projection assumptions, and oscillating projections.

10.3.1   "Fudging"

In projection analysis, "fudging" may be defined as the manipulation of assumptions to make projections take on particular values. Thus, for example, an analyst projecting consumer-goods imports for the coming year may know of a projection presumed to be highly authoritative. It is simple enough to set the projected elasticity of consumer-goods imports with respect to the value of world commerce in bananas so as to make the projection come out to the presumably authoritative projection. Suppose that the consumer-goods import volume depends only on real GDP, whose growth rate is given by "g," and that the authoritative

---

[89]   Commercial bankers involved in the concerted debt operations of the 1980s involving countries caught up in the debt crisis preferred wherever possible to set out prospective financing flows in sources-and-uses terms, since these were more in keeping with commercial banks' practices in general.

projection of consumer-goods volume growth is given by h*. Since $1 + h = (1 + g)^a$, where "a" is the elasticity of consumer-goods import volume with respect to real GDP, if the cell entry for the elasticity is set to the formula $\ln(1 + h*)/\ln(1 + g)$, with h* the authoritative numerical value and "g" the cell address of the growth rate of real GDP, the value of "h" will always be h*, regardless of the value of "g."[90]

Fudging is especially useful just after a year concludes, when it is still too early to treat the year just ended as a historical year, but for which estimated data values will gradually arrive. Thus, for example, preliminary data for 2008 exports and imports may arrive by February 2009. Even though 2008 is still a projection year, the analyst will want "to project" the estimated actual export values and volumes. In this case, she may set, say, the export elasticities so as to produce the estimated results as projections. No one should object in principle to using fudging in this way.

On the other hand, there are instances in which fudging seems rather more dubious. Many, perhaps most, people who have worked on business and economics projections have been asked by superiors and clients to fudge assumptions to bring about specified projection outcomes. Thus, for example, approval of loans by multilateral agencies often hinge on projections that external-accounts financing requirements will remain relatively low; sellers of sovereign bonds need to persuade would-be purchasers that the economy in question will be capable of sustaining the debt service. In such contexts, analysts may have to fudge to make their results come out as "required."

Some analysts believe fudging for purposes like these is ethically dubious, if not fundamentally unprofessional. There is no question that in some contexts fudging, depending on how and why it is carried out, can raise ethical issues. Analysts, it hardly needs saying, need to be careful about their work and the uses to which it is put: economic projections may be applied in policy and other decisions that have

---

[90] Spreadsheet programs often include iterative procedures in their "tool kits" ("goal seek" in Excel) For the present example, instead of placing a formula in the cell for "a," the value of "h" could be forced to h* by using the goal-seek procedure to calculate the required value for "a." The advantage of having a formula is that it would include h*, and so could easily be adjusted if the value of h* is changed.

consequences for people, and analysts should therefore take care to produce the projections in fully professional ways.

This said, it is also true that fudging can be perfectly ethical and professional. For example, there is no reason not to take advantage of "authoritative" projections of particular line items, or at least to test their consequences and implications. When fudging to bring about someone else's projection result, though, the analyst should make a point of examining the value of the parameter fudged. If, say, a fudged elasticity is unusually large or small, or significantly different from the "default" assumption, the analyst may wish to look into the reasons why, and in this way understand the bases and implications of the assumption deemed "authoritative." For example, the authoritative assumption might be based on a different projection of real-GDP growth. The analyst may wish to determine the assumed real-GDP growth rate that would bring about the authoritative projection under default assumptions, and then consider whether this growth rate is likely to prove feasible. (It is always possible, of course, that a supposedly authoritative projection is based on inappropriate assumptions.)

If a fudged projection assumption is hopelessly unrealistic, then the value being forced is probably unrealistic. Good judgment is very much the point here. It is one thing to have a near-term projection set a government-deficit projection to a targeted value using a fudged elasticity of income-tax revenue with respect to nominal GDP of 1.3, but quite another if the fudged value of the elasticity would have to be around 35.[91]

---

[91] Some analysts have had the experience of being asked to write over projection results in ways that either made them mutually inconsistent or arbitrary. For example, on one occasion, an analyst with whom this writer worked was asked to revise a multiannual projection for the loan documents of a proposed multilateral adjustment loan to a government. The projection incorporated highly optimistic assumptions for capital formation and rapid export growth, both of which were regarded as important to secure approval of the loan. Through the national-accounts identity, these assumptions implied that real per-capita private consumption would have to decline sharply. The loan documents had to be completed under a tight deadline, and the analyst was asked simply to show positive growth rates for the private-consumption projections. With this change, the national-accounts expenditure identity was no longer satisfied. Fudging of this kind should be regarded as inappropriate. It was necessary to recognize, of course, that the results implied that the assumptions for capital formation and export growth were simply too high, and to scale them back accordingly.

The validity of any particular fudging procedure depends on the purpose of the projection exercise. It is reasonable enough to fudge to force a result that is already known. This apart, broadly speaking, it matters whether the projection exercise is being done *to determine whether* a given program is likely to prove feasible, or whether it is done *to make a persuasive case* that a given program will prove feasible. If the purpose is to *determine whether* a program is likely to prove feasible, it is best to use default, or, in any case, conservative assumptions. When presenting an argument that a given program *is likely to prove* feasible, fudging an assumption or two to produce a target outcome may be reasonable enough, but even in this case, however, the fudged parameter assumption should be reasonable and defensible. (In addition, it may be appropriate to say in the projection write-up that one or more assumptions were fudged and, if necessary, to explain why their values should be considered reasonable.)[92]

10.3.2 *Econometric parameter estimates (and the stability of structural parameters)*

Econometric estimates are often formulated from time-series data for such parameters as money-demand parameters, elasticities of export and import volumes with respect to real GDP, and tax-revenue determinants. It is generally inadvisable to use such estimates as projection assumptions in the kind of exercise this book discusses, for several reasons. One is that the behavioral parameters relating two or more economic series may be unstable over time. In general, for many economies, parameter stability is a strong assumption, and econometric estimates based on past performance may therefore be inappropriate for projections of future performance. A closely related point is that past instability and data inadequacies may imply that econometric estimates are often inefficient — i.e., characterized by wide confidence intervals — and even subject to bias.

---

[92]   A write-up could say, for example, that "The current-account deficit is projected to be just one per cent of GDP when the elasticity of import volumes with respect to real GDP is (say) 0.97," where 0.97 is the fudged value required to bring about the one per cent current-account deficit.

For most structural parameters, it is likely to be more appropriate to use default assumption values, particularly if these fall within estimated confidence intervals. In general, where parameter assumptions have meaningful default values (see Section 10.2 above), analysts are usually best advised to apply them, unless there is a specific reason to set different assumptions.

Easterly 2002 argues that the instability of their assumed structural parameters implies that IMF programming exercises — and, by extension, exercises like the one this book describes — are fatally flawed. The fact that this writer has written this book shows that he is not completely persuaded. Parameter instability is a fact of life for economic models, and analysts must keep it in mind. All the same, taxpayers, donors, and other stakeholders entrust governments with substantial financial resources, and in many cases dedicate large amounts of time and efforts to the government's activities as well. Governments accordingly owe it to their stakeholders to make the best possible efforts to program their resource use. Methodologies of the kind this book describes, with all their limitations, are probably the best, or least bad, ways to do so. The challenge of programming, indeed of business planning in general, is precisely that it must be carried out against wide-ranging uncertainty.

10.3.3 Feasible assumptions

The purpose of the projection exercise is to gauge the *financial* feasibility of a macroeconomic program. It is important to be sure, however, that the assumptions of the program itself are feasible in other ways before subjecting them to the financial-feasibility test. Plainly enough, with the apparent exception of China, few countries have been able to sustain real-GDP growth rates higher than 7 or 8 per cent per year. Few countries could sustain the capital-formation rates that higher rates would imply without running into absorption-capacity constraints, let alone the limits to consumption that the required saving rates would require.

In any case, unfeasibly high real-GDP growth rates would tend to imply unfeasible financing requirements. The assumptions about which analysts need to be especially careful are those that effectively reduce financing constraints — that effectively assume away the constraints. For example, a macroeconomic program incorporating unfeasibly optimistic export-growth assumptions will imply low projected external-financing requirements. Economic analysts sometimes cite the so-called "small-country" hypothesis, according to which a small economy can export just about anything it can produce into large world markets. In reality, it is unusual for export volumes to sustain faster growth rates than those of the world markets into which they are being sold. In any case, supply constraints can tighten surprisingly quickly, especially if the exports in question are resource-based. High export growth can take place over a couple of years, especially if an economy is in the early stages of its expansion, but analysts must be careful not to assume that such growth rates can be remain high over projection years.

Time paths for projection assumptions: The time pattern of any given line of projection assumptions can obviously make an important difference for the results of a multiannual projection exercise. As noted in Section 10.2 above, many parameters have default values, and it is best to use these for the longer term assumptions, even if smaller or larger values are used for the shorter term.

There are several simple ways to formulate a projection in which an assumed parameter sets out at a value higher or lower than one but then adjusts gradually toward one. Suppose, for example, that a parameter has a value of H_0 in the base year and is assumed to rise or fall gradually to the value H^*, in such a way that each year's value is a fraction λ of the preceding year's value. In each projection year, then, each year's parameter value would be the maximum of (i) λ times the preceding year's value and (ii) one. This would be a kind of "radioactive-decay" adjustment. For gradual adjustment, suppose it is also assumed that the parameter will reach one in ten years from the initial projection year. A slightly different, but similar, approach would be to have the value of H adjust gradually from H_0 in the base year to H_T, T years later. In any projection year t after the base year, H_t would be given by $H_{t-1} [H_T/H_0]^{(1/T)}$, where N would be the number of years between t=0 to t=T. These adjustment processes could be applied with initial values in the base year or with starting, perhaps "fudged," values in the initial projection year.

"Radioactive-decay" and "gradual" patterns can be useful for a variety of parameter assumptions. A gradual pattern can be used, for example, to reflect improving efficiency of capital formation, by having the ICOR decline gradually from an initial to a longer-term value. To be sure, it is best to avoid using assumptions of this kind to make higher longer-term growth rates seem more feasible by reducing their capital-formation requirements. On the other hand, radioactive and gradual assumption projections, or something like them, may be used gradually to project the gradual adjustment of any parameter whose initial-year and presumable longer-term default values differ.

"Oscillating" projections. Projection exercises involving period-average and period-end variables can sometimes produce "oscillating" values. Projected year-end price-index, exchange-rate, and money-demand values, for example, may simply move up and down from year to year, rather than follow a simple trend. This could cause other key results, such as external- and fiscal-accounts financing requirements, to oscillate as well. In general, oscillating projections should be considered highly suspect, if not downright nonsensical, and steps should be taken to determine and remedy their causes. (Section 3.7 above explains why oscillating results can arise through projections of average and year-end values, and why and how projection assumptions should be revised to prevent this.)

10.4   Multiannual macroeconomic projection analysis in government budget-processing cycles

Modern governments prepare their annual budgets in processing cycles encompassing preparation, executive and legislative approval, execution, revision, and closure. The preparation and approval aspects of the process presumably take place over the year before the fiscal year to which the budget applies.[93] Budget cycles begin and conclude at different times of the year preceding the budget year in different economies. Some governments begin as early as nine or ten months before the start of the budget year, at least informally, while others begin as late as three or four months before the start of the budget cycle. The preparation process characteristically encompasses consultations, planning exercises, and preparation of early drafts. In the usual approach, finance ministries and budget offices define "ceilings," both for total expenditure and for the various expenditure components, and then define the expenditures to be carried out. The approval phase characteristically encompasses advanced drafts and rounds of approval by the executive and legislative branches of government. Budgets may then undergo revision over the course of the budget year, as execution proceeds. (Budget cycles typically conclude several months after the budget year concludes, with preparation of final accounts and reports.)

Multiannual exercises of the kind this book describes can play helpful roles through budget-preparation and execution cycles. The basic application of a multiannual exercise would be to determine how revenue and expenditure decisions for the current budget are likely to affect subsequent budgets. Tax-policy settings for the current budget are likely to remain in place over many years. No less important, expenditure decisions for the current budget are likely to have implications for future expenditure. Staff hired for the current budget are likely to remain on the payroll many years into the future; similarly, expenditure on goods and services contracted in the present year is likely to persist; investment projects are likely to extend over more than one year and, at least in some instances, may effectively commit maintenance and other operating resources in subsequent years; and, to the extent the current budget involves deficit finance, it generates future debt-service commitments.

Any year's budget incorporates a large amount of previously committed expenditure programs, that is, expenditure effectively contracted through laws and contracts set in earlier years. It is only to

---

[93] Many governments' "fiscal years" coincide with calendar years, but many differ. The United States' Federal fiscal year 2010 commenced in October 2009; the Government of India's fiscal year 2010 commenced in April 2009.

the extent prospective revenue and available financing together exceed its committed expenditures that a government has discretion to hire new staff, to increase payments on goods and services, or to develop new projects. To the extent it exercises its discretion in favor of authorizing new expenditures, however, it increases committed expenditure in subsequent years. People hired will acquire tenure in their position, new buildings constructed will require services, investment projects commenced will tend to continue to completion and may require maintenance, debt issued must be serviced, and so on. These considerations imply that any current budget proposal should be incomplete unless it includes a discussion of implications for future budgets.

A typical budget-preparation cycle commences with formulation of broad programming assumptions. Government analysts then apply these assumptions to calculate revenue and borrowing projections. (These assumptions should also be applied, using techniques like those this book describes, to calculate projections of the national, external and monetary accounts, to help gauge the overall feasibility of the macroeconomic program.) Meanwhile, "line" ministries and other public agencies will be developing their expenditure programs, presumably on the basis of the government's explicit or implicit sectoral policy objectives. In many economies, the recurrent and non-recurrent aspects of the budget are prepared separately. As the preparation phase of the cycle proceeds, the macroeconomic programming assumptions, revenue and borrowing projections, and the expenditure programs are updated, revised and refined, and brought into mutual consistency. Inevitably, this process involves negotiation among the various government agencies involved, and possibly foreign creditors and donors as well. Several months before the fiscal year begins, the budget is drafted and submitted to the legislature, for debate, further revision, and final approval — if all goes well, before the fiscal year begins. Once approved, the annual budget must be translated into a payments "calendar," i.e., a detailed program of cash expenditures and payments over the fiscal year. Governments characteristically formulate this calendar as a projection for the year as a whole and a relatively firm program for the first month or quarter. The analysts formulating this calendar must need to take account of revenue seasonality, timing of borrowing and debt-service payments, and other factors affecting the budget cash flow.

As the budget-preparation process advances through the year before the actual budget year, analysts and policy-makers will continually formulate new drafts of the coming year's budget, based on evolving assumptions about the state of the world, the basic macroeconomic variables, the financing program, and revised expenditure plans. As new drafts are formulated, the macroeconomic projection exercise should be used to formulate new multiannual projections. Each time, the idea would be to ensure that the projected macroeconomic program is financially feasible. When the budget is submitted to the executive and legislative branches for final approval, the budget documents should include tables and charts from the projection exercise that show that the budget is financially feasible over coming years.

At any moment, many, if not most, governments have separate multiannual projections of revenue, expenditure, and external and internal debt. Their central banks are likely to have multiannual balance-of-payments projections, and may have multiannual projections of their monetary system's performance. A macroeconomic-projection exercise would, or should, encompass projections in all these areas. Indeed, one of the purposes of the macroeconomic-projection exercise is to set out projections in all these areas that are coordinated and consistent — constructed, that is, from the same "state-of-the-world" assumptions and the same macroeconomic program. It would determine financing requirements in the full range of macroeconomic accounts, and ensure that they are all feasible.

The government's and central bank's projection exercises need not be consistent at every instant with the macroeconomic-projection exercise. Among other things, the various exercises should be used to project the consequences of changes, or possible changes, in "state-of-the-world" and programming assumptions. At certain moments, however, it is important that the various projection exercises be substantially consistent with one another and with the macroeconomic-projection exercise. When the annual budget is submitted for approval to

the executive and legislature for approval, for example, it is important
that the main projection exercises be consistent. Similarly, when the
government agrees to an IMF program, or when it agrees on an overall
macroeconomic program as part of a poverty-reduction strategy, then
the various projection analyses should be premised on consistent
assumptions and should give broadly consistent results.

10.5   Sensitivity analysis

Sensitivity analysis may be defined generally as the systematic
examination of the consequences of varying selected assumptions in a
projection exercise. It can be a particularly valuable application for any
business or economic projection exercise, and especially for the
macroeconomic programming exercises discussed here. In the general
approach, certain projection assumptions are designated to take on
varying values. Each set, or "vector," of assumptions subject to variation
in this way constitutes a "scenario." Each scenario's assumption settings
are then used to calculate a projection, and the different scenario results
may be evaluated and compared.

In general, as noted, the basic objective of the multiannual
projection exercise is to determine whether the financing requirements
implied by the assumed evolution of international export markets, import
prices, and interest rates, as well as internal exogenous variables; the
economy's structural parameters; policy-makers' objectives for real
growth, the price level, and the exchange rate; and government policy
settings for expenditure and revenue would be feasible. The general
point of sensitivity analysis would then be to determine how different
assumptions for states of the world and policy settings would affect this
feasibility.

It has become something near standard practice in business and
economic projection analysis to work with "base," "low" (i.e.,
pessimistic) and "high" (i.e., optimistic) scenarios. This can be done for
the projection exercise this book describes — say, with different settings
for real growth rates. It is important to remember, though, that scenarios
need not always fall into base, low and high categories. They can

represent changes of mixed character — involving, say, different rates of exchange-rate depreciation, or combinations of shifts in assumptions.

Thus, for example, an oil-exporting economy, a "high" scenario might have, *inter alia*, a higher oil-export price and lower world interest rates than the base scenario; a "low" scenario could have, *inter alia*, lower oil-export prices and higher world interest rates. On the other hand, an alternative scenario might have a higher oil-export price and *higher* world interest rates than the base scenario. The comparison of the two scenarios would then be mixed, rather than one being "higher" and the other "lower." Each of these "state-of-the-world" scenarios might then be associated with different combinations of real-GDP growth, inflation and real-effective exchange-rate assumptions. Indeed, *within* each "state-of-the-world" scenario, it may be possible and useful to set out "subsidiary" base-, high-, and low "macroeconomic" scenarios, with different combinations of policy objectives and settings.

There is no general best way to develop alternative scenarios from a base scenario. When structuring sensitivity analyses, however, it is important to be clear about the nature of the specific questions they are intended to address. Sensitivity analysis for varying states of the world is likely to be designed address the issue of how vulnerable the economy would be to events beyond its control. The subsidiary sensitivity analysis could therefore address the feasibility of policy settings given the state-of-the-world context.

It is perfectly possible to carry out a sensitivity analysis in which the growth rates of the main "exogenous" variables — e.g., real world economic growth, the world price level, world interest rates (LIBOR), and the real world oil price — vary from year to year, that is, in which each projection year amounts to a separate projection exercise.[94] In such a year-by-year projection analysis, the assumptions may be set so as to

---

[94] The growth rates of these exogenous variables could be formulated randomly, according to a multivariate normal distribution relating them to one another by assumed correlation coefficients. If this is done, a "Monte-Carlo" methodology can be applied. This would consist of maintaining a given set of policy settings and carrying out the projection exercise a large number of times. Since the assumptions for each "run" of the projection exercise would be different, the results would be different. The average results can then be evaluated.

produce episodes of crisis and episodes of "non-crisis" macroeconomic performance. Policy settings could then be adjusted to best advantage against these exogenous variables. Analysis of this kind is complex and usually not interesting. This is because projecting crisis and non-crisis episodes over time as assumptions would be so arbitrary. For most purposes, it is best to vary the growth rates of these variables for the projection period as a whole, so that each full projection, with a specific "vector" of growth rates, constitutes a projection exercise. In such exercises, the point would be to set stable multiannual policy settings, to determine whether they are likely to bring about feasible programs.

Section 10.6 below describes illustrative sensitivity-analysis projections for the Pacífica exercise.

10.6 Sensitivity analysis for "Pacífica"

The sensitivity analysis described here for the Pacífica projection is intended mainly to be illustrative. Its scenarios deal with changes to internal policy settings: world and other exogenous conditions are maintained unchanged in all scenarios, at the values used in the projection exercise as described thus far. Much can be learned from varying world and other exogenous conditions, of course, but the present purpose is to illustrate the sensitivity-analysis technique, and restricting the exercise to internal policy settings helps keep it simple.

The "base" scenario, "Scenario 1," comprises the policy settings in the projection exercise as described thus far. Table 31 gives the key scenario assumptions as well as the national-, fiscal-, external-, and monetary-accounts projection results for Pacífica discussed in the preceding chapters. Under this scenario, although the external debt-GDP ratio would diminish slightly, the fiscal deficit would remain significant, the current-account deficit would tend to widen, the growth rate of per-capita real non-government consumption would be fairly low, and the government's internal debt-GDP ratio would increase.

The first sensitivity comparison addresses the question of whether and how exchange-rate depreciation could improve the projection results. Accordingly, the second scenario is the same in all respects as the base scenario, with the single exception that the real-effective exchange rate is assumed to depreciate further than in the base scenario: rather than remaining at 9.60 per U.S. dollar after December 2009, the exchange rate is assumed to depreciate over 2010 to end the year at 10 per dollar, but remain at that value thereafter.

Table 32 shows the two scenarios' comparative results. To be sure, the single change in the assumptions between the first and second scenarios is a simplification, made only for the present illustrative purposes. (Among other things, the higher export proceeds resulting from the depreciated exchange rate beginning in 2009 would be likely to stimulate output, and to this extent the analyst might wish to incorporate a higher real-GDP growth rate in the higher-depreciation scenario compared with the base scenario. Moreover, the higher nominal growth rate in the exchange rate may imply a higher inflation rate. In general, since policy programs tend to involve a broad range of policy variables, realistic sensitivity analysis regarding policy choice may involve scenarios involving a relatively large number of changes in assumptions.)

Table 32 shows that, all other things being equal, the additional exchange-rate depreciation would reduce the average current-account deficit as a percentage of GDP over the years 2009–2015 from 1.4 to 1.0 per cent of GDP. (The annual current-account deficit would average US$406 million under Scenario 1 but US$292 million under Scenario 2. Note that the U.S. dollar value of GDP would be lower under Scenario 2 on account of the exchange-rate depreciation.) The additional exchange-rate depreciation would also reduce the average non-financial central-government deficit slightly, because of the specific structure of Pacífica's central-government accounts: the deficit would average 2 per cent of GDP under Scenario 1 but 1.8 per cent of GDP under Scenario 2. (Whether higher exchange-rate depreciation would tend to increase or reduce the government deficit is an empirical matter depending on the specific structure of the country's government accounts. If, say, the government derived less revenue from oil exports or had larger external debt-service charges, faster exchange-rate depreciation might *widen* the public deficit.)

Total external debt, which includes the unidentified non-guaranteed private debt, would end 2015 slightly *higher* as a percentage of GDP in the higher-depreciation scenario compared with the base scenario — 25.8 per cent of GDP compared with 25.5 per cent, even though the lower current-account deficit would lead to a smaller external financing need as percentage of GDP. This is because the depreciation would reduce the measured value of GDP in U.S. dollars, which would tend to increase any external debt-GDP ratios. Public and publicly-guaranteed debt would end 2015 *higher* as a percentage of GDP in Scenario 2 compared with Scenario 1, 22.1 per cent compared with 21.3 per cent. But private non-guaranteed debt, including the unidentified debt required to fill the financing gap, would come out significantly *lower* as a percentage of GDP in Scenario 2 compared with Scenario 1, 0.9 per cent compared with 1.6 per cent.

The central government's net internal financing would average 1.3 per cent of GDP in the higher-depreciation scenario, somewhat lower than the 1.5 per cent of GDP projected for the base scenario. Against the improved fiscal result, however, the faster depreciation would entail some reduction in living standards: over the years 2009–2015 average real non-government consumption would be 3.7 per cent lower in the higher-depreciation scenario than in the base scenario. This is partly the consequence of the assumption that real-GDP growth would not change despite the increase in exports and decrease in imports resulting from the exchange-rate depreciation. A higher real-GDP growth rate would imply, all other things being the same, a *higher* real non-government consumption level. It is important to remember, however, that if the real-GDP growth rate is assumed to be higher in Scenario 2, the overall capital-formation rate would be higher, which would at least partially offset the effect of the higher real GDP on non-government consumption.

The third scenario is the same in all respects as the base scenario, with the single exception that the value-added tax rate is assumed to rise from 12 to 14 per cent on January 1, 2010 and to remain at that value thereafter. Because the higher tax rate would probably encourage more avoidance and evasion, the collection efficiency is assumed to decline from 49.1 per cent in 2009 to 47.1 per cent in 2010, although it increases thereafter by 0.5 per cent per year. These changes would directly affect the fiscal accounts. The average central-government deficit over 2009–2015 would be 1 per cent, compared with 2 per cent in the base scenario. The smaller deficit would imply that the central government's internal financing requirement would be smaller. Central-government internal debt would end 2015 at 25.2 per cent of GDP in the higher-value-added-tax scenario, compared with 27.9 per cent in the base scenario.

One important point to note here is that real per-capita non-government consumption would not differ between the higher-value-added-tax and base scenarios, despite the increased tax collection in the higher-value-added-tax scenario. This is unrealistic, of course. It comes about through the simplified way in which the national-accounts projection is formulated in this exercise — that is, by having consumption imports depend on real GDP rather than on disposable income (see Chapter 6). (In effect, non-government saving is assumed to decline by the full amount of the increased tax.) Table 34 compares a fourth scenario with the base scenario. The projection assumptions under the fourth scenario are exactly the same as under the base scenario, with the single exception that real GDP growth would rise gradually from -4.5 per cent in 2009 to 6 per cent in 2015 in the higher-growth scenario, rather than to 5 per cent as in the base scenario. The programmed average real growth rate over the years 2009–2015 would be 2.3 per cent in the higher-growth scenario, compared with 1.9 per cent in the base scenario. With all other assumptions the same, higher growth would bring about higher living standards: per-capita real non-government consumption would grow at an annual average rate of 1.8 per cent over the years 2009–2015 in the higher-growth scenario. This would still be a rather low rate, but it would be well above the 1.2 per cent annual average rate in the base scenario. The higher-growth scenario would allow better progress on poverty reduction: in the higher-growth scenario, the overall poverty incidence and the extreme-poverty incidence would decline to 14.9 and 6.2 per cent respectively in 2015, compared with 15.5 and 6.6 per cent in the base scenario.

Meanwhile, the average current-account deficit would average 1.7 per cent of (a larger) GDP in the higher-growth scenario, compared with 1.4 per cent of GDP in the base scenario. The basic reason, of course, is that higher growth rate would lead to higher imports. The average central-government deficit would be about the same as a percentage of GDP in both the higher-growth and the base scenarios, about 2 per cent of GDP. Higher growth would generate higher government revenue, but GDP itself would also be higher.

Total external debt would end 2015 at 24.8 per cent of GDP, at US$8.8 billion, in the higher-growth scenario, compared with 25.5 per cent of GDP or US$8.2 billion in the base scenario. Perhaps unexpectedly, however, government internal debt would end 2015 at 24.5 per cent of GDP in the higher-growth scenario, a slightly *lower* figure than the base scenario's 25.8 per cent. This is because GDP would be higher in the higher-growth scenario. This illustrates an important point about how GDP growth assumptions affect the macroeconomic balances. Higher real growth rates tend to deepen current-account deficits, and will widen government deficits if expenditure grows more than revenue with higher GDP. When measured as percentages of GDP, however, the increased deficits may be offset by the higher GDP.

As noted, these sensitivity comparisons are intended as illustrative. The main point is simply that the projection exercise this book describes lends itself to sensitivity analysis, and that this sensitivity analysis can provide useful and even counterintuitive results. When results are counterintuitive, analysts may want to examine the full range of assumptions and results to understand the reasons the projection behaves as it does.

10.7 *Sensitivity analysis involving debt-reduction exercises*

Sensitivity analysis is the obvious methodological choice to analyze the consequences of debt-reduction exercises. At one level, the exercise could consist of a straightforward comparison of the results of a debt-reduction scenario and a base scenario. The debt-reduction scenario could incorporate the debt reduction but otherwise be the same as the base scenario. Comparison of the results of the two scenarios could focus on total external debt and central-government internal debt as percentages of GDP at the end of the projection period. It may be more practically meaningful, though, to compare the average current-account and central-government deficits over the projection period. This is because the reduction in these deficits resulting from debt reduction would indicate the degree to which policy-makers would have scope to stimulate real-GDP growth and to increase government expenditure on development and poverty reduction.

In any case, the analyst may wish to do the exercise in a different way. The presumable objectives of the debt-reduction exercise are to permit higher growth rates in real GDP, per-capita real non-government consumption, and government social-sectors expenditure. The analyst may therefore wish to incorporate changes besides the debt reduction in the debt-reduction scenario's assumptions, including higher real-GDP growth rates and higher social-sectors expenditure. Comparison of the results of the two scenarios could focus on per-capita real non-government consumption, poverty incidence, and per-capita real social-sectors expenditure, in addition to total external debt and central-government internal debt as percentages of GDP at the end of the projection period and on the average current-account and central-government deficits over the projection period.

For Pacífica, the debt-reduction exercise considered is an exchange with sovereign bondholders, under which the debt outstanding is repurchased for debt on the same terms but half the value. The fifth scenario, accordingly, is the same as the base scenario except for the single difference that the sovereign-debt stock is assumed to decline by 50 per cent over 2009.

Table 35 shows the comparative results of the debt-reduction and base scenarios. The reduced interest bill would narrow the current-account and central-government deficits. With the debt reduction, the current-account deficit would average 1.2 per cent of GDP over the 2009–2015 projection period, compared with 1.4 per cent of GDP without the debt reduction. With the debt reduction, the central-government deficit would average 1.8 per cent of GDP over the 2009–2015 projection period, compared with 2 per cent of GDP without the debt reduction. The external and fiscal borrowing requirements would be lower following the debt reduction. With debt reduction, the total external-debt stock would end 2015 at 22.7 per cent of GDP compared with 25.5 per cent of GDP without debt reduction, while the central government's internal debt stock would end 2015 at 24.8 per cent of GDP compared with 25.8 per cent of GDP without debt reduction.

Table 36 reports the results of one last exercise. Scenario 6 has the same debt reduction as Scenario 5, but in Scenario 6 the real-GDP growth rates rise gradually to 6 per cent, not 5 per cent, in 2015. With this additional change in the assumptions, average per-capita real non-government consumption would turn out 1.4 per cent higher over 2009–2015 than in the base scenario: per-capita real non-government consumption would grow at an average annual rate of 1.8 per cent over the projection period rather than 1.2 per cent. The poverty and extreme-poverty incidence would decline to 14.9 and 6.2 per cent in 2015, compared with 15.5 and 6.6 per cent. The central-government deficit would average 1.8 per cent in Scenario 6 rather than 2 per cent as in Scenario 1 over the projection period. The total external-debt stock would end 2015 at 22.3 per cent rather than 25.8 per cent, and the central government's internal debt stock would end 2015 at 24.9 per cent of GDP compared with 25.8.

Curiously, the current-account deficit would still average 1.4 per cent of GDP over the projection period, as in the base scenario. The time pattern of the current-account deficit would be somewhat different from that of the base scenario: it would be smaller in the earlier years of the projection period, but then higher toward the end of the projection period, as real-GDP growth ran at a higher rate.

As noted in Section 5.4 above, under the Highly-Indebted Poorest Countries initiative, an economy's public debt stock was characterized as "sustainable" if its net present value was within 150 per cent of net exports of goods and non-factor services. This book suggests taking a different approach to analyzing sustainability, however. An economy's debt stock could be characterized as sustainable if projection analysis indicates that the debt service, and in particular interest due, would remain steady or diminish over time as a percentage of GDP, so long as the economy could maintain adequate growth, poverty reduction, and government expenditure on development and poverty reduction. This definition of sustainability seems more directly practical than the HIPC definition, and in any case makes sustainability a dynamic concept, as it should be.

For better or worse, the HIPC sustainability definition has become more or less standard for analysts. The net-present-value calculation was essential for debt-reduction operations involving multiple creditors, because it was necessary to perform the calculations needed to determine their "burden sharing." Nevertheless, it is important to bear in mind that an external-debt stock's eventual "burden" for an economy is the debt service, not the stock *per se*. It stands to reason, then, that a proper evaluation of what is commonly understood as debt sustainability — that is, an economy's continuing capacity to maintain its debt service — should focus on whether the current-account and government deficits — and, in particular, the external interest bill — would be likely to grow over time, *given* that the growth rates of real GDP, per-capita real non-government consumption, and government expenditure on development and social services remain adequate.

10.8 A concluding note

The basic purpose of a multiannual macroeconomic programming exercise is to address the following question: Is the government macroeconomic program — encompassing assumptions about the state of the world, the evolution of the economy's basic macroeconomic variables, the government financing program, and the government's non-interest expenditure program — likely to prove financially feasible over coming years? For many reasons, some obvious and some perhaps less so, it is useful for a government to be able to assure itself and its various stakeholders that its macroeconomic program is indeed likely to prove financially feasible over coming years. A government may therefore find it worth dedicating resources to develop, maintain, and routinely apply a macroeconomic programming exercise for this purpose.

This book has presented a broad methodological approach to macroeconomic consistency analysis, intended as a help for macroeconomic policy planning in developing economies. The approach is intentionally general, open to adaptation and variation according to the economy under consideration and the specific questions that need to be addressed.

This writer has found this methodology useful to address a broad range of policy issues. Its structure can helpfully elucidate the linkages among the various macroeconomic sub-systems. It can be useful for policy planning. It can also help address issues of vulnerability. It cannot be emphasized too strongly, however, that it is not useful for every type of macroeconomic analysis. Given the characteristics of its methodology, it should especially not be considered useful for *prediction* of economic outcomes. Nor would it be especially useful for understanding the processes that change macroeconomic equilibria and then drive the economy toward them. Even where and when consistency analysis of the kind this book describes is the appropriate methodology, results must be interpreted and applied with care. As always, when a projection exercise produces counter-intuitive results, the analyst should examine the results and the underlying intermediate results to figure out what drives them.

A large body of what may be described as folk wisdom has accumulated among people who work with computer "models" of different kinds. For people who develop and apply the kinds of exercise this book describes, this folk wisdom is highly relevant, and should be sought out and applied as eagerly as carefully as any of the macroeconomic principles. One of the most important aspects of this folk wisdom is summarized in the aphorism "KISS" — "Keep it simple, stupid." The exercise should never become more complicated than necessary, and above all never more complicated than the analysts applying and using it can comprehend. Changes should be lucidly documented, especially if the exercise is to be used over a long period of time, and especially if there is turnover among the analysts who work with it. When an analyst sets assumptions at values different from default values, specific reasons for doing so should be indicated. (Excel and other spreadsheet programs permit comments to be placed in cells, and these can and should be used to explain unusual assumptions.)

Another long-standing body of folk wisdom in the computer-modeling trade is summarized in the well-known aphorism "GIGO," or "Garbage in, garbage out." To state the point just a bit less cynically, it is important to bear in mind that anything a computer projection exercise ever reveals is the consequence of its data and assumptions. A macroeconomic model can project continually rising external debt, for example, only because it incorporates an excessively high value for the elasticity of imports with respect to real GDP. In general, when setting assumptions, analysts are best advised to give careful thought beforehand about how these assumptions should be expected to affect projection results, and to watch out for and explain unanticipated consequences.

The kinds of spreadsheet exercise this book describes are intended to be used for several years, during which they will inevitably undergo fundamental revision and development. To the extent possible, revision and development should include simplification. It may be useful to maintain a manual, describing procedures and methodologies, and to update it as the exercise is revised. As analysts understand more clearly how the exercise is used and applied, opportunities to simplify are likely to become clearer. Paradoxically, spreadsheet simplification is often a complicated and difficult process, but it is important to keep spreadsheets as transparent as possible.

Spreadsheets of the kind this book describes should incorporate as many "checks" as possible, ensuring such things as (i) proper summation of identities, (ii) consistency of projection values across worksheets, and (iii) appropriate signs for projected variables — e.g., debt stocks, disbursements and repayment flows should never be projected to turn negative. It is nearly fair enough to say that analysts should include all calculation checks they can think of, and use them to guide any debugging that may be needed. Worksheets should include a cell in a highly visible location indicating whether all checks are satisfied.[95]

For developing economies, given the widespread experience of excessive public indebtedness and calamitous macroeconomic instability over the past thirty years, governments owe it to their various "stakeholders" — taxpaying citizens as well as international agencies

---

[95] It cannot be too strongly emphasized that errors accumulate all too easily in Excel workbooks. The larger and the more complicated the workbook, the faster it has been constructed, and the larger the number of people who work on it, the more likely errors are to seep in. Those with long experience of computer programming recognize this reality as a fact of life. Careful review; continual, probing examination of results; and incorporation of checks are the best remedies.

and foreign investors — to formulate their public expenditure and financing programs with care, discipline, and transparency, and with a multiannual perspective, to ensure not only that expenditure programs address priority national needs, but also that they are financially sustainable. As they formulate their own plans, international agencies and foreign investors owe it to their own stakeholders to ensure that their activities are grounded in careful programming. The macroeconomic projection exercise this book describes can be useful for these ends.

Chapter annexes

*Chapter 2, Annex 1. Summary of steps to formulate a
macroeconomic projection for each year*

This Annex summarizes the procedure for formulating a multiannual macroeconomic projection. The basic idea is to project, for each year in the projection period, "all but one line" in each of the basic accounts systems — the national, fiscal, external, and monetary accounts — on the basis of common programming assumptions. The one line in each set of accounts that is not projected from assumptions is the "residual" account. In each set of accounts, this residual is calculated from the other accounts in the system, using that system of accounts' basic accounting identity. Its magnitude is used to judge whether the projection is likely to prove feasible.

In the methodology this book describes, the solution procedure for the national, fiscal, external, and monetary accounts taken together is simultaneous, not sequenced, because each sub-sector's solution procedure draws from other sub-sectors' projections. To understand how a macroeconomic program is used to formulate a projection, however, it is helpful, if not really quite "right," to view the solution procedure as if it were in a sequence. For each year, then, the sequence would be as follows:

Assumptions:

1. Set assumptions for such ***structural parameters*** as the incremental capital-output ratio (ICOR), tax-administration

279

indicators, elasticities governing the export and import flows, elasticities of the demand for money with respect to real GDP and expected inflation, etc.

2. Set assumptions for **international conditions**, including prices of and world-trade growth in main exports, import prices, interest rates, etc.

3. Set assumptions for relevant **internal exogenous variables**, such as population growth.

4. Set the key macroeconomic programming assumptions, including (i) **real-GDP** growth, possibly including sectoral real growth rates; (ii) growth rates of the year-end and year-average **price level**, possibly including sectoral growth rates; (iii) growth rates of the year-average (real-effective) and year-end **exchange rates**; and (iv) the central bank's **gross foreign-exchange reserve holdings**.

5. Program relevant **policy variables**, including tax-rate settings, monetary-policy variables, etc.

6. Program **government consumption and capital-formation expenditure**.

7. Program **net public-sector external and internal borrowing**.

National-expenditure accounts:

8. Project **overall capital formation**, by applying assumed relationships between programmed real GDP growth in later years (excluding the terms-of-trade effect) and capital formation.

9. Project the increase in **inventory holdings** over the year.

10. Project **exports and imports of goods and non-facto services**.

11. Apply assumptions for **government consumption and capital formation**. *Residually* calculate **non-government consumption and capital formation**. *Determine whether the implied growth rates of per-capita real non-government consumption and real*

non-government capital formation would be feasible — i.e., high enough.

External accounts:

12. Bring in the U.S. dollar values of the projections of *exports and imports of goods and non-factor services* from the national-accounts exercise.
13. Project *all other "above-the-line" non-debt flows*, including unrequited transfers and non-debt capital-account flows (including the foreign-investment, short-term capital, and net errors-and-omissions flows).
14. Project the "below-the-line" *central-bank net international-reserve inflows*.
15. Project the *disbursement, repayment and valuation-change flows* of the various classes of *external debt*, as well as the implied debt stocks and interest charges.

Fiscal accounts:

16. *Residually* calculate the *disbursement of unidentified private external debt or accumulation of central-bank foreign-exchange reserves* that would reconcile the above- and below-the-line balance-of-payments flows (taking account of unprogrammed interest). *Determine whether this residual would be feasible — i.e., low enough.* Project *tax and non-tax revenue.*
17. Project *non-interest expenditure flows*, including the assumed consumption and capital-formation expenditure and transfers and subsidies.
18. Bring in the projected *disbursement, repayment, interest due and stocks outstanding of public external debt*, from the external-accounts exercise.

19. Project *disbursement, repayment, interest, and stocks outstanding of identified public internal debt.* Also, project *net increases in public-sector bank deposits and other public-sector asset holdings.*

20. *Residually* calculate the *increase in unidentified public-sector internal debt or deposits at the central bank* required to reconcile the above- and below-the-line public-accounts flows (taking account of unprogrammed interest). *Determine whether this residual would be feasible — i.e., low enough.* Project the *year-average and year-end money stocks* that the public is willing to hold, as well as the change over the year in the money stock, by applying the basic projection assumptions.

Monetary accounts:

21. Project the increase in the *monetary base* using the assumed marginal money multiplier.

22. Bring in the flow increase in the *central bank's net international assets* from the external-accounts projection (i.e., the U.S. dollar flow value is multiplied by the average exchange rate).

23. Project the flow increases in the **central bank's net internal asset position**. Residually calculate the increase in the **central bank's non-monetary liability position** required "to close" the monetary flows. Determine whether this increase is feasible — i.e., small enough.

24. Project the flow increases in the *commercial banks' consolidated balance sheet.*

Chapter 2, Annex 2. *Macroeconomic consistency and sustainability: a simplified version of the projection exercise*

Equations [*(1)–(20)*] below make up a summary macroeconomic projection exercise encompassing the fiscal, external, national, and monetary accounts. The main purpose is to show the basic macroeconomic system structure in a simplified way, in equations, and so to help make the more detailed projection exercise the book presents easier to understand. Even so, the simplified exercise as presented here can be applied to construct useful, if "stylized," spreadsheet projections for actual economies.

The essence of the approach is to program real growth rates of (a) GDP, (b) exports of goods and non-factor services, (c) government expenditure, (d) external government debt, and (e) population for each future year, and then to use them to calculate implied growth rates of (i) per-capita non-government consumption, (ii) non-government external debt and (iii) government internal debt. Inadequate (or even negative) per-capita non-government consumption growth and/or very rapid growth of non-government external debt and government internal debt would imply that, taken together, the programmed growth rates of GDP, government expenditure, and government external debt would not be feasible.

In this simplified version of the exercise, the macroeconomic aggregates — i.e., GDP and the various components of expenditure — are all taken to be in real terms. (If applied in an actual projection exercise, it is generally useful to express them in constant dollars, i.e., dollar values at a base year's prices and exchange rate.) This simplified exercise therefore abstracts from such important variables as the price level, the exchange rate, and the terms of trade. It does, however, encompass (a) the GDP-capital formation relationship, (b) the national accounts, (c) the general-government accounts, (d) the external accounts, and (e) the monetary accounts.

Define the following variables:

Y	real GDP;
I	total real capital formation (including government capital formation);
K'	year-end real capital stock;
T	real government revenue;
Z	real external transfers to government;
G	real government consumption expenditure;
J	real government capital formation;
H	real government internal transfers and subsidies;
X	real exports of goods and non-factor services;
Q	real imports of goods and non-factor services;
F	net real current-account inflows excluding net exports, real external transfers to government, and net interest due;
W	net real non-debt capital inflows;
E'	real year-end stock of government external debt;
L'	real year-end stock of central-bank external liabilities;
A'	real year-end stock of central-bank external assets;
U'	real year-end stock of non-government external debt;
D'	real year-end stock of government internal debt;
M'	real year-end money stock;
B'	real year-end monetary base;
V'	real year-end central-bank net internal assets;
S	real non-government saving, and
P	real government primary surplus.

The primes following the variables E', L', A', U', and D' indicate that they are year-end stock values. The variables E, L, A, U, and D (that is, without the prime) are the year-average values corresponding to the year-end values:

$$E = (E'_{-1} + E')/2 = E'_{-1} + (\Delta E'/2), \text{ where } \Delta E' = E' - E'_{-1};$$

likewise for the year-average values L, A, U and D.

The following variables are projection assumptions:

v   incremental capital-output ratio, net of capital depreciation;
v'   capital-output ratio;
d   depreciation rate of the capital stock;
r_U interest rate on non-government external debt;
r_D interest rate on government internal debt;
r_E interest rate on government external debt;
r_L interest rate on central-bank external liabilities;
r_A interest rate on central-bank external assets;
m   marginal money multiplier;
t   elasticity of T with respect to Y;
q   elasticity of Q with respect to Y;
f   ratio of F to Y; and
w   ratio of W to Y.

In general, the growth rate of any variable "x" is given by $(x/x_{-1})-1$. The values of the following variables are programming assumptions:

$a = A'/(Q/12)$,
$g_Y = (Y/Y_{-1})-1$;
$g_Z = (Z/Z_{-1})-1$;
$g_G = (G/G_{-1})-1$;
$g_H = (H/H_{-1})-1$;
$g_J = (J/J_{-1})-1$;
$g_L = (L'/L'_{-1})-1$;
$g_E = (E'/E'_{-1})-1$; and
$g_N = (N'/N_{-1})-1$.

The real flows of interest due on government internal and external debt and on non-government external debt are taken to be based on the year-average debt stock. Thus, interest due on the government's external debt is given by

$$r_E\, E = r_E\, (E'_{-1} + E')/2 = r_E\, E'_{-1} + r_E\, \Delta E'/2, \quad \text{where}$$

$$\Delta E' = E' - E'_{-1} = E'_{-1}\, g_E.$$

The first equation of the projection system gives **gross fixed capital formation** in year t as a function of (i) the programmed growth rate "g_Y" in the following year, (ii) the incremental capital-output ratio for capital formation carried out in year t, and (iii) the capital-depreciation rate d,

(1) $$I = Y v \left[g_{Y(+1)} + d \right].$$

This is because GDP growth in year t+1 is given by

$$\Delta Y_{+1}/Y = (I/Y)/v - d \, (K'_{-1}/Y)/v'$$

$$= \left[(I/Y)/v + d \right],$$

(since by definition $(K'_{-1}/Y) = v'$).

Next, **government revenue** (excluding external transfers) is given by

(2) $$T = T_{-1} \left[(1 + g_Y)^t \right],$$

where "t" is a policy-programming assumption. External transfers to government are given by

(3) $$Z = Z_{-1} \left[1 + g_Z \right].$$

The non-interest government-expenditure flows are based on the assumptions for "g_G", "g_J" and "g_H." These are **government consumption expenditure**,

(4) $$G = G_{-1} \left[1 + g_G \right];$$

government expenditure on **gross fixed capital formation**,

(5) $$J = J_{-1} \left[1 + g_J \right];$$

and **government internal transfers and subsidies**,

(6) $$H = H_{-1} \left[1 + g_H \right].$$

Exports and imports of goods and non-factor services follow from the assumptions for g_X and q. ***Exports of goods and non-factor services*** are given by

(7) $$X = X_{-1} [1 + g_X]$$

(as explained below, the growth rate of exports *should not* be linked positively to real-GDP growth), and ***imports of goods and non-factor services*** by

(8) $$Q = Q_{-1} [(1 + g_Y)^q].$$

Non-government consumption is then determined residually using the national-accounts expenditure identity so as to be consistent with the projections of G, I, X and Q,

(9) $$C = Y - [(G + J) + (I - J) + (X - Q)]$$

$$= Y - (G + I + X - Q).$$

One basic purpose of the exercise is to determine whether the growth rates g_Y, g_X, g_G, g_J, and g_H taken together constitute a feasible macroeconomic "program," given the other assumptions and initial conditions of the economy.

In the balance of payments, *"other" current-account flows* — that is, current-account flows other than net exports of goods and non-factor services, net interest, and external transfers to government, encompassing non-interest factor-service net exports and all other net unrequited transfers — are given by

(10) $$F = f Y.$$

Non-debt financial account flows (including net investment, short-term non-debt financial flows, and net errors and omissions) are given by

(11) $$W = w Y.$$

One of this exercise's basic "strategic" approaches is *to program* — that is, to assume — the growth rates of the government external debt and the central bank's net external liabilities. It is then possible to calculate *both* the net increase in non-government net external liabilities, U', that would be required to complete the financing of the external accounts, *and* the net increase in the government's net internal liabilities, D', that would be required to complete the financing of the fiscal accounts. If the growth rates of either U' or D' would need to be significantly higher than the respective sources of finance would be likely to be willing and able to provide — in particular, if they significantly exceed the growth rate of real GDP — then the programmed macroeconomic policy and government expenditure would presumably be unfeasible, and would need to be adjusted.

That is, applying the programmed values g_E and g_L, the *flow increases* in the ***government's external debt*** and the ***central bank's external debt*** are given by

$$(12) \qquad\qquad\qquad \Delta E' = g_E\, E'_{-1}$$

and

$$(13) \qquad\qquad\qquad \Delta L' = g_L\, L'_{-1}.$$

Using the programmed value "a" (in months of imports of goods and non-factor services) the *flow increase in the central bank's external asset stock* (basically, gross international reserves) is given by

$$(14) \qquad\qquad \Delta A' = [a\,(Q/12)] - A'_{-1}.$$

Applying the assumptions for the interest rates on government and non-government external debt to the year-average debt stocks, and the assumptions for the interest rates on central-bank external assets to the year-average asset stock, the *flow increase in non-government external debt* is given by

$$(15) \qquad \Delta U' = r_U\, U + r_E\, E + r_L\, L - r_A\, A - (X - Q + Z + F + W)$$

$$- \Delta E' - \Delta L' + \Delta A'.$$

This equation is simply a rearrangement of the balance-of-payments identity. That is, the sum of the current and financial accounts is

$$[(X - Q) + r_A A - (r_U U + r_E E) + Z + F] + [\Delta E' + \Delta U' + W],$$

and the central-bank financing of the balance-of-payments *deficit* is given by

$$\Delta L' - \Delta A'.$$

Equation (15) may be solved for $\Delta U'$, making use of

$$U = U'_{-1} + (\Delta U'/2):$$

$$\Delta U' = [(r_U U'_{-1}) + (r_E E) + (r_L L) - (r_A A) - (X - Q + F + W)$$

$$- \Delta E' - \Delta L' + \Delta A']/[1 - (r_U/2)].$$

The primary surplus P is given by

(16) $$\Delta P = T + Z - (G + H + J).$$

Applying the assumptions for the interest rates on government external and internal debt to their year-average stocks, the *flow increase in government internal debt* is given by

(17) $$\Delta D' = r_D D + r_E E - P - \Delta E',$$

since the government deficit is given by

$$\Delta D' + \Delta E' = r_D D + r_E E - P.$$

Equation (17) can be solved for $\Delta D'$, making use of

$$D = D'_{-1} + (\Delta D'/2):$$

$$\Delta D' = [(r_D D'_{-1}) + (r_E E) - P - \Delta E']/[1 - (r_D/2)].$$

Two equations describe the monetary aggregates. Assume that the economy's average money holding over each year, M, is given (as a percentage of GDP). Since

$$M = M'_{-1} + (\Delta M'/2)$$

the *flow increase in the money supply* is given by

$$\Delta M' = 2 \, (M - M'_{-1}).$$

The *flow increase in the monetary base* is then given by

(18) $\Delta B' = \Delta M'/m,$

and the *flow increase in the central bank's net internal assets* is given by

(19) $\Delta V' = \Delta B' + (\Delta L' - \Delta A').$

That is, $\Delta V'$ is whatever amount is required to ensure that the monetary authority's flow balance identity is satisfied, with the increase in assets $\Delta V'$ and $\Delta A'$ "backing" the increase in liabilities $\Delta L'$ and $\Delta B'$.

    The system's final equation gives the *year-average population*,

(20) $N = N_{-1} \, [1 + g_N].$

This is used to calculate projected per-capita values.

    In summary, for each projection year t, the analyst would program the government expenditure assumptions, "g_G," "g_J," "g_H,", as well as the growth rates of real GDP and (real) government external debt "g_Y" and "g_E." The equations listed can then be used to solve for the growth rate of per-capita non-government consumption,

$$g_{C/N} = [(C/C_{-1})/(1 + g_N)] - 1;$$

the year-end non-government external-debt stock as a percentage of GDP,

$$U'/Y = (U'_{-1} + \Delta U')/Y; \text{ and}$$

the year-end government internal-debt stock as a percentage of GDP,

$$D'/Y = (D'_{-1} + \Delta D')/Y.$$

    These projected values would then be examined to determine whether they are sufficiently high, in the case of per-capita non-government consumption, or sufficiently low, in the cases of the debt ratios, to ensure the program's feasibility.

This projection exercise can be straightforwardly adapted for spreadsheet use. Although too simplified for detailed policy analysis, it can provide some useful indicators of orders of magnitude. One way to apply this simplified exercise would be to program the growth rates of E and L to equal that of GDP, thus maintaining the ratios of E and L to GDP unchanged, and then determine whether the implied growth rates of U and D would be less than or greater than that of GDP. If both growth rates turn out smaller than the growth rate of GDP, an interesting exercise may then be to test smaller and smaller growth rates of E, to determine how rapidly the government's external-debt burden could be reduced. For debt-reduction exercises, one obvious approach would be to reduce the starting ratio E/Y to some new level — possibly along with policy changes affecting other variables, such as government revenue or government consumption expenditure — and then to set the future growth rates of E so as to maintain that ratio thereafter. The resulting growth rates of U and D would then indicate whether the debt reduction — and accompanying policy changes — would ensure "sustainability."

Different solution strategies would be possible, of course. For example, the growth rate of the net government internal debt (D) could be programmed, and the growth rates of the net government and non-government external debt then determined so as "to close" the government and external accounts. The advantage of programming the government external debt and solving for the growth rates of the government internal and non-government external debt is that doing so more explicitly addresses the sustainability characteristics that would result from a specified government external-debt strategy.

In this exercise, the export growth rate, g_X, should be considered independent of the real-GDP growth rate. In particular, it is inadvisable to assume, in this or in any projection exercise, that the real export growth rate will be linked positively to the real GDP growth rate. Linking the export and GDP growth rates positively has the effect of assuming away the basic external-accounts constraint, i.e., that faster GDP growth will induce import growth, at least in the short and probably in the medium term, without there being any way to increase export earnings. Over the longer term, a small commodity-exporting economy would presumably tend to grow at the same real rate as the value of its

exports. In the short and medium term, however, the real growth rates of
its export value and GDP could diverge. All other things — in particular,
the terms of trade — being equal, if export growth is less than GDP
growth, external debt would tend to grow faster, while if export growth
exceeds GDP growth, non-government consumption would tend to grow
slower.

The *net* external non-government and internal government debt
stocks could come out equal to or less than zero in any given year. If the
net non-government external debt fell below zero, this would indicate
that the economy's non-government sectors had acquired external assets
in excess of their external liabilities. If the net internal government debt
fell below zero, this would indicate that the government had acquired
assets (including deposit balances) exceeding its internal liabilities.

Some care must be taken in projecting interest rates on external
debt. To the extent the programmed real-GDP growth rate is below the
projected external world interest rates, the more likely it would be that
the macroeconomic-policy and government-expenditure programs would
prove unsustainable, since U/Y and D/Y would tend to grow faster.

The following table lists the variables in the simplified
projection exercise.

Table. List of variables and parameters in the simplified projection exercise

Definition	*Variable*
Central-bank external assets	A
Monetary base	B
Non-government consumption	C
Government internal debt	D
Government external debt	E
Net current-account inflows excluding net exports and net interest due	F
Government consumption expenditure	G
Government internal transfers and subsidies	H
Total gross fixed capital formation	I
Government capital formation	J
Capital stock	K
Central-bank external liabilities	L
Broad money supply	M
Population	N

Table. (*Continued*)

Definition	*Variable*
Government primary surplus	P
Imports of goods and non-factor services	Q
Government interest due	R
Non-government saving	S
Government revenue	T
Non-government external debt	U
Central-bank net internal assets	V
Net non-debt capital inflows	W
Exports of goods and non-factor services	X
Gross domestic product	Y
	Z
A'/(Q/12)	a
C/(C+S)	c
annual physical capital depreciation rate	d
F/Y	f
growth rate of…	$g_{()}$
H/Y	h
J/Y	j
ΔM'/ΔB'	m
Elasticity of Q with respect to Y	q
interest rate on…	$r_{()}$
S/(C+S)	s
Elasticity of T with respect to Y	t
incremental capital-output ratio (ICOR) (net of depreciation)	v
capital-output ratio	v'
W/Y	w

Inflation and exchange rates — real-effective or nominal — play no role in this simplified exercise. The exercise's flows and stocks are all in real terms — base-year dollars, for example. Price-level and exchange-rate movements figure in none of the equations and are assumed, in effect, not to affect macroeconomic behavior in any way. This limits the exercise's usefulness, of course. The larger, more detailed exercise described in this book's remaining chapters incorporates programming assumptions for price-level and exchange-rate movements and represents their consequences for a wide range of macroeconomic behavior.

This said, it can be useful to incorporate projections of the price-level and exchange-rate evolution in the simplified exercise described here, in order to present the projection results in units of account besides the real units. Thus, for example, the flows and stocks of the national, external, fiscal and monetary accounts can all be expressed as percentages of GDP, U.S. dollars, or national currency. Let p_t and e_t represent the period-average price level and exchange rate (national currency per U.S. dollar) respectively for period t, and let p'_t and e'_t represent the corresponding period-end values. The projected values can be formulated from assumptions for their growth rates. (Section 3.7 explains how to ensure that the projected values of p_t can be kept consistent with those of p'_t and that the projected values of e_t can be kept consistent with those of e'_t.)

To express, say, the year-t capital-formation flow in current U.S. dollars, multiply the real (base-year U.S. dollar) flow by e_t/e_0, where e_t is the year-average exchange rate for that year and e_0 is the year-average base-year exchange rate. To express the same flow in current domestic-currency units, multiply by $(p_t/p_0)\,(1/e_0)$, where p_t and p_0 are the year-average price levels for year t and the base year respectively. To express, say, the *year-end* year-t international-reserve stock in current U.S. dollars, multiply by e'_t/e'_0, where e'_t is the *year-end* exchange rate for that year and e'_0 is the *year-end* base-year exchange rate.

Different units of account are useful in different ways for interpreting the projection results of this simplified exercise as well as the more detailed exercise. It is always helpful "to scale" flow and even stock values by expressing them as percentages of GDP. A unit of account that can be especially useful for macroeconomic analysis generally is the per-capita real value, obtained simply by dividing the value in question by the (year-average) population. Once a projection has been formulated in real terms, price-level and exchange-rate projections are not needed to set the results in either of these units of account.

Chapter 2, Annex 3. An extension of the simplified version of the projection exercise to cover the banking system's lending capacity

By adding two additional projection assumptions, the projection exercise described in Annex 2.2 can be extended to provide an indicator of the banking system's period-end lending capacity. First, let "k" represent the maximum of (i) the banking system's minimum required reserve ratio and (ii) the reserve ratio that banks maintain. Next, let "z" represent the ratio of currency holdings to bank deposits. The money multiplier is given by

$$m = (z + 1)/(z + k).^{96}$$

Finally, suppose the minimum capital-adequacy is "b" times the risk-weighted asset base.

Assume for simplicity that commercial banks have no significant liabilities other than their deposit base, that they lend all available resources, and that their assets consist exclusively of the minimum amount required of (riskless) bank reserves and (risky) loans. Let **D'**, **N'**, **C'**, **R'**, and **W'** (bold-faced to distinguish them from previously defined variables) represent the banking system's year-end deposit base, loan balance, currency in circulation, bank-reserve stock, and capital position, respectively. It is straightforward to calculate formulas for these values in terms of M, B, k, and b. Since

$$M' = C' + D' \text{ and}$$

---

[96] For present purposes only, if **C'** represents currency in circulation, **R'** bank reserves, and **D'** bank deposits, since the money multiplier is defined as m = M'/B' and M' = **C'** + **D'**, B' = **C'** + **R'**, k = R'/D', and z = **C'**/D',

$$m = M'/B' = [C' + D']/[C' + R']$$

$$= [(C'/D') + (D'/D')]/[(C'/D') + (R'/D') = (z + 1)/(z + k).$$

If "m" and "k" are given, then the implied currency-deposit ratio would be given by solving this last formula for "z": z = (1 - mk)/(m - 1).

$$B' = C' + R',$$

$$M' - B' = D' - R'.$$

Since $\mathbf{R'} = k\,\mathbf{D'}$,

$$(1 - k)\,\boldsymbol{D'} = M' - B', \text{ or}$$

$$\boldsymbol{D'} = (M' - B')/(1 - k), \text{ and}$$

$$\boldsymbol{R'} = (M' - B')\,k/(1 - k).$$

Since $\mathbf{W'} = b\,\mathbf{N'}$, and $\mathbf{R'} + \mathbf{N'} = \mathbf{D'} + \mathbf{W'}$ (the banking-sector balance-sheet identity),

$$\boldsymbol{L'} = (D' - R')/(1 - b)$$

$$= (M' - B')/(1 - b), \text{ and}$$

$$\boldsymbol{W'} = (M' - B')\,b/(1 - b).$$

$\mathbf{R'}$, $\mathbf{N'}$, $\mathbf{D'}$, and $\mathbf{W'}$ are the four basic components of the consolidated commercial banks' balance sheet. $\mathbf{N'}$ would be the maximum credit stock the banks could provide given $\mathbf{M'}$; the banks taken together might elect to provide less, of course. The year-average credit stock $\mathbf{N}$ may be computed from $\mathbf{N}$ and $\mathbf{N'_{-1}}$ and the growth rates of $\mathbf{N}$ and Y may then be compared. A growth rate of $\mathbf{N}$ far below that of Y would suggest that the growth rate of the credit stock might prove insufficient to enable real GDP to grow at its programmed rate. (Section 9.4 sets out a more detailed projection exercise for commercial-banking performance.)

Chapter 3, Annex 1 (review). Gross domestic product, net domestic product, capital stock, capital depreciation, gross national product, and national income

An economy's **"gross domestic product"** (GDP) is defined as the aggregate value of *final* goods and services produced within its geographic frontiers during a specified time period (year, semester or quarter). "Final" goods are those sold and consumed or set in place as new capital equipment or structures (homes and factories), but *not* those used as inputs in final products. An economy's gross domestic product is calculated by estimating the *quantity* of each kind of good and service produced over the year, multiplying each such quantity by its average market *price* to obtain the total *value* of each kind of good and service produced, and summing all the values. The figure so calculated is in units of national-currency units per year. By excluding component products, the calculation avoids double-counting the total value of what is produced.

An economy's (physical) **capital stock** at any given moment is the aggregate value of its productive plant and equipment and residential housing, calculated by summing all their estimated values. An economy's **capital depreciation** is the estimated value lost through the physical wear and obsolescence of the capital stock over a given time period. The depreciation flow is estimated by applying "rules of thumb" regarding the average length of time each kind of equipment or structure is likely to remain productive. (Such rules are ordinarily unrelated to tax laws governing companies' depreciation of capital assets when reporting such expenses to calculate taxable profits.) Thus, for example, a piece of machinery with a productive life of ten years presumably depreciates by something like one tenth of its value each year. An economy's **"net domestic product"** (NDP) is defined as its GDP less estimated capital depreciation occurring over the same time period.

An economy's GDP, as noted above, is the aggregate value of what is produced within an economy's frontiers, regardless of who receives the income deriving from it. An economy's **gross national product** (GNP) is the GDP, less what foreign nationals receive in income from this production, plus what the country's own nationals (i.e., excluding residents) receive in income from other economies. An economy's **national income** is the total amount received as income by the economy's nationals, from the economy's own production and any external sources. The amount they received in income from the economy's own production is reduced by capital depreciation and by taxes on goods and services, since no individual or firm receives these as income.

Chapter 3, Annex 2 (review). Nominal and real gross domestic product and the choice of base period

Imagine a simple economy that produced 5,000 boxes of apples, 10,000 tons of bananas, and 25,000 cartons of cigarettes during the year 1999. If the average market prices of boxes of apples, tons of bananas, and cartons of cigarettes were 100, 50 and 20 pesos respectively, then **1999 GDP at market prices** was the sum of

1,000,000 pesos = 200 pesos per box of apples times 5,000 boxes
  500,000 pesos = 50 pesos per ton of bananas times 10,000 tons
  500,000 pesos = 20 pesos per carton of cigarettes times
                 25,000 cartons, or 2,000,000 pesos.

Suppose that in the following year, 2000, the prices of all three commodities doubled, but the quantities produced remained the same. So-called "**nominal**" **GDP** would then have doubled to P/4,000,000, but "**real**" GDP would not have changed. It is often useful to refer, say, to "GDP in 2000 measured at 1999 prices," or "GDP in the years 1999 and 2000 measured at 2000 prices." These would be measures of real GDP in those years.

     Suppose now that instead of remaining unchanged the quantity of apples produced rose 50 per cent between 1999 and 2000, from 5,000 to 7,500 boxes; the quantity of bananas produced remained unchanged; and the quantity of cigarettes produced fell by half, from 25,000 to 12,500 cartons. GDP in 2000 at 1999 prices would be 2,250,000 pesos, 12.5 per cent higher in 2000 than in 1999. In this example, it would make no difference whether the two years' GDP is measured at 1999 or

2000 prices, *as long as they are both measured at the same prices.* The "real" growth rate — the percentage increase from 1999 to 2000 — would be precisely the same, 12.5 per cent. This is because the three prices all simply doubled from one year to the next, preserving their *relative* values.

In general, however, using 1999 or 2000 prices makes a difference for the calculated 2000 real-GDP growth rate. Suppose, for instance, the price of bananas had quadrupled while the other prices had only doubled. If the 1999 and 2000 real GDP flows are measured at 1999 prices, the real growth rate would still be 12.5 per cent. It is straightforward to verify, however, that if the 1999 and 2000 GDP flows are measured at 2000 prices, the real growth rate would be only 10 per cent. This is because the higher relative banana price in 2000 assigns a higher weight in 2000 GDP measured at 2000 prices to a commodity whose output did not grow.

Chapter 3, Annex 3 (review). International comparisons of GDP using nominal and purchasing-power-parity conversion

To compare one nation's GDP with another's, the two GDPs must be converted to a common currency. The conventional way to do this is calculate the two economies' U.S. dollar GDPs, by dividing each economy's GDP by its period-average exchange rate for the U.S. dollar. Many economists believe this approach over-estimates the gap between more and less developed economies, because non-traded goods and services tend to have lower U.S. dollar prices in less-developed economies. To address this concern, when comparing two or more economies' GDPs, many economists prefer to work with recalculated GDP estimates using common prices for such goods and services. Thus, for example, haircuts are generally cheaper in Bolivia than in the United States. The argument is that when comparing Bolivia's GDP with that of the U.S., Bolivian haircuts should be priced the same as haircuts in the U.S. If this is systematically done, the gap between the United States' and Bolivia's per-capita GDPs would presumably be smaller.

Reasonable as the argument may seem, however, there is an important, if subtle, objection. In any economy, haircuts are priced according to the marginal product of labor in the economy's *material* output. If at any instant they happened to be priced higher, some labor would stop producing material output and move to providing haircuts. Microeconomic theory implies that this would lead to some combination of an increase to the marginal product of labor and reduction in the price of haircuts, until equilibrium were restored. Bolivia's relative underdevelopment implies that the marginal product of labor in its material output is lower than that of the United States. Even if Bolivian haircuts differ in no essential way from New York haircuts, the two kinds of haircuts are, on this reasoning, appropriately valued in their respective economies, and should be incorporated accordingly in their respective GDPs at their respective values. That is, what is really being *valued* is not the service, but the factors of production used to produce it.

Chapter 3, Annex 4 (review). The price level, the GDP deflator, and price indices in general

An economy's **price level** is defined as the rate at which its currency unit exchanges for goods and services at any moment, or on average over any time interval. It may also be defined in an "inverse" sense: if "p" represents the price level, 1/p represents the monetary unit's purchasing power in goods and services.

The price level in any economy can only be estimated. One familiar estimate for the average price level over a year (or semester or quarter) is the so-called **GDP deflator**, calculated by dividing each year's nominal GDP by the same year's real GDP at a given base year's prices and multiplying the results by a constant (usually 100) (see Annex 3.4). For the base year, for which nominal and real GDP measures are equal by definition, the GDP deflator would be equal to the constant. Once a series of annual values for the GDP deflator has been calculated, the real value of any year's GDP — that is, the value of that year's GDP at the base year's prices — may be calculated by dividing nominal GDP by the deflator and multiplying the result by the constant.

In actual economies, GDP, and hence the GDP deflator, can be calculated only after some delay from the period in question, because it takes time to compile and process the survey data. For practical short-term purposes, many economies measure price-level changes using consumer- or wholesale-price indices (CPIs and WPIs), which measure the cost of specified commodity "baskets." The prices that go into these indices are typically collected in mid-month price surveys. A typical monthly CPI, for example, would be calculated from survey observations made over the middle five to ten working days of each month. When news reports speak of a CPI growing by "x per cent" from one month to the next, what they mean more precisely is that prices were x per cent higher on average in the middle days of the second month compared with the middle days of the first.

Price indices in general are *weighted* averages of an economy's goods and services prices. In the case of a CPI, the "relative importances," or weights, assigned to all commodities whose prices figure in the index are calculated from a base-year consumer survey, which estimates the proportion of consumer expenditure going to each commodity. The year selected as the base makes a difference, since consumer expenditure patterns evolve over time. Relative importances must be updated from time to time to keep a CPI current. It is important also to bear in mind that poorer people's consumption patterns differ from those of wealthier people. (Brazil, for example, calculates consumer price indices for different income levels.)

Because it is an "index series," the values of a price index over a sequence of months can be "rebased." Suppose that in months 1, 2 and 3 an index takes on the values 150, 156, and 168. This may be read to mean that a given basket of goods and services, in quantities proportioned to people's consumption patterns, costs 150, 156, and 164 pesos in the middle days of months 1, 2 and 3. Since another basket containing precisely half of every kind of commodity in this basket is equivalent, the series could just as well be the same numbers all divided by two — 75, 78, and 84. What is important is that the ratios 78/75 and 84/75 are equal, respectively, to 156/150 and 168/150. It follows, of course, that two index series corresponding to the same dates are equivalent if their respective growth rates are equal.

It is often convenient to rebase an index series so that its value for a particular date, or for the average of several dates, is 100. Suppose that the idea is to rebase an index series x_1, x_2 and x_3 so the first month's value is 100. This is readily accomplished by multiplying all the values in the series by $(100/x_1)$. If this were done with the series above, the new series would be 100, 104, 112. If the series were rebased so the *average* of the three figures were 100, it would become (approximately) 94.9, 98.7, and 103.3. These figures result from multiplying all the values in the series by $[100/\text{average}(x_1, x_2, x_3)]$.

Chapter 3, Annex 5 (review). Exchange-rate management "regimes"

"Exchange rates" are the prices in a nation's currency for foreign exchange. As such, they mediate the supply and demand for foreign exchange. Exchange rates determined through supply and demand with no official intervention are said to be "freely floating." This is rare: monetary authorities almost always intervene, one way or another, in foreign-exchange markets. Even if they do not actually buy or sell foreign exchange, they can influence the exchange rate indirectly through their control of the money supply, interest rates, and credit conditions. Exchange rates allowed to float but *with* official intervention are said to be in "managed float."

The "opposite" of a floating exchange rate is a "fixed" exchange rate. In a fixed-rate regime, the monetary authority stands ready to purchase or sell foreign exchange at the fixed rate until further notice. This requires the monetary authority to have sufficient foreign exchange on hand "to make the exchange rate credible." If buyers and sellers believe the monetary authority has insufficient foreign exchange to hold its price down, or that it would prefer not to use the foreign exchange, they may bid up the foreign-exchange price — that is, bring about exchange-rate depreciation. This may take place within officially-sanctioned foreign-exchange markets, or in "parallel" markets (or "black" markets if they are illegal). A fixed exchange rate may prove unsustainable, within or outside "legal" markets. The authorities find they have to accept the existence of a parallel market.

Most economies have had variants of these exchange-rate "regimes." Some monetary authorities have used "crawling-peg" exchange rates, devaluing fixed rates gradually (in some instances with the objective of maintaining more or less constant "real-effective" exchange rates, as discussed in Annex 3.6). Some monetary authorities have allowed exchange rates to float within announced "bands," which the authorities may also adjust. For several years in the mid-1990s, for example, Ecuador's Central Bank allowed its exchange rate to float within a pre-announced band whose "floor" and "ceiling" depreciated according to a crawling peg (see Annex 3.10). Some monetary authorities have made do with no declared policy, adjusting their exchange rates up or down or allowing them to float as conditions and policy objectives warranted. Some economies have adopted "hard" fixed rates.

Under "convertibility" policies, some monetary authorities have firmly committed themselves to specific fixed exchange rates, and to buy and sell foreign exchange at these rates without restriction. Argentina maintained such a policy for about ten years (1991–2001). It was forced to abandon it, however, when balance-of-payments pressures and deepening recession made it unsustainable. Some monetary authorities have supported convertibility with rules requiring them to hold the equivalent of their money supply in foreign exchange — what is known as a "currency board." The "hardest" possible "fix" is full "dollarization," in which an economy simply gives up its own money and uses foreign exchange instead. Even this "fix" can be relaxed, of course, by introducing a new currency.

Chapter 3, Annex 6 (review). The real-effective exchange-rate concept

Imagine a small town divided between two nations, Atlántica and Pacífica. People may pass freely between the two nations, and a short stroll separates any two places in the combined town. Pacífica's currency is the peso; Atlántica uses dollars. In each part of town McDonald's restaurants sell identical "Big Mac" hamburgers. Neither nation taxes hamburger sales.

The exchange rate of pesos for dollars can be expected to be such that Big Mac prices are equivalent in both parts of town. Pacifica's peso price would be the same as Atlántica's dollar price multiplied by the pesos-for-dollars exchange rate. If a Big Mac costs a dollar in Atlántica and five pesos are worth one dollar, a Big Mac should cost five pesos in Pacífica. If this equivalence did not hold, Big Mac prices could be expected to adjust until it did. If Big Macs cost, say, six pesos in Pacífica, no one would buy any there. People could go to Atlántica, and purchase a dollar for the five pesos and then a Big Mac with the dollar. Pacífica's restaurant would sell no Big Macs until it cut its price to five pesos, or until Atlántica's Big Mac price rose to US$1.20 — or until Pacífica's exchange rate depreciated from five to six pesos per dollar. (This illustrates "the **Law of One Price**": if people can choose to buy or sell the same commodity in two different markets, supply and demand should, sooner or later, drive the two markets' prices to equivalence.)

If "e" represents the exchange rate (pesos per dollar), "p" the Pacífica Big Mac peso price, and p* the Atlántica Big Mac dollar price, the "Law of One Price" implies that "in equilibrium" — when "**purchasing-power parity**" holds — the ratio ep*/p would equal one. If this ratio happened to be less than one, the peso would be "overvalued" in dollar terms. With the Atlántica price of ep* less than the Pacífica price of "p," people in Pacífica possessing, say, 100 pesos could buy *more* hamburgers in Atlántica with them than in Pacífica. If the ratio exceeded one, Pacífica's peso would be "undervalued." A given quantity of pesos could buy *fewer* hamburgers in Atlántica than in Pacífica — or, a given quantity of dollars could buy *more* hamburgers in Pacífica than in Atlántica.

To discuss actual exchange rates economists use price indices instead of the Big Mac prices in the ratio above. If "p" represents one country's consumer-price index, and p* a world dollar price index, then the evolution of the ratio ep*/p indicates whether the exchange rate is "really" depreciating or appreciating. This ratio is the "**real-effective exchange rate**." When it rises, prices of the country's goods and services generally become more attractive — i.e., lower — to foreign purchasers. In this sense, a higher value of the ratio indicates a "more competitive" exchange rate for an exporting economy. At the same time, when the ratio rises, prices of foreign goods and services generally become less attractive — i.e., higher — from internal purchasers' perspective.

(The London *Economist* has calculated a Big Mac index since the 1980s, determining real-effective exchange rates on the basis of nations' Big Mac prices. Big Macs are essentially "non-tradable," and so the Law of One Price does not operate on their prices. Nevertheless, although the *Economist* has presented the index in a tongue-in-cheek spirit, it has proven a respectable indicator of relative exchange-rate valuation.)

Chapter 3, Annex 7 (review). Estimating an economy's historical trade-weighted real-effective exchange rates

Estimates of an economy's trade-weighted real-effective exchange rates over any historical period can be calculated as a weighted average of the economy's bilateral real-effective exchange rates with its more important trading partners. Practical steps in a spreadsheet calculation would be as follows.

The first step is to compile time series, for the country in question and for each of its more significant trading partners, for (i) the period-average exchange rate and (ii) the period-average price index (for monthly calculations, a consumer-price index, and for annual calculations, the GDP deflator). The best data source for most economies is the International Monetary Fund's *International Financial Statistics*. These data can be used then to calculate a time series of bilateral real-effective exchange rates, as defined in Annex 3.5, corresponding to each of the country's trading partners.

The next step is to determine the weights of each bilateral real-effective exchange rate in the overall bilateral exchange rate, by calculating the total merchandise trade between the economy and each trading partner over the entire period. The best data source for most economies would be the IMF's *Direction of Trade Statistics*. Total merchandise trade with each trading partner is the sum of the economy's merchandise exports to *and* merchandise imports from the partner over the period in question. The economy's *total* merchandise trade with all trading partners included in the calculation is then computed as the sum of merchandise exports to and merchandise imports from all trading partners included in the calculation over the entire period. The weight of each trading partner's bilateral exchange rate in the calculation of the overall real-effective exchange rate is the ratio of the economy's merchandise trade with each partner to its total merchandise trade. It is important to remember that the trade weights chosen can make a significant difference to the calculated series. (It is difficult to justify this weighting approach on theoretical grounds — but perhaps more difficult to imagine a better weighting approach.)

In calculating bilateral exchange rates, if both nations have both wholesale and consumer price indices, either can be used in the calculation. It is possible, and in general desirable, to use both, by averaging together the growth rates of the two indices in each nation.

A real-effective exchange-rate series is an index series, and so may be rebased to any year deemed convenient.

Chapter 3, Annex 8 (review). International reserves

Central banks are the usual holders of nations' "official" international reserves, although in some nations other entities may also hold at least some of them. A central bank's international-reserve holdings form part of its asset base. International reserves include such assets as gold, IMF Special Drawing Rights, and others, but "foreign exchange" accounts for the bulk of most nations' international reserves.

By definition, a central bank's **gross foreign-exchange reserves** is the aggregate of foreign-exchange holdings — in the main, deposit balances in "hard-currency" accounts in overseas commercial banks, but possibly also placements in foreign-exchange bonds. (Central banks will also hold relatively small amounts of foreign exchange in cash for local transactions purposes.) Modern central banks "manage" their reserve holdings, placing them so as to earn some yield and capital gains while remaining liquid.

Many central banks maintain some **gold holdings**, but these are now far less important than they were just a few decades ago. For several decades, declining value has discouraged central banks from holding gold. In any case, central banks find it far more convenient to use foreign exchange for international operations.

Central banks typically also have **foreign-exchange liabilities**. These may have varying maturities, ranging what used to be called "liabilities constituting assets of other central banks" to longer-term loans to multilateral institutions or the International Monetary Fund. ("Liabilities constituting assets of other central banks" were checks drawn by foreign banks on banks within this economy, which the central bank has cleared for payment but not yet paid at the instant represented by the central bank's closing balance sheet.)

Central banks may maintain foreign-exchange assets and liabilities that they do not define as reserve assets and liabilities. These include assets considered insufficiently liquid to count as reserves. Reserve liabilities are those owed to the IMF and to other special reserve facilities.

A central bank's **net foreign-exchange reserves** are, by definition, the difference between its foreign-exchange reserve assets and its reserve liabilities — that is, the central bank's net foreign-exchange position. Different concepts of "net foreign-exchange reserves" may be appropriate for different purposes. If the purpose is to indicate how much foreign exchange a central bank has immediately available, one would like to net out only the short-term liabilities owed to other central banks, perhaps along with principal and interest due within, say, thirty days on the longer-term foreign-exchange liabilities. If the purpose is simply to indicate the central bank's foreign-exchange balance-sheet position, then the full amount of the foreign-exchange liabilities should be netted out. For example, in its statistical publications Perú's central bank has for many years reported several different "concepts" of its international liquidity: overall reserves, including gold and silver holdings (at accounting values or at market values); gross foreign-exchange reserves; and three concepts of net reserves, calculated as (i) gross reserves less short-term obligations, (ii) gross reserves less short-term obligations and obligations to the IMF; and (iii) gross reserves less all foreign-exchange liabilities.

Special drawing rights (SDR) are liabilities issued by the IMF that central banks may use in transactions with other central banks. The Fund first issued them in the late 1960s, in an attempt to enhance the international financial system's liquidity. The quantity issued since then has been relatively small. The SDR's unit value is fixed in terms of a basket of currencies. This unit value has been useful as a unit of account, in particular for the IMF's own loans.

Chapter 3, Annex 9 (review). "Elasticities"

In setting out the assumptions for projection analysis, it is often useful to express the relationship between two variables in terms of an "elasticity" of one with respect to the other. If "z" and "x" are two variables, the elasticity of "z" with respect to "x" is usually defined quantitatively as the percentage change in "z" associated with each percentage point of change in "x." That is, if β represents the elasticity, then

$$g_z = \beta\, g_x.$$

For example, suppose that each percentage-point increase in the price of a commodity reduces demand for the commodity by two percentage points. In this case, the "price elasticity of demand" for the commodity would be minus two.

This book uses a slightly different definition, however. Here, the elasticity is defined as α such that

$$(1 + g_z) = (1 + g_x)^{\alpha}.$$

This way of formulating the definition turns out to be more convenient when writing equations involving compounding growth rates. The two definitions are precisely equivalent only when the growth rates of "z" and "x" are understood to be "instantaneous", i.e., the growth rates over an instantaneous time interval (a calculus concept). For most purposes, however, little is lost by using the second rather than the first definition as an assumption to characterize the relationship between two variables. For relatively low values of the elasticity and of the growth rates in question, α is approximately the ratio of the growth rates of "z" to "x".

The following table shows the relationship between the two elasticity definitions. Suppose that the variable "x" grows at the periodic rates of 1, 2, 5, and 10 per cent. When the elasticity as defined in the second way (α) is the value given in the first column, the corresponding elasticity as defined in the first way (β) would be as given in the columns to the right. For low values of α and "x," the corresponding values of β are close to those of α.

	Percentage growth rate of "x":			
α:	*1.0*	*2.0*	*5.0*	*10.0*
2.0	*2.0*	*2.0*	*2.1*	*2.1*
4.0	*4.1*	*4.1*	*4.3*	*4.6*
6.0	*6.2*	*6.3*	*6.8*	*7.7*
8.0	*8.3*	*8.6*	*9.5*	*11.4*
10.0	*10.5*	*10.9*	*12.6*	*15.9*
20.0	*22.0*	*24.3*	*33.1*	*57.3*
100.00	*170.5*	*312.2*	*2610.0*	*137796.1*

Chapter 3, Annex 10. Ecuador's real-effective exchange rates

Ecuador's exchange-rate experience over the Twentieth Century's last three decades was especially varied, and so provides an illustrative case study of the real-effective exchange-rate concept. (Beckerman and Solimano 2002 reviews Ecuador's evolution toward full "dollarization.")

All other things being equal, the more depreciated an economy's real-effective exchange rate happens to be at any given moment, the greater the incentive to export and the smaller the incentive to import would be (see Section 6.4). As a rule, unprocessed and semi-processed commodity exports tend to be less sensitive to — i.e., less elastic with respect to — the real-effective exchange rate than manufactured exports. This is basically because a relatively small exporting economy's internal markets for unprocessed commodities are likely to be limited, and so, as long as the price they receive covers the cost of producing and shipping, producers are likely to export a large share of their output. On the other hand, exports of goods with a substantial internal market could be affected by the real-effective exchange rate. All other things being equal, a more appreciated exchange rate encourages manufacturers to sell in internal markets rather than export. Consumer-, intermediate- and capital-goods imports may be more or less sensitive to the real-effective price, depending on the circumstances. Among consumer goods, food imports are likely to be less sensitive to the real-effective price, while luxury-goods imports are likely to be more sensitive. Intermediate-goods imports are likely to be influenced more by (real) GDP, and capital-goods imports are likely to be influenced more by (real) capital formation, but these kinds of imports may also be somewhat sensitive to price incentives.

For macroeconomic analysis, it helps to think of the real-effective exchange rate as affecting the economy's "resource deficit," that is, net imports (that is, imports less exports) of goods and factor services. The orders of magnitude of the ratios of these exports and imports, respectively, to GDP, are best thought of as reflecting the "fundamental" characteristics of the economies in question. (In particular, small economies are more likely to export and import larger percentages of GDP.) Net imports of goods and factor services, however, may be thought of as the economy's external-saving inflow (which is more of a macroeconomic phenomenon). A more (less) appreciated real-effective exchange rate would generally lead to a larger (smaller) net external-saving flow.

Three decades of data from Ecuador provide an example of the typical relationship between the real-effective exchange rate and export and import performance. This Annex's Figure 1 shows Ecuador's monthly trade-weighted exchange rate as it evolved between January 1970 and December 2001. The series has been calculated using the method outlined in Annex 3.6. The series divides fairly neatly into five periods, (1) the 1970s, (2) the 1980s, (3) 1990-March 1998, (4) March 1998–December 1999, and (5) January 2000 and afterward. From August 1970 through May 1982, the nominal exchange rate was fixed at 25 per dollar. Since Ecuador's inflation exceeded world inflation, the real-effective exchange rate gradually appreciated. A series of devaluations carried out between May 1982 and 1990 brought the real-effective exchange rate to its relatively depreciated 1990 level. Between 1993 and 1998, Ecuador's currency (the *sucre*) was allowed to depreciate in nominal terms. This was because the authorities maintained a policy of allowing it to "float" — i.e., to be determined by the exchange markets — within a pre-announced "crawling-peg" band. That is, the monetary authority let the markets know the lower and upper boundaries within which supply and demand would be allowed to determine the exchange rate, and made it clear that it would intervene to hold the exchange rate within the band. Nevertheless, the exchange rate gradually appreciated in real-effective terms, reaching a point of relative maximum appreciation (after 1990) in early 1998 (although the exchange rate remained significantly more depreciated throughout the 1990s than it had been in the 1970s).

Chapter 3, Annex 1, Figure 1. Ecuador: Monthly nominal and real-effective exchange rates, 1970–2001

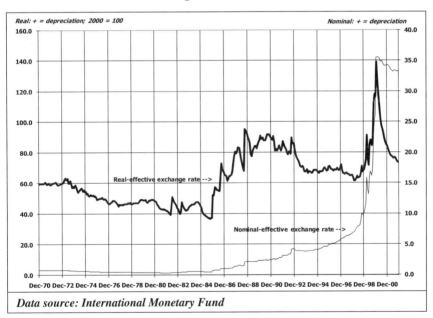

Data source: International Monetary Fund

The evolution of Ecuador's exchange rate affected, and was in turn affected by, the performance of net exports. With its real-effective exchange-rate depreciation over the latter part of the 1980s, Ecuador's net-exports flow went basically from deficit into surplus (see this Annex's Figure 2). The balance returned to deficit briefly in 1987, when an earthquake temporarily interrupted oil exports, and in 1998, when exports declined while lagging exchange-rate adjustment encouraged increased imports. For the most part, however, Ecuador maintained its net-export surplus over the 1980s and 1990s, until 1998. This was a matter of deliberate policy. Like other Latin American economies, Ecuador's external debt had grown so large by the early 1980s that it undermined the country's financial solvency. Over the 1980s the authorities used the depreciated real-effective exchange rate to hold net exports high, and in this way to remove the need for additional external borrowing to finance the balance of payments.

Chapter 3, Annex 1, Figure 2. Ecuador: Exports and imports of goods and non-factor services (per cent of GDP), 1971–2001

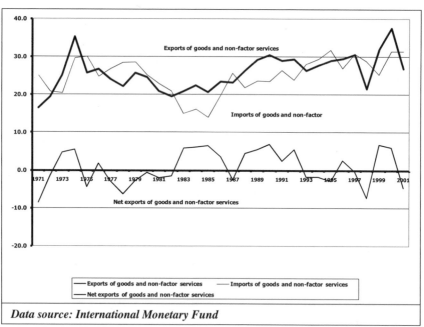

Data source: International Monetary Fund

Beginning in March 1998, Ecuador experienced heavy reserve loss on account of sharply lower oil-export prices and damage to export crops by unusually heavy rains (associated with the world "El Niño weather cycle). This forced the authorities to devalue the pre-announced crawling-peg band's ceiling. In September 1998 they had to carry out yet another "maxi-devaluation." Part of the reason imports were relatively high in 1998 was that importers anticipated the exchange-rate depreciation, and so increased their orders for inventory. In February 1999, persisting international reserve loss finally forced the authorities to allow the exchange rate to float freely.

These developments had at least one unfortunate fiscal consequence. Before oil-export prices declined, any exchange-rate depreciation tended *to reduce* the fiscal deficit, basically because the resulting increase in the *sucre* equivalent of revenue deriving from oil and from tariffs exceeded the increase in the *sucre* equivalent of debt service. The decline in oil prices was so severe, however, that this relationship reversed: during 1998 and 1999 any exchange-rate depreciation tended *to widen* the fiscal deficit.

Over the first three months of 1999 the exchange rate depreciated sharply. Expectations of further depreciation became self-fulfilling, and hyperinflationary processes appeared to be developing. One consequence was that commercial banks suffered heavy losses, because a large proportion of their loans were in dollars to people and firms that had no dollar income, and who therefore defaulted. As bank losses intensified, depositors, fearing their deposits were in danger, withdrew, adding liquidity pressure to the banks' difficulties. In March 1999 the authorities took the desperate step of freezing bank deposits. With the supply of *sucres* suddenly sharply restricted, the exchange rate appreciated briefly, but the collapse of bank operations plunged the economy into recession. Over the remainder of the year, in an effort to restore normal bank operations, the authorities gradually released the frozen deposit balances. As withdrawals and purchases of dollars intensified, however, the exchange rate once again resumed its rapid depreciation. Inflation picked up over 1999, and drove and was driven by the exchange rate in a gathering vicious cycle.

During 1999, as the exchange rate depreciated sharply in real-effective terms and the recession turned severe, imports declined precipitously. Merchandise imports responded to the combination of depreciation, recession and the interruption of banking operations, falling from US$5.5 billion in 1998 to just over US$3 billion in 1999. Real GDP declined by about 6.3 per cent. The import-GDP ratio dropped from 23.5 to 18.2 per cent. Exports rose in 1999, although mainly on account of recovering oil-export prices.

From the beginning of November 1999 to January 9, 2000 the *sucre* lost a third of its nominal value against the U.S. dollar. Over the first week of 2000 alone it lost a quarter of its value. At this point, facing incipient hyperinflation, the authorities announced that Ecuador would "dollarize" at the exchange rate of the moment, 25,000 per dollar. Under legislation approved in early March, the Central Bank used part of its U.S. dollar holdings to buy in all its outstanding *sucre* issues, and changed the nation's currency unit to the U.S. dollar.

With dollarization, Ecuador moved to what amounted to a rigorously fixed exchange rate. Because it dollarized at a moment just following a few weeks of severe nominal and real-effective exchange rate depreciation, the export incentive was unusually high and the import incentive unusually low. Over 2000 and 2001, however, in the wake of the move to dollarization, internal prices rose toward international parity levels. As a consequence, the real-effective exchange rate appreciated over those years from the sharply depreciated level at which dollarization commenced. Over 2000 the depreciated real-effective exchange rate discouraged imports and helped maintain a positive merchandise-trade surplus. In 2001, however, reviving real GDP growth and the appreciating real-effective exchange rate steadily reduced the trade surplus. In the latter part of the year it slid into deficit.

Summarizing, in the 1970s the oil boom and the inflow of external financing enabled Ecuador to maintain a fixed exchange rate and an appreciating real-effective exchange rate. In the 1980s, however, as Ecuador struggled to meet its inflated external obligations, it used exchange-rate depreciation to generate and then to sustain an export surplus. Exchange-rate instability largely explains why depositors and commercial banks preferred increasingly to hold wealth in dollars rather than *sucres*, and why banks therefore had to lend in dollars. Over most of the 1990s the authorities were able to maintain adequate external balance with a crawling-peg exchange rate. In 1998, however, when external circumstances thrust the country's balance of payments into crisis, massive exchange-rate depreciation resulted. This pretty much forced the economy to dollarize in early 2000.

Chapter 4, Annex 1. A nation's future primary education payroll: a "back-of-the-envelope" calculation

A simple calculation can be used to project the growth rate of a national public primary education system's payroll that would be necessary to serve a growing student population. Let "w" represent real average remuneration for teachers and administrative staff; "a" the ratio of school-age persons to the total population; "q" the ratio of enrolled to total school-age persons; "n" the total population; "r" the teacher-student ratio; "s" the ratio of administrative staff to teachers; and "y" represent real GDP. The growth rate of the total remuneration bill as a percentage of GDP, W/Y, is given then by

$$[(1 + g_w)(1 + g_a)(1 + g_q)(1 + g_n)(1 + g_r)(1 + g_s)/(1 + g_y)] - 1,$$

where g_w represents the (decimal) growth rate of w, g_n represents the (decimal) growth rate of n, and so on. If the real wage grows at the rate of per-capita GDP,

$$g_w = [(1 + g_y)/(1 + g_n)] - 1,$$

and the growth rate of the total remuneration bill as a percentage of GDP would be given by

$$[(1 + g_a)(1 + g_q)(1 + g_r)(1 + g_s)] - 1.$$

Suppose it is a longer-term policy objective to achieve universal education by year T_q. The required annual growth rate of "q" would be given then by

$$1 + g_{q*} = (1/q_0)^{[1/(T_q - T_0)]}$$

where q_0 is the value of "q" in the base year 0. Other growth rates could be defined in similar ways. For example, assume that the ratio of administrative staff to teachers "s" is to grow (or decline) to a level s* by time T_s, and that the teacher-student ratio "r" is to grow (or decline) to a level r* by time T_r:

Paul Beckerman

$$g_q = (q^*/q_0)^{[1/(T_q - T_0)]},$$

$$g_s = (s^*/s_0)^{[1/(T_s - T_0)]},$$

and

$$g_r = (r^*/r_0)^{[1/(T_r - T_0)]}.$$

Suppose it is now 2005. In 2004, 80 per cent of school-age children were enrolled. Suppose the basic policy objective is to achieve 100 per cent enrollment by the year 2020. Additional objectives include a reduction in the student-teacher ratio from 33.3 in 2004 to 25 in 2020 and a reduction in the ratio of administrative to teaching staff from 30 to 25 per cent. Suppose that population and real GDP are expected to grow at average annual rates of 2 and 4.5 per cent respectively, and that average real staff remuneration would grow at the same rate as per-capita real GDP. If the nation's primary educational payroll amounted to 2 percent of GDP in 2004, it would rise to 2.4 per cent in 2020.

Chapter 5, Annex 1 (review). Types of external debt in developing economies

Since the early 1980s, the World Bank has published estimates of developing economies' external debt. Its country-by-country figures classify external debt in four broad categories: (i) public and publicly-guaranteed term debt (excluding the central bank's debt to the IMF); (ii) non-guaranteed private term debt; (iii) the central bank's debt to the IMF; and (iv) short-term debt, including accumulated interest arrears on the government's term debt. Public and publicly-guaranteed term debt encompasses (a) debt owed to official entities and (b) debt owed to private entities. Debt to official entities encompasses, in turn, (1) debt owed to multilateral lenders, such as the World Bank and the various regional development banks, and (2) debt owed to bilateral lenders. Debt to private entities may be owed to commercial banks; holders of the government's "sovereign" bond issues; and suppliers (e.g., foreign companies that have sold aircraft, ships, turbines, and other "large" pieces of capital equipment), among others.

The listing following shows a "generic" structure of a developing economy's external debt, more or less as the World Bank's Global Development Finance has shown it for most economies.

Term debt:
    Public and publicly guaranteed term debt:
        Official creditors:
            Multilateral creditors
            Bilateral creditors
        Private creditors:
            Commercial banks
            Bondholders
            Suppliers
            Other creditors
    Private non-guaranteed term debt
    International Monetary Fund
Short-term debt:
    Interest arrears
    Other short-term debt (including trade credit)

Chapter 6, Annex 1 (review). Expenditure accounts in the national accounts: definitions

In the national accounts' standard classification, aggregate expenditure on an economy's gross domestic product over any given time interval comprises residents' expenditure on **consumption**, residents' expenditure on **investment**, and non-residents' expenditure on the economy's **exports of goods and non-factor services** (i.e., "final" services), *less* residents' expenditure on **imports of goods and non-factor services**.

	Gross domestic product	
=	**Consumption:**	
		Non-government consumption
		Government consumption
+	**Gross investment:**	
		Gross fixed capital formation:
		Non-government capital formation
		Government capital formation
		Net increase in inventory stocks
+	**Net exports of goods and non-factor services:**	
		Exports of goods and non-factor services
		Imports of goods and non-factor services

Consumption expenditure goes for goods and services that disappear — i.e., are "consumed" — during the period in question. Investment expenditure goes for goods that will still exist at the end of the period, whether capital goods or inventories. Export expenditure goes for goods and services that are removed from the economy; import expenditure goes for goods and services produced outside but brought into the economy. The consumption-investment distinction is sometimes a bit blurry. Consumption expenditure comprises expenditure on consumer "non-durable" goods, which literally cease to exist within the period, and "durable" goods — household vehicles, furniture, appliances, and so on — which "disappear" into people's homes.

Investment comprises **gross fixed capital formation** and the **net increase in inventory holdings** over the period. "Gross fixed capital formation" is "gross" in the sense of making no allowance for depreciation of the existing capital stock (see Annex 3.1). Gross fixed capital formation comprises (1) new plant and machinery and (2) new "structures," including roads, bridges, tunnels, dams, ports, and buildings (including residences). "Net" fixed capital formation is gross fixed capital formation less estimated capital depreciation.

Most economies' national accounts classify expenditure on consumption and capital formation into government and non-government categories. The government categories conventionally *exclude* state-owned business enterprises, so their capital-formation expenditure is classified as "non-government." Government consumption and investment expenditure account for all government expenditure, except interest, subsidies, and so-called transfers. These are government transfers of income, not expenditure on goods and services.

Chapter 6, Annex 2 (review). Expenditure accounts in developing and developed economies

The relative proportions of the expenditure components vary considerably among economies. Gross fixed capital formation amounting to 20 per cent of GDP is more or less average performance in developing economies. Economies undergoing severe economic crises have sometimes had ratios below 10 per cent; while rapidly growing economies may have ratios exceeding 30 per cent. Brazil's gross fixed capital formation averaged 21.7 per cent of GDP over the years 1970–1998, varying between 16.5 per cent (in 1984) and 28.6 per cent (in 1989) while its annual real growth rate averaged 4.6 per cent. South Korea's gross fixed capital formation averaged 31.2 per cent of its GDP over the same years, while its annual real growth rate averaged 7.2 per cent Exports and imports tend to be larger percentages of the economies of smaller economies. Thus, for example, Argentina's exports of goods and non-factor services averaged 7.7 per cent of GDP over 1971–2000, Ecuador's averaged 26.3 per cent of GDP over the same years. "Net exports of goods and non-factor services" is defined as exports less imports of goods and non-factor services. (This value is sometimes called the "resource balance.") In principle, one would expect this flow to be negative for developing economies and positive for developed economies, on the view that developing economies would tend to import capital equipment for their investment. In recent years, however, the United States has run persistent net-export deficits. Ecuador, on the other hand, has tended to run surpluses since the mid-1980s — partly because it is an oil exporter, but also because it has had to manage policy so as to generate a surplus in order to meet its servicing obligations on its large external debt.

It cannot be over-emphasized that any nation's national-accounts aggregates are estimates formulated from surveys. Unfortunately, there is simply no way to determine how far they differ from their "true" values.

Chapter 6, Annex 3. A procedure for projecting capital formation

This Annex outlines a practical approach to formulating a capital-formation projection, taking account of the points mentioned in Section 6.2 above. The aim is to project capital formation in current prices as a percentage of GDP at current prices. The approach works with GDP and capital formation at *constant* prices, with the same base year. No less important, it works with an assumption for the "incremental capital-*potential* output ratio," the "ICPOR." Assume that capital formation carried out this year will generate incremental output over three years immediately following. For any projection year, the projection procedure may be summarized as follows:

a. For the given year, the real GDP growth rates in subsequent years, g_{+1}, g_{+2}, g_{+3} are assumptions. Real GDP for each of those years, y_{+1}, y_{+2}, y_{+3}, may be projected by applying the assumed growth rate to the preceding year's real-GDP flow.

b. Divide y_{+1}, y_{+2}, y_{+3}, by the respective assumed capacity-utilization rates, c_{+1}, c_{+2}, c_{+3}, to obtain the projected potential GDP, z_{+1}, z_{+2}, z_{+3}.

c.   Subtract each year's projected potential GDP from the preceding year's potential GDP to obtain the projected increases in potential GDP, $\Delta z_{+1}, \Delta z_{+2}, \Delta z_{+3}$.

d.   Multiply the preceding year-end capital stock k'_{-1} by the assumed depreciation rate δ to calculate the projected real depreciation of the capital stock, $d = \delta\, k'_{-1}$.

e.   Real gross fixed capital formation "i" for the year in question would be given then by

$$i = d + v\, [(a_{+1}\, z_{+1}) + (a_{+2}\, z_{+2}) + (a_{+3}\, z_{+3})]$$

where "v" is the ICPOR that characterizes capital formation in the year being projected and a_{+t} is the fraction of capital formation in the current year that will produce incremental output in year t, such that $a_{+3} = 1 - a_{+1} - a_{+2}$.

f.   The year-end real capital stock can then be projected as

$$k' = k'_{-1} + i - d.$$

g.   Let "h" represent the growth rate of capital-goods prices. The capital-formation flow at current prices "I" would be given then by

$$I = I_{-1}\, (i/i_{-1})\, (1 + h),$$

and the investment rate would be given by I/Y where Y represents nominal GDP.

This projection procedure should be relatively straightforward to implement in a spreadsheet exercise.

Chapter 6, Annex 4. Aggregate national income and the terms-of-trade effect

For certain purposes in the projection exercise, the "aggregate economic-activity" variable that matters is, or should be, aggregate *national income* rather than GDP. For example, economic agents within an economy would presumably base decisions regarding consumption or consumption-goods imports on their income. By definition, aggregate national income in any period is the sum of all factor incomes, including wages, interest, rents, and profits. Unfortunately, relatively few developing economies carry out the surveys required to estimate aggregate national income, much less its component factor incomes. The main reason is that credible estimation is costly and technically difficult, particularly in developing economies' circumstances.

In the national accounts, aggregate national income is identically equal to GDP *less* capital depreciation and "indirect" taxes, *plus* government transfers (in particular subsidies) from government to business, net factor income from (and to) foreign sources, and net unrequited transfers from (and to) foreign sources. (If factor incomes are estimated, the identity would also imply that there would be a statistical discrepancy in any historical year.)

All the same, partly because few developing economies have credible national-income estimates, and because national income and its component factor incomes are relatively complicated both to measure and to project, the exercise this book describes makes a point of avoiding national-income. Non-government consumption is calculated residually, thus avoiding the use of aggregate income. Consumption-goods imports and tax proceeds are taken, for simplicity, to depend on (real) GDP rather than (real) aggregate income.

If aggregate national income is the variable that really matters for consumption imports, then a case could be made for incorporating the effect of changes in the economy's terms of trade in the formulas that determine import volumes. In effect, the real income that an economy's residents perceive would grow or decline in any year not only through increased income, but also through *real* increases in the external unit values of (merchandise and non-factor service) exports and *real* decreases in the external unit values of (merchandise and non-factor service) imports. That is, economic agents within an economy should perceive a positive income effect to the extent the ratio of export prices to import prices increases.

When estimating or projecting the terms-of-trade effect, the idea is to capture the net increase (or decrease) in the economy's aggregated purchasing power arising solely from the changes in export and import prices from one period to the next. If "p" represents the GDP deflator, "e" the (period-average) exchange rate, X and Q exports and imports of goods and non-factor services, and p_X^* and p_Q^* their respective (U.S. dollar) price indices, then the real net increase in the economy's purchasing power deriving from the changes in the export and import price indices could be estimated or projected by

$$e \, [(X_{-1} \, \Delta p_X^*) - (Q_{-1} \, \Delta p_Q^*)]/p.$$

The value of the increase as a percentage of GDP would be given by

$$e \, [(X_{-1} \, \Delta p_X^*) - (Q_{-1} \, \Delta p_Q^*)]/Y,$$

where Y represents GDP.[97]

Chapter 6, Annex 5. Saving concepts: National, foreign, internal and external saving; inflation adjustment; and non-physical capital formation

This Annex discusses three issues relating to the calculation of saving aggregates. The first is the relationships among national, foreign, internal and external saving, and the question of which of these saving concepts is appropriate for different questions of analysis. The second is the rationale for adjusting government saving flows for inflation. The third is the point that the conventional national-accounts definitions do not take account of human- (as opposed to physical-) capital formation, so that, for example, government expenditure on education — i.e., human-capital formation is conventionally considered government-consumption expenditure.

---

[97] To be sure, the terms-of-trade effect on perceived real income is a different concept from the growth rate of the terms of trade. The growth rate of the terms of trade is given simply by

$$\{[1 + g_{p^*(X)}]/[1 + g_{p^*(Q)}]\} - 1,$$

where p*(X) and p*(Q) represent the price indices of exports and imports respectively.

Projected aggregate saving flows for any given year can be derived from the national-accounts expenditure projections. Define the following variables (for this Annex only):

Y	gross domestic product;
I	gross non-government capital formation;
J	gross government capital formation;
ΔV	net inventory accumulation;
C	non-government consumption;
G	government consumption;
X	exports of goods and non-factor services;
Q	imports of goods and non-factor services;
T	government tax receipts;
S	gross non-government (household and company) saving;
D	gross internal saving, $S + (T - G)$;
N	gross national saving;
B	balance-of-payments current-account deficit ("foreign" saving);
H	resource gap, or "external" saving, Q-X.

Rearranging the basic national-accounts identity,

$$(C + G) + (I + \Delta V + J) + (X - Q) \equiv Y,$$

total gross investment is identically equal to

$$I + J + \Delta V \equiv [Y - (C + G)] + [Q - X]$$

$$\equiv (Y - C - T) + (T - G) + (Q - X)$$

$$\equiv [S + (T - G)] + (Q - X)$$

$$\equiv D + H.$$

That is, total gross internal investment identically equals the sum of internal saving and the "resource gap."

The resource gap is the "external" saving flow effectively transferred into the economy. Define the following variables:

L	net interest and transfer payments from non-government sectors outside the country;

R   net interest and transfer payments from the government outside the country; and

F   net interest and transfer payments from non-government sectors to the government.

Simultaneously adding in and subtracting F, L, and R to and from the right-hand side of the last formula,

$$I + \Delta V + J \equiv (S - L + F) + (T - G - F + R) + (M - L + R + Q - X)$$

$$\equiv N + B,$$

where

$$N = (S - L + F) + (T - G - F + R)$$

and

$$B = (M - L + R + Q - X)$$

— that is, gross internal investment identically equals the sum of national saving and the current-account deficit, or foreign saving. The current-account deficit measures the extent to which the rest of the world transfers real resources to and accepts financial obligations from an economy, and to this extent indicates the extent to which foreigners provide the economy saving.

Macroeconomists generally take the view that national saving is the most appropriate measure of an economy's saving performance (see Schmidt-Hebbel and Serven 1999). Nevertheless, the internal-saving measure should not be discarded entirely. Broadly speaking, which indicator is more appropriate depends on what question about macroeconomic performance is being addressed.

The point can be understood by noting the distinction between external and foreign saving. Assume for the moment that the entire difference between external and foreign saving is external interest due less interest income, or net external interest due, as is very nearly the case in many heavily indebted developing economies. In a country that accrues net interest due to the rest of the world over any given time period, foreign saving exceeds external saving (and internal saving exceeds national saving) by an amount equal to the net interest due.

It is plainly problematic to regard the overseas interest payments a country makes (or accrues) as constituting part of the foreign saving flows contributing to the financing of the country's capital formation. On the internal side, national saving excludes interest payments made overseas. Again, however, it is uncertain whether doing so yields a more "indicative" aggregate of the economy's saving effort. The economy forgoes consumption, regardless of whether the proceeds are "used" to pay for capital formation or for external interest.

Broadly speaking, a foreign interest bill may be regarded as a "wedge" between an economy's aggregate saving and investment. This suggests that a useful distinction may be drawn between *the overall saving effort the economy makes*, best conveyed by the internal-saving concept, and *the saving flow available for capital formation*, best conveyed by the national-saving concept. Thus, when the focus of analysis is an economy's saving *performance*, the internal-saving concept is presumably more useful; when the focus of analysis is the *availability* of saving resources for investment, the national-saving concept is presumably more useful.

Internal and national saving may each be sub-divided into government and non-government components. National saving may be divided into a non-government component, $(S - L + H)$, and a government component $(T - G - H + R)$.

Adjustment of measured saving flows to take account of inflation is another controversial (and often misunderstood) issue. In economies where inflation rates are high, so-called "nominal" interest rates tend also to be high. One consequence is that in such economies government dissaving and non-government saving tend to be overstated. This is because, where inflation is significant, it erodes the purchasing power of any amount lent. In an economic sense, part of the interest paid on funds lent is not really saving, but restoration of value to outstanding principal stocks. *Ex ante*, financial-market forces will tend to set nominal interest rates so they compensate lenders for anticipated loss of purchasing power on the amounts they lend because of inflation. *Ex post*, some part of the nominal interest payment presumably effects this compensation, leaving whatever remains to remunerate the lender for the lending service. Thus, where inflation rates are high, interest paid by borrowers effectively comprises two components. One, the "real" component, effectively compensates the lender for the service of lending funds. The other compensates the lender for the loss through inflation in the real value of the loan principal over the maturity of the loan.

The component of the interest bill that compensates, *ex post*, for inflationary erosion in this way may be estimated, for any given time period, by

$$Z = V/(1 + x),$$

where V is the average stock of national-currency debt outstanding at the beginning of the year and "x" the inflation rate over the year (December-December). With this adjustment, the non-government and government components of national saving would become $(S - L + H - Z)$ and $(T - G + R - H + Z)$ respectively. That is, over any period in which the price level rises by "x" (in decimal terms), outstanding debt diminishes in real terms by the proportion $[x/(1 + x)]$. The government dissaves to the extent it pays interest on its debt, but saves to the extent inflation reduces the real value of its outstanding debt. To measure the government saving deriving from this latter effect, the nominal interest bill must be adjusted by subtracting the product of $[x/(1 + x)]$ and the average outstanding debt stock. Mirroring the government accounts, non-government holders of government debt *save* to the extent they receive interest and monetary correction on government debt, but *dissave* to the extent inflation reduces the value of their holdings. (Brazilian economists and policy makers have applied the term "operational" to refer to flows of government interest payments, government saving, and overall deficits adjusted for the effects of inflation on outstanding debt.)

Finally, as noted in Section 6.5 above, there is a measure of arbitrariness in the classification of certain classes of government expenditure as "consumption." As defined in the national accounts, capital formation refers only to physical assets and excludes human or natural capital. From this broader perspective, education, for example, is human-capital formation. If its value could be measured (say, at the cost of the factors producing it), it could be added to physical capital formation to obtain a measure of total (i.e., physical and human) capital formation. It would then have a saving offset (presumably through an imputed government transfer to individuals, which they would then be presumed to save in correspondence with their acquisition of human capital).

At the same time, natural-resources depletion and environmental degradation constitute depreciation of natural capital, and as such constitute dissaving. This could be treated as depreciation of assets owned "collectively" by the private sector.

Some attempts have been made to improve international national-accounting methodology by incorporating more relevant saving concepts (see World Bank 1997). "Broadly-defined" net saving, for example, could be defined as total net saving (i.e., total gross saving less capital depreciation) less natural-capital depletion. In national economies examined by the 1997 World Bank study, taking account of natural-capital depletion leads to significant differences in absolute levels and changes in measured saving. At present, however, measurement and conceptual problems appear still to be too large to incorporate more relevant saving concepts in national-accounting systems. Still, policy-makers need to be mindful of how much the conventional definition of saving misses. The fact that increased government education expenditure counts as increased government dissaving, for example, is a revealing reminder of the limitations of the conventional national-accounts framework.

Chapter 6, Annex 6. A method for projecting poverty incidence

An economy's poverty incidence may be projected for future years on the basis of (i) a base-year per-capita non-government consumption figure, (ii) the base-year poverty line, (iii) the base-year poverty incidence, (iv) assumed future annual growth rates for per-capita real non-government consumption, and (v) assumptions regarding the evolution of the consumption distribution. The projection methodology described here is based on two strong assumptions. The first is that the base-year distribution of real consumption over the population is roughly the same as the household consumption distribution. (Poverty incidence is estimated on the basis of household survey data.) The second is that the consumption distribution over the population is and will remain *log-normally* distributed.

If the base-year consumption distribution is log-normal, the three pieces of information given for the base year — the log of the economy's average per-capita real non-government consumption, the log of the poverty line, and the proportion of the population below the poverty line — suffice to characterize the log-normal distribution. The distribution mean is the log of the economy's average per-capita real consumption. It is then straightforward to calculate the distribution's standard deviation.[98]

If the standard deviation is assumed to remain constant in the future, the consumption distribution would remain unchanged, although the average would grow at the assumed future growth rates. On this assumption, it is straightforward to determine the resulting reduction over time in the proportion of the population below the poverty line. Alternatively, the standard deviation may be assumed to widen or shrink over time. Widening would correspond to a worsening (more unequal) consumption distribution, while shrinkage would correspond to an improving (more equal) distribution. All other things being equal, a widening standard deviation would slow projected improvement of poverty incidence, while a shrinking standard deviation would enhance projected improvement.

---

[98] A spreadsheet projection exercise could use a standard function — in Excel,

$$log\,(L) = NORMINV\,[P,\,log(A),\,s]\,,$$

where L represents the poverty line, P the proportion of the population with real consumption below L, A the mean real per-capita consumption, and "s" the standard deviation — to make this calculation. Given L, P, and A, the calculation procedure is to use iteration (in Excel, the "goal-seek" feature) to determine "s" so as to make the two sides of the equation equal.

Since each future year's projected consumption distribution can be transformed straightforwardly into a cumulative distribution, it is also straightforward to calculate decile limits (i.e., the consumption flows corresponding to between 10 and 20 per cent, 20 and 30 per cent, and so on of the population), as well as each decile's average per-capita consumption flow. These figures can be used then to calculate implied Gini coefficients for the future years. Gini coefficients will rise (i.e., show increasing inequality) if the standard deviation widens, remain unchanged if the standard deviation remains constant, and diminish if the standard deviation shrinks.

Chapter 7, Annex 1 (review). *Balance-of-payments accounts*

Formally, a nation's "balance-of-payments" accounts (by convention, in U.S. dollars) quantitatively "explain" how its central bank's holdings of "international reserves" evolved as they did over a given period. By convention, the net international-reserve flows whose evolution is to be explained are shown "below the line," in the lower part of the accounts listing (see Annex 7.2). These show the changes in the central bank's asset and liability foreign-exchange accounts, and in any non-central bank accounts defined as official foreign-exchange reserves. The asset-flow accounts include net increases in the central bank's (i) foreign-exchange holdings (cash and overseas deposit accounts in "convertible" currencies); (ii) gold holdings; and (iii) positions in such international entities as the International Monetary Fund. The liability-flow accounts include net increases in the central bank's (i) obligations to the IMF and (ii) shorter-term obligations. Total increases in asset stocks less total increases in liability stocks give the net increase in the central bank's net foreign reserves. The part of this increase arising from valuation changes — e.g., changes in the value of reserve holdings in currencies other than the U.S. dollar — is subtracted from the net increase in the central bank's net foreign exchange position to obtain the overall net international-reserve inflow.

The above-the-line accounts quantitatively explain how this overall net inflow came about. They have three main components, the (i) "current," (ii) "capital and financial," and (iv) "errors-and-omissions" accounts. Receipts increase and payments decrease net international reserves.

The current account has two main components. The first, "net exports of goods and non-factor services," is conceptually the same as in the national accounts' expenditure accounts, but in U.S. dollars rather than national currency. The second is "net factor receipts and unrequited-transfers inflows." These figure in national income but not national expenditure. Depending on the level of detail in any given presentation, the accounts under net exports of goods and non-factor services may include merchandise and services exports and imports, and even specific export and import categories. The accounts under net factor receipts and unrequited transfer inflows may show accrued interest receipts and payments, other factor service inflows and outflows, and official and non-official "unrequited" transfer receipts and payments.

The financial accounts have four main components. The first, called the "capital account," comprises financial transfers, including project-financing grants. It may also include debt relief and other kinds of valuation adjustment. The second is "net foreign investment," consisting basically of foreigners' acquisition of equity positions in companies less residents' acquisition of equity positions in foreign companies. Its name notwithstanding, this account is not directly related to the national-accounts investment accounts. It records financial inflows and outflows applied to claims on yields from productive assets. "Direct foreign investment" consists of funds used to purchase substantial shares of company equity (by convention, ten per cent or more). "Portfolio" investment comprises funds used to purchase other equity shares. The third financial-accounts component is "net debt flows" — disbursement less repayment flows, giving rise to changes in external-debt stocks. These include net inflows of short-term debt used to finance trade and other intra-year uses. The fourth financial-accounts component is "other" financial movements, consisting basically of cross-border movements of funds into and out of bank accounts and other short-term instruments. Although these flows are sometimes characterized as "hot money," in "normal" times — that is, when there are no perceived crises causing people to move money in or out — they are mostly the ebb and flow of bank accounts resulting from every-day transactions.

The net errors-and-omissions account is a discrepancy account. For any given year, it gives the difference between the increase in the central bank's net international-reserve position, as determined by the central bank's accounting system, and the above-the-line accounts. The above-the-line accounts are largely estimated. For any actual economy, a discrepancy can therefore be expected to arise between these estimated accounts and the recorded international-reserve flows, and this is recorded in the errors-and-omissions account. The more precisely the above-the-line accounts are estimated, the lower the discrepancy would presumably be. (It is important to remember, though, that the discrepancy can turn out low even if the estimated accounts are far off, if errors just happen to be offsetting.)

Chapter 7, Annex 2 (review). Balance-of-payments accounts structure

The listing following shows the "generic" structure of an economy's balance-of-payments accounts. These are flow accounts over a given time interval. Balance-of-payments accounts are conventionally denominated in U.S. dollars, although in principle any currency could be used. The sum of the "above-the-line" accounts "identically equals" the sum of the "below-the-line" accounts. For historical data, as explained in Annex 7.1, the net errors-and-omissions inflow is computed so as to set them equal.

Current-account surplus:

    Goods and non-factor services:

        Net merchandise trade:

            Merchandise exports

            Merchandise imports

        Net non-factor services:

            Receipts

            Payments

    Net factor receipts and transfer inflows:

        Factor services:

            Income:

                Interest income

                Other factor income

            Payments:

                Interest due

                Other factor payments

        Net unrequited transfers:

            Net official unrequited transfers

            Net private unrequited transfers

<u>**Financial-account surplus:**</u>

    Net capital inflows:

            Capital inflows

            Capital outflows

    Net foreign investment inflows:

            Direct foreign investment:

                    Net direct-foreign-investment inflow

                    Net direct-foreign-investment outflow

            Portfolio investment:

                    Net portfolio inflow

                    Net portfolio outflow

            Other net foreign-investment inflows

    Net debt inflows:

            Disbursements

            Repayment

    Other net financial inflows

<u>**Net errors and omissions inflow**</u>

≡

<u>**Net increase in international reserves:**</u>

    Increase in gross international reserves (less increase in valuation)

    Decrease in international-reserve liabilities (less decrease in valuation)

Chapter 7, Annex 3. Sources and uses of external finance

It is sometimes useful to present an economy's balance of payments in "sources-and-uses" format, showing more explicitly which entities are providing loan disbursements ("sources") and the purposes for which the funds will be used ("uses"). The sources-and-uses structure is derived from the balance-of-payments "identity" (see Annex 7.2) by adding and subtracting component accounts to or from "above" and "below" the line. Begin with the structure described in Annex 7.2, summarized to simplify the exposition:

Current-account surplus
Capital-account surplus:
>   Net foreign investment inflows
>   Net debt inflow:
>>   Disbursements
>>   Repayment
>   Other net financial inflows

Net errors and omissions inflow

≡:

Net increase in international reserves:
>   Increase in gross international reserves
>   Decrease in international-reserve liabilities

Subtract all the accounts listed above the line except for disbursements from above and below the line, to obtain one version of the sources-and-uses structure:

<u>Sources</u>:
>   Disbursements (excl. IMF)

≡

<u>Uses</u>:
>   Current-account deficit
>   Non-debt financial outflows:
>>   Net foreign investment outflows
>>   Other net financial capital outflows
>   Repayment of debt outstanding
>   Net errors and omissions inflow
>   Net increase in international reserves:
>>   Increase in gross international reserves
>>   Decrease in international-reserve liabilities
>>>   Net increase in obligations to the IMF:
>>>>   Disbursements by the IMF
>>>>   Repayment to the IMF
>>>   Net increase in other international-reserve liabilities

This way of setting out the format shows the uses to which the disbursements, excluding those from the IMF, are put. Subtracting "repayment of debt outstanding" from the top and the bottom makes the above-the-line total become net disbursements (i.e., disbursements less repayment).

Chapter 8, Annex 1 (review). Fiscal, budget, accrual, and cash surpluses and deficits

Over any time interval, any government entity has revenue and expenditure flows. The excess of revenue over expenditure is the entity's "surplus." A negative surplus is, of course, a "deficit." An entity that runs a surplus can *apply it* to some combination of repaying outstanding debt, purchasing assets, and adding to its deposit accounts in the central bank or other financial institutions. An entity that runs a deficit must *finance it* through some combination of additional debt, asset sales, and deposit withdrawals. (To the extent an entity running a deficit nevertheless *adds* to its deposits, it must take on even more debt.)

Tables giving fiscal accounts conventionally show the revenue and expenditure accounts in the upper part and the financing accounts in the lower part. Revenue and expenditure accounts are therefore said to be "above-the-line," while financing and asset-accounts flows are "below-the-line." Government budgets are sometimes presented, however, on a "budget" basis, as opposed to a "fiscal" basis. When shown on a budget basis, the only account below the line would be the net increase in the government's deposit accounts. Borrowing and proceeds of asset sales are shown above the line as inflows; repayment of debt and amounts spent on asset purchases are shown above the line as outflows. When shown on a fiscal basis, expenditure and revenue are shown above the line, and the financing of the difference between them — the "deficit" — is shown below the line. The deficit is financed by net borrowing — borrowing less repayment — and by withdrawals from the government's deposit balances. (Grants to governments, such as development aid, are sometimes shown above the line as non-tax revenue and sometimes below the line as a type of financing.) If the accounts are presented in sufficient detail, it should be possible to restructure a budget-basis presentation as a fiscal-basis presentation (and *vice versa*).

It is important to remember that all the transactions that make up the government accounts are recorded in "double entries." That is, in principle, any particular transaction affects at least two accounts. For example, any government cash expenditure is recorded above the line as an expenditure flow and as a reduction in the government's deposit account. The above-the-line total for any given time period must therefore precisely equal the below-the-line total. In reality, since errors almost always arise in compiling the figures, most fiscal accounts include a discrepancy account — analogous to the balance-of-payments errors-and-omissions account. It is best to assume that the financing flows are "correct," in which case the discrepancy account would be above the line — it would be calculated so as to make the above- and below-the-line sums equal.

Any given expenditure can be recorded on a "cash" or an "accrual" basis. Either way, if the expenditure is legally or contractually due and actually paid, it is recorded. The difference arises for expenditure that is legally or contractually due but *not* paid. Under *accrual*-basis accounting, expenditure that is contractually due is recorded *whether paid or not*. If not paid, it is also recorded below-the-line as an increase in accumulated arrears. In effect, the increase in arrears "finances" the expenditure — in effect, the expenditure's recipient "finances" the expenditure — non-contractually, to be sure — by failing to receive it. Under *cash*-basis accounting, expenditure that is contractually due is recorded *only if actually paid*. For example, suppose a government fails to pay a supplier on the contracted date. Under accrual accounting, the full amount of the payment purchase is recorded above the line and is, or should be, recorded below the line as financed by an increase in the outstanding stock of arrears. Under cash accounting, the purchase would not be recorded at all until actually paid.

Fiscal accounts are often on a "mix" of cash and accrual basis. For example, expenditure accounts may record interest payments when due, whether paid or not, but may fail to record government salaries due but not paid, or may fail to record goods-and-services purchases made but not yet paid.

Chapter 8, Annex 2. The primary government deficit consistent with maintaining a constant debt-GDP ratio

A simple algebraic formula can be used to estimate the primary (i.e., non-interest) government deficit that would be consistent with maintaining any given debt-GDP ratio, given (i) the nominal GDP growth rate and (ii) the nominal interest rate on the debt. By definition, the government's deficit over any period is equal to the change in its net debt stock:

$$\Delta D = N + i\, D,$$

where D represents the government's period-average net debt stock (i.e., gross debt less assets), N the government's primary deficit, and "i" the (nominal) interest rate on the (net) debt (so that the right-hand side represents the flow deficit). Divide both sides of this equation by D:

$$\Delta D/D = N/D + i\, D/D,\ \text{or}$$

$$g_D = N/D + i.$$

Multiply N/D by (1/Y)/(1/Y):

$$g_D = (N/Y)/(D/Y) + i,$$

$$= n/d + i,$$

where $g_D = \Delta D/D$, $n = N/Y$ and $d = D/Y$. Subtract the growth rate of GDP from both sides to obtain

$$g_D - g_Y = n/d + i - g_Y.$$

(If "i" is a nominal interest rate, g_Y should be the nominal GDP growth rate; if "i" is a real interest rate, then g_Y should be the real GDP growth rate.) Set $g_d = g_D - g_Y$ equal to zero and solve for "n." By definition, this would be the value of "n" that would be consistent with maintaining "d" constant:

$$n = d\,(g_Y - i).$$

Several important points may be noted about this formula. If $(g_Y - i)$ is less than zero, the required primary "deficit" would be negative, i.e., the primary balance would have to be in surplus to hold "d" unchanging. If $(g_Y - i)$ is greater than zero, the primary deficit could be positive. Moreover, smaller values for "d" imply smaller positive values of n^*. That is, the smaller the debt-GDP ratio to be kept unchanged, the smaller the primary deficit would need to be.

This calculation can be applied to help analyze debt-reduction exercises. Suppose that a government's maximum feasible longer-term primary surplus can be determined. The formula can then be applied to determine the level to which the debt-GDP ratio would have to be reduced to be sustainable. For example, suppose that real GDP grows at a long-term annual average rate of about 3 per cent while the government pays annual real interest of about seven percent. If it can run a primary surplus equal to one per cent of GDP, then the formula implies that the government could sustain a debt-GDP ratio equal to 25 per cent. This assumes, to be sure, that the long-term real-GDP growth is independent of the primary-surplus level.

Chapter 8, Annex 3. Sources and uses of fiscal financing

Like the balance-of-payments projections (see Chapter 7, Annex 3), the fiscal-accounts projections can be shown in a revealing sources-and-uses format. Begin from the standard fiscal-accounts presentation,

```
   Expenditure
 - Revenue
 = Deficit
 ≡ Financing:
         Net external financing
         Net internal financing.
```

Add "Revenue" to both the above- and below-the-line accounts to obtain

```
      Uses:
            Expenditure

 ≡    Sources:
            Revenue
            Net external financing
            Net internal financing.
```

That is, simply enough, the fiscal sources-and-uses presentation shows total expenditure "financed" by revenue, net external financing, and net internal financing flows.

Chapter 8, Annex 4. Public-sector economic structures

From the economic perspective, national public sectors may be categorized first into non-financial and financial components (see Figure 11 above). A "financial public sector" would comprise (i) the central bank and (ii) any other publicly-owned financial institutions, including commercial and development banks. One of the present projection exercise's objectives is to show how a non-financial public-sector deficit is to be financed. Public-sector financial institutions are themselves possible financing sources, and their operations may therefore be projected separately. (Holders of these institutions' liabilities, including the central bank's "monetary base," are the "ultimate" financing source.)

The non-financial public sector comprises "government" and "non-government" entities. Government entities comprise the "central" government and the various "sub-national" governments, including those of regions, territories, states, provinces, departments, municipalities, and so on. In most national-accounts systems, the consumption and investment expenditure of these entities counts as "government" consumption and investment expenditure. Public enterprises' consumption and investment, however, is effectively included in the *non*-government accounts, since most economies' national accounts treat such enterprises as businesses like any other. Separate government entities, including regulatory bodies, research agencies, cultural entities, universities, and so on, generally count as belonging to the government, although some countries' national accounts may classify specific public entities as non-government. The important point about such entities is that their financial management is usually separate from that of the national treasury: the central administration typically "transfers" funds to them. One important kind of entity from the financial perspective is the public pensions (social-security) system, since even in many developing economies pensions are quantitatively significant components of public-sector activities.

A central administration's budget may incorporate receipts from and transfers and explicit subsidies to other public- and private-sector entities. Thus, for example, a central administration may receive dividends from public-sector enterprises, or may provide transfers to specialized agencies entities or to sub-national governments; or, a government may provide explicit subsidies to certain private or public enterprises.

The following listing outlines the structure of a "generic" public-sector structure:

Non-financial public sector:
    Government:
        Central government:
            Government proper (central administration)
            Separate government entities (excl. the pensions
                system)
            Pensions system
        Sub-national (regional, state/provincial, municipal)
            governments:
            Government proper (administration)
            Separate entities
    Public-sector enterprises
Public-sector financial institutions:
    Central bank
        Publicly-owned commercial banks, investment
        banks, other financial institutions

Chapter 8, Annex 5. Consolidating public-sector surpluses and deficits

Public-sector structures and budgets differ significantly from economy to economy. In some economies, what is called the "national budget" encompasses only the central administration. In others, it encompasses all central-government entities, either on a consolidated or non-consolidated basis. It may even encompass some or all of the government enterprises. Some nations' legislatures consider, approve and monitor the budgets of all public entities. Others confine themselves only to the central administration's budget.

Surpluses and deficits of two or more public entities may be consolidated simply by summing their revenues, expenditures, and financing values. If one entity purchased goods and services or borrowed funds from the other, of course, the transactions in question would "net out" in the consolidation. Thus, for example, an overall central-government surplus could be calculated by consolidating the accounts of the central administration and any other central-government entities.

When consolidating, it is important to know which accounts are on an "accrual" or "cash" basis, and to adjust the consolidated accounts accordingly. A particular problem arises when consolidating government and public-enterprise accounts, even when both are on an accrual basis. One might think first to consolidate the government deficit and the public-enterprise profit-and-loss accounts, but this simply may be inappropriate. Government accounts, as noted, record revenues and expenditure: the overall deficit they together imply is financed through a combination of borrowing, asset sales, and net deposit withdrawals. Public-enterprise accounts, in contrast, are more likely to be conventional corporate accounts. The "profit-and-loss" account indicates the change in the corporation's net-worth position deriving from its operations. A loss indicated by a profit-and-loss statement is therefore conceptually distinct from a government deficit. One notable difference is that government expenditure on capital formation leads to an increase in the government deficit, whereas expenditure on capital formation by an enterprise does not in itself affect a corporation's profit.

Chapter 9, Annex 1 (review). The "demand for money" and the price level

By definition, the **demand for money** at any given moment as the stock of money an individual, or an economy as a whole, is willing and able to hold. Over the Twentieth Century a significant branch of the literature of macroeconomics dealt with the theoretical and empirical determinants of the demand for money. The broad conclusions of this literature were that the demand for money increases with nominal GDP, increases to the extent money offers a positive real rate of return, and diminishes to the extent other wealth-holding alternatives offer higher returns. The earliest theories maintained that demand for money was grounded exclusively on its usefulness for transactions, and that since money generally earned no return demand for money was probably not influenced by the rates of return on other forms of wealth holding.   John Maynard Keynes' *General Theory of Employment, Interest and Money* argued, however, that if people perceived that other forms of holding wealth were likely to offer a reduced or negative yield, people might prefer to hold more of their wealth in money — what Keynes called the "speculative" demand for money. In addition, as inflation became increasingly important in many economies, many analysts pointed out that expected inflation would reduce the demand for money (see Annexes 9.2 and 9.4).

The lengthy scholarly literature on monetary dynamics also concluded that if demand for money differs from the supply of money at any moment, real economic activity, the price level, and rates of return on other assets would tend to adjust to bring about equality. A large number of possible dynamic adjustment processes has been described, depending on assumed circumstances.   In one textbook adjustment process, if the amount of money people hold exceeds the amount they wish to hold, they would move some of their wealth from money into bonds and equities. In so doing, they would raise the prices of bonds and equities, reducing interest rates and lifting stock-market valuations. This would stimulate production and income, and increase the demand for money. In this particular adjustment process, price-level adjustment plays no role.

The price level (see Annex 3.4) is likely, however, to figure in the adjustment process whenever money demand and money supply are unequal. Very simply, if money demand exceeds money supply, one way they could come into alignment would be through a reduction in the price level. That is, if people in the aggregate prefer to hold more money than they have — that is, if money demand exceeds money supply — they will retain money, inducing would-be sellers of goods and services to reduce their prices, thus reducing the overall price level and so reducing money demand. If, on the other hand, money supply exceeds money demand, people would attempt to exchange money for goods and services, bidding up prices of goods and services in the process, and so increasing money demand.

Expected inflation is likely to reduce money demand because rising prices amount to a reduction in the purchasing power of money. All other things being equal, to the extent people anticipate rising prices, they are likely to prefer to hold less money. (Annex 9.2 discusses the concept of the "real rate of return on money," and its relationship with the price level.)

Chapter 9, Annex 2 (review). The real rate of return on money and on other assets

Like any other financial asset, over any time interval a unit of money has a real rate of return. This would be defined as the percentage increase in its purchasing power from one end of the period to the other. Let p' represent the period-end price level. The purchasing power of each unit of money would be $(1/p')$. The real rate of return on money would then be given by

$$-\pi = [(1/p')/(1/p'_{-1})] - 1$$

$$= (p'_{-1}/p') - 1$$

$$= (p'_{-1} - p')/p'$$

$$= [p'_{-1} - p'_{-1}(1 + g_{p'})]/[p'_{-1}(1 + g_{p'})]$$

since

$$p' = p'_{-1} (1 + g_{p'}).$$

Multiplying this last formula by p'_{-1}/p'_{-1} gives

$$-\pi = g_{p'}/(1 + g_{p'}).$$

(With this definition π has the same sign as the inflation rate.) This expression defines the real rate of return on money over any time interval for which the inflation rate is $g_{p'}$. Thus, for example, over any period in which prices double, the inflation rate is 100 per cent while the real rate of return on money is -50 per cent (i.e., money loses half its purchasing power). Over any period in which prices rise 25 per cent the real rate of return on money is -20 per cent (i.e., money loses a fifth of its purchasing power).

Note that

$$1 + \pi = [(1 + g_{p'})/(1 + g_{p'})] - g_{p'}/(1 + g_{p'}) = 1/(1 + g_{p'}).$$

The real rate of return on an interest-bearing asset denominated in money units can be calculated in a similar way. Any asset worth one peso yielding nominal interest of "n" over a time period for which the inflation rate is $g_{p'}$ would have a real value of $(1 + n)/(1 + g_{p'})$ at the end of the period. The real rate of return on the asset over the period would be given then by

$$\{[(1 + n)/(1 + g_{p'})] - 1\}/1,$$

or

$$(n - \pi)/(1 + \pi).$$

For low values of π, this would be approximately equal to n - π.

Chapter 9, Annex 3 (review). *The money multiplier*

The "money multiplier" is defined as the ratio of the money stock to the monetary base. The money stock would be defined as currency in circulation excluding commercial banks' holdings plus total deposits in commercial banks, while the monetary base would be defined as the central bank's monetary liability, that is, total currency issues plus commercial banks' deposits at the central bank. The "marginal money multiplier" is defined as the ratio of the *increase* in the money stock to the *increase* in the monetary base over a given time period.

Intuitively, the money multiplier arises because commercial banks will hold only a percentage of their total deposit liabilities as "bank reserves" — that is, as deposits at their central bank and "vault cash." They will hold the larger of (i) the minimum legal reserve ratio and (ii) the minimum amount their management feels they need to hold to meet withdrawal demand. Thus, for example, suppose that a commercial bank's authorities (or its risk-averse management) require it to hold at least 10 per cent of its deposits in bank reserves. Suppose the bank receives a deposit in currency of 100 pesos. Having created a deposit liability of 100 pesos, the bank will now be in a position to provide new loans amounting to as much as 900 pesos. In the process, the bank would create additional deposits of 900 pesos, since this is the form in which it would provide the loans. Doing so will bring its reserve-deposit ratio down to the 10 per cent minimum. In this sense, once the 100 pesos enter the banking system, they would be "multiplied" into ten times as much money. In general, the smaller the proportion of its money that the non-bank public prefers to hold in currency, or — the same thing — the larger the amount of its money holdings that the public prefers to place in bank deposits, the higher the money multiplier will be.

Let M' represent the total money supply, B' the monetary base, C' currency in circulation (excluding commercial banks' holdings), D' total deposits in commercial banks, and R' total reserve holdings of commercial banks (including currency held as bank reserves). By definition, the money supply and monetary base would be given, respectively, by

$$M' = C' + D'$$

and

$$B' = C' + R'.$$

The "stock" money multiplier would be given then by

$$m = M'/B' = (C' + D')/(C' + R')$$

$$= [(C'/D') + (D'/D')]/[(C'/D') + (R'/D')].$$

The "marginal" money multiplier would be given, similarly, by

$$m' = [(\Delta C'/\Delta D') + (\Delta D'/\Delta D')]/[(\Delta C'/\Delta D') + (\Delta R'/\Delta D')].$$

The behavioral relationships that determine the stock and marginal money multipliers' values are (i) banks' reserve holdings in relation to their deposit obligations (if they exceed the "required" reserve ratio — otherwise, presumably, the required reserve ratio would be binding) and (ii) the holdings maintained by the economy, commercial banks apart, of currency in relation to money. Let "k" represent the marginal ratio of bank reserves to deposits, $\Delta R'/\Delta D'$ and let "z" represent the economy's marginal currency/deposit ratio, $\Delta C'/\Delta D'$. The marginal money multiplier is given then by

$$m' = (z + 1)/(z + k)].$$

Higher values of "z" and "k" imply smaller values for the money multiplier. Since

$$\Delta B' = \Delta C' + \Delta R' = z \, \Delta D' + k \, \Delta D',$$

$$\Delta D' = \Delta B'/(z + k).$$

Chapter 9, Annex 4 (review). "Seignorage" and the inflation tax

By issuing money that the economy is willing to hold at an interest rate of zero, a central bank effectively captures income, amounting to the interest it would have had to pay if it had borrowed at market interest rates. This profit flow is called "seignorage." (Historically, the term referred to the percentages that sovereigns retained as payment for coining precious metals for circulation.) A central bank's earnings flow over a given year from seignorage may therefore be estimated by applying a market interest rate to the average monetary liability stock. (If the monetary liabilities pay interest, the seignorage would be estimated by multiplying the average stock of the monetary liabilities over the year by the difference between the market interest rate and the interest rate on the monetary liabilities.)

Central banks often pass on seignorage earnings from money issue. To the extent a government borrows from the central bank at an interest rate below what the market rate, it effectively shares in the central bank's seignorage earnings. In addition, commercial banks that take monetary deposits at interest rates lower than those on less liquid bank liabilities earn a kind of seignorage. Again, some of these earnings may be captured by borrowers in the form of lower interest rates than they would otherwise pay.

Some analysts prefer a conceptually different measure of seignorage, the net issue of central-bank monetary liabilities over a given time interval (in real terms or as a percentage of GDP). In effect, each year's issue of monetary liabilities permits the central bank to acquire an equal quantity of assets at no charge in real resources. This second measure will generally be larger than the first. Both measures are widely used.

The "inflation tax" is a component of the seignorage flow (according to the first definition). All other things being the same, to the extent the central bank's, or indeed any commercial bank's, monetary liability diminishes in real terms over any time interval, the entity's real profits will have increased. A simple estimate of the inflation tax paid on an economy's average money holdings over the time interval can be calculated by multiplying the average money stock by the real rate of return on money (see Annex 9.2) and expressing the result in real terms or as a percentage of GDP to make it comparable with other time periods. Thus, in an economy whose average money supply over a year is 50 per cent of GDP and whose December-December inflation rate is 25 per cent, the real rate of return on money is -20 per cent and the inflation tax proceeds would amount to 10 per cent of GDP.

A well-known calculation first suggested by Cagan (1956) can be used to determine an "optimal" inflation rate at which the inflation-tax proceeds would be maximized. If the formula for the (year-average) demand for money is M = A $(1 - \pi)^\beta$, where -π represents the real rate of return on money, then the inflation-tax proceeds would be

$$\pi A (1 - \pi)^\beta.$$

Using the standard calculus procedure to maximize this expression with respect to π (i.e., calculating the first derivative and setting it equal to zero, then ensuring that the second derivative is less than zero) gives

$$1 - \pi = \beta,$$

i.e., the inflation tax is maximized when π is equal to $(1 - \beta)$.

Chapter 9, Annex 5 (review). Performance conditions in International Monetary Fund programs

From its inception in the mid-1940s, the International Monetary Fund has served several different purposes. One basic, defining purpose, however, has always been to provide "stand-by" financial support for member economies whose international-reserve holdings have fallen too low. The idea is to give the authorities time to implement policies to reverse the reserve loss, with less exchange-rate depreciation and credit tightening than might otherwise be necessary. In simple terms, the basic IMF transaction is a foreign-exchange loan disbursed in tranches. The objective is to lift the borrowing economy's international-reserve stock to a level appropriate to stabilize its exchange rate and permit normal international business operations, while policy-makers implement corrective policy measures to bring external accounts flows to more appropriate magnitudes.

     The loan tranche disbursements are therefore subject to "conditionality," intended to ensure that they will proceed only if and as policy-makers carry out necessary corrective measures. These conditions are set out in terms of certain quantitative indicators, "performance criteria." If the economy's performance meets or exceeds these indicators, the economy is presumed to be recovering sustainably.

     "Textbook" IMF programs have four basic performance criteria. The first is a ***minimum increase in net international reserves***, defined as the change in the stock of international reserves held by the central bank less the central bank's international-reserve liabilities — in particular, less the reserves borrowed from the Fund. The point is to ensure that the central bank's international-reserve position is indeed recovering, as a consequence of the policy changes and not just because of the resources borrowed from the Fund. The second performance criterion is a *maximum increase in the accumulation of public-sector external debt.* The point of this criterion is partly to ensure that the international-reserve position is not improving simply through public borrowing, and partly to ensure that future debt-servicing obligations will not reverse the recovery of international reserves. The third performance criterion is a *maximum public-sector deficit.* This is partly intended to limit internal demand, which contributes to demand pressure affecting imports. It is also intended to limit the government's borrowing requirement, to help reduce pressure on the central bank to take on government obligations. The fourth performance criterion is a *maximum increase in the central bank's "net domestic assets,"* defined as the difference between the monetary base and the net international reserve stock. The point of this condition is to limit money creation by the central bank. This helps limit inflation which, all other things being equal, makes the economy less competitive with other economies, discouraging exports and encouraging imports.

In general, the conditions are calculated through a monetary-programming procedure like the one described here, and first set out by Jacques J. Polak (see Polak 1957) (see Annex 9.6).

Chapter 9, Annex 6. Formulating programming targets for "IMF-type" programs

Although the monetary-programming aspects of the exercise this book describes are set out in annual terms, the formal approach is similar to the Fund's quarterly monetary-programming approach. In principle, it could be used to set out annual consistency indicators for an IMF-type program, and to examine their feasibility. Suppose, for example, that an economy's policy-makers choose to emphasize maintenance of exchange-rate and price-level stability over the coming two years, and wish to set out their macroeconomic program for the two years accordingly. The exercise this book describes could be used to calculate performance indicators similar to (and consistent with) those of a quarterly IMF program and to determine whether they are likely to prove feasible.

The procedure would be broadly as follows. First, target values for real GDP growth, inflation, and the exchange rate path would be set out as described in Chapter 3. At the same time, target values would be set out for the main non-interest government-expenditure flows. The projection exercise described in Chapter 8 above would then be used to determine (1) the implied public deficit. Next, a target year-end gross international reserve position would be set (calculated as some number of months of imports of goods and non-factor services), along with a program of public-sector external borrowing. The projection exercise described in Chapter 7 above could then be applied to determine (2) the implied central-bank net international-reserve position and (3) the implied accumulation of public external debt. The projection exercise described in Section 9.2 above could then be used to compute (4) the implied increase in the central bank's net internal assets.

These four values would be the implied basic "performance targets" for an IMF-supported stabilization program (see Annex 9.5). In practice, the analyst would want to examine other projection results to gauge the program's feasibility. The national-accounts projection discussed in Chapter 6 would indicate whether the program would imply too large a decline in real non-government consumption. The external-accounts projection of Chapter 7 would indicate whether the program would imply an excessive external-financing flow to close the balance of payments. The fiscal-accounts projection of Chapter 8 would indicate whether the program would imply an excessively large amount of internal public borrowing. And finally, the monetary-accounts projection discussed in Section 9.2 would indicate whether the monetary authority would have to carry out an excessively large amount of offsetting monetary policy to hold money-supply growth within the program limits. Should any of these projection results seem too ambitious, the analyst would presumably recommend that the policy program's assumptions and performance indicators be adjusted accordingly.

Chapter 9, Annex 7. A central bank's "sustainable" capital base

From the projection of its flow balance-sheet variables, it is a straightforward step to project the central bank's period-end balance sheet. A multi-period projection can be carried out to see whether the central bank's net-worth position would be tending either to deteriorate or to grow. Unfortunately, as discussed above, analysts have not yet discovered persuasive criteria that can be used to determine a central bank's appropriate net worth-asset ratio. (The same is true for commercial banks — the "Basel" ratios are essentially arbitrary, even if practice and custom over time have begun to make them seem less so.) All the same, suppose that a particular monetary authority believes its central bank should maintain a specified net worth-net asset ratio, even if the ratio it chooses is, of necessity, arbitrary. It should be helpful to consider conditions under which a central bank could maintain this ratio over time.

One approach is to determine the rate of return a central bank would have to maintain on its net-asset position in order to maintain a specified net worth-net asset ratio. To do so, return to the simplified central-bank balance sheet discussed in Section 9.2 above, but now assume, for simplicity, that the central bank issues no sterilization instruments. The central bank's balance sheet therefore comprises aggregated net assets Z', monetary base B', and net worth V'. (Alternatively, assume that the aggregated net assets Z' include the stock of sterilization instruments, with a negative value.) Assuming there is no other source of change in the central bank's net worth, and maintaining the assumption that $r_B = 0$,

$$\Delta V' = X$$

$$= r_Z (Z'_{-1} + Z')/2$$

$$= r_Z [Z'_{-1} + (\Delta Z'/2)].$$

The flow balance-sheet identity implies that

$$\Delta Z' = \Delta B' + \Delta V',$$

and so that

$$\Delta Z' = \Delta B' + r_Z [Z'_{-1} + (\Delta Z'/2)].$$

Divide both sides by Z'_{-1} and rearrange to obtain

$$\Delta Z'/Z'_{-1} = \Delta B'/Z'_{-1} + r_Z + (r_Z/2)(\Delta Z'/Z'_{-1}),$$

or, since $g_{Z'} = \Delta Z'/Z'_{-1}$ and $g_{B'} = \Delta B'/B'_{-1}$,

$$g_{Z'} = g_{B'}(B'_{-1}/Z'_{-1}) + r_Z + (r_Z/2) g_{Z'}.$$

Rearrange this into an expression for r_Z:

$$r_Z = \{g_{Z'} - g_{B'}(B'_{-1}/Z'_{-1})\}/\{1 + (g_{Z'}/2)\}.$$

Since the balance-sheet identity implies that

$$B'_{-1}/Z'_{-1} = 1 - (V'_{-1}/Z'_{-1}),$$

$$r_Z = \{g_{Z'} - g_{B'}[1 - (V'_{-1}/Z'_{-1})]\}/\{1 + (g_{Z'}/2)\}.$$

In the "steady state" — that is, for V'/Z' to come out equal to V'_{-1}/Z'_{-1} — the growth rates of the balance-sheet components would have to be precisely equal:

$$g_{Z'} = g_{B'} = g_{V'}.$$

The previous expression would then become

$$r_Z = \{g_{B'} - g_{B'}[1 - (V'_{-1}/Z'_{-1})]\}/\{1 + (g_{Z'}/2)\}$$
$$= \{g_{B'}(V'_{-1}/Z'_{-1})]\}/\{1 + (g_{B'}/2)\}.$$

If this is the rate of return on the net asset position over the period, then the period-end net worth-net asset ratio (V'/Z') will be equal to the preceding period-end ratio (V'_{-1}/Z'_{-1}). That is, suppose the monetary program calls for the monetary base to grow at the rate $g_{B'}$ and for the net worth-net asset ratio to end the period at a value equal to what it was at the end of the preceding period. The expression above gives the rate of return on the central bank's net-asset position that would meet these programming objectives. If the rate of return on the net asset position is higher (lower) than the expression above shows, then the net worth-net asset ratio will end the period higher (lower) than its preceding period-end value.

In reality, to be sure, for any central bank the value of r_Z would vary over time, rising and falling over time under a variety of pressures — including tightening and easing monetary policy. Over the longer term, however, if the value of r_Z maintained the average value indicated by the preceding expression while the monetary base grew at an average value of $g_{B'}$, then the central bank would maintain the capital-asset ratio roughly at (V'_{-1}/Z'_{-1}).

The table following shows the value of r_Z that would be required to maintain the given capital-asset ratio (V'_{-1}/Z'_{-1}) for given growth rates of the monetary base. The vertical axis shows various capital-asset ratios to maintain constant, and the horizontal axis shows various monetary-base growth rates. That is, for each pair of capital-asset ratio and monetary-base growth rate, the table gives the rate of return on the central bank's net-asset position that would be required to maintain the capital-asset ratio. For relatively lower capital-asset ratios shown, the required rates of return are reassuringly low. Not surprisingly, though, a central bank determined to maintain a high net worth-net asset ratio would have to earn relatively high rates of return on its assets.

Rate of return on the central bank's net-asset position required to maintain the capital-asset ratio V_{-1}/Z_{-1} given the monetary-base growth rate $g_{B'}$

	3.0%	5.0%	7.5%	10.0%	15.0%	g(B)
8.0%	0.2%	0.4%	0.6%	0.8%	1.1%	
10.0%	0.3%	0.5%	0.7%	1.0%	1.4%	
12.0%	0.4%	0.6%	0.9%	1.1%	1.7%	
15.0%	0.4%	0.7%	1.1%	1.4%	2.1%	
20.0%	0.6%	1.0%	1.4%	1.9%	2.8%	
50.0%	1.5%	2.4%	3.6%	4.8%	7.0%	
100.0%	3.0%	4.9%	7.2%	9.5%	14.0%	
V'(-1)/Z'(-1)						

Source: Calculations by the writer.

Chapter 10, Annex 1. Suggestions for spreadsheet design

This Annex offers suggestions for setting up spreadsheets for macroeconomic projection analysis, based on this writer's experience. Analysts, and their superiors, have different preferences about how best to organize spreadsheets. This writer's most basic recommendation is that spreadsheets should be set up in ways that are easy to understand for the people who will need to work with them. It is impossible to over-emphasize the importance of making spreadsheets as transparent and straightforward as possible. Detailed documentation is drudge work, but has large rewards. Because transparency and documentation make it much easier to work with a spreadsheet, they make it more likely that the spreadsheet will be used. (They also help the analyst remember what she herself has done.)

The suggestions noted here are reflected in the "Pacífica" spreadsheet. This writer has found they have worked well in practical applications, in the sense that they help formulate spreadsheets that are efficient and relatively easy for other users to understand. In addition, they help reduce the likelihood of errors. The Pacífica spreadsheet is in Microsoft Excel, but the suggestions following should apply to any kind of spreadsheet.

Worksheet table structure: The Pacífica exercise has years in columns and the accounts in rows. This is generally preferable for multiannual projection exercises, since it usually makes the tables easier to read: labels for account titles and assumptions are longer than date labels, and account and assumption titles can be written at greater length at the left-hand ends of rows than in column headings.

Just about any spreadsheet projection exercise may be said to comprise four different activities: (i) historical-data input; (ii) assumption setting; (iii) processing of historical data and assumptions to formulate projections; and (iv) presentation of results in tables and charts. In putting together a "workbook" (in Microsoft Excel's terminology, a set of linked spreadsheets, or "worksheets"), it may be helpful to have each worksheet specialize one of these four types of task. (The Pacífica workbook combines assumption setting and processing of historical data and assumptions in "projection" worksheets.)

Data input: Historical-data worksheets should, if possible, be set up in the formats in which data are received. Thus, for example, if annual tax-revenue data come from the revenue agency, it is helpful to have the data-input worksheet in precisely the same format as the worksheets on which revenue agency provides the data. This makes it far easier than it would otherwise be to update the data bases. (It may even be possible, if lines and columns are precisely aligned, simply to copy the entire worksheet as received from the revenue agency directly into the data sheet.)

Projection assumptions: The most important advice regarding projection assumptions is that they should be set out as *explicitly* as possible. (In particular, where an assumption has two components, the two components should be set out separately. Thus, for example, suppose that the growth rate of the world coffee trade volume is an assumption. If that assumption is related through an elasticity to the growth rate of the overall world-trade volume, the elasticity and the growth rate of the overall world-trade volume should be set out explicitly as assumptions.) In assumptions worksheets, it is helpful to highlight each line of assumptions over the projection period (say, by "shading" cells containing projection assumptions in a particular color). It is helpful also (or alternatively) to number the lines containing projection assumptions sequentially. In these ways users will know all the assumptions they must set so as to formulate a complete projection.

On each assumption line, in addition to setting out the assumptions for future years, it is helpful to calculate the implicit assumption values corresponding to historical periods. Thus, for just one simple example, while real GDP would be projected over the future by having assumed real-GDP growth rates for each projection year, it is also helpful to show the implicit real-GDP growth rates for each historical year. These implicit growth rates would be calculated from the historical real-GDP data. Similarly, if the projected import volume of intermediate goods is projected using assumed elasticities of import volume with respect to real GDP, the implicit values of the elasticities could be shown for the historical years.

The ***projection worksheets*** transform base-year data and projection assumptions into projections. Some analysts may prefer to have projection assumptions on worksheets separate from the projection worksheets, and to have the assumptions all grouped together on one worksheet. Other analysts may prefer to place projection assumptions within the projection worksheets to which they are relevant. This has the advantage of having each sector's projections and related assumptions on the same worksheet. (The Pacífica exercise mixes these two approaches: assumptions of general importance likely to be varied in sensitivity analysis are given in one worksheet, and assumptions relevant to particular sectors are given in the worksheets relevant to those sectors.)

If the projection worksheets are structured with both projections and assumptions, it may be helpful to think of them as having northwest, northeast, southeast, and southwest areas. The northwest would show historical data, the northeast would show projections, and the southeast would show the assumptions that generate the projections. The southwest would show the "implicit" assumptions, that is, the parameter assumptions that would have generated the actual outcomes. The northwest and southwest would conclude with the "base" year, while the northeast and southeast would commence with the initial projection year. Thus, for example, the series for historical GDP at 1995 prices would be in the northwest and the projected values for the same series would continue on the same row over the northeast. The assumed growth rates that generate the projection would be in the southeast, while the real growth rates implied by the historical data series would be in the southwest.[99]

Finally, it is helpful to have separate worksheets for *tables* that are to be printed and/or placed in documents. These worksheets would draw data, assumptions and projection results from the projection worksheets. Tables are often formatted, adjusted and modified to meet

---

[99]   One problem that can arise when calculating implicit growth rates of an historical data series is that when this year's datum is non-zero but the previous year's is zero the implicit growth rate would be undefined. One way to keep the calculation from showing an undefined value would be to substitute a very small figure for the previous year's datum. The calculated growth rate would then be very large, but at least the calculation could then continue without generating "errors."

various needs, and it is useful to be able to do this without affecting the projection worksheets. The same table can be used to generate (say) versions in national currency, U.S. dollars, and percentage of GDP. For this, construct the table in (say) national-currency terms, but have all entries multiplied by a common coefficient given in a particular cell for each year, so they can be multiplied into any desired unit of account.

The tables worksheet can be used to set up *charts*. It is difficult to overstate the power of well-designed charts to convey information efficiently.

Cell conventions: It is helpful to make consistent use of cell formatting conventions. For example, cells containing figures could be indicated in (say) blue font, while cells containing formulas could be indicated in black font. Cells containing assumptions could be indicated with other font colors, or shaded (or "painted"). Font colors or shading may also be used to indicate cells in one worksheet that contain formulas involving cells in other worksheets. This writer generally employs red font to indicate figures or formulas that should be regarded as subject to revision (such as values estimated in advance of obtaining actual data or programming assumptions requiring further discussion). Any convention will do to convey such information to other analysts, as long as it is clearly defined and used consistently.

Projection worksheets: In the Pacífica workbook, the different macroeconomic accounts systems are projected on separate worksheets — that is, the balance-of-payments, external-debt, monetary-and-banking, fiscal and national accounts projections are carried out on separate, but linked, worksheets. These worksheets' columns all correspond to the same years — that is, Column AQ gives 1999 figures in all worksheets. This makes it easier to compose formulas on one worksheet incorporating variables from other worksheets.

Summation and other checks: The Pacífica workbook incorporates a number of "summation" checks, to flag errors and to assist in debugging. Thus, for example, for each year the spreadsheet calculates the difference of the above- and below-the-line balance-of-payments projections, to be sure that their difference equals to zero. The workbook also incorporates several other kinds of check — for example, to ensure that no external-debt stock falls below zero as a consequence of excessive repayment, or that values that should be equal in different worksheets are so in fact.[100] Each worksheet in the Pacífica workbook shows the sum of all such checks in a cell at the top of the worksheet, enabling the user to see quickly whether any check in the worksheet is non-zero. In addition, each worksheet shows the sum of all sums of checks in all worksheets, enabling the user to see quickly whether any check in the *workbook* is non-zero. The checks can then be used to help correct the worksheet.

Circularities: Under the methodology and calculation procedures this book describes, there is no reason for the projection spreadsheet ever to incorporate a circularity.[101] If a circularity is inadvertently introduced, the workbook may fail to calculate completely, and the results then cannot be assumed to be valid. Accordingly, the workbook must be debugged to remove any circularity.[102]

Links with other workbooks: Cells in one workbook may be drawn from another workbook, by means of formulas. Care must be taken, however, when working with one workbook while the other is not open, since changes — especially elimination or insertion of rows or columns — can throw off the linkages. When using spreadsheet linkages, this writer has found it helpful to have all linkages between two workbooks carried out through twinned worksheets in the two workbooks set up in precisely the same way. Cell formulas in the receiving worksheet would simply refer

---

[100]   "Conditional formatting" can be used to highlight cells containing check formulas when they indicate errors. For example, suppose the balance-of-payments check for a given projection year is the absolute value of the difference between the above- and below-the-line balance-of-payments sums. The cell font could be conditionally set to white if the check is less than (say) 0.00000000001 but to red if it is greater.

[101]   A circularity is an instance in which, say, the formula in cell A1 includes cell A2 and the formula in cell A2 includes cell A1.

[102]   Workbooks that (unlike the exercise this book describes) use iterative solution procedures may have circularities, which are resolved by the iteration process. One disadvantage of having any circularity in place is that other, unintended circularities may go undetected.

to the corresponding addresses in the transmitting worksheet, and this transmitting worksheet would draw from the transmitting workbook's other worksheets. These two linkage worksheets would never be changed except when both workbooks are open, and then always so that they always "line up" with one another.

Spreadsheet "Boolean" functions; the "CHOOSE" function: The various "Boolean" functions are especially useful for spreadsheet projection work. In Microsoft Excel, these include the "IF," "OR," "AND," and "NOT" functions. (Spreadsheet programs other than Microsoft Excel have the same or similar functions.) In Excel, the function IF (*relational, a, b*) returns the value "a" if the "relational" expression is true and "b" if it is false. (A "relational" expression is an expression like "$1 = 2$" or "$5 < B6$"). The function AND (*relational1, relational2, relational3...*) returns the value "one" if *all* the relational arguments are true and "zero" if *any* are untrue, while the function OR (*relational1, relational2, relational3...*) returns the value "one" if *any* of the relational arguments are true and "zero" if *all* are untrue. The NOT (*relational*) function returns the value "one" if the relational is *not* true and "zero" if it is true. (Refer to an Excel manual or the help menu tab on a worksheet screen.)

A simple example of the use of the "IF" function would be the following. Suppose the economy is projected to consume "c" barrels of oil and produce "p" barrels during a given year. Suppose that if "p" exceeds "c" the economy would export the difference, while if "c" exceeds "p" the economy would import the difference. The volume exported could be set using the function

$$+IF(p > c, p - c, 0)$$

and the volume imported could be set using the function

$$+IF(p < c, c - p, 0).$$

The IF function is especially useful in projection worksheets organized in the "northwest, northeast, southeast, southwest" structure mentioned above, with historical data in the northwest, projections in the northeast, assumptions in the southeast, and implicit assumptions in the southwest. In the Pacífica workbook, the IF function allows the same formula to be used across any row in the north of any projection worksheet, by writing it as follows:

$$+IF[t < IPY, \; \varphi(historical\ data), \; \varphi(projection)],$$

where "t" is the year, IPY is the initial projection year, and φ(historical data) and φ(projection) are the data-reporting and projection functions for historical-data and projection years respectively.

The CHOOSE(a, b_1, b_2, b_3...) function can also be remarkably useful. In its Microsoft Excel version, it returns the value b_i if "a" is equal to "i". For example, suppose the cells J3:M3 contain the years 1995, 1996, 1997 and 1998. Suppose the function +CHOOSE(j3-(j3-1), 45,50,55,60) is placed in cells J4:M4 directly below. This function would return 45 in J4 under 1995, 50 in K4 for 1996, 55 in L4 for 1997, and 60 in M4 for 1998. One obvious application of this function is to set "scenarios" for sensitivity analysis. Suppose an analyst wishes to determine the consequences of a 10 per cent exchange-rate depreciation in a future year. Suppose that the cell A1 is set as the "scenario" cell. Suppose that the exchange rate would be 10 per dollar if there were no depreciation and 11 per dollar if there were. The cell for the exchange rate setting in the future year could then contain the function

$$+CHOOSE(\$A\$1, 10, 11).$$

By setting A1 alternatively equal to 1 and 2 and comparing the projection results, the analyst could determine the implications of the more depreciated exchange rate.

Another application of the CHOOSE function is to have titles change with changing scenarios, choices of units, or even language. Thus for example, the function

$$+CHOOSE(a, \text{"Base scenario"}, \text{"High scenario"}, \text{"Low scenario"})$$

returns the scenario title according to whether "a" equals 1, 2, or 3; similarly,

+CHOOSE(a, "English","castellano","français","português")

returns the language title according to whether "a" equals 1, 2, 3, or 4.

Macros to help conserve diskette space: In multiannual projection exercises, many of the formulas for historical and for projection years are repeated year after year. In the Pacífica workbook this is exploited to reduce the workbook's size. Before saving, a macro ("eraser," shortcut ctrl-shift-J) can be executed to delete all but one column of historical formulas (except for data) and all but one column of projection formulas (except for projection assumptions). Upon opening, another macro ("copier," shortcut ctrl-shift-C) can be used to copy the appropriate formulas into all historical and projection columns. The Pacífica workbook has a macro ("saver," shortcut ctrl-shift-S) that runs the macro "eraser" and then saves the workbook. It also has another macro ("quick," shortcut ctrl-shift-Q) that runs the "saver" and "copier" macros in succession, so that the user can save the workbook and return to work on it.

Chapter 10, Annex 2. A simple "open-economy Phillips curve"[103]

The accounts structure with which this book works is structured so as to evaluate the financial feasibility implied by a "vector" of macroeconomic outcomes, including the (i) real-GDP growth rate, (ii) price level (GDP deflator), (iii) (real-effective) exchange rate, (iv) capacity-utilization percentage, and others. For any given projection year, the selection of a vector is pretty much arbitrary. The discussion thus far at no point considers the macroeconomic relationships among the vector's variables.

The Phillips-curve concept goes back to a scholarly article that the Australian economist A. W. Phillips published in 1958, called "The relationship between unemployment and the rate of change of money

---

[103] I am grateful to Andrés Solimano for suggesting the basic approach described here.

wages in the United Kingdom 1861–1957." That article was an empirical examination of the relationship between wage increases and unemployment. A lengthy literature grew from this article. The underlying idea was that, all other things being equal, in any economy higher wages ought to be associated with diminished labor demand, hence with higher unemployment, all other things being the same. The so-called "Phillips curve" was the presumed relationship between an economy's short-term wage level and its unemployment rate — and, by extension, between its wage level and its capacity utilization, or, on the assumption that wage and price inflation were positively related, between its inflation rate and its capacity utilization.

The essential idea was that, at least in the relatively short term, higher inflation rates were associated with higher output, higher capacity utilization and lower unemployment. Or, in other words, that inflation rates would tend to be negatively correlated with lower unemployment. Policy-makers, as the idea was set out, could set policies at any moment so as to select from a "trade-off" range of inflation-unemployment pairings, ranging from a high inflation-low unemployment pairing to a low inflation-high unemployment pairing.

The conventional Phillips curve is in two dimensions, with an economic-activity indicator on the abscissa and an inflation indicator on the ordinate. A three-dimensional Phillips curve would add a dimension for a measure of an economy's international financial position — say, the stock of gross international reserves, or the stock of gross international reserves less the stock of public external debt. This would better represent the full range of pressures on policy-makers struggling to set short-term policies.

This Annex develops a simple "open-economy Phillips curve," which could be used to structure relationships among the components of a macroeconomic programming vector. That is, given projection assumptions for the growth rates of real GDP and the real-effective exchange rate, as well as for the international price level, relationships could be structured and parameters assumed for (a) the wage level in function of the price level, capacity utilization, and employment; (b) capacity utilization in function of the wage level, the price level and the real-effective exchange rate; and (c) the price level in function of the wage level, the exchange rate, and capacity utilization. By making projection assumptions for the parameters of these relationships, a somewhat less arbitrary set of base assumptions can be formulated. These base assumptions could then be applied in the projection exercise.

More precisely, the point is to determine the growth rate of the price level that would be consistent with the assumed or programmed growth rates of potential productivity per worker, the real-effective exchange rate, and the international price level. To do so, define the following variables:

y   real GDP;

p   price level (GDP deflator);

p*   international price level;

e   exchange rate (national currency/U.S. dollar);

E   real-effective exchange rate (+ = depreciation);

w   average wage rate;

n   employment rate;

z   potential real GDP; and

c   capacity utilization.

By definition, the growth rate of labor productivity is given by

$$g_{y/n} = [(1 + g_y)/(1 + g_n)] - 1. \tag{1}$$

By definition, the real-effective exchange rate is given by

$$g_E = [(1 + g_e)(1 + g_{p*})/(1 + g_p)] - 1. \tag{2}$$

Capacity utilization is defined by

$$y = c\,z \tag{3}$$

and is taken to be determined by

$$1 + g_c = (1 + g_w)^\lambda (1 + g_E)^\mu (1 + g_p)^\nu; \qquad (4)$$

where the behavioral parameter λ is presumably less than zero and μ and ν are presumably greater than zero. The average wage level is taken to be determined by

$$1 + g_w = [1 + g_p]^\delta [(1 + g_y)/(1 + g_n)]^\varepsilon$$

$$= (1 + g_p)^\delta (1 + g_c)^\varepsilon (1 + g_{z/n})^\varepsilon \qquad (5)$$

where the behavioral parameters δ and ε are presumably greater than zero. The price level is taken to be determined by

$$1 + g_p = (1 + g_w)^\alpha (1 + g_e)^\beta (1 + g_c)^\gamma, \qquad (6)$$

where the behavioral parameters α, β and γ are all presumably greater than zero.

These equations may be solved together to obtain an expression for the growth rate of the price level consistent with given growth rates of the real-effective exchange rate, potential productivity per worker, and the international price level. Begin by solving equations (1), (3), (4) and (5) together to obtain

$$1 + g_c = (1 + g_{z/n})^{h\varepsilon\lambda} (1 + g_E)^{h\mu} (1 + g_p)^{hk}, \qquad (7)$$

where

$$h = 1/(1 - \varepsilon\lambda)$$

and

$$k = \lambda\delta + \nu.$$

Substitute equations (2) and (7) into (6) to obtain, first,

$$1 + g_p = (1 + g_{z/n})^{\alpha\varepsilon} (1 + g_E)^\beta (1 + g_{p*})^{-\beta} (1 + g_c)^m (1 + g_{p*})^q, \qquad (8)$$

where $m = \alpha\varepsilon + \gamma$ and $q = \alpha\delta + \beta$, and then

$$1 + g_p = [(1 + g_{z/n})^{\varepsilon(\alpha + h\lambda m)} (1 + g_E)^{(\beta + mh\mu)} (1 + g_{p*})^{-\beta}]^{[1/(1-s)]}, \qquad (9)$$

where s = hkm + q. This formula gives the growth rate of the price level that would be consistent with the assumed or programmed growth rates of potential productivity per worker, the real-effective exchange rate, and the international price level.

Determining the parameters of these "Phillips-Curve" relationships to be used in the projection exercise requires a certain amount of data analysis. It may be possible in some economies to apply econometric techniques to past data, but for most economies the determination of the appropriate parameters will require at least a measure of guesswork combined with trial and error.

Tables for the Pacífica exercise

Table 1. Pacífica: Summary macroeconomic indicators, 2004–2008

	2004	2005	2006	2007	2008
Initial projection year: **2009**					
Gross domestic product (US$ million)	$19,492.4	$20,732.6	$22,380.7	$24,396.8	$26,563.8
Gross domestic product (million pesos)	163,009.8	180,935.9	200,129.1	219,571.1	239,075.0
Real GDP growth rate	4.0%	4.9%	5.5%	5.7%	6.0%
US$ per capita at prices and exchange rate of... *2005*					
Gross domestic product	$2,623.5	$2,697.6	$2,791.4	$2,893.5	$3,006.0
Non-government consumption	$1,774.8	$1,812.4	$1,725.4	$1,840.3	$1,934.2
Inflation (growth rates):					
Implicit GDP deflator	6.9%	5.8%	4.8%	3.8%	2.8%
Consumer prices (Dec.-Dec.)	4.1%	2.9%	2.7%	2.8%	2.7%
Exchange rate (per US$):					
Year-average	8.4	8.7	8.9	9.0	9.0
December average	8.6	8.9	9.0	9.0	9.0
Real-effective exchange rate (1995 = 100)	98.3	100.0	101.0	100.6	100.0
Population (million)	7.5	7.7	7.8	8.0	8.2
Growth rate	*2.0%*	*2.0%*	*2.0%*	*2.0%*	*2.0%*
Per cent of GDP:					
Total investment (saving):	**19.4%**	**19.7%**	**21.2%**	**19.8%**	**19.6%**
Gross fixed capital formation	19.5%	20.0%	21.1%	19.8%	19.7%
Net increase in inventories	-0.1%	-0.2%	0.0%	0.1%	-0.1%
Current-account surplus (deficit):	**-1.2%**	**-1.3%**	**1.7%**	**1.0%**	**1.4%**
Net exports of merchandise and non-factor services	**-0.8%**	**-1.0%**	**2.3%**	**1.0%**	**0.9%**
Exports of merchandise and non-factor services	19.7%	23.0%	26.2%	27.0%	27.7%
Exports of oil products	8.1%	11.2%	14.0%	15.0%	16.1%
Crude-oil export price (US$/bbl)	*$37.8*	*$53.4*	*$64.3*	*$71.1*	*$95.9*
Other exports of merchandise and non-factor services	11.6%	11.8%	12.2%	12.0%	11.6%
Imports of merchandise and non-factor services	20.5%	24.0%	23.8%	26.0%	26.7%
General government surplus (déficit)	**-1.7%**	**-1.1%**	**-0.7%**	**-1.6%**	**-0.5%**
Total revenue:	**22.8%**	**24.5%**	**25.7%**	**25.9%**	**26.6%**
Oil-based revenue (taxes and royalties)	2.9%	4.3%	5.2%	5.3%	5.5%
Transfer receipts from external sources	0.6%	0.5%	0.5%	0.5%	0.5%
Other revenue (incl. non-oil tax revenue)	19.4%	19.6%	19.9%	20.0%	20.6%
Total expenditure (incl. statistical discrepancy):	**-24.6%**	**-25.5%**	**-26.3%**	**-27.4%**	**-27.1%**
Government gross fixed capital formation	-4.7%	-5.1%	-5.4%	-5.5%	-5.7%
Interest due:	-2.7%	-2.7%	-2.7%	-2.7%	-2.7%
External	-1.6%	-1.6%	-1.5%	-1.5%	-1.4%
Domestic	-1.1%	-1.1%	-1.1%	-1.2%	-1.2%
Other expenditure	-17.2%	-17.8%	-18.3%	-19.2%	-18.7%
Public and publicly guaranteed external debt	**25.1%**	**24.5%**	**23.6%**	**22.9%**	**22.0%**
Year-end central-bank foreign-exchange reserves (US$ million):	**$1,318.0**	**$1,556.1**	**$1,824.5**	**$2,316.7**	**$2,971.8**
(Months of imports of goods, non-factor services)	*3.8*	*3.7*	*4.1*	*4.4*	*5.0*
International indicators:					
U.S. GDP deflator (US$; annual average)	109.5	113.0	116.7	119.8	122.4
Growth rate	*2.9%*	*3.2%*	*3.3%*	*2.7%*	*2.2%*
LIBOR (6 mos., US$; average; per cent per year)	1.8%	3.8%	5.3%	5.3%	3.0%

Source: Pacífica projection exercise.

369

Table 2. Pacífica: World-context and macroeconomic programming assumptions, 2008–2015

	2008	2009	2015	Average, 2009-15
Initial projection year: **2009**				
Assumptions for exogenous world variables:				
Average LIBOR (U.S. dollars, 6 mos., annual percentage rate)	3.0%	1.7%	4.0%	2.8%
Growth rates (per cent per year):				
Real world commerce volume	4.1%	-4.5%	5.5%	3.6%
World price level (U.S. GDP deflator)	2.2%	0.0%	2.0%	1.6%
Exports:				
Crude oil:				
Unit price:	34.8%	-31.6%	2.8%	-1.3%
World trade volume:	4.1%	-0.5%	0.5%	0.4%
Bananas and plantain:				
Unit price:	17.4%	-9.1%	2.9%	1.2%
World trade volume:	4.1%	-0.9%	1.1%	0.7%
Manufactures:				
Unit price:	2.2%	0.0%	2.0%	1.6%
World trade volume:	4.1%	-2.3%	2.7%	1.8%
Assumptions for macroeconomic variables:				
Growth rates (per cent per year):				
Gross domestic product:				
Real GDP	6.0%	-4.5%	5.0%	1.9%
GDP deflator	2.8%	2.4%	2.0%	1.8%
Consumer prices:				
year-average	2.8%	2.4%	2.0%	1.8%
December-December	2.7%	2.2%	2.0%	1.7%
Exchange rate (per U.S. dollar):				
year-average	0.0%	3.3%	0.0%	0.9%
December-December	0.0%	6.7%	0.0%	1.0%
Real-effective exchange rate	-0.6%	0.8%	0.0%	0.7%
Population	**2.0%**	**2.0%**	**2.0%**	**2.0%**
Gross foreign-exchange reserves:				
(months of imports of goods, non-factor services)	5.0	4.0	4.0	4.0

Source: Pacífica projection exercise.

Table 3. Pacífica: Summary national-accounts projections, 2008–2015

	2008	2009	2015	Average, 2009-15
Initial projection year: 2009				
Expenditure (per cent of GDP):	**100.0%**	**100.0%**	**100.0%**	**100.0%**
Consumption:	**79.4%**	**84.3%**	**82.8%**	**82.7%**
Non-government (residual)	*64.3%*	*68.9%*	*66.6%*	*66.8%*
Government	15.1%	15.5%	16.2%	15.9%
Gross investment:	**19.6%**	**17.5%**	**21.1%**	**19.2%**
Gross fixed capital formation:	**19.7%**	**17.5%**	**21.0%**	**19.2%**
Non-government (residual)	*13.9%*	*11.8%*	*15.2%*	*13.4%*
Government	5.7%	5.7%	5.8%	5.8%
Increase in inventories	**-0.1%**	**0.0%**	**0.1%**	**0.0%**
Resource balance:	**0.9%**	**-1.8%**	**-3.8%**	**-2.0%**
Exports of goods and non-factor services	27.7%	23.3%	24.2%	24.8%
Imports of goods and non-factor services	-26.7%	-25.1%	-28.0%	-26.8%
Gross national saving (per cent of GDP):	**21.0%**	**16.3%**	**17.8%**	**17.8%**
Non-government	15.7%	12.9%	15.1%	14.7%
Government	5.3%	3.3%	2.7%	3.1%
Gross domestic saving	**20.6%**	**15.7%**	**17.2%**	**17.3%**
Net external factor and transfer receipts	**0.4%**	**0.6%**	**0.5%**	**0.6%**
Foreign saving (current-account déficit; per cent of GDP)	**-1.4%**	**1.2%**	**3.3%**	**1.4%**
Growth rates (per cent per year):				
Nominal GDP:	**8.9%**	**-2.2%**	**7.1%**	**3.7%**
Real GDP	6.0%	-4.5%	5.0%	1.9%
GDP deflator	2.8%	2.4%	2.0%	1.8%
Non-government consumption	**$2,095.7**	**$2,083.3**	**$2,282.9**	**$2,077.9**
Growth rate (per cent per year):	*8.0%*	*-0.6%*	*5.6%*	*1.3%*
Gross domestic product (million pesos)	**239,075.0**	**233,900.1**	**308,245.8**	**263,121.4**

Source: Pacífica projection exercise.

Table 4. Pacífica: Summary external-accounts projections, 2008–2015

	2008	2009	2015	Average, 2009-15
Initial projection year: **2009**				
External accounts (per cent of GDP):				
Current-account surplus:	**1.4%**	**-1.2%**	**-3.3%**	**-1.4%**
Net exports of goods and non-factor services:	**0.9%**	**-1.8%**	**-3.8%**	**-2.0%**
Exports of goods and non-factor services	27.7%	23.3%	24.2%	24.8%
Imports of goods and non-factor services	-26.7%	-25.1%	-28.0%	-26.8%
Interest due on external debt	**-1.7%**	**-1.6%**	**-1.5%**	**-1.6%**
Interest due on public and publicly-guaranteed external debt	-1.4%	-1.4%	-1.3%	-1.4%
Interest due on other external debt	-0.2%	-0.2%	-0.2%	-0.2%
Net other current account	**2.1%**	**2.2%**	**2.0%**	**2.2%**
Financial-account surplus, errors and omissions:	**2.9%**	**1.8%**	**4.1%**	**2.6%**
Investment transactions	2.5%	2.7%	2.4%	2.6%
Net debt flows:	0.5%	-0.8%	1.7%	0.1%
Programmed	0.5%	-0.8%	0.5%	-0.1%
Programmed (residual)	*0.0%*	*0.0%*	*1.2%*	*0.2%*
Other capital-account items, errors and omissions	-0.1%	-0.1%	-0.1%	-0.1%
Increase in net international reserves:	**4.2%**	**0.6%**	**0.7%**	**1.2%**
Increase in gross foreign-exchange reserves	4.2%	0.6%	0.7%	1.2%
Programmed	4.2%	-3.4%	0.7%	0.0%
Unprogrammed (residual)	*0.0%*	*4.0%*	*0.0%*	*1.2%*
Other reserve accounts	0.0%	0.0%	0.0%	0.0%
Net international reserves (year-end stocks; US$ millión):	**$3,239.4**	**$3,376.0**	**$5,450.2**	**$4,510.6**
Gross international reserves (year-end stocks; US$ million):	**$3,213.5**	**$3,352.7**	**$5,442.4**	**$4,495.0**
of which, foreign-exchange reserves	$2,971.8	$3,108.4	$5,182.6	$4,243.0
(in months of imports of goods,non-factor services)	*5.0*	*5.9*	*6.9*	*6.8*
International reserve liabilities (-)	**-$25.9**	**-$23.3**	**-$7.8**	**-$15.5**
Year-end external debt:	**25.2%**	**26.5%**	**25.5%**	**25.8%**
(World Bank Global Development Finance; US$ million):				
Public and publicly guaranteed	22.0%	23.4%	21.3%	22.5%
Private non-guaranteed	0.2%	0.3%	1.6%	0.5%
International Monetary Fund	0.1%	0.1%	0.0%	0.1%
Short-term debt (including interest arrears)	2.9%	2.8%	2.6%	2.8%
Gross domestic product (US$ million)	**$26,563.8**	**$25,163.6**	**$32,108.9**	**$27,522.6**

Source: Pacífica projection exercise.

Table 5. Pacífica: Summary government-accounts projections, 2008–2015

	2008	2009	2015	Average, 2009-15
Initial projection year: **2009**				
General government accounts (per cent of GDP):				
Total revenue	**26.6%**	**25.1%**	**25.2%**	**25.4%**
Total expenditure:	**-27.1%**	**-27.5%**	**-28.3%**	**-28.0%**
Interest due:	**-2.7%**	**-2.7%**	**-2.8%**	**-2.8%**
External	-1.4%	-1.4%	-1.3%	-1.4%
Domestic	-1.2%	-1.3%	-1.5%	-1.4%
Central-government education and health current expenditure:	-5.9%	-6.1%	-6.5%	-6.4%
Government gross fixed capital formation	-5.7%	-5.7%	-5.8%	-5.8%
Other expenditure:	-12.7%	-12.9%	-13.2%	-13.1%
Surplus	**-0.5%**	**-2.4%**	**-3.1%**	**-2.6%**
Financing:	**0.5%**	**2.4%**	**3.1%**	**2.6%**
Net external financing:	**0.9%**	**0.2%**	**1.0%**	**0.5%**
Net domestic financing (residual)	*-0.5%*	*2.2%*	*2.1%*	*2.1%*
General-government year-end debt outstanding	**45.5%**	**50.4%**	**52.9%**	**52.4%**
(per cent of GDP):				
External debt	**22.0%**	**24.2%**	**21.3%**	**22.6%**
Domestic debt	**23.5%**	**26.2%**	**31.6%**	**29.8%**
General-government deposit accounts	**-0.3%**	**-0.3%**	**-0.8%**	**-0.5%**
Gross domestic product (million pesos)	**239,075.0**	**233,900.1**	**308,245.8**	**263,121.4**

Source: Pacífica projection exercise.

Table 6. Pacífica: Summary monetary-accounts projections, 2008–2015

	2008	2009	2015	Average, 2009-15
Initial projection year: **2009**				
Monetary accounts (per cent of GDP):				
Broad money supply (year-average stock):	**50.0%**	**54.4%**	**54.1%**	**54.3%**
Monetary base (year-average stock)	**16.9%**	**17.9%**	**19.0%**	**18.4%**
Central-bank accounts: flow increases (per cent of GDP):				
Liabilities and net worth:	**2.1%**	**1.2%**	**1.4%**	**1.3%**
External liabilities	0.0%	0.0%	0.0%	0.0%
Monetary base	1.7%	0.6%	1.5%	1.0%
Public-sector deposits at the central bank	0.2%	0.0%	0.1%	0.0%
Central-bank non-monetary obligations (residual)	*-0.1%*	*0.0%*	*0.0%*	*0.3%*
Central-bank net worth:	0.2%	0.7%	-0.2%	-0.1%
Exchange-rate revaluation of foreign-exchange accounts	-1.8%	-0.8%	0.0%	-0.1%
Other	1.9%	1.5%	-0.2%	0.1%
Assets:	**2.1%**	**1.2%**	**1.4%**	**1.3%**
External assets	2.5%	1.4%	0.7%	1.3%
Central-bank holdings of financial-system and private obligations	-0.1%	0.0%	0.0%	0.0%
Central-bank holdings of public-sector obligations	-0.3%	-0.2%	0.7%	0.0%
Other net assets	0.0%	0.0%	0.0%	0.0%
Gross domestic product (million pesos)	239,075.0	233,900.1	308,245.8	263,121.4

Source: Pacífica projection exercise.

Table 7. Pacífica: Basic macroeconomic projection variables, 2008–2015

	2008	2009	2015	Average, 2009-15
Initial projection year: **2009**				
Gross domestic product (US$ million):	**$26,563.8**	**$25,163.6**	**$32,108.9**	**$27,522.6**
GDP (P/ million)	239,075.0	233,900.1	308,245.8	263,121.4
GDP at 1995 prices (P/ million)	100,809.9	96,273.5	114,825.6	103,308.4
GDP deflator (1995 = 100)	237.2	243.0	268.4	254.2
Consumer prices (year-end)	**239.1**	**244.2**	**269.6**	**255.0**
Exchange rate (pesos/U.S. dollar)				
Year-end (December average)	9.0	9.6	9.6	9.6
Year-average:	9.0	9.3	9.6	9.6
Purchasing-power parity rate	9.0	9.2	9.1	9.2
Real-effective exchange rate -- base 100 = 1995	100.0	100.8	105.1	104.3
Population (million)	**8.2**	**8.3**	**9.4**	**8.8**
U.S. GDP deflator -- base 100 = 2000:	**122.4**	**122.4**	**136.5**	**128.9**

Source: Pacífica projection exercise.

Paul Beckerman

Table 8. Pacífica: Central-government non-interest expenditure assumptions, 2008–2015

	2008	2009	2015	Average, 2009-15
Initial projection year: **2009**				
Central-government non-interest expenditure:				
Growth rates:				
Non-interest current expenditure:				
Consumption expenditure:				
Staff-remuneration expenditure				
Payroll (number of persons)				
(1) Average remuneration per staff member:	6.7%	-3.1%	6.1%	2.7%
Average real remuneration per staff member:				
Goods-and-services expenditure				
Non-interest, non-consumption current expenditure:				
(2) Central-government transfers to sub-national governments	8.9%	-2.2%	7.1%	3.7%
Central-government transfers to non-government entities:	8.9%	-2.2%	7.1%	3.7%
(3) Central-government subsidies	8.9%	-2.2%	7.1%	3.7%
(4) Central-government transfers to persons	8.9%	-2.2%	7.1%	3.7%
(5) Other central-government non-consumption expenditure	8.9%	-2.2%	7.1%	3.7%
Capital expenditure:				
(6) Fixed-capital formation expenditure:	11.6%	-2.2%	7.1%	3.7%
Other capital expenditure:				
(7) Central-government transfers to sub-national governments	0.0%	-2.2%	7.1%	3.7%
(8) Central-government transfers to non-government entities:	0.0%	-2.2%	7.1%	3.7%
(9) Other capital expenditure	8.9%	-2.2%	7.1%	3.7%
Elasticities of...				
(10) payroll with respect to population	1.2	1.5	1.0	1.2
(11) goods-and-services expenditure with respect to population	9.8	1.5	1.0	1.2
Armed-forces expenditure:				
Growth rates:				
Non-interest current expenditure:				
Consumption expenditure:				
Staff-remuneration expenditure				
Payroll (number of persons)				
(12) Average remuneration per staff member:	6.7%	-3.1%	6.1%	2.7%
Average real remuneration per staff member:				
Goods-and-services expenditure				
Non-interest, non-consumption current expenditure:				
(13) Central-government transfers to sub-national governments	0.0%	-2.2%	7.1%	3.7%
Central-government transfers to non-government entities:	0.0%	0.0%	0.0%	0.0%
(14) Central-government subsidies	0.0%	-2.2%	7.1%	3.7%
(15) Central-government transfers to persons	0.0%	0.0%	0.0%	0.0%
(16) Other central-government non-consumption expenditure	0.0%	0.0%	0.0%	0.0%
Capital expenditure:				
(17) Fixed-capital formation expenditure:	8.9%	-2.2%	7.1%	3.7%
Other capital expenditure:				
(18) Central-government transfers to sub-national governments	0.0%	-2.2%	7.1%	3.7%
(19) Central-government transfers to non-government entities:	0.0%	-2.2%	7.1%	3.7%
(20) Other capital expenditure	8.9%	-2.2%	7.1%	3.7%
Elasticities of...				
(21) payroll with respect to population	2.2	1.3	1.0	1.1
(22) goods-and-services expenditure with respect to population	4.8	1.3	1.0	1.1
(continues)				

Source: Pacífica projection exercise.

Table 8 (*Continued*)

		2008	2009	2015	Average, 2009-15
	Initial projection year: 2009				
	Public-security expenditure:				
	Growth rates:				
	Non-interest current expenditure:				
	Consumption expenditure:				
	Staff-remuneration expenditure				
	Payroll (number of persons)				
(23)	Average remuneration per staff member:	6.7%	-3.1%	6.1%	2.7%
	Average real remuneration per staff member:				
	Goods-and-services expenditure				
	Non-interest, non-consumption current expenditure:				
(24)	Central-government transfers to sub-national governments	0.0%	-2.2%	7.1%	3.7%
	Central-government transfers to non-government entities:	0.0%	0.0%	0.0%	0.0%
(25)	Central-government subsidies	0.0%	0.0%	0.0%	0.0%
(26)	Central-government transfers to persons	0.0%	0.0%	0.0%	0.0%
(27)	Other central-government non-consumption expenditure	0.0%	-2.2%	7.1%	3.7%
	Capital expenditure:				
(28)	**Fixed-capital formation expenditure:**	8.9%	-2.2%	7.1%	3.7%
	Other capital expenditure:				
(29)	Central-government transfers to sub-national governments	0.0%	-2.2%	7.1%	3.7%
(30)	Central-government transfers to non-government entities:	0.0%	-2.2%	7.1%	3.7%
(31)	Other capital expenditure	8.9%	-2.2%	7.1%	3.7%
	Elasticities of...				
(32)	payroll with respect to population	2.5	1.3	1.0	1.1
(33)	goods-and-services expenditure with respect to population	5.0	1.3	1.0	1.1
	Financial administration expenditure:				
	Growth rates:				
	Non-interest current expenditure:				
	Consumption expenditure:				
	Staff-remuneration expenditure				
	Payroll (number of persons)				
(34)	Average remuneration per staff member:	6.7%	-3.1%	6.1%	2.7%
	Average real remuneration per staff member:				
	Goods-and-services expenditure				
	Non-interest, non-consumption current expenditure:				
(35)	Central-government transfers to sub-national governments	8.9%	-2.2%	7.1%	3.7%
	Central-government transfers to non-government entities:	148.3%	-2.2%	7.1%	3.7%
(36)	Central-government subsidies	0.0%	-2.2%	7.1%	3.7%
(37)	Central-government transfers to persons	148.3%	-2.2%	7.1%	3.7%
(38)	Other central-government non-consumption expenditure	-100.0%	-2.2%	7.1%	3.7%
	Capital expenditure:				
(39)	**Fixed-capital formation expenditure:**	8.9%	-2.2%	7.1%	3.7%
	Other capital expenditure:				
(40)	Central-government transfers to sub-national governments	0.0%	-2.2%	7.1%	3.7%
(41)	Central-government transfers to non-government entities:	0.0%	-2.2%	7.1%	3.7%
(42)	Other capital expenditure	8.9%	-2.2%	7.1%	3.7%
	Elasticities of...				
(43)	payroll with respect to population	2.6	1.5	1.0	1.2
(44)	goods-and-services expenditure with respect to population	5.1	1.5	1.0	1.2
	(continues)				

Source: Pacífica projection exercise.

Table 8 (*Continued*)

		2008	2009	2015	Average, 2009-15
	Initial projection year: **2009**				
	Economic expenditure (including public works):				
	Growth rates:				
	Non-interest current expenditure:				
	Consumption expenditure:				
	Staff-remuneration expenditure				
	Payroll (number of persons)				
(45)	Average remuneration per staff member:	6.7%	-3.1%	6.1%	2.7%
	Average real remuneration per staff member:				
	Goods-and-services expenditure				
	Non-interest, non-consumption current expenditure:				
(46)	Central-government transfers to sub-national governments	0.0%	-2.2%	7.1%	3.7%
	Central-government transfers to non-government entities:	0.0%	0.0%	0.0%	0.0%
(47)	Central-government subsidies	0.0%	0.0%	0.0%	0.0%
(48)	Central-government transfers to persons	0.0%	0.0%	0.0%	0.0%
(49)	Other central-government non-consumption expenditure	0.0%	-2.2%	7.1%	3.7%
	Capital expenditure:				
(50)	**Fixed-capital formation expenditure:**	8.9%	-2.2%	7.1%	3.7%
	Other capital expenditure:				
(51)	Central-government transfers to sub-national governments	0.0%	-2.2%	7.1%	3.7%
(52)	Central-government transfers to non-government entities:	0.0%	-2.2%	7.1%	3.7%
(53)	Other capital expenditure	8.9%	-2.2%	7.1%	3.7%
	Elasticities of...				
(54)	payroll with respect to population	2.6	1.6	1.0	1.3
(55)	goods-and-services expenditure with respect to population	5.1	1.6	1.0	1.3
	Education expenditure:				
	Growth rates:				
	Non-interest current expenditure:				
	Consumption expenditure:				
	Staff-remuneration expenditure				
	Payroll (number of persons)				
(56)	Average remuneration per staff member:	6.7%	-3.1%	6.1%	2.7%
	Average real remuneration per staff member:				
	Goods-and-services expenditure				
	Non-interest, non-consumption current expenditure:				
(57)	Central-government transfers to sub-national governments	0.0%	-2.2%	7.1%	3.7%
	Central-government transfers to non-government entities:	0.0%	0.0%	0.0%	0.0%
(58)	Central-government subsidies	0.0%	0.0%	0.0%	0.0%
(59)	Central-government transfers to persons	0.0%	0.0%	0.0%	0.0%
(60)	Other central-government non-consumption expenditure	0.0%	-2.2%	7.1%	3.7%
	Capital expenditure:				
(61)	**Fixed-capital formation expenditure:**	8.9%	-2.2%	7.1%	3.7%
	Other capital expenditure:				
(62)	Central-government transfers to sub-national governments	0.0%	-2.2%	7.1%	3.7%
(63)	Central-government transfers to non-government entities:	0.0%	-2.2%	7.1%	3.7%
(64)	Other capital expenditure	8.9%	-2.2%	7.1%	3.7%
	Elasticities of...				
(65)	payroll with respect to population	2.9	1.6	1.0	1.3
(66)	goods-and-services expenditure with respect to population	5.4	1.6	1.0	1.3
(continues)					

Source: Pacífica projection exercise.

Table 8 (*Continued*)

		2008	2009	2015	Average, 2009-15
	Initial projection year: 2009				
	Health and other social-services expenditure:				
	Growth rates:				
	Non-interest current expenditure:				
	Consumption expenditure:				
	Staff-remuneration expenditure				
	Payroll (number of persons)				
(67)	Average remuneration per staff member:	6.7%	-3.1%	6.1%	2.7%
	Average real remuneration per staff member:				
	Goods-and-services expenditure				
	Non-interest, non-consumption current expenditure:				
(68)	Central-government transfers to sub-national governments	0.0%	-2.2%	7.1%	3.7%
	Central-government transfers to non-government entities:	0.0%	0.0%	0.0%	0.0%
(69)	Central-government subsidies	0.0%	0.0%	0.0%	0.0%
(70)	Central-government transfers to persons	0.0%	0.0%	0.0%	0.0%
(71)	Other central-government non-consumption expenditure	0.0%	-2.2%	7.1%	3.7%
	Capital expenditure:				
(72)	**Fixed-capital formation expenditure:**	8.9%	-2.2%	7.1%	3.7%
	Other capital expenditure:				
(73)	Central-government transfers to sub-national governments	0.0%	-2.2%	7.1%	3.7%
(74)	Central-government transfers to non-government entities:	0.0%	-2.2%	7.1%	3.7%
(75)	Other capital expenditure	8.9%	-2.2%	7.1%	3.7%
	Elasticities of...				
(76)	payroll with respect to population	2.9	1.6	1.0	1.3
(77)	goods-and-services expenditure with respect to population	5.4	1.6	1.0	1.3

Source: Pacífica projection exercise.

Table 9. Pacífica: Functional-*cum*-economic structure of government expenditure (per cent of GDP), 2008–2015

	2008	2009	2015	Average, 2009-15
Initial projection year: 2009				
Expenditure (per cent of GDP):				
Non-interest expenditure:	**19.0%**	**19.4%**	**20.0%**	**19.8%**
Non-interest current expenditure:	**14.4%**	**14.7%**	**15.4%**	**15.2%**
Consumption expenditure:	**11.5%**	**11.9%**	**12.6%**	**12.3%**
Staff-remuneration expenditure	8.9%	9.1%	9.9%	9.5%
Goods-and-services expenditure	2.5%	2.7%	2.6%	2.8%
Non-interest, non-consumption current expenditure:	**2.9%**	**2.9%**	**2.9%**	**2.9%**
Capital expenditure:	**4.6%**	**4.6%**	**4.6%**	**4.6%**
Fixed-capital formation expenditure	4.4%	4.4%	4.4%	4.4%
Other capital expenditure	0.2%	0.2%	0.2%	0.2%
Armed-forces expenditure:				
Non-interest expenditure:	**2.7%**	**2.7%**	**2.8%**	**2.8%**
Non-interest current expenditure:	**2.0%**	**2.0%**	**2.1%**	**2.1%**
Consumption expenditure:	**2.0%**	**2.0%**	**2.1%**	**2.1%**
Staff-remuneration expenditure	1.4%	1.4%	1.6%	1.5%
Goods-and-services expenditure	0.5%	0.6%	0.5%	0.6%
Non-interest, non-consumption current expenditure:	**0.0%**	**0.0%**	**0.0%**	**0.0%**
Capital expenditure:	**0.7%**	**0.7%**	**0.7%**	**0.7%**
Fixed-capital formation expenditure	0.7%	0.7%	0.7%	0.7%
Other capital expenditure	0.0%	0.0%	0.0%	0.0%
Public-security expenditure:				
Non-interest expenditure:	**0.7%**	**0.7%**	**0.7%**	**0.7%**
Non-interest current expenditure:	**0.5%**	**0.5%**	**0.5%**	**0.5%**
Consumption expenditure:	**0.5%**	**0.5%**	**0.5%**	**0.5%**
Staff-remuneration expenditure	0.4%	0.4%	0.4%	0.4%
Goods-and-services expenditure	0.1%	0.1%	0.1%	0.1%
Non-interest, non-consumption current expenditure:	**0.0%**	**0.0%**	**0.0%**	**0.0%**
Capital expenditure:	**0.2%**	**0.2%**	**0.2%**	**0.2%**
Fixed-capital formation expenditure	0.2%	0.2%	0.2%	0.2%
Other capital expenditure	0.0%	0.0%	0.0%	0.0%
Financial administration expenditure:				
Non-interest expenditure:	**3.2%**	**3.2%**	**3.2%**	**3.2%**
Non-interest current expenditure:	**3.1%**	**3.1%**	**3.2%**	**3.1%**
Consumption expenditure:	**0.3%**	**0.3%**	**0.3%**	**0.3%**
Staff-remuneration expenditure	0.2%	0.2%	0.2%	0.2%
Goods-and-services expenditure	0.1%	0.1%	0.1%	0.1%
Non-interest, non-consumption current expenditure:	**2.9%**	**2.9%**	**2.9%**	**2.9%**
Capital expenditure:	**0.1%**	**0.1%**	**0.1%**	**0.1%**
Fixed-capital formation expenditure	0.1%	0.1%	0.1%	0.1%
Other capital expenditure	0.0%	0.0%	0.0%	0.0%
(continues)				

Source: Pacífica projection exercise.

Table 9 (*Continued*)

	2008	2009	2015	Average, 2009-15
Initial projection year: 2009				
Financial administration expenditure:	**1.3%**	**1.4%**	**1.4%**	**1.4%**
Non-interest current expenditure:	**1.0%**	**1.0%**	**1.1%**	**1.1%**
Consumption expenditure:	**1.0%**	**1.0%**	**1.1%**	**1.1%**
Staff-remuneration expenditure	0.7%	0.7%	0.8%	0.8%
Goods-and-services expenditure	0.3%	0.3%	0.3%	0.3%
Non-interest, non-consumption current expenditure:	**0.0%**	**0.0%**	**0.0%**	**0.0%**
Capital expenditure:	**0.3%**	**0.3%**	**0.3%**	**0.3%**
Fixed-capital formation expenditure	0.3%	0.3%	0.3%	0.3%
Other capital expenditure	0.0%	0.0%	0.0%	0.0%
Education expenditure:				
Non-interest expenditure:	**4.8%**	**4.9%**	**5.2%**	**5.1%**
Non-interest current expenditure:	**3.6%**	**3.7%**	**3.9%**	**3.9%**
Consumption expenditure:	**3.6%**	**3.7%**	**3.9%**	**3.9%**
Staff-remuneration expenditure	2.6%	2.7%	2.9%	2.8%
Goods-and-services expenditure	1.0%	1.1%	1.0%	1.1%
Non-interest, non-consumption current expenditure:	**0.0%**	**0.0%**	**0.0%**	**0.0%**
Capital expenditure:	**1.2%**	**1.2%**	**1.2%**	**1.2%**
Fixed-capital formation expenditure	1.2%	1.2%	1.2%	1.2%
Other capital expenditure	0.1%	0.1%	0.1%	0.1%
Health and other social-services expenditure:				
Non-interest expenditure:	**3.1%**	**3.2%**	**3.3%**	**3.3%**
Non-interest current expenditure:	**2.3%**	**2.4%**	**2.5%**	**2.5%**
Consumption expenditure:	**2.3%**	**2.4%**	**2.5%**	**2.5%**
Staff-remuneration expenditure	1.7%	1.7%	1.9%	1.8%
Goods-and-services expenditure	0.6%	0.7%	0.7%	0.7%
Non-interest, non-consumption current expenditure:	**0.0%**	**0.0%**	**0.0%**	**0.0%**
Capital expenditure:	**0.8%**	**0.8%**	**0.8%**	**0.8%**
Fixed-capital formation expenditure	0.7%	0.7%	0.7%	0.7%
Other capital expenditure	0.0%	0.0%	0.0%	0.0%
Administrative, legislative, and judicial expenditure:				
Non-interest expenditure:	**3.2%**	**3.2%**	**3.4%**	**3.3%**
Non-interest current expenditure:	**1.9%**	**1.9%**	**2.1%**	**2.0%**
Consumption expenditure:	**1.9%**	**1.9%**	**2.1%**	**2.0%**
Staff-remuneration expenditure	1.9%	2.0%	2.1%	2.0%
Goods-and-services expenditure	-0.1%	-0.1%	-0.1%	-0.1%
Non-interest, non-consumption current expenditure:	**0.0%**	**0.0%**	**0.0%**	**0.0%**
Capital expenditure:	**1.3%**	**1.3%**	**1.3%**	**1.3%**
Fixed-capital formation expenditure	1.3%	1.3%	1.3%	1.3%
Other capital expenditure	0.0%	0.0%	0.0%	0.0%

Source: Pacífica projection exercise.

Paul Beckerman

Table 10. Pacífica: Year-end external debt outstanding and disbursed (per cent of GDP), 2008–2015

	2008	2009	2015	Average, 2009-15
Initial projection year: 2009				
Year-end total debt outstanding (incl. short-term debt):	25.2%	26.5%	25.5%	25.8%
Total term debt (incl. debt to IMF):	22.3%	23.7%	22.9%	23.0%
Term debt excl. debt to IMF:	22.2%	23.7%	22.9%	23.0%
Public and publicly guaranteed debt:	22.0%	23.4%	21.3%	22.5%
Official creditors:	13.7%	15.2%	15.6%	15.5%
Multilateral debt:	10.2%	11.3%	11.6%	11.5%
Non-concessional multilateral debt:	10.2%	11.3%	11.6%	11.5%
World Bank (IBRD)	6.7%	7.5%	7.7%	7.6%
Other non-concessional multilateral debt:	3.4%	3.8%	3.9%	3.9%
Concessional multilateral debt:	0.0%	0.0%	0.0%	0.0%
International Development Association (IDA)	0.0%	0.0%	0.0%	0.0%
Other concessional multilateral debt:	0.0%	0.0%	0.0%	0.0%
Bilateral debt:	3.5%	3.9%	4.0%	4.0%
Non-concessional bilateral debt:	3.5%	3.9%	4.0%	4.0%
Concessional bilateral debt:	0.0%	0.0%	0.0%	0.0%
Debt to private creditors:	8.3%	8.2%	5.7%	7.0%
Soveriegn bonds	5.1%	5.2%	4.9%	5.1%
Debt to commercial banks	3.2%	3.0%	0.8%	1.9%
Debt to other private creditors	0.0%	0.0%	0.0%	0.0%
Private non-guaranteed debt:	0.2%	0.3%	1.6%	0.5%
Historical/programmed	0.2%	0.3%	0.2%	0.2%
Unidentified	0.0%	0.0%	1.4%	0.2%
Use of IMF credit	0.1%	0.1%	0.0%	0.1%
Short-term debt:	2.9%	2.8%	2.6%	2.8%
Interest arrears on public term debt	0.0%	0.0%	0.0%	0.0%
Other short-term debt: trade credit, credit lines to banks, etc.	2.9%	2.8%	2.6%	2.8%

Source: Pacífica projection exercise.

Table 11. Pacífica: National-accounts projection assumptions, 2008–2015

		2008	2009	2015	Average, 2009-15
	Initial projection year: 2009				
	Gross capital-formation determinants:				
	Incremental capital-potential output ratio in year t for...				
(1)	net fixed capital formation	16.7	7.3	1.5	2.6
	gross fixed capital formation	48.8	34.4	3.8	10.2
	Incremental capital-output ratio in year t	-12.5	11.8	4.2	6.2
	for gross fixed capital formation (implicit)				
	For each year t...				
	percentage of the increase in potential real GDP deriving				
	from capital formation...				
	in the year t-1	50.0%	50.0%	50.0%	50.0%
(2)	in the year t-2	33.3%	33.3%	33.3%	33.3%
(3)	in the year t-3	16.7%	16.7%	16.7%	16.7%
(4)	Capital depreciation	3.5%	3.5%	3.5%	3.5%
	(per cent of previous year-end capital stock)				
(5)	GDP/potential GDP (capacity utilization)	78.7%	74.8%	80.0%	77.4%
	Per cent of GDP:				
(6)	Increase in inventories	-0.1%	0.0%	0.1%	0.0%

Source: Pacífica projection exercise.

Table 12. Pacífica: Projection assumptions for non-factor goods-and-services exports and imports, 2008–2015

	2008	2009	2015	Average, 2009-15
Growth rates: *Initial projection year: 2009*				
World price level (US$)				
Real world commerce volume	2.2%	0.0%	2.0%	1.6%
Period-average real-effective exchange rate	4.1%	-4.5%	5.5%	3.6%
Real GDP excluding the terms-of-trade effect	-0.6%	0.8%	0.0%	0.7%
Real gross fixed-capital formation	6.0%	-4.5%	5.0%	1.9%
	3.7%	-19.4%	9.4%	3.6%
Crude-oil exports:				
Growth rates (per cent):				
(1) Real unit price				
(2) World trade volume	31.9%	-31.6%	0.8%	-2.9%
(3) Export tax (-) or subsidy (+)	4.1%	-0.5%	0.5%	0.4%
Elasticities of volume with respect to...	-10.0%	-10.0%	-10.0%	-10.0%
(4) Commodity world-trade volume				
(5) Real effective price	1.0	1.0	1.0	1.0
Oil-derivatives exports:	-0.7	0.0	0.0	0.0
Growth rates (per cent):				
(6) Real unit price				
(7) World trade volume	-6.9%	-31.6%	0.8%	-2.9%
(8) Export tax (-) or subsidy (+)	4.1%	-0.5%	0.5%	0.4%
Elasticities of volume with respect to...	0.0%	0.0%	0.0%	0.0%
(9) Commodity world-trade volume				
(10) Real effective price	1.0	1.0	1.0	1.0
Bananas and plantain exports:	-0.7	0.2	0.2	0.2
Growth rates (per cent):				
(11) Real unit price				
(12) World trade volume	14.9%	-9.1%	0.9%	-0.4%
(13) Export tax (-) or subsidy (+)	4.1%	-0.9%	1.1%	0.7%
Elasticities of volume with respect to...	-10.0%	-10.0%	-10.0%	-10.0%
(14) Commodity world-trade volume				
(15) Real effective price	1.0	1.0	1.0	1.0
Manufactured products exports:	-0.9	0.2	0.2	0.2
Growth rates (per cent):				
(16) Real unit price				
(17) World trade volume	0.0%	0.0%	0.0%	0.0%
(18) Export tax (-) or subsidy (+)	4.1%	-2.3%	2.7%	1.8%
Elasticities of volume with respect to...	0.0%	0.0%	0.0%	0.0%
(19) Commodity world-trade volume				
(20) Real effective price	1.1	1.0	1.0	1.0
Non-factor service exports:	6.6	0.7	0.7	0.7
Growth rates (per cent):				
(21) Real unit price				
(22) World trade volume	0.0%	0.0%	0.0%	0.0%
Elasticities of volume with respect to...	4.1%	-4.5%	5.5%	3.6%
(23) Commodity world-trade volume				
(24) Real effective price	1.0	1.0	1.0	1.0
(continues)	-2.0	0.3	0.3	0.3

Source: Pacífica projection exercise.

Table 12 (*Continued*)

		2008	2009	2015	Average, 2009-15
	Initial projection year: 2009				
	Consumer goods:				
	Growth rates (per cent):				
(25)	Real unit price	0.0%	0.0%	0.0%	0.0%
(26)	Tariff (+) or subsidy (-) rate	10.0%	10.0%	10.0%	10.0%
	Elasticities of volume with respect to...				
(27)	Real GDP	1.1	1.0	1.0	1.0
(28)	Real-effective import price	-13.5	-0.5	-0.5	-0.5
	Oil derivatives imports:				
	Growth rates (per cent):				
(29)	Real unit price	31.9%	-31.6%	0.8%	-2.9%
(30)	Tariff (+) or subsidy (-) rate	10.0%	10.0%	10.0%	10.0%
	Elasticities of volume with respect to...				
(31)	Real GDP	1.0	1.0	1.0	1.0
(32)	Real-effective import price	-1.3	-0.5	-0.5	-0.5
	Non-oil intermediate goods:				
	Growth rates (per cent):				
(33)	Real unit price	-6.9%	-31.6%	0.8%	-2.9%
(34)	Tariff (+) or subsidy (-) rate	10.0%	10.0%	10.0%	10.0%
	Elasticities of volume with respect to...				
(35)	Real GDP	1.1	1.0	1.0	1.0
(36)	Real-effective import price	-0.8	-0.2	-0.2	-0.2
	Capital goods:				
	Growth rates (per cent):				
(37)	Real unit price	0.0%	0.0%	0.0%	0.0%
(38)	Tariff (+) or subsidy (-) rate	10.0%	10.0%	10.0%	10.0%
	Elasticities of volume with respect to...				
(39)	Real gross fixed-capital formation	1.1	1.0	1.0	1.0
(40)	Real-effective import price	-0.8	-0.2	-0.2	-0.2
	'C.I.F./F.O.B.' ratio (per cent)	**10.0%**	**10.0%**	**10.0%**	**10.0%**

Source: Pacífica projection exercise.

Table 13. Pacífica: National-accounts projections, 2008–2015

	2008	2009	2015	Average, 2009-15
Initial projection year: 2009				
Per cent of GDP:				
Expenditure:	**100.0%**	**100.0%**	**100.0%**	**100.0%**
Consumption plus investment:	**99.1%**	**101.8%**	**103.8%**	**102.0%**
Consumption:	**79.4%**	**84.3%**	**82.8%**	**82.7%**
Non-government	64.3%	68.9%	66.6%	66.8%
Government	15.1%	15.5%	16.2%	15.9%
Investment:	**19.6%**	**17.5%**	**21.1%**	**19.2%**
Gross fixed capital formation:	**19.7%**	**17.5%**	**21.0%**	**19.2%**
Non-government	13.9%	11.8%	15.2%	13.4%
Government	5.7%	5.7%	5.8%	5.8%
Increase in inventories	**-0.1%**	**0.0%**	**0.1%**	**0.0%**
Resource balance:	**0.9%**	**-1.8%**	**-3.8%**	**-2.0%**
Exports of merchandise and non-factor services	27.7%	23.3%	24.2%	24.8%
Imports of merchandise and non-factor services	-26.7%	-25.1%	-28.0%	-26.8%
Gross national saving:	**21.0%**	**16.3%**	**17.8%**	**17.8%**
Non-government	15.7%	12.9%	15.1%	14.7%
Government	5.3%	3.3%	2.7%	3.1%
Gross domestic saving	20.6%	15.7%	17.2%	17.3%
Net external factor and transfer receipts	0.4%	0.6%	0.5%	0.6%
Foreign saving (current-account déficit):	**-1.4%**	**1.2%**	**3.3%**	**1.4%**
Resource déficit (imports less exports)	-0.9%	1.8%	3.8%	2.0%
Net external factor and transfer payments:	-0.4%	-0.6%	-0.5%	-0.6%
Interest on external debt	-1.7%	-1.6%	-1.5%	-1.6%
Other net external factor and transfer payments:	1.2%	1.0%	1.0%	1.0%
Gross domestic product (million pesos)	239,075.0	233,900.1	308,245.8	263,121.4

Source: Pacífica projection exercise.

Table 14. Pacífica: External-accounts projection assumptions, 2008–2015

		2008	2009	2015	Average, 2009-15
	Initial projection year: 2009				
	International reserves:				
	Gross foreign-exchange reserves (year-end):				
(1)	Months of imports of goods, non-factor services	5.0	4.0	4.0	4.0
	Growth rates (in SDRs):				
(2)	SDR holdings (year-end)	3.3%	0.0%	0.0%	0.0%
(3)	Reserve position in the IMF (year-end)	3.3%	0.0%	0.0%	0.0%
	Growth rates:				
(4)	Central-bank gold holdings (thousand Troy ounces)	0.0%	0.0%	0.0%	0.0%
(5)	Unit national gold valuation (U.S. dollars/Troy ounce)	0.7%	0.0%	0.0%	0.0%
(6)	**Interest rate on foreign-exchange reserves**	1.0%	1.0%	0.0%	0.9%
	Real growth rates:				
(7)	Factor receipts excl. interest, profit remittances	2.7%	0.0%	2.0%	1.6%
(8)	Factor payments excl. interest, profit remittances	-20.8%	0.0%	2.0%	1.6%
(9)	Transfers received by government	3.4%	0.0%	2.0%	1.6%
(10)	Transfers received by non-government public entities	0.0%	0.0%	2.0%	1.6%
(11)	Transfers received by private entities	6.2%	0.0%	3.5%	1.7%
(12)	Unrequited transfer outflows	3.4%	0.0%	2.0%	1.6%
(13)	Direct investment abroad	0.0%	0.0%	2.0%	1.6%
(14)	Direct investment in rep. econ., nie	55.1%	1.0%	3.0%	2.6%
(15)	Portfolio investment assets	0.0%	0.0%	2.0%	1.6%
(16)	Portfolio investment liabilities	0.0%	1.0%	3.0%	2.6%
(17)	Other investment assets	3.4%	0.0%	2.0%	1.6%
(18)	Other investment liabilities	3.4%	0.0%	2.0%	1.6%
(19)	Other net non-debt capital flows	-23.6%	0.0%	2.0%	1.6%
(20)	Net errors and omissions	-139.3%	0.0%	0.0%	0.0%

Source: Pacífica projection exercise.

Table 15. Pacífica: Projected balance-of-payments current account
(per cent of GDP), 2008–2015

	2008	2009	2015	Average, 2009-15
Initial projection year: 2009				
Current-account surplus:	1.4%	-1.2%	-3.3%	-1.4%
Goods and non-factor services:	0.9%	-1.8%	-3.8%	-2.0%
Merchandise trade	2.5%	-0.4%	-2.7%	-0.8%
Non-factor services	-1.6%	-1.4%	-1.1%	-1.2%
Exports of goods and non-factor services:	27.7%	23.3%	24.2%	24.8%
Merchandise exports:	24.6%	20.3%	20.5%	21.4%
Oil	16.1%	11.7%	11.7%	12.4%
Non-oil commodities	3.0%	2.8%	2.8%	2.9%
Other exports	5.6%	5.8%	6.0%	6.2%
Income from non-factor services	3.0%	3.1%	3.6%	3.4%
Imports of goods and non-factor services:	-26.7%	-25.1%	-28.0%	-26.8%
Merchandise imports:	-22.1%	-20.7%	-23.2%	-22.2%
Consumer goods	-2.9%	-2.9%	-3.0%	-3.0%
Oil derivatives	-0.9%	-0.6%	-0.4%	-0.5%
Non-oil intermediate goods	-7.2%	-7.2%	-7.5%	-7.4%
Capital goods	-11.1%	-10.0%	-12.4%	-11.3%
Payments for non-factor services:	-4.6%	-4.4%	-4.7%	-4.6%
Insurance, freight for merchandise imports	-2.3%	-2.1%	-2.4%	-2.3%
Other non-factor service payments	-2.3%	-2.3%	-2.4%	-2.4%
Factor services and unrequited transfers:	0.4%	0.6%	0.5%	0.6%
Factor services:	-2.0%	-1.9%	-1.7%	-1.8%
Income:	0.7%	0.7%	0.7%	0.7%
Interest earned on international reserves	0.1%	0.1%	0.2%	0.1%
'Historical/programmed	0.1%	0.1%	0.1%	0.1%
'Unprogrammed	0.0%	0.0%	0.1%	0.1%
Other factor income:	0.6%	0.6%	0.5%	0.5%
Payments due:	-2.6%	-2.6%	-2.4%	-2.5%
Interest payments due:	-1.7%	-1.6%	-1.5%	-1.6%
'Historical/programmed	-1.7%	-1.6%	-1.5%	-1.6%
'Unprogrammed	0.0%	0.0%	0.0%	0.0%
Other factor payments	-0.9%	-1.0%	-0.9%	-1.0%
Net unrequited transfers:	2.4%	2.5%	2.2%	2.4%
Transfer receipts:	2.5%	2.7%	2.4%	2.6%
Official	0.5%	0.5%	0.4%	0.5%
Other	2.1%	2.2%	1.9%	2.1%
Transfer payments	-0.2%	-0.2%	-0.1%	-0.2%
Gross domestic product (US$ million)	$26,563.8	$25,163.6	$32,108.9	$27,522.6

Source: Pacífica projection exercise.

Table 16. Pacífica: Projected balance-of-payments financial accounts (per cent of GDP), 2008–2015

	2008	2009	2015	Average, 2009-15
Initial projection year: 2009				
Financial-accounts surplus:				
Capital-accounts surplus:	3.0%	1.9%	4.2%	2.7%
Investment transactions:	0.0%	0.0%	0.0%	0.0%
Direct foreign investment:	2.5%	2.7%	2.4%	2.6%
In-country investment by foreign nationals	1.9%	2.0%	1.8%	2.0%
Investment abroad by country nationals	1.9%	2.0%	1.8%	2.0%
Portfolio and other investment:	0.0%	0.0%	0.0%	0.0%
In-country investment by foreign nationals	0.6%	0.7%	0.6%	0.6%
Investment abroad by country nationals:	0.7%	0.8%	0.7%	0.7%
Other capital flows:	-0.1%	-0.1%	-0.1%	-0.1%
Net term borrowing:	0.5%	-0.8%	1.7%	0.1%
Public and publicly guaranteed debt:	0.9%	0.2%	2.2%	0.7%
Disbursements	0.9%	0.2%	1.0%	0.5%
Repayment	2.8%	2.5%	3.5%	2.8%
Private non-guaranteed debt:	-1.9%	-2.3%	-2.5%	-2.4%
Disbursements	0.0%	0.0%	1.2%	0.2%
Historical/programmed	0.0%	0.0%	1.3%	0.2%
Unprogrammed	0.0%	0.0%	0.0%	0.0%
Repayment	*0.0%*	*0.0%*	*1.2%*	*0.2%*
Net increase in short-term debt:	0.0%	0.0%	0.0%	0.0%
Net accumulation of interest arrears	0.2%	-0.3%	0.1%	0.0%
Net increase in short-term trade credit,	0.0%	0.0%	0.0%	0.0%
credit lines to banks, etc.	0.2%	-0.3%	0.1%	0.0%
Other net capital inflows:				
Errors and omissions	-0.6%	-0.7%	-0.6%	-0.6%
	-0.1%	-0.1%	-0.1%	-0.1%
Gross domestic product (US$ million)	$26,563.8	$25,163.6	$32,108.9	$27,522.6

Source: Pacífica projection exercise.

Table 17. Pacífica: Balance-of-payments international-reserves account (per cent of GDP), 2008–2015

	2008	2009	2015	Average, 2009-15
Initial projection year: 2009				
Increase in net international reserves:	4.2%	0.6%	0.7%	1.2%
Increase in gross reserves and related items:	4.2%	0.5%	0.7%	1.2%
(+ =increase):				
Foreign exchange:	4.2%	0.5%	0.7%	1.2%
Historical/programmed	4.2%	-3.4%	0.7%	0.0%
Unprogrammed	*0.0%*	*4.0%*	*0.0%*	*1.2%*
Other reserve holdings:	0.0%	0.0%	0.0%	0.0%
SDR holdings	0.0%	0.0%	0.0%	0.0%
Reserve position in the IMF	0.0%	0.0%	0.0%	0.0%
Gold holdings	0.0%	0.0%	0.0%	0.0%
International reserve liabilities:	0.0%	0.0%	0.0%	0.0%
International Monetary Fund:	0.0%	0.0%	0.0%	0.0%
Net change in outstanding balance	0.0%	0.0%	0.0%	0.0%
Valuation change	0.0%	0.0%	0.0%	0.0%
Other reserve liabilities	0.0%	0.0%	0.0%	0.0%
Balance-of-payments unadjusted financing gap	0.0%	4.0%	-1.2%	1.0%
Gross domestic product (US$ million)	$26,563.8	$25,163.6	$32,108.9	$27,522.6

Source: Pacífica projection exercise.

Table 18. Pacífica: Projected external assets and liabilities (per cent of GDP), 2008–2015

	2008	2009	2015	Average, 2009-15
Initial projection year: **2009**				
Net international reserves (year-end stocks):	12.1%	13.3%	16.9%	16.2%
International reserve assets:	12.2%	13.4%	17.0%	16.3%
Total reserves minus gold:	11.2%	12.4%	16.2%	15.4%
SDR holdings	0.0%	0.0%	0.0%	0.0%
Reserve position in the IMF	0.1%	0.1%	0.0%	0.1%
Foreign-exchange reserves:	11.2%	12.4%	16.1%	15.3%
Historical/programmed	11.2%	8.4%	9.3%	8.9%
Unprogrammed	0.0%	4.0%	6.8%	6.4%
Gold (national valuation):	1.0%	1.0%	0.8%	0.9%
Thousand fine Troy ounces	*414.0*	*414.0*	*414.0*	*414.0*
International reserve liabilities:	-0.1%	-0.1%	0.0%	-0.1%
Central-bank debt to the IMF	-0.1%	-0.1%	0.0%	-0.1%
Other international reserve liabilities	0.0%	0.0%	0.0%	0.0%
Foreign-exchange reserves: months of imports of goods, non-factor services	*5.0*	*5.9*	*6.9*	*6.8*
External debt (World Bank Global Development Finance; year-end stock):				
Debt outstanding and disbursed:	25.2%	26.5%	25.5%	25.8%
Public and publicly guaranteed:	22.0%	23.4%	21.3%	22.5%
Private non-guaranteed:	0.2%	0.3%	1.6%	0.5%
programmed	0.2%	0.3%	0.2%	0.2%
unprogrammed	0.0%	0.0%	1.4%	0.2%
International Monetary Fund	0.1%	0.1%	0.0%	0.1%
Short-term debt:	2.9%	2.8%	2.6%	2.8%
Accumulated interest arrears on public and publicly guaranteed debt	0.0%	0.0%	0.0%	0.0%
Short-term trade credit, credit lines to banks, etc.	2.9%	2.8%	2.6%	2.8%
Gross domestic product (US$ million)	$26,563.8	$25,163.6	$32,108.9	$27,522.6

Source: Pacífica projection exercise.

**Table 19. Pacífica: Projected sources and uses of external financing
(per cent of GDP), 2008–2015**

	2008	2009	2015	Average, 2009-15
Initial projection year: **2009**				
Uses of finance:	4.8%	4.1%	6.6%	4.9%
Current-account déficit	-1.4%	1.2%	3.3%	1.4%
Repayment of term debt:	1.9%	2.4%	2.6%	2.4%
Public and publicly guaranteed debt	1.9%	2.3%	2.5%	2.4%
Private non-guaranteed debt	0.0%	0.0%	0.0%	0.0%
Central-bank debt to the IMF	0.0%	0.0%	0.0%	0.0%
Net increase in international-reserve assets	4.2%	0.5%	0.7%	1.2%
and related items:				
Foreign exchange:	4.2%	0.5%	0.7%	1.2%
Historical/programmed	4.2%	-3.4%	0.7%	0.0%
Unprogrammed	*0.0%*	*4.0%*	*0.0%*	*1.2%*
Other reserve holdings	0.0%	0.0%	0.0%	0.0%
Sources of finance:	4.8%	4.1%	6.6%	4.9%
Disbursement of term debt:	2.8%	2.6%	4.8%	3.1%
Public and publicly guaranteed debt:	2.8%	2.5%	3.5%	2.8%
Private non-guaranteed debt:	0.0%	0.0%	1.3%	0.2%
programmed (incl. Global Development Finance, other)	0.0%	0.0%	0.0%	0.0%
programmed	*0.0%*	*0.0%*	*1.2%*	*0.2%*
Central-bank debt to the IMF	0.0%	0.0%	0.0%	0.0%
Net accumulation of interest arrears	0.0%	0.0%	0.0%	0.0%
Net increase in short-term trade credit,	0.2%	-0.3%	0.1%	0.0%
credit lines to banks, etc.				
Net non-debt financial inflows:	1.7%	1.9%	1.7%	1.9%
Investment transactions	2.5%	2.7%	2.4%	2.6%
Other net capital inflows	-0.6%	-0.7%	-0.6%	-0.6%
Errors and omissions	-0.1%	-0.1%	-0.1%	-0.1%
Gross domestic product (US$ million)	$26,563.8	$25,163.6	$32,108.9	$27,522.6

Source: Pacífica projection exercise.

Paul Beckerman

Table 20. Pacífica: Government-revenue projection assumptions, 2008–2015

		2008	2009	2015	Average, 2009-15
	Initial projection year: **2009**				
	General-government revenue:				
	Oil-based revenue (taxes and royalties):				
	from crude-oil exports:				
(1)	Ad valorem tax rate	38.0%	38.0%	38.0%	38.0%
(2)	Collection efficiency	87.9%	87.9%	87.9%	87.9%
	from oil-derivatives exports:				
(3)	Ad valorem tax rate	0.0%	0.0%	0.0%	0.0%
(4)	Collection efficiency	#N/A	#N/A	#N/A	#N/A
	from crude-oil imports:				
(5)	Ad valorem tax rate	0.0%	0.0%	0.0%	0.0%
(6)	Collection efficiency	#N/A	0.0%	0.0%	0.0%
	from oil-derivatives imports:				
(7)	Ad valorem tax rate	3.0%	3.0%	3.0%	3.0%
(8)	Collection efficiency	90.2%	90.2%	90.2%	90.2%
	from domestic oil-derivatives sales:				
(9)	Domestic price (national currency)	17.4%	-6.1%	2.9%	2.1%
	Crude export price (national currency)				
(10)	Domestic sales volume (national currency)	6.0%	-4.5%	5.0%	1.9%
	Elasticity of...				
(11)	domestic price with respect to crude export price	1.0	1.0	1.0	1.0
(12)	domestic sales volume with respect to real GDP	1.0	1.0	1.0	1.0
(13)	revenue flow with respect to domestic sales	0.5	1.0	1.0	1.0
	Non-oil internal revenue:				
	Internal tax revenue:				
	Domestic value-added tax (VAT):				
(14)	Value-added tax rate	12.0%	12.0%	12.0%	12.0%
(15)	Collection efficiency (GDP)	48.8%	49.1%	50.6%	49.8%
	Excises:				
(16)	Elasticity with respect to nominal non-govt. consumption	1.3	1.0	1.0	1.0
	Income tax (personal and business):				
(18)	Elasticity with respect to nominal GDP	1.3	1.0	1.0	1.0
	Financial transactions:				
(19)	Elasticity with respect to nominal GDP	#N/A	1.0	1.0	1.0
	Property and other subnational-government taxes:				
(20)	Elasticity with respect to nominal GDP	0.9	0.9	0.9	0.9
	(continues)				

Source: Pacífica projection exercise.

Table 20 (*Continued*)

		2008	2009	2015	Average, 2009-15
	Initial projection year: 2009				
	Internal non-tax, non-interest revenue:				
	Growth rates:				
	Transfer receipts received by government (national currency):				
	Transfer receipts received by...				
(21)	government from public enterprises	#N/A	0.0%	0.0%	0.0%
(22)	government from non-public entities	#N/A	0.0%	0.0%	0.0%
(23)	Other non-interest internal non-tax revenue	11.3%	0.0%	0.0%	0.0%
	Tariff and other external-source revenue:				
	Tariff revenue (US$m):				
	Consumption-goods imports:				
	Tariff rate	10.0%	10.0%	10.0%	10.0%
(24)	Collection efficiency	94.6%	94.6%	94.6%	94.6%
	Fuels and lubricants:				
	Tariff rate	10.0%	10.0%	10.0%	10.0%
(25)	Collection efficiency	94.6%	94.6%	94.6%	94.6%
	Non-oil intermediate goods imports:				
	Tariff rate	10.0%	10.0%	10.0%	10.0%
(26)	Collection efficiency	94.6%	94.6%	94.6%	94.6%
	Capital-goods imports:				
	Tariff rate	10.0%	10.0%	10.0%	10.0%
(27)	Collection efficiency	94.6%	94.6%	94.6%	94.6%
	Value-added tax revenue from imports (US$m):				
	Consumption-goods imports:				
(28)	Value-added tax rate	12.0%	12.0%	12.0%	12.0%
(29)	Collection efficiency	90.7%	90.7%	90.7%	90.7%
	Fuels and lubricants:				
(30)	Value-added tax rate	12.0%	12.0%	12.0%	12.0%
(31)	Collection efficiency	90.7%	90.7%	90.7%	90.7%
	Non-oil intermediate goods imports:				
(32)	Value-added tax rate	12.0%	12.0%	12.0%	12.0%
(33)	Collection efficiency	90.7%	90.7%	90.7%	90.7%
	Capital-goods imports:				
(34)	Value-added tax rate	12.0%	12.0%	12.0%	12.0%
(35)	Collection efficiency	90.7%	90.7%	90.7%	90.7%
	Other revenue from external transactions:				
	Growth rates:				
(36)	Exchange transactions	-4.0%	-35.2%	10.1%	1.9%
	Growth rate (US$)	#N/A	-5.3%	7.1%	2.8%
(37)	Departure tax	28.3%	-31.6%	2.8%	-1.3%
	Growth rate (US$)	#N/A	0.0%	0.0%	0.0%
(38)	Other revenue from external transactions	14.5%	-35.2%	10.1%	1.9%
	Growth rate (US$)	#N/A	-5.3%	7.1%	2.8%
	Transfer receipts from external sources (national currency)	8.9%	-31.6%	2.8%	-1.3%
	Transfer receipts from external sources (US$m)	3.4%	0.0%	2.0%	1.6%

Source: Pacífica projection exercise.

Table 21. Pacífica: Central-government financing projection assumptions, 2008–2015

		2008	2009	2015	Average, 2009-15
	Initial projection year: 2009				
	Per cent going to central government of total...				
	Oil revenue	**100.0%**	**100.0%**	**100.0%**	**100.0%**
	Non-oil internal revenue excl. interest:				
	Internal tax revenue:				
(1)	Domestic value-added tax (VAT)	100.0%	100.0%	100.0%	100.0%
(2)	Excises	100.0%	100.0%	100.0%	100.0%
(3)	Income tax (personal and business)	100.0%	100.0%	100.0%	100.0%
	Internal non-tax revenue:				
(4)	**Transfer receipts from external sources**	100.0%	100.0%	100.0%	100.0%
	Transfer receipts from...				
	sub-national governments:	8.9%	9.1%	6.9%	8.1%
(5)	current transfer receipts	0.0%	0.0%	0.0%	0.0%
(6)	capital transfer receipts	0.0%	0.0%	0.0%	0.0%
(7)	**Other non-interest internal non-tax revenue**	14.4%	14.4%	14.4%	14.4%
(8)	Tariff revenue	100.0%	100.0%	100.0%	100.0%
(9)	Value-added tax (VAT) on imports	100.0%	100.0%	100.0%	100.0%
(10)	Other revenue from external transactions	0.0%	0.0%	0.0%	0.0%
	Net external financing (US$m):				
	Net external borrowing:	**$5,834.1**	**$5,888.9**	**$6,826.5**	**$6,172.8**
	Disbursements	$756.3	$638.3	$1,131.4	$791.1
	Repayment of principal	-$505.6	-$583.4	-$814.1	-$649.3
	Net accumulation of interest arrears:	**$4.6**	**$0.0**	**$0.0**	**$0.0**
	Gross accumulation of interest arrears	$0.2	$0.2	$0.0	$0.0
	Payment of interest arrears	$0.0	-$4.9	$0.0	-$0.7
	Growth rates:				
	Programmed net internal borrowing	3.4%	-1.9%	6.4%	3.4%
	Programmed deposits in commercial banks	-128.0%	0.0%	7.1%	4.0%
	Interest rates:				
	Internal debt outstanding:				
	Contractual debt:				
(11)	Historical/programmed	5.0%	5.0%	5.0%	5.0%
(12)	Unprogrammed	0.0%	5.0%	5.0%	5.0%
(13)	Accumulated interest arrears	0.0%	0.0%	0.0%	0.0%
	Internal assets (-):				
	Deposits (-):				
(14)	Deposits at the central bank	0.0%	1.0%	1.0%	1.0%
	Deposits at commercial banks:				
(15)	Historical/programmed	0.0%	0.0%	0.0%	0.0%
(16)	Unprogrammed	0.0%	0.0%	0.0%	0.0%
(17)	Non-deposit assets (-)	0.0%	0.0%	0.0%	0.0%

Source: Pacífica projection exercise.

Table 22. Pacífica: Projected public-sector surplus (per cent of GDP), 2008–2015

	2008	2009	2015	Average, 2009-15
Initial projection year: 2009				
Overall public-sector surplus:	**1.1%**	**-1.7%**	**-3.3%**	**-2.7%**
Overall non-financial public-sector surplus:	**-0.5%**	**-2.4%**	**-3.1%**	**-2.6%**
General-government consolidated surplus:	**-0.5%**	**-2.4%**	**-3.1%**	**-2.6%**
Central government (excl. public pension system)	-0.4%	-2.0%	-2.1%	-2.0%
Other government (excl. public pension system)	-0.1%	-0.4%	-1.0%	-0.6%
Non-financial public-enterprise surplus				
Public pension-system surplus				
Central-bank profit	1.6%	0.7%	-0.2%	-0.1%
Gross domestic product (million pesos)	239,075.0	233,900.1	308,245.8	263,121.4

Source: Pacífica projection exercise.

Table 23. Pacífica: Projected central-government revenue (per cent of GDP), 2008–2015

	2008	2009	2015	Average, 2009-15
Initial projection year: 2009				
Total revenue:				
Oil-based revenue (taxes and royalties):	21.4%	20.2%	20.7%	20.7%
Non-oil revenue:	4.1%	3.0%	3.0%	3.1%
Tax and other domestic-source revenue:	17.3%	17.2%	17.7%	17.5%
Tax revenue:	12.3%	12.5%	12.5%	12.5%
Value-added tax (VAT)	12.0%	12.2%	12.3%	12.2%
Excises	5.9%	5.9%	6.1%	6.0%
Income tax	2.1%	2.2%	2.2%	2.2%
Other taxes	4.1%	4.1%	4.1%	4.1%
Transfer receipts:	0.0%	0.0%	0.0%	0.0%
from sub-national governments	0.1%	0.1%	0.1%	0.1%
from other sources	0.1%	0.1%	0.1%	0.1%
Interest receipts:	0.0%	0.0%	0.0%	0.0%
Deposits in the central bank	0.0%	0.0%	0.0%	0.0%
Other assets:	0.0%	0.0%	0.0%	0.0%
Historical/programmed	0.0%	0.0%	0.0%	0.0%
Unprogrammed (residual)	0.0%	0.0%	0.0%	0.0%
Other domestic central-government revenue	0.2%	0.3%	0.2%	0.2%
Tax and tariff revenue from external trade	4.5%	4.2%	4.7%	4.5%
Transfer receipts from external sources	0.5%	0.5%	0.4%	0.5%
Gross domestic product (million pesos)	239,075.0	233,900.1	308,245.8	263,121.4

Source: Pacífica projection exercise.

Table 24. Pacífica: Projected central-government expenditure (per cent of GDP), 2008–2015

	2008	2009	2015	Average, 2009-15
Initial projection year: 2009				
Total expenditure:	21.8%	22.2%	22.8%	22.7%
Interest due:	2.6%	2.7%	2.6%	2.7%
External interest	1.4%	1.4%	1.3%	1.4%
Internal interest	1.2%	1.3%	1.4%	1.4%
Programmed contractual debt	1.2%	1.2%	1.1%	1.2%
Unprogrammed contractual debt	0.0%	0.1%	0.3%	0.2%
Non-interest expenditure:	19.1%	19.5%	20.2%	20.0%
Non-interest current expenditure	14.4%	14.7%	15.4%	15.2%
Current expenditure on education and health:	5.9%	6.1%	6.5%	6.4%
Personnel remuneration	4.3%	4.4%	4.8%	4.6%
Goods and services	1.6%	1.7%	1.7%	1.7%
Current transfers:	0.0%	0.0%	0.0%	0.0%
to sub-national governments	0.0%	0.0%	0.0%	0.0%
other current transfers	0.0%	0.0%	0.0%	0.0%
Other current expenditure	0.0%	0.0%	0.0%	0.0%
Non-interest, non-social-sectors current expenditure:	8.5%	8.6%	9.0%	8.8%
Personnel remuneration	4.6%	4.7%	5.1%	4.9%
Goods and services	0.9%	1.0%	1.0%	1.0%
Current transfers:	1.8%	1.8%	1.8%	1.8%
to sub-national governments	1.0%	1.0%	1.0%	1.0%
other current transfers	0.8%	0.8%	0.8%	0.8%
Other current expenditure	1.0%	1.0%	1.0%	1.0%
Capital expenditure:	4.8%	4.8%	4.8%	4.8%
Fixed capital expenditure	4.4%	4.4%	4.4%	4.4%
Other capital expenditure	0.3%	0.3%	0.3%	0.3%
Gross domestic product (million pesos)	239,075.0	233,900.1	308,245.8	263,121.4

Source: Pacífica projection exercise.

Paul Beckerman

Table 25. Pacífica: Projected central-government financing (per cent of GDP), 2008–2015

	2008	2009	2015	Average, 2009-15
Initial projection year: 2009				
Central-government surplus (excl. public pension system):	-0.4%	-2.0%	-2.1%	-2.0%
Interest due	-2.6%	-2.7%	-2.6%	-2.7%
Primary (non-interest) surplus	2.2%	0.7%	0.5%	0.7%
Financing (per cent of GDP):	0.4%	2.0%	2.1%	2.0%
Net external financing	0.9%	0.2%	1.0%	0.5%
Net domestic borrowing:	-0.6%	1.8%	1.1%	1.5%
Increase in domestic contractual debt:	0.7%	1.8%	1.4%	1.6%
Historical/programmed	0.7%	-0.5%	1.4%	0.7%
Unprogrammed (residual)	0.0%	2.2%	0.0%	0.9%
Increase in domestic payments arrears	0.0%	0.0%	0.0%	0.0%
Decrease in other assets:	-1.3%	0.0%	-0.2%	-0.1%
Net increase in deposits (-):	0.0%	0.0%	0.0%	0.0%
Net increase in deposits at the central bank (-)	-0.2%	0.0%	-0.1%	0.0%
Net increase in deposits at commercial banks (-):	-1.1%	0.0%	-0.2%	0.0%
Historical/programmed	-1.1%	0.0%	-0.1%	0.0%
Unprogrammed (residual)	0.0%	0.0%	-0.1%	0.0%
Net increase in non-deposit assets (-):	0.0%	0.0%	0.0%	0.0%
Unadjusted central-government financing gap	0.0%	2.2%	-0.1%	0.9%
Year-end net debt:				
Net external debt:	22.0%	24.2%	21.3%	22.6%
External debt outstanding:	22.0%	24.2%	21.3%	22.6%
Debt outstanding and disbursed	22.0%	24.2%	21.3%	22.6%
Accumulated interest arrears	0.0%	0.0%	0.0%	0.0%
External assets (-)	0.0%	0.0%	0.0%	0.0%
Net internal debt:	20.4%	22.7%	24.6%	24.8%
Internal debt outstanding:	23.5%	25.8%	27.9%	27.9%
Contractual debt:	23.5%	25.8%	27.9%	27.9%
ʳHistorical/programmed	23.5%	23.6%	22.9%	23.3%
ʳUnprogrammed	0.0%	2.2%	5.0%	4.6%
Accumulated interest arrears	0.0%	0.0%	0.0%	0.0%
Internal assets (-):	-3.1%	-3.1%	-3.3%	-3.2%
Deposits (-):	-3.1%	-3.1%	-3.2%	-3.2%
Deposits at the central bank	-2.0%	-2.0%	-2.1%	-2.0%
Deposits at commercial banks:	-1.1%	-1.1%	-1.1%	-1.1%
Historical/programmed	-0.9%	-0.9%	-1.0%	-0.9%
Unprogrammed (residual)	-0.9%	-0.9%	-0.9%	-0.9%
Non-deposit assets (-)	0.0%	0.0%	-0.1%	0.0%
Gross domestic product (million pesos)	239,075.0	233,900.1	308,245.8	263,121.4

Source: Pacífica projection exercise.

Table 26. Pacífica: Sources and uses of central-government financing (per capita U.S. dollars at 2005 prices and exchange rate), 2008–2015

	2008	2009	2015	Average, 2009-15
Initial projection year: 2009				
Uses of finance:	**$654.4**	**$625.0**	**$680.7**	**$644.8**
Non-interest expenditure:	**$575.4**	**$549.4**	**$602.5**	**$567.4**
Current non-interest expenditure	**$431.8**	**$414.9**	**$460.0**	**$431.6**
Capital expenditure	**$143.6**	**$134.5**	**$142.4**	**$135.8**
Interest due:	**$79.0**	**$75.6**	**$78.2**	**$77.5**
External interest	$43.5	$40.3	$37.4	$38.7
Internal interest:	$35.6	$35.3	$40.8	$38.8
Programmed contractual debt	$35.6	$33.7	$33.4	$32.8
Unprogrammed contractual debt	$0.0	$1.6	$7.5	$6.0
Sources of finance:	**$654.4**	**$625.0**	**$680.7**	**$644.8**
Revenue:	**$493.1**	**$436.5**	**$462.8**	**$445.0**
Oil-based revenue	$122.5	$84.0	$88.8	$89.4
Non-oil internal tax revenue	$361.0	$343.0	$366.4	$346.9
Non-oil internal non-tax revenue	$9.6	$9.5	$7.7	$8.6
Non-oil external revenue	$135.2	$118.5	$140.9	$128.3
External transfers	$14.5	$14.3	$13.2	$13.9
Net external financing	**$28.4**	**$5.6**	**$29.5**	**$13.8**
Net internal financing	**-$16.7**	**$50.0**	**$34.2**	**$43.8**
Gross domestic product (million pesos)	239,075.0	233,900.1	308,245.8	263,121.4
Gross domestic product (per-capita US$ at 2005 prices and exchange rate)	$3,006.0	$2,814.5	$2,980.7	$2,841.5

Source: Pacífica projection exercise.

Table 27. Pacífica: Monetary-accounts projection assumptions, 2008–2015

		2008	2009	2015	Average, 2009-15
	Initial projection year: **2009**				
	Broad money supply:				
	Per cent, at year end:				
(1)	Foreign-currency deposits (in national currency)/broad money supply				
	Elasticities of year-average national-currency money stock with respect to				
(2)	Real GDP	1.0	-0.8	1.0	0.7
(3)	December-December percentage 'real rate of return on money'	41.5	0.1	0.1	0.1
	Elasticities of year-average foreign-currency deposits with respect to				
(4)	Real GDP	1.0	-0.7	1.3	0.8
(5)	'Percentage 'real rate of return on the U.S. dollar', December-December	-1.5	-0.1	-0.1	-0.1
	Geometric averaging exponent:				
(6)	**Money supply in national currency**	**0.5**	**0.5**	**0.5**	**0.5**
(7)	**Bank deposits in foreign currency**	**0.5**	**0.5**	**0.5**	**0.5**
	Marginal money multiplier for money in national currency:	**2.6**	**2.6**	**2.6**	**2.6**
(8)	Marginal currency-deposit ratio	47.9%	48.1%	49.6%	48.8%
(9)	Marginal bank reserve-deposit ratio	8.3%	8.3%	8.3%	8.3%
	Per cent, at year end:				
(10)	**Reserves held at the central bank**	**9.0%**	**9.0%**	**9.0%**	**9.0%**
	against foreign-currency deposits:				
	Growth rates:				
	Assets:				
	Net foreign assets:				
	Net reserve assets				
	Net non-reserve assets				
(11)	Claims on central government	-10.9%	-50.0%	-50.0%	-50.0%
(12)	Claims on other government entities:	0.0%	-2.2%	7.1%	3.7%
(13)	Claims on sub-national governments	0.0%	-2.2%	7.1%	3.7%
(14)	Claims on pension system	0.0%	-2.2%	7.1%	3.7%
(15)	Claims on non-financial public enterprises	0.0%	-2.2%	7.1%	3.7%
(16)	Claims on private sector	0.0%	-2.2%	7.1%	3.7%
(17)	Claims on deposit-money banks	-37.1%	-2.2%	7.1%	3.7%
(18)	Claims on other banking institutions	0.0%	-2.2%	7.1%	3.7%
(19)	Claims on non-bank financial institutions	0.0%	-2.2%	7.1%	3.7%
(20)	**Liabilities and net worth:**				
	Reserve money (period-end)	11.2%	-2.2%	7.1%	3.7%
(21)	Currency in circulation	11.2%	-2.2%	7.1%	3.7%
(22)	Time, savings, fgn. curr. deposits	0.0%	-2.2%	7.1%	3.7%
	Bonds	-17.9%	0.0%	0.0%	-11.9%
(23)	Restricted deposits	0.0%	-2.2%	7.1%	3.7%
(24)	Foreign liabilities	0.0%	-2.2%	7.1%	3.7%
(25)	Long-term foreign liabilities	0.0%	-2.2%	7.1%	3.7%
(26)	Central-government deposits	25.4%	-2.2%	7.1%	3.7%
(27)	Central-government lending funds	0.0%	-2.2%	7.1%	3.7%
(28)	Other-government deposits	0.0%	-2.2%	7.1%	3.7%
(29)	Deposits of non-financial public enterprises	25.4%	-2.2%	7.1%	3.7%
(30)	Deposits of the public pension system	8.9%	-2.2%	7.1%	3.7%
	Capital accounts	-4.9%	-17.3%	5.4%	2.2%
(31)	Other items (net)	0.0%	-2.2%	7.1%	3.7%
(continues)					

Source: Pacífica projection exercise.

Table 27 (*Continued*)

		2008	2009	2015	Average, 2009-15
	Initial projection year: 2009				
	U.S.-dollar interest rates:				
(32)	Net external assets excl. reserves	3.8%	3.8%	3.8%	3.8%
(33)	External liabilities excl. reserve liabilities	3.8%	3.8%	3.8%	3.8%
	Nominal interest rates:				
	Central-bank holdings of financial-system and private obligations	1.5%	1.5%	1.5%	1.5%
	Central-bank holdings of public-sector obligations:				
	Central government:	0.0%	0.0%	0.0%	0.0%
	Other government	2.0%	2.0%	2.0%	2.0%
	Public enterprises	2.0%	2.0%	2.0%	2.0%
	Public pension system	2.0%	2.0%	2.0%	2.0%
	Other internal assets	0.0%	0.0%	0.0%	0.0%
	Public-sector deposits at the central bank:				
	Central government	1.0%	1.0%	1.0%	1.0%
	Other government	1.0%	1.0%	1.0%	1.0%
	Public enterprises	1.0%	1.0%	1.0%	1.0%
	Public pension system	1.0%	1.0%	1.0%	1.0%
	Other internal assets	1.0%	1.0%	1.0%	1.0%
	Real interest rates:				
(34)	Central-bank holdings of financial-system and private obligations	-1.2%	-0.6%	-0.5%	-0.2%
	Central-bank holdings of public-sector obligations:				
(35)	Central government:	-2.7%	-2.1%	-2.0%	-1.7%
(36)	Other government	-0.7%	-0.2%	0.0%	0.3%
(37)	Public enterprises	-0.7%	-0.2%	0.0%	0.3%
(38)	Public pension system	-0.7%	-0.2%	0.0%	0.3%
(39)	Other internal assets	-2.7%	-0.2%	0.0%	0.3%
(40)	Public-sector deposits at the central bank:				
(41)	Central government	-1.7%	-1.1%	-1.0%	-0.7%
(42)	Other government	-1.7%	-1.1%	-1.0%	-0.7%
(43)	Public enterprises	-1.7%	-1.1%	-1.0%	-0.7%
(44)	Public pension system	-1.7%	-1.1%	-1.0%	-0.7%
(45)	Other internal assets	-1.7%	-1.1%	-1.0%	-0.7%
	Per cent of GDP:				
(46)	**Operating expenditure**	0.2%	0.2%	0.2%	0.2%
	Transfer of accumulated earnings...				
(47)	to the central government	0.0%	0.0%	0.0%	0.0%
(48)	to other entities	0.0%	0.0%	0.0%	0.0%
	Capital contributions...				
(49)	by the central government	0.0%	0.0%	0.0%	0.0%
(50)	by other entities	0.0%	0.0%	0.0%	0.0%

Source: Pacífica projection exercise.

Table 28. Pacífica: Projected monetary accounts (per cent of GDP), 2008–2015

	2008	2009	2015	Average, 2009-15
Initial projection year: 2009				
Broad money supply:				
Year-average stock	50.0%	54.4%	54.1%	54.3%
Year-end stock	52.4%	55.2%	56.0%	55.6%
Increase in year-end stock	4.8%	1.6%	3.9%	2.5%
Percentage increase	*0.1*	*0.1*	*0.1*	*0.1*
Percentage increase deflated by the GDP deflator	*0.1*	*0.1*	*0.0*	*0.0*
Bank deposits:				
Year-end stock	38.0%	37.2%	37.0%	37.2%
Increase in year-end stock	3.3%	-1.6%	2.4%	1.2%
Percentage increase	*0.1*	*0.0*	*0.1*	*0.0*
Central bank:				
Flow increases:				
Liabilities and net worth:	2.1%	1.2%	1.4%	1.3%
International liabilities:	0.0%	0.0%	0.0%	0.0%
International-reserve liabilities	0.0%	0.0%	0.0%	0.0%
Other international liabilities	0.0%	0.0%	0.0%	0.0%
Monetary base:	1.7%	0.6%	1.5%	1.0%
Currency in circulation	1.5%	0.5%	1.3%	0.8%
Bank reserves	0.3%	0.1%	0.2%	0.1%
Deposits at the central bank:	0.2%	0.0%	0.1%	0.0%
Central-government deposits at the central bank	0.2%	0.0%	0.1%	0.0%
Other deposits at the central bank	0.0%	0.0%	0.0%	0.0%
Non-monetary central-bank obligations (residual)	-0.1%	0.0%	0.0%	0.3%
Historical/programmed	-0.1%	0.0%	0.0%	0.0%
Unprogrammed	0.0%	0.0%	0.0%	0.3%
Other central-bank liabilities	0.0%	0.0%	0.0%	0.0%
Central-bank net worth	0.2%	0.7%	-0.2%	-0.1%
Assets:	2.1%	1.2%	1.4%	1.3%
International assets:	2.5%	1.4%	0.7%	1.3%
International reserves	2.5%	1.4%	0.7%	1.3%
Other international assets	0.0%	0.0%	0.0%	0.0%
Central-bank holdings of commercial-bank obligations	-0.1%	0.0%	0.0%	0.0%
Central-bank holdings of government obligations	-0.3%	-0.2%	0.7%	0.0%
Other central-bank assets	0.0%	0.0%	0.0%	0.0%
Central-bank unadjusted financing gap	0.0%	-1.1%	-0.7%	0.0%
Per cent of GDP:				
Indicators of policy stance				
(positive values indicate expansionary policy):				
Central bank - credit to commercial banks				
less non-monetary obligations:				
Flow increase	0.0%	0.0%	0.0%	-0.3%
Year-end stock	-0.1%	1.0%	0.1%	-0.3%
Central bank - credit to government				
less government deposits:				
Flow increase	-0.5%	-0.1%	0.6%	0.0%
Year-end stock	1.4%	0.2%	-1.1%	-0.7%
Gross domestic product (million pesos)	239,075.0	233,900.1	308,245.8	263,121.4

Source: Pacífica projection exercise.

Table 29. Pacífica: Projected central-bank capitalization flow (per cent of GDP), 2008–2015

	2008	2009	2015	Average, 2009-15
Initial projection year: 2009				
Change in net worth:	**1.5%**	**0.5%**	**-0.3%**	**-0.2%**
Profits/losses:	**1.5%**	**0.5%**	**-0.3%**	**-0.2%**
Net interest earnings:	**0.0%**	**-0.1%**	**-0.1%**	**-0.1%**
Interest earnings:	**0.0%**	**0.0%**	**0.0%**	**0.0%**
Foreign-exchange reserves	0.1%	0.1%	0.2%	0.1%
Other international assets	0.0%	0.0%	0.0%	0.0%
Central-bank holdings of financial-system and private obligations	0.0%	0.0%	0.0%	0.0%
Central-bank holdings of public-sector obligations:	0.0%	0.0%	0.0%	0.0%
Other internal assets	0.0%	0.0%	0.0%	0.0%
Interest payments:	**0.0%**	**-0.1%**	**-0.1%**	**-0.1%**
International reserve liabilities	0.0%	0.0%	0.0%	0.0%
Other external liabilities	0.0%	0.0%	0.0%	0.0%
Bank reserves	0.0%	-0.1%	-0.1%	-0.1%
Public-sector deposits at the central bank	0.0%	0.0%	0.0%	0.0%
Other internal liabilities	0.0%	0.0%	0.0%	0.0%
Non-monetary central-bank obligations (residual)	0.0%	0.0%	0.0%	0.0%
Revaluation of net international assets	**1.8%**	**0.8%**	**0.0%**	**0.1%**
Operating expenditure	**-0.2%**	**-0.2%**	**-0.2%**	**-0.2%**
Transfer of earnings to the central government	**0.0%**	**0.0%**	**0.0%**	**0.0%**
Capital contributions by the central government	**0.0%**	**0.0%**	**0.0%**	**0.0%**
Gross domestic product (million pesos)	239,075.0	233,900.1	308,245.8	263,121.4

Source: Pacífica projection exercise.

Table 30. Pacífica: Projected central-bank assets and liabilities (per cent of GDP), 2008–2015

	2008	2009	2015	Average, 2009-15
Initial projection year: 2009				
Central bank:				
Year-end stocks:				
Liabilities and net worth:	**-14.8%**	**-16.4%**	**-19.2%**	**-18.1%**
International liabilities:	**-0.1%**	**-0.1%**	**0.0%**	**-0.1%**
International-reserve liabilities	-0.1%	-0.1%	0.0%	-0.1%
Other international liabilities	0.0%	0.0%	0.0%	0.0%
Monetary base:	**-16.9%**	**-17.9%**	**-19.0%**	**-18.4%**
Currency in circulation	-14.4%	-15.3%	-16.3%	-15.7%
Bank reserves	-2.5%	-2.6%	-2.7%	-2.7%
Deposits at the central bank:	**-1.2%**	**-1.2%**	**-1.2%**	**-1.2%**
Central-government deposits at the central bank	-1.1%	-1.1%	-1.1%	-1.1%
Other deposits at the central bank	-0.2%	-0.2%	-0.2%	-0.2%
Non-monetary central-bank obligations (residual)	**-0.2%**	**-0.2%**	**-2.2%**	**-1.7%**
Historical/programmed	-0.2%	-0.2%	-0.2%	-0.2%
Unprogrammed	0.0%	0.0%	-2.0%	-1.5%
Other central-bank liabilities	**0.0%**	**0.0%**	**0.0%**	**0.0%**
Central-bank net worth	**3.7%**	**3.1%**	**3.3%**	**3.3%**
Assets:	**14.8%**	**16.4%**	**19.2%**	**18.1%**
International assets:	**12.2%**	**13.9%**	**17.0%**	**16.4%**
International reserves	12.2%	13.9%	17.0%	16.4%
Other international assets	0.0%	0.0%	0.0%	0.0%
Central-bank holdings of commercial-bank obligations	**0.1%**	**0.1%**	**0.1%**	**0.1%**
Central-bank holdings of government obligations	**2.5%**	**2.4%**	**2.1%**	**1.6%**
Other central-bank assets	**0.0%**	**0.0%**	**0.0%**	**0.0%**
Gross domestic product (million pesos)	239,075.0	233,900.1	308,245.8	263,121.4

Source: Pacífica projection exercise.

Table 31. Pacífica: "Base" scenario assumptions and results, 2008–2015

		2008	2009	2015	Average, 2009-15
	Initial projection year: *2009*				
Assumptions:					
World economic variables:					
Growth rate of the world price level (US$)		2.2%	0.0%	2.0%	1.6%
Real world commerce volume		4.1%	-4.5%	5.5%	3.6%
LIBOR (per cent per year)		3.0%	1.7%	4.0%	2.8%
Real crude-oil price (percentage increase over previous year)		31.9%	-31.6%	0.8%	-2.9%
Macroeconomic programming and policy variables:					
Growth rates:					
Real GDP		6.0%	-4.5%	5.0%	1.9%
Consumer prices (Dec.-Dec.)		2.7%	2.2%	2.0%	1.7%
Real-effective exchange rate		-0.6%	0.8%	0.0%	0.7%
Value-added tax (internal transactions):					
Tax rate (per cent)		12.0%	12.0%	12.0%	12.0%
Tax productivity (per cent)		48.8%	49.1%	50.6%	49.8%
Gross foreign-exchange reserves:					
year-end; months of imports of goods, non-factor services		*5.0*	*4.0*	*4.0*	*4.0*
Results:					
Per-capita U.S. dollars at prices and exchange rate of...	*2005*				
Gross domestic product (GDP)		**$3,006.0**	**$2,814.5**	**$2,980.7**	**$2,841.5**
Non-government consumption		**$2,095.7**	**$2,083.3**	**$2,282.9**	**$2,077.9**
Percentage:					
Poverty incidence		17.0%	17.1%	15.5%	17.2%
Extreme poverty incidence		7.4%	7.5%	6.6%	7.5%
Per cent of GDP:					
Gross investment/saving:		**19.6%**	**17.5%**	**21.1%**	**19.2%**
Gross fixed capital formation		19.7%	17.5%	21.0%	19.2%
Net increase in inventories		-0.1%	0.0%	0.1%	0.0%
National saving		21.0%	16.3%	17.8%	17.8%
Balance-of-payments current-account deficit		-1.4%	1.2%	3.3%	1.4%
Internal saving		20.6%	15.7%	17.2%	17.3%
Net imports of goods and non-factor services		-0.9%	1.8%	3.8%	2.0%
General-government déficit:		**0.5%**	**2.4%**	**3.1%**	**2.6%**
External financing		-0.9%	-0.2%	-1.0%	-0.5%
Internal financing		1.4%	2.6%	4.1%	3.1%
Year-end total external debt:		**25.2%**	**26.5%**	**25.5%**	**25.8%**
of which, public and publicly guaranteed (excl. IMF)		22.0%	23.4%	21.3%	22.5%
of which, private non-guaranteed		0.2%	0.3%	1.6%	0.5%
Year-end government net internal debt		**20.4%**	**22.7%**	**24.6%**	**24.8%**
Net increase in non-monetary central-bank obligations		**-0.1%**	**0.0%**	**0.0%**	**0.3%**
Months of imports of goods, non-factor services:					
Gross foreign-exchange reserves		**5.0**	**5.9**	**6.9**	**6.8**
Per-capita U.S. dollars at prices and exchange rate of...	*2005*				
Central government:					
Tax and other internal-source revenue		**$370.6**	**$352.5**	**$374.1**	**$355.6**
Interest due:		**$79.0**	**$75.6**	**$78.2**	**$77.5**
External		$43.5	$40.3	$37.4	$38.7
Internal		$35.6	$35.3	$40.8	$38.8
Current education and health expenditure		**$177.6**	**$172.6**	**$193.1**	**$181.0**
Capital expenditure		**$143.6**	**$134.5**	**$142.4**	**$135.8**
Gross domestic product (US$ billion)		**$26.6**	**$25.2**	**$32.1**	**$27.5**

Source: Pacífica projection exercise.

Table 32. Pacífica: Macroeconomic-projection sensitivity analysis, comparing the base and higher-depreciation scenarios (1 and 2 respectively), 2008–2015

		2008	2009	2015	Average, 2009-15	2008	2009	2015	Average, 2009-15
Initial projection year:	*2009*		*Scenario 1*				*Scenario 2*		
Assumptions:									
World economic variables:									
Growth rate of the world price level (US$)		2.2%	0.0%	2.0%	1.6%	2.2%	0.0%	2.0%	1.6%
Real world commerce volume		4.1%	-4.5%	5.5%	3.6%	4.1%	-4.5%	5.5%	3.6%
LIBOR (per cent per year)		3.0%	1.7%	4.0%	2.8%	3.0%	1.7%	4.0%	2.8%
Real crude-oil price (percentage increase over previous year)		31.9%	-31.6%	0.8%	-2.9%	31.9%	-31.6%	0.7%	-2.9%
Macroeconomic programming and policy variables:									
Growth rates:									
Real GDP		6.0%	-4.5%	5.0%	1.9%	6.0%	-4.5%	5.0%	1.9%
Consumer prices (Dec.-Dec.)		2.7%	2.2%	2.0%	1.7%	2.7%	2.2%	2.0%	1.7%
Real-effective exchange rate		-0.6%	0.8%	0.0%	0.7%	-0.6%	0.8%	0.0%	1.3%
Value-added tax (internal transactions):									
Tax rate (per cent)		12.0%	12.0%	12.0%	12.0%	12.0%	12.0%	12.0%	12.0%
Tax productivity (per cent)		48.8%	49.1%	50.6%	49.8%	48.8%	49.1%	50.6%	49.8%
Gross foreign-exchange reserves:									
year-end; months of imports of goods, non-factor services		*5.0*	*4.0*	*4.0*	*4.2*	*5.0*	*4.0*	*4.0*	*4.2*
Results:									
Per-capita U.S. dollars at prices and exchange rate of...	*2005*								
Gross domestic product (GDP)		$3,006.0	$2,814.5	$2,980.7	$2,841.5	$3,006.0	$2,814.5	$2,980.7	$2,841.5
Non-government consumption		$2,095.7	$2,083.3	$2,282.9	$2,077.9	$2,095.7	$2,083.3	$2,179.6	$2,002.1
Percentage:									
Poverty incidence		17.0%	17.1%	15.5%	17.2%	17.0%	17.1%	16.3%	17.9%
Extreme poverty incidence		7.4%	7.5%	6.6%	7.5%	7.4%	7.5%	7.0%	7.9%
Per cent of GDP:									
Gross investment/saving:		19.6%	17.5%	21.1%	19.2%	19.6%	17.5%	21.1%	19.2%
Gross fixed capital formation		19.7%	17.5%	21.0%	19.2%	19.7%	17.5%	21.0%	19.2%
Net increase in inventories		-0.1%	0.0%	0.1%	0.0%	-0.1%	0.0%	0.1%	0.0%
National saving		21.0%	16.3%	17.8%	17.8%	21.0%	16.3%	18.2%	18.2%
Balance-of-payments current-account deficit		-1.4%	1.2%	3.3%	1.4%	-1.4%	1.2%	2.9%	1.0%
Internal saving		20.6%	15.7%	17.2%	17.3%	20.6%	15.7%	17.6%	17.6%
Net imports of goods and non-factor services		-0.9%	1.8%	3.8%	2.0%	-0.9%	1.8%	3.5%	1.6%
General-government déficit:		0.5%	2.4%	3.1%	2.6%	0.5%	2.4%	2.8%	2.4%
External financing		-0.9%	-0.2%	-1.0%	-0.5%	-0.9%	-0.2%	-1.0%	-0.5%
Internal financing		1.4%	2.6%	4.1%	3.1%	1.4%	2.6%	3.8%	2.9%
Year-end total external debt:		25.2%	26.5%	25.5%	25.8%	25.2%	26.5%	25.8%	26.5%
of which, public and publicly guaranteed (excl. IMF)		22.0%	23.4%	21.3%	22.5%	22.0%	23.4%	22.1%	23.2%
of which, private non-guaranteed		0.2%	0.3%	1.6%	0.5%	0.2%	0.3%	0.9%	0.3%
Year-end government net internal debt		20.4%	22.7%	24.6%	24.8%	20.4%	22.7%	22.8%	24.1%
Net increase in non-monetary central-bank obligations		-0.1%	0.0%	0.0%	0.3%	-0.1%	0.0%	0.0%	0.6%
Months of imports of goods, non-factor services:									
Gross foreign-exchange reserves		5.0	5.9	6.9	6.8	5.0	5.9	7.8	7.4
Per-capita U.S. dollars at prices and exchange rate of...	*2005*								
Central government:									
Tax and other internal-source revenue		$370.6	$352.5	$374.1	$355.6	$370.6	$352.5	$373.7	$355.2
Interest due:		$79.0	$75.6	$78.2	$77.5	$79.0	$75.6	$78.4	$78.0
External		$43.5	$40.3	$37.4	$38.7	$43.5	$40.3	$38.9	$39.9
Internal		$35.6	$35.3	$40.8	$38.8	$35.6	$35.3	$39.4	$38.1
Current education and health expenditure		$177.6	$172.6	$193.1	$181.0	$177.6	$172.6	$193.1	$181.0
Capital expenditure		$143.6	$134.5	$142.4	$135.8	$143.6	$134.5	$142.4	$135.8
Gross domestic product (billion pesos)		239.1	233.9	308.2	263.1	239.1	233.9	308.2	263.1
Gross domestic product (US$ billion)		$26.6	$25.2	$32.1	$27.5	$26.6	$25.2	$30.8	$26.6

Source: Pacífica projection exercise.

Paul Beckerman

Table 33. Pacífica: Macroeconomic-projection sensitivity analysis, comparing the base and higher-value-added-tax scenarios (1 and 3 respectively), 2008–2015

		2008	2009	2015	Average, 2009-15	2008	2009	2015	Average, 2009-15
Initial projection year:	*2009*		Scenario 1				Scenario 3		
Assumptions:									
World economic variables:									
Growth rate of the world price level (US$)		2.2%	0.0%	2.0%	1.6%	2.2%	0.0%	2.0%	1.6%
Real world commerce volume		4.1%	-4.5%	5.5%	3.6%	4.1%	-4.5%	5.5%	3.6%
LIBOR (per cent per year)		3.0%	1.7%	4.0%	2.8%	3.0%	1.7%	4.0%	2.8%
Real crude-oil price (percentage increase over previous year)		31.9%	-31.6%	0.8%	-2.9%	31.9%	-31.6%	0.7%	-2.9%
Macroeconomic programming and policy variables:									
Growth rates:									
Real GDP		6.0%	-4.5%	5.0%	1.9%	6.0%	-4.5%	5.0%	1.9%
Consumer prices (Dec.-Dec.)		2.7%	2.2%	2.0%	1.7%	2.7%	2.2%	2.0%	1.7%
Real-effective exchange rate		-0.6%	0.8%	0.0%	0.7%	-0.6%	0.8%	0.0%	0.7%
Value-added tax (internal transactions):									
Tax rate (per cent)		12.0%	12.0%	12.0%	12.0%	12.0%	12.0%	14.0%	13.7%
Tax productivity (per cent)		48.8%	49.1%	50.6%	49.8%	48.8%	49.1%	48.3%	47.9%
Gross foreign-exchange reserves:									
year-end; months of imports of goods, non-factor services		*5.0*	*4.0*	*4.0*	*4.2*	*5.0*	*4.0*	*4.0*	*4.2*
Results:									
Per-capita U.S. dollars at prices and exchange rate of...	*2005*								
Gross domestic product (GDP)		$3,006.0	$2,814.5	$2,980.7	$2,841.5	$3,006.0	$2,814.5	$2,980.7	$2,841.5
Non-government consumption		$2,095.7	$2,083.3	$2,282.9	$2,077.9	$2,095.7	$2,083.3	$2,282.9	$2,077.9
Percentage:									
Poverty incidence		17.0%	17.1%	15.5%	17.2%	17.0%	17.1%	15.5%	17.2%
Extreme poverty incidence		7.4%	7.5%	6.6%	7.5%	7.4%	7.5%	6.6%	7.5%
Per cent of GDP:									
Gross investment/saving:		19.6%	17.5%	21.1%	19.2%	19.6%	17.5%	21.1%	19.2%
Gross fixed capital formation		19.7%	17.5%	21.0%	19.2%	19.7%	17.5%	21.0%	19.2%
Net increase in inventories		-0.1%	0.0%	0.1%	0.0%	-0.1%	0.0%	0.1%	0.0%
National saving		21.0%	16.3%	17.8%	17.8%	21.0%	16.3%	17.8%	17.8%
Balance-of-payments current-account deficit		-1.4%	1.2%	3.3%	1.4%	-1.4%	1.2%	3.3%	1.4%
Internal saving		20.6%	15.7%	17.2%	17.3%	20.6%	15.7%	17.2%	17.3%
Net imports of goods and non-factor services		-0.9%	1.8%	3.8%	2.0%	-0.9%	1.8%	3.8%	2.0%
General-government déficit:		0.5%	2.4%	3.1%	2.6%	0.5%	2.4%	1.9%	1.6%
External financing		-0.9%	-0.2%	-1.0%	-0.5%	-0.9%	-0.2%	-1.0%	-0.5%
Internal financing		1.4%	2.6%	4.1%	3.1%	1.4%	2.6%	2.9%	2.1%
Year-end total external debt:		25.2%	26.5%	25.5%	25.8%	25.2%	26.5%	25.5%	25.8%
of which, public and publicly guaranteed (excl. IMF)		22.0%	23.4%	21.3%	22.5%	22.0%	23.4%	21.3%	22.5%
of which, private non-guaranteed		0.2%	0.3%	1.6%	0.5%	0.2%	0.3%	1.6%	0.5%
Year-end government net internal debt		20.4%	22.7%	24.6%	24.8%	20.4%	22.7%	14.8%	20.3%
Net increase in non-monetary central-bank obligations		-0.1%	0.0%	0.0%	0.3%	-0.1%	0.0%	0.0%	0.3%
Months of imports of goods, non-factor services:									
Gross foreign-exchange reserves		5.0	5.9	6.9	6.8	5.0	5.9	6.9	6.8
Per-capita U.S. dollars at prices and exchange rate of...	*2005*								
Central government:									
Tax and other internal-source revenue		$370.6	$352.5	$374.1	$355.6	$370.6	$352.5	$394.6	$372.2
Interest due:		$79.0	$75.6	$78.2	$77.5	$79.0	$75.6	$74.2	$74.9
External		$43.5	$40.3	$37.4	$38.7	$43.5	$40.3	$37.4	$38.7
Internal		$35.6	$35.3	$40.8	$38.8	$35.6	$35.3	$36.8	$36.2
Current education and health expenditure		$177.6	$172.6	$193.1	$181.0	$177.6	$172.6	$193.1	$181.0
Capital expenditure		$143.6	$134.5	$142.4	$135.8	$143.6	$134.5	$142.4	$135.8
Gross domestic product (billion pesos)		239.1	233.9	308.2	263.1	239.1	233.9	308.2	263.1
Gross domestic product (US$ billion)		$26.6	$25.2	$32.1	$27.5	$26.6	$25.2	$32.1	$27.5

Source: Pacífica projection exercise.

Table 34. Pacífica: Macroeconomic-projection sensitivity analysis, comparing the base and higher-growth scenarios (1 and 4 respectively), 2006–2010

	2008	2009	2015	Average, 2009-15	2008	2009	2015	Average, 2009-15
Initial projection year: **2009**		Scenario 1				Scenario 4		
Assumptions:								
World economic variables:								
Growth rate of the world price level (US$)	2.2%	0.0%	2.0%	1.6%	2.2%	0.0%	2.0%	1.6%
Real world commerce volume	4.1%	-4.5%	5.5%	3.6%	4.1%	-4.5%	5.5%	3.6%
LIBOR (per cent per year)	3.0%	1.7%	4.0%	2.8%	3.0%	1.7%	4.0%	2.8%
Real crude-oil price (percentage increase over previous year)	31.9%	-31.6%	0.8%	-2.9%	31.9%	-31.6%	0.7%	-2.9%
Macroeconomic programming and policy variables:								
Growth rates:								
Real GDP	6.0%	-4.5%	5.0%	1.9%	6.0%	-4.5%	6.0%	2.3%
Consumer prices (Dec.-Dec.)	2.7%	2.2%	2.0%	1.7%	2.7%	2.2%	2.0%	1.7%
Real-effective exchange rate	-0.6%	0.8%	0.0%	0.7%	-0.6%	0.8%	0.0%	0.7%
Value-added tax (internal transactions):								
Tax rate (per cent)	12.0%	12.0%	12.0%	12.0%	12.0%	12.0%	12.0%	12.0%
Tax productivity (per cent)	48.8%	49.1%	50.6%	49.8%	48.8%	49.1%	50.6%	49.8%
Gross foreign-exchange reserves:								
year-end; months of imports of goods, non-factor services	*5.0*	*4.0*	*4.0*	*4.2*	*5.0*	*4.0*	*4.0*	*4.2*
Results:								
Per-capita U.S. dollars at prices and exchange rate of... **2005**								
Gross domestic product (GDP)	$3,006.0	$2,814.5	$2,980.7	$2,841.5	$3,006.0	$2,814.5	$3,066.7	$2,869.3
Non-government consumption	$2,095.7	$2,083.3	$2,282.9	$2,077.9	$2,095.7	$2,083.3	$2,375.9	$2,107.6
Percentage:								
Poverty incidence	17.0%	17.1%	15.5%	17.2%	17.0%	17.1%	14.9%	17.0%
Extreme poverty incidence	7.4%	7.5%	6.6%	7.5%	7.4%	7.5%	6.2%	7.4%
Per cent of GDP:								
Gross investment/saving:	**19.6%**	**17.5%**	**21.1%**	**19.2%**	**19.6%**	**17.5%**	**21.1%**	**19.2%**
Gross fixed capital formation	19.7%	17.5%	21.0%	19.2%	19.7%	17.5%	21.0%	19.2%
Net increase in inventories	-0.1%	0.0%	0.1%	0.0%	-0.1%	0.0%	0.1%	0.0%
National saving	21.0%	16.3%	17.8%	17.8%	21.0%	16.3%	17.0%	17.6%
Balance-of-payments current-account deficit	-1.4%	1.2%	3.3%	1.4%	-1.4%	1.2%	4.1%	1.7%
Internal saving	20.6%	15.7%	17.2%	17.3%	20.6%	15.7%	16.5%	17.0%
Net imports of goods and non-factor services	-0.9%	1.8%	3.8%	2.0%	-0.9%	1.8%	4.5%	2.2%
General-government déficit:	**0.5%**	**2.4%**	**3.1%**	**2.6%**	**0.5%**	**2.4%**	**3.1%**	**2.6%**
External financing	-0.9%	-0.2%	-1.0%	-0.5%	-0.9%	-0.2%	-1.2%	-0.6%
Internal financing	1.4%	2.6%	4.1%	3.1%	1.4%	2.6%	4.3%	3.2%
Year-end total external debt:	**25.2%**	**26.5%**	**25.5%**	**25.8%**	**25.2%**	**26.5%**	**26.5%**	**26.0%**
of which, public and publicly guaranteed (excl. IMF)	22.0%	23.4%	21.3%	22.5%	22.0%	23.4%	21.2%	22.5%
of which, private non-guaranteed	0.2%	0.3%	1.6%	0.5%	0.2%	0.3%	2.8%	0.7%
Year-end government net internal debt	**20.4%**	**22.7%**	**24.6%**	**24.8%**	**20.4%**	**22.7%**	**22.8%**	**24.2%**
Net increase in non-monetary central-bank obligations	-0.1%	0.0%	0.0%	0.3%	-0.1%	0.0%	0.0%	0.3%
Months of imports of goods, non-factor services:								
Gross foreign-exchange reserves	5.0	5.9	6.9	6.8	5.0	5.9	6.7	6.7
Per-capita U.S. dollars at prices and exchange rate of... **2005**								
Central government:								
Tax and other internal-source revenue	$370.6	$352.5	$374.1	$355.6	$370.6	$352.5	$385.4	$359.2
Interest due:	**$79.0**	**$75.6**	**$78.2**	**$77.5**	**$79.0**	**$75.6**	**$78.8**	**$77.6**
External	$43.5	$40.3	$37.4	$38.7	$43.5	$40.3	$38.1	$38.9
Internal	$35.6	$35.3	$40.8	$38.8	$35.6	$35.3	$40.7	$38.7
Current education and health expenditure	$177.6	$172.6	$193.1	$181.0	$177.6	$172.6	$197.3	$182.3
Capital expenditure	$143.6	$134.5	$142.4	$135.8	$143.6	$134.5	$146.5	$137.1
Gross domestic product (billion pesos)	239.1	233.9	308.2	263.1	239.1	233.9	317.1	265.9
Gross domestic product (US$ billion)	$26.6	$25.2	$32.1	$27.5	$26.6	$25.2	$33.0	$27.8

Source: Pacífica projection exercise.

Table 35. Pacífica: Macroeconomic-projection sensitivity analysis, comparing the base and debt-reduction scenarios (1 and 5 respectively), 2008–2015

		2008	2009	2015	Average, 2009-15	2008	2009	2015	Average, 2009-15
Initial projection year:	*2009*		Scenario 1				Scenario 5		
Assumptions:									
World economic variables:									
Growth rate of the world price level (US$)		2.2%	0.0%	2.0%	1.6%	2.2%	0.0%	2.0%	1.6%
Real world commerce volume		4.1%	-4.5%	5.5%	3.6%	4.1%	-4.5%	5.5%	3.6%
LIBOR (per cent per year)		3.0%	1.7%	4.0%	2.8%	3.0%	1.7%	4.0%	2.8%
Real crude-oil price (percentage increase over previous year)		31.9%	-31.6%	0.8%	-2.9%	31.9%	-31.6%	0.8%	-2.9%
Macroeconomic programming and policy variables:									
Growth rates:									
Real GDP		6.0%	-4.5%	5.0%	1.9%	6.0%	-4.5%	5.0%	1.9%
Consumer prices (Dec.-Dec.)		2.7%	2.2%	2.0%	1.7%	2.7%	2.2%	2.0%	1.7%
Real-effective exchange rate		-0.6%	0.8%	0.0%	0.7%	-0.6%	0.8%	0.0%	0.7%
Value-added tax (internal transactions):									
Tax rate (per cent)		12.0%	12.0%	12.0%	12.0%	12.0%	12.0%	12.0%	12.0%
Tax productivity (per cent)		48.8%	49.1%	50.6%	49.8%	48.8%	49.1%	50.6%	49.8%
Gross foreign-exchange reserves:									
year-end; months of imports of goods, non-factor services		*5.0*	*4.0*	*4.0*	*4.2*	*5.0*	*4.0*	*4.0*	*4.2*
Results:									
Per-capita U.S. dollars at prices and exchange rate of...	*2005*								
Gross domestic product (GDP)		$3,006.0	$2,814.5	$2,980.7	$2,841.5	$3,006.0	$2,814.5	$2,980.7	$2,841.5
Non-government consumption		$2,095.7	$2,083.3	$2,282.9	$2,077.9	$2,095.7	$2,083.3	$2,282.9	$2,077.9
Percentage:									
Poverty incidence		17.0%	17.1%	15.5%	17.2%	17.0%	17.1%	15.5%	17.2%
Extreme poverty incidence		7.4%	7.5%	6.6%	7.5%	7.4%	7.5%	6.6%	7.5%
Per cent of GDP:									
Gross investment/saving:		19.6%	17.5%	21.1%	19.2%	19.6%	17.5%	21.1%	19.2%
Gross fixed capital formation		19.7%	17.5%	21.0%	19.2%	19.7%	17.5%	21.0%	19.2%
Net increase in inventories		-0.1%	0.0%	0.1%	0.0%	-0.1%	0.0%	0.1%	0.0%
National saving		21.0%	16.3%	17.8%	17.8%	21.0%	16.4%	18.0%	18.1%
Balance-of-payments current-account deficit		-1.4%	1.2%	3.3%	1.4%	-1.4%	1.1%	3.1%	1.2%
Internal saving		20.6%	15.7%	17.2%	17.3%	20.6%	15.7%	17.2%	17.3%
Net imports of goods and non-factor services		-0.9%	1.8%	3.8%	2.0%	-0.9%	1.8%	3.8%	2.0%
General-government déficit:		0.5%	2.4%	3.1%	2.6%	0.5%	2.3%	2.9%	2.4%
External financing		-0.9%	-0.2%	-1.0%	-0.5%	-0.9%	-0.2%	-0.9%	-0.4%
Internal financing		1.4%	2.6%	4.1%	3.1%	1.4%	2.5%	3.7%	2.8%
Year-end total external debt:		25.2%	26.5%	25.5%	25.8%	25.2%	23.8%	22.7%	23.1%
of which, public and publicly guaranteed (excl. IMF)		22.0%	23.4%	21.3%	22.5%	22.0%	20.7%	18.7%	19.8%
of which, private non-guaranteed		0.2%	0.3%	1.6%	0.5%	0.2%	0.3%	1.4%	0.4%
Year-end government net internal debt		20.4%	22.7%	24.6%	24.8%	20.4%	22.6%	23.5%	24.1%
Net increase in non-monetary central-bank obligations		-0.1%	0.0%	0.0%	0.3%	-0.1%	0.0%	0.0%	0.4%
Months of imports of goods, non-factor services:									
Gross foreign-exchange reserves		5.0	5.9	6.9	6.8	5.0	5.9	7.2	7.1
Per-capita U.S. dollars at prices and exchange rate of...	*2005*								
Central government:									
Tax and other internal-source revenue		$370.6	$352.5	$374.1	$355.6	$370.6	$352.5	$374.1	$355.6
Interest due:		$79.0	$75.6	$78.2	$77.5	$79.0	$72.5	$71.0	$71.0
External		$43.5	$40.3	$37.4	$38.7	$43.5	$37.2	$31.4	$33.0
Internal		$35.6	$35.3	$40.8	$38.8	$35.6	$35.2	$39.6	$38.0
Current education and health expenditure		$177.6	$172.6	$193.1	$181.0	$177.6	$172.6	$193.1	$181.0
Capital expenditure		$143.6	$134.5	$142.4	$135.8	$143.6	$134.5	$142.4	$135.8
Gross domestic product (billion pesos)		239.1	233.9	308.2	263.1	239.1	233.9	308.2	263.1
Gross domestic product (US$ billion)		$26.6	$25.2	$32.1	$27.5	$26.6	$25.2	$32.1	$27.5

Source: Pacífica projection exercise.

Table 36. Pacífica: Macroeconomic-projection sensitivity analysis, comparing the base and debt-reduction scenarios (1 and 6 respectively), 2008–2015

	2008	2009	2015	Average, 2009-15	2008	2009	2015	Average, 2009-15
Initial projection year: 2009		*Scenario 1*				*Scenario 6*		
Assumptions:								
World economic variables:								
Growth rate of the world price level (US$)	2.2%	0.0%	2.0%	1.6%	2.2%	0.0%	2.0%	1.6%
Real world commerce volume	4.1%	-4.5%	5.5%	3.6%	4.1%	-4.5%	5.5%	3.6%
LIBOR (per cent per year)	3.0%	1.7%	4.0%	2.8%	3.0%	1.7%	4.0%	2.8%
Real crude-oil price (percentage increase over previous year)	31.9%	-31.6%	0.8%	-2.9%	31.9%	-31.6%	0.8%	-2.9%
Macroeconomic programming and policy variables:								
Growth rates:								
Real GDP	6.0%	-4.5%	5.0%	1.9%	6.0%	-4.5%	6.0%	2.3%
Consumer prices (Dec.-Dec.)	2.7%	2.2%	2.0%	1.7%	2.7%	2.2%	2.0%	1.7%
Real-effective exchange rate	-0.6%	0.8%	0.0%	0.7%	-0.6%	0.8%	0.0%	0.7%
Value-added tax (internal transactions):								
Tax rate (per cent)	12.0%	12.0%	12.0%	12.0%	12.0%	12.0%	12.0%	12.0%
Tax productivity (per cent)	48.8%	49.1%	50.6%	49.8%	48.8%	49.1%	50.6%	49.8%
Gross foreign-exchange reserves:								
year-end; months of imports of goods, non-factor services	*5.0*	*4.0*	*4.0*	*4.2*	*5.0*	*4.0*	*4.0*	*4.2*
Results:								
Per-capita U.S. dollars at prices and exchange rate of... 2005								
Gross domestic product (GDP)	$3,006.0	$2,814.5	$2,980.7	$2,841.5	$3,006.0	$2,814.5	$3,066.7	$2,869.3
Non-government consumption	$2,095.7	$2,083.3	$2,282.9	$2,077.9	$2,095.7	$2,083.3	$2,375.9	$2,107.6
Percentage:								
Poverty incidence	17.0%	17.1%	15.5%	17.2%	17.0%	17.1%	14.9%	17.0%
Extreme poverty incidence	7.4%	7.5%	6.6%	7.5%	7.4%	7.5%	6.2%	7.4%
Per cent of GDP:								
Gross investment/saving:	19.6%	17.5%	21.1%	19.2%	19.6%	17.5%	21.1%	19.2%
Gross fixed capital formation	19.7%	17.5%	21.0%	19.2%	19.7%	17.5%	21.0%	19.2%
Net increase in inventories	-0.1%	0.0%	0.1%	0.0%	-0.1%	0.0%	0.1%	0.0%
National saving	21.0%	16.3%	17.8%	17.8%	21.0%	16.4%	17.2%	17.8%
Balance-of-payments current-account deficit	-1.4%	1.2%	3.3%	1.4%	-1.4%	1.1%	3.9%	1.4%
Internal saving	20.6%	15.7%	17.2%	17.3%	20.6%	15.7%	16.5%	17.0%
Net imports of goods and non-factor services	-0.9%	1.8%	3.8%	2.0%	-0.9%	1.8%	4.5%	2.2%
General-government deficit:	0.5%	2.4%	3.1%	2.6%	0.5%	2.3%	2.9%	2.4%
External financing	-0.9%	-0.2%	-1.0%	-0.5%	-0.9%	-0.2%	-1.0%	-0.5%
Internal financing	1.4%	2.6%	4.1%	3.1%	1.4%	2.5%	3.9%	2.9%
Year-end total external debt:	25.2%	26.5%	25.5%	25.8%	25.2%	23.8%	23.9%	23.3%
of which, public and publicly guaranteed (excl. IMF)	22.0%	23.4%	21.3%	22.5%	22.0%	20.7%	18.7%	19.8%
of which, private non-guaranteed	0.2%	0.3%	1.6%	0.5%	0.2%	0.3%	2.6%	0.7%
Year-end government net internal debt	20.4%	22.7%	24.6%	24.8%	20.4%	22.6%	21.7%	23.6%
Net increase in non-monetary central-bank obligations	-0.1%	0.0%	0.0%	0.3%	-0.1%	0.0%	0.0%	0.4%
Months of imports of goods, non-factor services:								
Gross foreign-exchange reserves	5.0	5.9	6.9	6.8	5.0	5.9	6.9	6.9
Per-capita U.S. dollars at prices and exchange rate of... 2005								
Central government:								
Tax and other internal-source revenue	$370.6	$352.5	$374.1	$355.6	$370.6	$352.5	$385.4	$359.2
Interest due:	$79.0	$75.6	$78.2	$77.5	$79.0	$72.5	$71.7	$71.2
External	$43.5	$40.3	$37.4	$38.7	$43.5	$37.2	$32.0	$33.2
Internal	$35.6	$35.3	$40.8	$38.8	$35.6	$35.2	$39.7	$38.0
Current education and health expenditure	$177.6	$172.6	$193.1	$181.0	$177.6	$172.6	$197.3	$182.3
Capital expenditure	$143.6	$134.5	$142.4	$135.8	$143.6	$134.5	$146.5	$137.1
Gross domestic product (billion pesos)	239.1	233.9	308.2	263.1	239.1	233.9	317.1	265.9
Gross domestic product (US$ billion)	$26.6	$25.2	$32.1	$27.5	$26.6	$25.2	$33.0	$27.8

Source: Pacífica projection exercise.

References

Allen, M. and G. Nankani (2004). "Debt Sustainability in Low-Income Countries — Proposal for an Operational Framework and Policy Implications" (International Monetary Fund and International Development Association: Washington, DC), February.

Allen, R. G. D. (1967). *Macro-Economic Theory: A Mathematical Treatment* (New York, NY: St. Martin's Press).

Anand, R. and S. van Wijnbergen (1989). "Inflation and the Financing of Government Expenditure: an Introductory Analysis with an Application to Turkey." *World Bank Economic Review*, Vol. 3, No. 1, pp. 17–38.

Baumol, W. J. (1952). "The Transactions Demand for Cash: An Inventory-Theoretic Approach." *Quarterly Journal of Economics* (November).

Beckerman, P. and A. Solimano (eds.) (2002). *Ecuador's Crisis and Dollarization.* (Washington, DC): World Bank.

Beckerman, P. (2000). "How Small Should an Economy's Fiscal Deficit Be?: A Monetary Programming Approach." (World Bank Policy Research Working Paper 2308) (March).

Beckerman, P. (1994). "External Debt and Growth: The 'Debt-Stabilizing' Real Growth Rate." *Journal of Developing Areas*, Vol. 28 (January), pp. 229–236.

Blejer, M. and A. Cheasty (1991). "Analytical and Methodological Issues in the Measurement of the Fiscal Deficit." *Journal of Economic Literature*, Vol. XXIX, No. 4 (December), pp. 1644–78.

Branson, W. H. (1972). *Macroeconomic Theory and Policy* (New York, NY: Harper and Row).

Braverman, J. D. (1979). *Fundamentals of Business Statistics.* (New York, NY: Academic Press).

Cagan, P. (1956). "The Monetary Dynamics of Hyperinflation." In *Studies in the Quantity Theory of Money*, M. Friedman, ed. (University of Chicago Press: Chicago, IL) pp. 25–117.

Claessens, S., E. Detragiache, R. Kanbur, and P. Wickham (1996). "Analytical Aspects of the Debt Problems of Heavily Indebted Poor Countries." (World Bank Policy Research Working Paper 1618).

Cline, W. R. (1983). *International Debt and the Stability of the World Economy*. Institute for International Economics (Cambridge, MA: MIT Press).

Devarajan, S., W. Easterly, and H. Pack (1999). "Is investment in Africa too high or too low?" World Bank, processed.

Domar, E. (1947). "Expansion and Employment." *American Economic Review*, Vol. 37, No. 1 (March), pp. 34–55.

Easterly, W. (2002). "An Identity Crisis?: Testing IMF Financial Programming." (Center for Global Development: Washington, DC), Working Paper No. 9 (August).

Economist (1998) "The Perils of Prediction." August 1.

Economist (2003) "McCurrencies" April 24.

Friedman, M. and A. J. Schwartz. *A Monetary History of the United States, 1867–1960* (Princeton, NJ; 1963).

Geithner, T. (2002). "Assessing Sustainability." IMF Policy Development and Review Department. May.

Harrod, R. (1959). "Domar and Dynamic Economics." *Economic Journal*, Vol. 69, No. 275 (September), pp. 451–464.

International Monetary Fund (1993). *Balance of Payments Manual* (Washington, DC).

International Monetary Fund. *Direction of Trade Statistics* (Washington, DC), monthly publication.

International Monetary Fund (2001). *Government Financial Statistics Manual* (Washington, DC).

International Monetary Fund. *International Financial Statistics* (Washington, DC), monthly publication.

International Monetary Fund (2000). *Monetary and Financial Statistics Manual* (Washington, DC).

International Monetary Fund and International Development Association (2001). "The Challenge of Maintaining Long-Term External Debt Sustainability." April.

Jones, H. (1975). *An Introduction to Modern Theories of Growth* (Nelson: London).

Keynes, J. M. (1936). *The General Theory of Employment, Interest and Money* (New York: 1964).

Lago Gallego, R. (1991). *Programación financiera y política macroeconómica: un modelo financiero de la economía mexicana* (*Centro de Estudios Monetarios Latinoamericanos*: Mexico, D.F.)

Le Houerou, P. and H. Sierra (1993). "Estimating Quasi-Fiscal Deficits in a Consistency Framework." World Bank Working Paper Series (Feb.), No. 1105.

Leontief, W. W. (1951). *The Structure of the American Economy, 1919–1939* (New York: Oxford University Press).

Olivera, J. (1967). "Money, Prices and the Fiscal Lag: A Note on the Dynamics of Inflation." *Banca Nazionale del Lavoro Quarterly Review* No. 26.

Payer, C. (1974). *The Debt Trap* (Monthly Review Press: New York).

Rajan, R. (2005). "Debt Relief and Growth." *Finance and Development* (June).

Phillips, A. W. (1958). "The Relationship between Unemployment and the Rate of Change of Money Wages in the United Kingdom 1861–1957." *Economica* 25 (100), pp. 283–99.

Polackova, H. (1998). "Contingent Government Liabilities." World Bank Working Paper Series (October), No. 1989.

Polak, J. J. (1957). "Monetary Analysis of Income Formation and Payments Problems." *Staff Papers*, International Monetary Fund (Washington, D.C., Vol. 5 (November).

Robinson, J. (1954). "The Production Function and the Theory of Capital." *Review of Economic Studies*, Vol. 21, No. 2, pp. 81–106.

Rodríguez, C. A. and Aquiles Almansi (1989). "*Reforma monetaria y financiera en hiperinflación.*" *Centro de Estudios Macroeconómicos de la Argentina* (CEMA), Buenos Aires, *Serie Documentos de Trabajo* No. 67 (August).

Sargent, T. and N. Wallace (1981). "Some Unpleasant Monetarist Arithmetic." *Federal Reserve Bank of Minneapolis Quarterly Review*, Fall, pp. 1–18.

Schmidt-Hebbel, K. and L. Serven (1999). *The Economics of Saving* (Cambridge, England: Cambridge University Press).

Solow, R. M. (1970). *Growth Theory: An Exposition* (Oxford, England: Oxford University Press).

Tanzi, V. (1977). "Inflation, Lags in Collection and the Real Value of Tax Revenue." *IMF Staff Papers*, No. 1.

van Trotsenburg, A. and A. MacArthur (1997). "The HIPC Initiative: Delivering Debt Relief to Poor Countries (International Monetary Fund and World Bank: Washington, DC), February.

World Bank. *Global Development Finance* (Washington, DC), annual publication.

World Bank (2003). HIPC website,
http://www.worldbank.org/hipc/about/hipcbr/hipcbr.htm

Index